Liberalism and Distributive Justice

Liberalism and Distributive Justice

SAMUEL FREEMAN

OXFORD

UNIVERSITY PRESS

OXFORD

UNIVERSITY PRESS

Oxford University Press is a department of the University of Oxford. It furthers
the University's objective of excellence in research, scholarship, and education
by publishing worldwide. Oxford is a registered trade mark of Oxford University
Press in the UK and certain other countries.

Published in the United States of America by Oxford University Press
198 Madison Avenue, New York, NY 10016, United States of America.

CIP data is on file at the Library of Congress
ISBN 978–0–19–069926–0

1 3 5 7 9 8 6 4 2
Printed by Sheridan Books, Inc., United States of America

Contents

Acknowledgments

I AM GRATEFUL to the many people with whom I have engaged over the years in helpful philosophical discussions and who have critically assessed the material in these chapters; they are mentioned at the end of each chapter. I am especially grateful to Samuel Scheffler, who has provided advice and support for twenty years, as have T.M. Scanlon, Joshua Cohen, Jay Wallace, Charles Beitz, and my current and former colleagues Kok-Chor Tan, Paul Guyer, and Rahul Kumar. I am also indebted to my former graduate students since 2005, including John Oberdiek, Paul Litton, Melina Bell, Matthew Lister, Douglas Weck, Jeppe von Platz, Douglas Paletta, Ryan Muldoon, Chris Melenovsky, Greg Hall and Collin Anthony, and to my current students, Justin Bernstein, Daniel Fryer, Pierce Randall, Chetan Cetty, Raj Patel, Dylan Manson, and Itamar Rosensweig. I have learned a great deal from my students, both graduate and undergraduate, at the University of Pennsylvania, who have given me the opportunity to teach and discuss with them my own ideas as well as others'. Thanks to all my colleagues in the Department of Philosophy at Penn, past and present, and the School of Arts and Sciences, which have provided me with such a supportive environment and a professional and intellectual home for thirty-three years. I am also thankful for my long-standing association with the School of Law, especially with its Law and Philosophy group, including Stephen Perry, Anita Allen, Claire Finklestein, William Ewald, Mitchell Berman, and formerly Matthew Adler. I am indebted to the School of Arts and Sciences and the University of Pennsylvania for the Avalon Chair in the Humanities and their ongoing financial support.

I was fortunate that Allauren Forbes agreed to assist me in the preparation of this manuscript. Her unusual combination of astute philosophical judgment and careful editing skills significantly enhanced the final version. Many thanks to Mardy Rawls for allowing me to use once again one of her marvelous watercolors of the Maine coast where Jack sailed and vacationed during the summer throughout much of his life. Peter Ohlin, the philosophy editor at Oxford University Press USA, has graciously supported this project; I appreciate his enthusiasm for it. Thanks to Isla Ng and Mary Becker for their fine editorial work.

Finally, I am most indebted to my wife, Annette Lareau, who for many years has been a constant source of support and companionship for me, both professionally and personally.

I dedicate this book to my daughter, Rachel De Dios Freeman, who is devoting her life to educating young people, and to Dillon Freeman, my son with autism.

January 28, 2018, Philadelphia

Most of the chapters in this book been published elsewhere. Some revisions have been made to each of them since initial publication.

Chapter 1: Originally published in *Social Philosophy and Policy* 28, no. 2 (July 2011): 19–55. Copyright 2011 by Cambridge University Press; reprinted by permission of the publisher.

Chapter 2: Originally published in *Philosophy and Public Affairs* 30, no. 2 (Spring 2001): 105–51. Copyright 2001 by Blackwell Publishing; reprinted by permission of the publisher.

Chapter 3: Originally published in *The Oxford Handbook of Distributive Justice*, ed. Serena Olsaretti (Oxford: Oxford University Press, 2018). Copyright 2017 by Oxford University Press; reprinted by permission of the publisher.

Chapter 4: Originally published in *Analyse & Kritik* 35, no. 1 (2013): 9–36. Copyright 2013 by *Analyse & Kritik*; reprinted by permission of the publisher.

Chapter 5: Has not been previously published.

Chapter 6: Originally published in *Cosmopolitanism versus Non-Cosmopolitanism: Critiques, Defenses, Reconceptualizations*, ed. Gillian Brock (Oxford: Oxford University Press, 2013). Copyright 2013 Oxford University Press; reprinted by permission of the publisher.

Chapter 7: Originally published in *A Companion to Rawls*, ed. Jon Mandle and David A. Reidy (Hoboken, NJ: John Wiley & Sons, 2013). Copyright 2013 John Wiley & Sons, Inc.; reprinted by permission of the publisher.

Chapter 8: Originally published in *Rutgers Law Journal* 43, no. 2 (April 2012): 169–209. Copyright 2012 by *Rutgers Law Journal*; reprinted by permission of the publisher.

Chapter 9: Originally published in *Contemporary Debates in Political Philosophy*, ed. Thomas Christiano and John Christman (Oxford: Wiley-Blackwell, 2009). Copyright 2009 Wiley-Blackwell; reprinted by permission of the publisher.

Abbreviations

ASU   Robert Nozick, *Anarchy, State, and Utopia*. New York: Basic
        Books, 1974.

CP   John Rawls, *Collected Papers*. Edited by Samuel Freeman. Cambridge,
        MA: Harvard University Press, 1999.

FP   G. A. Cohen, "Facts and Principles," *Philosophy & Public Affairs* 31, no. 3
        (2003): 211–45.

IJ   Amartya Sen, *The Idea of Justice*, Cambridge MA: Harvard University
        Press, 2009

JF   John Rawls, *Justice as Fairness: A Restatement* Edited by E. Kelly.
        Cambridge, MA: Harvard University Press, 2001.

LHPP   John Rawls, *Lectures on the History of Political Philosophy*. Edited by
        Samuel Freeman. Cambridge, MA: Harvard University Press, 2007.

LP   John Rawls, *The Law of Peoples*. Cambridge, MA: Harvard University
        Press, 1999.

PL   John Rawls, *Political Liberalism*. New York: Columbia University
        Press, 2005.

TJ   John Rawls, *A Theory of Justice*, rev. ed. Cambridge, MA: Harvard
        University Press, 1999.

TJ orig.   John Rawls, *A Theory of Justice*. Cambridge, MA: Harvard University
        Press, 1971.

Liberalism and Distributive Justice

Introduction

I. Liberalism

Liberalism is the predominant social and political doctrine, in theory and in practice, in the Western world. Given liberals' penchant for disagreement, it is not surprising that liberalism is such a contested idea, standing for different principles and values depending upon one's political point of view. In American public political culture, "liberal" is often used as a term of abuse and is rarely embraced by the persons and political party to whom it refers: those moderately left of center, mostly Democrats, who advocate a broad interpretation of personal and civil liberties, the regulation of business, and the generous provision of public goods, including social insurance, anti-poverty, health and education, and other programs designed to improve people's lives. "Conservatives" in the United States reject most if not all of these ideas and advocate expansive economic liberties, robust rights of property, free enterprise with unregulated markets, low taxes, the privatization of public functions, and minimal redistribution of income and wealth except for national defense and domestic security of persons and their property.

The irony is that American conservatism strongly resembles nineteenth-century classical liberalism, which provided the theoretical background for laissez-faire capitalism. Liberalism in Europe is still regarded in this way. The term "neo-liberalism" lately has been applied to the resurgence of laissez-faire economic liberalism and its extension to international trade and the increasing globalization of capitalism. This resurgence is due in part to the influence that the economists Friedrich Hayek and Milton Friedman respectively had on Margaret Thatcher and Ronald Reagan and their political parties in the last quarter of the twentieth century.

Left-of-center American liberalism is sometimes compared with social democracy, but it really has no close parallel in European politics, largely because those left of center in the United States who survived McCarthyism and anti-communism were never seriously influenced by socialism, unlike social democrats in Europe and the Labour Party in the United Kingdom. The established liberal Left in the United States has long embraced economic markets with private ownership of means of production, conjoining their support for capitalism with the regulatory welfare state. The division between neo-liberal conservatives and left-of-center liberals in the United States thus parallels the division between laissez-faire and welfare-state capitalism.

Here I understand liberalism more broadly, in a philosophical sense that encompasses a group of related political, social, and economic doctrines and institutions encompassing both classical and left liberalism, and including liberal market socialism. Liberalism in this more general sense is associated in political thought with non-authoritarianism, the rule of law, limited constitutional government, and the guarantee of civil and political liberties. A liberal society is tolerant of different religious, philosophical, and ethical views, and its citizens are free to express their views and their conflicting opinions on all subjects, as well as to live their lives according to their freely chosen life plans. In economic thought, liberalism is associated with a predominantly unplanned economy with free and competitive markets and, normally, private ownership and control of productive resources. In international relations, liberalism advocates freedom of trade and cultural relations, idealism instead of realism, international cooperation and institutions rather than isolationism, and the use of soft power instead of power politics. This is not to say that liberal governments are consistent in realizing these ideas in practice.

Certain values, principles, and ideals are also connected with social, political, and economic liberalism: liberty, of course, but also equality—of liberties, as well as opportunities and the civic status of citizens. Other liberal values commonly cited include tolerance, impartiality, fairness, consensus, non-interference, non-discrimination, free choice, entrepreneurship, and private property. To justify their position, liberals appeal to such abstract values and ideals as human dignity, equal respect, the moral equality of persons, autonomy, the public good, the general welfare, consent of the governed, diversity, human progress, and individuality. Liberals interpret some if not all of these values in different ways.

Liberalism is also a debate about how to interpret and structure certain basic social and political institutions that all liberals normally endorse: constitutionalism and the rule of law; equal basic rights and liberties; equality of opportunity; free competitive markets and private property; public goods and a social minimum; and the public nature of political power and (since the twentieth century) democratic government. In chapter 1, "Capitalism in the Classical and High Liberal Traditions,"[1] I distinguish classical liberalism from liberalism to its left, which was called "new" or "modern liberalism" in the twentieth century but which I call the "high liberal tradition"—both because the resurgence of classical liberalism renders its neighbor to the left neither new nor modern and because high liberalism is, I contend, the natural development of fundamental liberal values of the freedom and moral equality of persons in a democratic society. I discuss the two liberalisms' competing interpretations of these basic social and political institutions, and especially their attitudes toward capitalism. The chapter compares the two liberalisms' different positions regarding the rights and liberties each regards as most basic, as well as their positions regarding equality of opportunity and the distributive role of markets in establishing distributive justice, the other major theme of this book.

Classical liberals characteristically consider economic liberties and robust rights of property to be as important as, if not more important than, basic personal liberties such as freedom of conscience, expression, association, and freedom of the person. For example, Hayek said that the most important rights and liberties for a person are freedom from involuntary servitude, immunity from arbitrary arrest, the right to "work at whatever he desires to do," freedom of movement, and the right to own property. The liberties on this list were regarded as "the essential conditions of freedom" in the eighteenth and nineteenth centuries, and the list still "contains all the elements required to protect an individual against coercion."[2] Notably absent from Hayek's list of essential freedoms are the personal freedoms that J. S. Mill said were essential to individuality and the principle of liberty: freedoms of conscience, expression, association, and "tastes and pursuits."[3] Most contemporary classical liberals emphasize these important personal liberties too, along with economic liberties and rights of property, which together constitute what the nineteenth-century classical liberal Benjamin Constant called "the liberties of the moderns." Classical liberals, though they now accept constitutional democracy as the safest form of government, characteristically assign less importance to equal political rights to participate in government and in public life—Constant's "liberties of the ancients"—regarding political democracy as jeopardizing robust economic and personal liberties, but still preferable to other forms of government. Since high liberals assign greater priority to personal and political liberties than economic liberties, the priority that classical liberals assign to the economic liberties accounts for most of the differences between contemporary classical and high liberalism, including their conflicting positions regarding the justice of market distributions.

I introduce in this chapter the idea of distributive justice that was raised to prominence within the high liberal tradition in the twentieth century. Here I critically assess the classical liberal distributive principle that economic agents deserve to be rewarded according to their (marginal) contributions to economic product. The chapter concludes with some reflections upon the essential role that dissimilar conceptions of persons and society play in grounding the different positions on economic liberties and distributive justice that classical and high liberals advocate.

Chapter 2, "Illiberal Libertarians: Why Libertarianism Is Not a Liberal View," examines a third political conception that is often regarded as liberal, since it appears to have much in common with classical liberalism, including the prominence assigned to property rights and economic liberties. I argue that the resemblance between liberalism and libertarianism is superficial: upon close examination, it becomes apparent that libertarianism rejects the most basic liberal institutions discussed in chapter 1 and here in greater detail.

A clarification: the term "libertarian" refers most often to those who fervidly defend robust laissez-faire economic rights and liberties and have full confidence in capitalist markets' capacity to address social problems. The classical liberals Milton Friedman and Friedrich Hayek are sometimes called "libertarians," as is Ayn Rand. The term is also used for liberals mostly on the left, called "civil libertarians," who ardently defend personal and civil liberties, though not strong property rights and economic liberties.[4] I use the term "libertarian" in a philosophical sense, to refer to economic and personal libertarianism in its purest form, which is grounded in a doctrine of absolute property rights in one's person ("self-ownership") and in one's possessions. Libertarianism so construed is associated with its major philosophical spokesperson, Robert Nozick, and others who advocate similar social and political arrangements (e.g., Murray Rothbard and Jan Narveson).

One of the essential features of liberalism, I argue, is that it holds that legitimate political power is not simply limited: it is a *public power* that is to be *impartially* exercised and only for the *public good*. Libertarianism rejects each of these liberal ideas, conceiving of legitimate political power as a private power that is based in a network of economic contracts and that is to be sold and distributed, not impartially, but, like any other private good, according to individuals' willingness and ability to pay. Correctly understood, libertarianism resembles a view that liberalism historically defined itself against, the doctrine of private political power that underlies feudalism. Moreover, the primary institutions typical of the liberal political tradition—including inalienable basic rights and liberties, equality of opportunity, and government's role in maintaining fair and efficient markets, public goods, and a social minimum—are also rejected, I contend, by orthodox libertarianism.

The term "orthodox" suggests that there are other, more moderate accounts of libertarianism that do not reject all the basic liberal institutions I discuss and that regard themselves as versions of classical liberalism.[5] I do not discuss these here, but do so elsewhere in more recent work.[6] Characteristically, those who adhere to these non-orthodox positions, endorse, as liberals do, the inalienability of certain basic rights and liberties, especially freedom of the person, and reject the enforcement of contracts for involuntary servitude. But as libertarians they also usually reject the social safety net that is typical of modern classical liberal views and seek to privatize the provision of most public goods accepted by classical liberals. I regard these positions, including the minimization of government's role, which currently have a great deal of popular support in the Republican Party, as hybrid views, impoverished forms of liberalism that surrender consistency for the sake of certain fixed moral intuitions, especially moral revulsion to slavery and other morally repugnant practices even if voluntarily contracted into. Orthodox libertarians, such as Nozick, by contrast, take the idea of absolute property in one's person and possessions and absolute freedom of contract to the limit, and have no theoretical misgivings (whatever personal reservations they may feel) about the complete alienation of all one's rights and liberties. This is what makes orthodox libertarianism a distinct philosophical conception of justice and ultimately distinguishes it from liberalism.

II. Distributive Justice

In the three chapters in part II of the book, "Distributive Justice and the Difference Principle," I analyze and apply to economic systems and the private law John Rawls's, conception of justice, which embodies the major account of distributive justice set forth in the twentieth-century high liberal tradition. "Distributive justice," when used to refer to the just or fair distribution of income and wealth produced by economic cooperation, is a relatively modern idea that gained considerable prominence only with the socialist criticism of capitalism starting in the nineteenth century. But before that, David Hume addressed the subject when he said that it would be irrational to organize the economy so that income and wealth were distributed either equally or to reward individuals according to their virtue. Both proposals would soon meet with failure, reducing all to poverty. Instead, Hume said, the conventions of property, markets, and other consensual transfers, and contracts and similar agreements, are and should be organized to promote public utility.[7] Individuals should be permitted to sell what they produce, retain economic gains from their efforts and contributions, and pass their property to their offspring, because these conventions are useful to society. Adam Smith's doctrine of the invisible hand provided the economic framework for Hume's utilitarian account of justice. These ideas have long been developed by classical and neo-classical economists and have provided classical liberalism with the primary justification of market distributions in a capitalist economy.

Rawls presents his difference principle as an alternative to utilitarianism in order to structure economic institutions and productive relations and to distribute income and wealth. The difference principle requires that property and the economic system be organized so that income and wealth are distributed in a way that maximizes, not the welfare of society, but the economic position of the least advantaged members of society, making them economically better off than they would be in any alternative economic arrangement. Chapter 3, "Rawls on Distributive Justice and the Difference Principle," provides a thorough discussion of Rawls's account of distributive justice with particular focus on the difference principle. It begins with the requirements of distributive justice implicit in Rawls's principle of equal basic liberties and fair equality of opportunity. Rawls argues that economic inequalities should not become so large that they undermine either the fair value of citizens' equal political liberties or the fair equality of their opportunities to develop their capacities so they can compete for open occupational positions and enjoy the benefits of culture.

G. A. Cohen argued that the inequalities allowed by the difference principle are compatible with the vast inequalities typical of capitalism.[8] For example, the difference principle might be used to justify tax reductions for the wealthiest, on the assumption that they will invest in new jobs that marginally benefit the least advantaged. Leaving aside the fact that the great inequalities in our capitalist economy violate the fair value of equal political liberties and also fair equality of opportunity, Cohen's objection raises a problem in non-ideal theory that Rawls does not address. As I discuss here and in chapter 8 on ideal and non-ideal theory, Rawls's difference principle is chosen by the parties in the original position for an ideal well-ordered society where everyone accepts the same principles of justice and these principles are fully enacted into law. The difference principle can be narrowly applied in a well-ordered society in order to put in place measures that maximally benefit the least advantaged in those ideal circumstances. But in non-ideal circumstances that do not comply with the difference principle, such as a capitalist society with huge inequalities like those in the United States, the application of the difference principle is not as straightforward. If the best among the narrow measures currently available to maximally benefit the least advantaged only increase and permanently reinforce the gross inequalities that already exist, then, I argue, a society should forgo those maximin measures and instead adopt alternative measures which promote the eventual realization of just economic institutions that do not yet exist. This means that an unjust society has a duty to enact alternative measures that, even if they benefit the least advantaged less than the maximin measures currently available, reform unjust institutions in the direction of an economic system that eventually satisfies the difference principle. The difference principle must presuppose in non-ideal conditions a broad requirement that imposes on a society a duty of justice to reform its economic system so that eventually it makes the least advantaged class better off than does any alternative economic system. This may frequently require a society to enact measures in non-ideal conditions that, while they benefit the least advantaged, are nonetheless suboptimal for them in the short run. This is the appropriate response, I argue, to classical liberal trickle-down policies that increase and permanently solidify great inequalities in a capitalist society.

J. S. Mill was a fairly orthodox classical liberal when he first wrote *The Principles of Political Economy*, which Marx regarded as the testament of capitalism. But Mill had made the transition to high liberalism by the seventh edition of his treatise. He argued for the redistribution of large estates, large taxes on profits from rentier income on land, and most notably workers' private ownership and control of the firms they labored in within a market economy. His proposal was an early version of what has since come to be called "property-owning democracy."

In chapter 4, "Property-Owning Democracy and the Difference Principle," I take up where the preceding chapter leaves off and address the question, what social and economic system is capable of best realizing the principles of justice and maximizing the prospects of the least advantaged? Rawls says the main problem of distributive justice is the choice of a social system. Property-owning democracy is the social system that Rawls thought best realizes the requirements of his principles of justice, including the difference principle (though he leaves open the possibility that liberal market socialism might do so as well under some circumstances). This chapter discusses Rawls's conception of property-owning democracy and how it differs from welfare-state capitalism and other economic arrangements. I explain why Rawls thought that welfare-state capitalism could not fulfill his principles of justice and discuss the connection between welfare-state capitalism and utilitarianism. I also discuss the crucial role of democratic reciprocity and the social bases of self-respect in Rawls's argument for both the difference principle and property-owning democracy.

Chapter 5, "Private Law and Rawls's Principles of Justice," which has not been previously published, continues the discussion of the application of Rawls's principles of justice to liberal institutions, in this case to what is known as "private law"—the law of legal relationships between individuals—including primarily property, contract, and tort law. It has been argued that Rawls's principles of justice apply only to public law—laws affecting government's relationships to individuals, and the benefits government provides and the burdens it imposes. Public law includes constitutional law, taxation, and redistribution to pay for public goods, social insurance, and welfare programs, also criminal law, administrative law, and procedural law. I contend that, in addition to public law, the first principle plays a crucial role in assessing and determining the private law of property, contract, and tort; moreover, fair equality of opportunity and the difference principle are to be applied to the assessment of rules of property and contract law. But the role of the difference principle in tort law and its determinations of fault and liability are more limited. The reason for this difference is that the difference principle addresses the question of how a society is to fairly design and efficiently organize the institutions that make economic cooperation possible among free and equal persons actively engaged in productive activity, including the fair and efficient allocation of resources and the production, transfer, and fair distribution of goods and services that enable individuals to freely pursue their life plans. Certain core legal institutions, including property, economic contract, and other laws enabling the sale and transfer of goods, are necessary for economic cooperation and are among the institutions covered by the second principle of justice. Other bodies of law, including criminal law and the private law of torts, restitution, and family law are not directly concerned with matters of economic justice, and so are not regulated by the difference principle. In this respect, the role of the difference principle differs from the role assigned to the principle of efficiency in law and economics, which by its terms applies to all of private law, including the law of torts and compensation for accidents.

III. Institutions

The four chapters in part III, "Liberal Institutions and Distributive Justice," focus on the crucial role of liberal institutions and procedures in determinations of distributive justice. Social institutions in general and their laws and procedures play a fundamental role in defining a liberal government and society. We take for granted the rule of law and adherence to the rules and procedures of liberal social institutions—the constitution, the legal system, property, markets, and the economic system—since they provide background structure that affects nearly every aspect of social life. The importance of the rule of law and adherence to the procedures of a liberal constitution are especially palpable now that they are threatened by an administration in the US that has no respect for them.

In chapters 6, 7, and 8, I discuss the central role that basic social institutions play in determining the scope and requirements of distributive justice. Chapter 6, "The Social and Institutional Bases of Distributive Justice," addresses the question of whether distributive justice is "relational" and based in cooperative social institutions or whether it is non-relational and global in the reach of its requirements. Many so-called luck egalitarians contend that it is morally arbitrary whether a person is born into a wealthy or a poor society, just as it is morally arbitrary whether a person is born to wealthy or poor parents or with more or less intelligence or physical prowess. Liberal social egalitarians such as Rawls and Ronald Dworkin, who seek to neutralize the effects of social class, natural talents, and misfortune, should also neutralize, many claim, the effects of national boundaries and extend the scope of their distributive principles to the world at large. Distributive justice knows no boundaries, cosmopolitan egalitarians contend.

Chapter 6 argues that distributive justice is institutionally based. Certain cooperative institutions are basic: they are essential to economic production and the division of labor, trade and exchange, and distribution and consumption. These background institutions require principles to specify their terms and determine the justice of their distributions. Primary among these basic institutions are the legal institution of property; laws and conventions such as markets enabling transfers and distribution of goods and services; and the legal system of contracts and related transactions that make production, transfers, and distribution possible and productive. Political institutions are necessary to specify, interpret, enforce, and make effective the terms of these basic economic institutions. I conclude that the basic institutions that make economic cooperation possible are thus social in nature; they are realizable only within the context of social and political cooperation—this is a fixed empirical fact about cooperation among free and equal persons. Given the nature of social cooperation as a kind of reciprocity, distributive justice, I conclude, is primarily a question of social justice too.

The institutional account of distributive justice recognizes that many requirements of justice apply to international relations and institutions as well and to people the world over regardless of our relations with them. These requirements include not only respect for human rights and the law of peoples, and procedural and fairness requirements in our dealings with other societies, but also substantive requirements of economic justice. Societies have a duty to maintain fair trade relations with each other, for example, which means that wealthier societies should not exercise their economic power to take unfair advantage of or exploit others. This is a requirement of global economic justice. Distributive justice, however, I regard as a distinct form of economic justice; it originates with participants who are engaged in social cooperation doing their fair share to sustain basic social institutions and contribute to economic cooperation, and addresses the question of the fair distribution of the social product among those who contribute to its production. We cannot address the question of whether there are demands of distributive justice that stem from international/global institutions without investigating the particular nature and complexity of these institutions and their role in economic production and commerce. I do not rule out a global distribution requirement of economic justice that is in addition to societies' duties of assistance to burdened societies that are unable to provide for all their citizens' basic needs. But if there are international or global distribution requirements, they would not replace, but would supplement and remain dependent upon, the social and institutional bases of distributive justice.

Chapter 7, "The Basic Structure of Society as the Primary Subject of Justice," discusses the reasons Rawls assigns such a central role to social institutions and procedures in his liberal account of distributive justice. Rawls's liberal conception of free and equal moral persons, and of the social conditions necessary to realize fair reciprocity and citizens' fundamental interests, is integral to understanding why Rawls assigns such importance to principles of justice for the institutions of the basic structure of society. Rawls himself mentions two reasons for this primacy: the profound effects of basic social institutions on individuals' purposes and life prospects, and the need to maintain background justice in a liberal system that relies on pure procedural justice. In this chapter, I discuss the main reasons for the primacy Rawls assigns to principles of justice for the basic structure. First, it is necessary to apply the principles of justice to the basic structure instead of directly to individuals' conduct in order to maintain the freedom, equality, and independence of moral persons. Individuals are then left free to devote themselves to their special commitments and the pursuit of their conceptions of the good, secure in the knowledge that the achievement of the fair distribution of income and wealth will take place without their having to sacrifice their purposes, plans, and special commitments.

Second, Rawls's focus on the basic structure is a condition of economic reciprocity and fair distribution in a competitive market among free and equal citizens, each of whom contributes his or her fair share to economic product. In addition to legitimate distributive inequalities based on differences in individuals' efforts and other substantial contributions, markets tend toward inequalities based on arbitrary factors, such as differences in natural talent and social position, life's accidents and misfortunes, and good and bad market luck due to myriad factors beyond anyone's control (natural and man-made catastrophes, fluctuations in the labor supply, a surfeit or shortage of particular labor skills, etc.). In a liberal society that seeks to take advantage of economic markets' productive efficiency and to distribute income and wealth on grounds of pure procedural justice, it is necessary to maintain background justice by correcting the arbitrary distributions of markets so that individuals are rewarded their fair share on grounds of fair reciprocity and mutual respect. This is the role of the difference principle in structuring the basic institutions that make economic cooperation possible and productive.

Third, priority is assigned to the basic structure because it is required by moral pluralism to maintain the plurality of values and the diversity of reasonable conceptions of the good among free and equal persons. The values of justice clearly are not the only values worth pursuing, even if their requirements constrain and regulate the means individuals can adopt to pursue their valuable as well as merely permissible purposes. There are a plurality of values, moral principles, and reasons for acting in addition to those required by distributive justice. To morally require individuals themselves to directly apply principles of distributive justice, such as the difference principle, to their conduct and conform their actions to its direct demands, would not just severely limit their freedom and independence to pursue their conceptions of the good; it also would severely interfere with and in effect diminish the importance of equally important values that constitute individuals' reasonable conceptions of the good. By applying the principles of justice to the basic structure and requiring individuals to comply with rules for individuals that are based on these principles but that leave them free to pursue a wide range of reasonable conceptions of the good, Rawls's theory enables what Samuel Scheffler has called "the division of moral labor," including individuals' realization of a plurality of values as they freely pursue their purposes and commitments.[9]

Liberal social contract doctrine characteristically seeks to discover principles that free and equal persons in society can all reasonably agree on and accept as a matter of justice. Its method assumes an ideal society that is well ordered in that everyone agrees to and accepts the same principles of justice and everyone generally complies with these principles. Given such "full compliance," the question Kantian contract doctrine asks is, which public principles of justice could or would free and equal rational and reasonable persons all agree to as the basis for social cooperation in such a well-ordered society? The general thought is that free, equal, and independent persons ought to be able to publicly recognize and freely accept and endorse the fundamental principles of their society that structure their relations and determine their future prospects and the kinds of persons they are and can come to be. In chapter 8, "Ideal Theory and the Justice of Institutions,"[10] I address Amartya Sen's argument against Rawls's reliance on such an ideal theory of "a perfectly just society." I argue that the principles of justice chosen for such an ideal society are not redundant or irrelevant as Sen contends. The principles of justice that would be agreed to and fully complied with in a well-ordered society of free and equal persons are needed to determine the just distribution of equal basic rights and liberties, powers and opportunities, and income and wealth in our non-ideal society.

I also address Sen's rejection of Rawls's primary focus on the basic institutions of society in favor of an account of "consequence-sensitive" evaluation of "comprehensive outcomes." I argue that Rawls's institutional approach, without being consequentialist, is also consequence-sensitive in that the principles of justice are designed to realize an ideal of persons and society. I discuss some potential problems with a consequentialist interpretation of Sen's own comparative method of evaluating comprehensive outcomes and suggest that a pluralist interpretation of his account (one that combines deontological with consequentialist principles) is not as different from Rawls's approach as Sen intends it to be.

Finally, Rawls relies upon social and psychological facts about humans to argue for his principles of justice, especially the difference principle. Some of his main arguments against utilitarianism are that, given natural human propensities and our moral sense of justice, the principles of justice realize our rational and moral nature; by contrast, the principle of utility imposes unreasonable demands on human beings, requiring the less advantaged to sacrifice their well-being for the sake of those already more advantaged by nature and circumstance. Aggregate or average utility cannot be widely embraced by all members of a liberal society, especially the least advantaged, as a dominant social end; as a result a utilitarian society will always be unstable. Chapter 9, "Constructivism, Facts, and Moral Justification," responds to G. A. Cohen's criticisms of Rawls's reliance upon empirical facts about human psychological and social tendencies to justify the difference principle. Cohen contends that empirical facts are irrelevant to the justification of fundamental principles of justice and that Rawls's difference principle is not a fundamental principle but a principle of regulation designed to accommodate injustice due to human selfishness. I deny this interpretation and discuss three reasons why the first principles of a moral conception of justice should be "fact-sensitive," or presuppose general facts in their justification. First, a conception of justice should be compatible with our moral and psychological capacities. It should respond to basic human needs and our distinctly human capacities. Moreover, conscientious moral agents should be capable of developing appropriate attitudes enabling them to normally act upon and affirm the requirements of the principles of justice that structure society and determine their prospects. Second, a conception of justice should provide principles for practical reasoning and fulfill a social role in supplying a public basis for justification among persons with different conceptions of their good and diverse comprehensive religious, philosophical, and moral views. Third, a moral conception should not frustrate but rather affirm the pursuit of the human good, including the exercise and development of our moral capacities and sense of justice.

Notes

1. This chapter is a revised and somewhat expanded version of the original article.
2. Friedrich Hayek, *The Constitution of Liberty* (Chicago: University of Chicago Press, 2011), 70–71.
3. J. S. Mill, *"On Liberty" and Other Essays*, ed. John Gray (Oxford: Oxford University Press, 1991), chap. 1, 16–17.
4. The position known as "left libertarianism" has been defended relatively recently and is still waiting to be more fully developed. It seeks to combine redistributive egalitarianism with self-ownership and near-absolute personal, civil, and economic liberties. I do not address that position here. See the essays in Peter Vallentyne and Hillel Steiner, eds., *Left-Libertarianism and Its Critics* (New York: Palgrave MacMillan, 2000); Michael Otsuka, *Libertarianism without Inequality* (Oxford: Clarendon Press, 2005), and my review of Otsuka's book in *Mind*, 117 (2008): 709–15; and Hillel Steiner, *An Essay on Rights* (Oxford: Wiley-Blackwell, 1994).

5. See the helpful book by Jason Brennan, *Libertarianism: What Everyone Needs to Know* (Oxford: Oxford University Press, 2012), and Jason Brennan, Bas van der Vossen, and David Schmidtz, eds., *The Routledge Handbook of Libertarianism* (London: Routledge, 2017).

6. See Samuel Freeman, "Liberal and Illiberal Libertarianism," in Brennan et al., *The Routledge Handbook of Libertarianism*, 108–24.

7. David Hume. *An Enquiry Concerning the Principles of Morals*, 2nd ed. (Oxford: Clarendon Press, 1970), sect. III, 183–204.

8. G. A. Cohen, *Rescuing Justice and Equality* (Cambridge, MA: Harvard University Press, 2008), chaps. 3–4; see e.g. 138.

9. Samuel Scheffler, Equality and Tradition, (New York: Oxford University Press, 2010), chap. 4.

10. This chapter is a shortened version of the original article.

PART I

*Liberalism, Libertarianism,
and Economic Justice*

I

Capitalism in the Classical and High Liberal Traditions

1. Introduction: Essential Features of Liberalism

Liberalism holds that there are certain individual liberties that are of fundamental political significance. These liberties are fundamental or basic in that they are preconditions of the pursuit of other social values, such as achieving economic efficiency, promoting the general welfare, and moderating the degree of inequality in the distribution of income and wealth. None of these liberties are absolute, but the reasons for limiting their exercise are to protect other basic liberties and maintain essential background conditions for their effective exercise. For example, freedom of speech and expression can be limited when it imminently endangers others' safety or the freedom of their person, but not because the ideas expressed are found to be offensive by vast majorities of people. Liberal basic liberties are also inalienable: they cannot be given up voluntarily or permanently transferred to anyone else, though some liberties are forfeitable upon criminal conviction for serious crimes. No liberal government would enforce a contract in which a person sold himself into permanent servitude, or alienated his freedom to change religions, or legally bound himself to vote only as his employer insisted. An integral feature of a liberal constitution is the protection of the basic rights and liberties necessary to establish and maintain the equal civic status of citizens.

What liberties do liberals generally find to have this extraordinary status? Liberals now would all agree that among the basic liberties are freedom of thought, expression, and inquiry, freedom of conscience and of association, freedom and security of the person, and free choice of occupation. They also agree that the right to hold personal property is part of freedom of the person, since control over personal belongings and the security of one's living space is necessary for individuals' independence and sense of self-respect. Finally, nearly all contemporary liberals accept that individuals have a basic right to live under a democratic government with universal franchise (though this was not seen as a basic liberty by classical liberals prior to the twentieth century). All citizens, then, should enjoy equal political rights and liberties, including the right to vote, hold office, and freely participate in political life.

Where liberals primarily disagree among themselves is on the nature and status of economic rights and liberties, including the extent of freedom of contract and rights to private property in land, raw materials, and other productive resources. Classical liberals generally hold that the economic liberties are to be regarded and guaranteed as among the basic liberties; or if they are not strictly basic liberties, then they resemble basic liberties in that they can be restricted only for special reasons.[1] Freedom of contract and rights of property are not absolute for classical liberals; for example, the inalienability of the basic liberties itself puts restrictions on freedom of contract and rights of property. Nor would classical liberals, or liberals generally, accept or see as legally enforceable individuals' attempts to permanently alienate their rights to equal opportunities to educate themselves and compete for open employment positions or their right not to be discriminated against on grounds of race, religion, gender, or other classifications. One of the primary distinctions between classical liberalism and libertarianism is that libertarians regard freedom of coercively enforceable contracts as of such fundamental importance that it overrides the liberal restriction on the inalienability of basic liberties and also overrides equality of opportunity and equal rights to apply and compete for open positions.[2] For liberals, by contrast, one cannot alienate the basic rights, liberties, and opportunities that define one's equal status as a person or citizen.

While classical liberals regard the economic liberties as having great importance, they do not really regard them as basic liberties in every respect. Classical liberals have generally recognized that freedom of economic contract and rights of property differ from basic liberties in that they can be restricted for reasons other than maintaining others' basic liberties and rights to equal opportunities. For example, classical liberals today accept that contracts for the purpose of fixing prices or putting restraints on trade and competition should not be enforceable; for in addition to foreclosing economic opportunities for others, such contracts are economically inefficient. Unregulated monopolies on certain resources are generally forbidden by classical liberals when they lead to economic inefficiencies. Also, contemporary classical liberals accept governments' powers of eminent domain for public purposes (on the condition that compensation is provided for any government "taking"). And most can accept zoning restrictions of certain kinds, for example, noise restrictions or the exclusion of manufacturing and commercial development in residential neighborhoods.[3] Zoning restrictions do not protect any basic liberty or opportunity but are issued as a matter of convenience, or to maintain property values, or to keep out unwanted neighbors. And classical liberals recognize other restrictions on the economic liberties that they would not extend to the basic freedoms of expression, conscience, association, and other basic liberties.

This suggests that however much the economic liberties are revered by classical liberals, they are not really among the class of basic liberties that all liberals recognize. For while classical liberals reject restrictions on the basic liberties (except to protect those liberties), they generally allow for restrictions and regulations on the economic liberties in order to procure and maintain the conditions necessary for free competitive markets and economic efficiency, as well as maintaining health and safety, and procuring other public goods.[4] The most enduring and (I believe) persuasive classical liberal justification of the economic liberties is cast in terms of the conditions required to establish and maintain economically efficient market allocations of resources and distributions of income and wealth. The enforcement of a scheme of private economic rights and liberties within a system of free competitive markets designed to achieve conditions of economic efficiency in both the allocation and the distribution of income and wealth is, as I understand it, the most fundamental feature of capitalism. It is also the primary feature of classical liberalism that distinguishes it from what I call the "high liberal tradition" (discussed in section 2).

Karl Marx understood capitalism partly as a social and economic system, the predominant feature of which is the existence of two distinct and mutually exclusive economic classes with different functions and conflicting interests: the class of capitalists own and control the means of production; and the class of workers own no capital but own and control their labor power. The "petit bourgeoisie"— the class of shopkeepers, craftspeople, and other small businesspersons who own both their labor power and means of production—Marx found to be of no economic or historical significance. Since small businesses have always occupied a central position within the US economy, and the United States is emblematic of contemporary capitalism, Marx's class-based definition of "capitalism" was never really adequate to describe capitalism or class conditions in the United States. While it may be true that during certain historical periods capitalism has been marked by class divisions and conflict, this seems incidental to what I will take to be central to a capitalist economy.

Capitalism (as Marx and the classical economists recognized) is not simply an economic system but also a social and political system. For essential to capitalism is the political specification and legal enforcement of a complicated system of extensive property and contract rights and duties that are all conditions of economic production, transfer, and consumption, as well as the political specification and enforcement of laws and regulations needed to maintain the fluidity of markets and competitive enterprise (laws restricting monopolies, price fixing, and other restraints on trade).

Rather than accepting Marx's class-based definition, I regard capitalism as an economic and social/political system that enforces a scheme of extensive private economic rights and liberties within a system of free markets, wherein these economic rights and liberties are specified and markets are designed to achieve conditions of maximal productive output and economic efficiency in both the allocation and distribution of income and wealth. Essential to this understanding of capitalism, then, is (1) a political system of extensive private property and contract rights, and other legal background conditions, (2) that are specified and adjusted to achieve efficient markets and the resulting maximization of productive output and, therewith, (3) maximal opportunities for consumption among those willing and able to pay for goods and services thereby produced. Finally, (4) the capitalist standard for the just distribution of income and wealth is fundamentally tied to market outcomes.

So defined, capitalism is not the only economic system that relies upon markets and private property in the means of production. An alternative will be discussed later (namely, property-owning democracy). But capitalism in this pure sense is the economic system that is defended by classical liberals, particularly the classical economists and their modern heirs. Thus, it should come as no surprise that capitalism, like the liberalism of the classical economists, has been closely associated with utilitarianism and attuned to utilitarian arguments, especially within the Anglo-American tradition.[5]

On this understanding, a system of robust private property rights and wide-ranging freedom of contract is not sufficient for capitalism. Capitalism also requires a system of free and efficient markets for the allocation of productive resources and the distribution of income and wealth. Liberals generally, including classical liberals, maintain that, when markets break down due to a monopolistic concentration of market power, or when markets are incapable of adequately supplying goods or services that are important for individuals' independence and well-being, it is government's role to intervene and address such "externalities" or "neighborhood effects" by restoring competition and providing for these "public goods."[6] Thus, Adam Smith writes:

> According to the system of natural liberty, the sovereign has only three duties to attend to . . . first [national defense]; secondly, the duty of protecting . . . every member of society from the injustice or oppression of every other member, or the duty of establishing an exact administration of justice; and, thirdly, the duty of erecting and maintaining certain publick works and certain publick institutions, which it can never be for

the interest of any individual, or small number of individuals, to erect and maintain; because the profit could never repay the expence to any individual, or small number of individuals, though it may frequently do much more than repay it to a great society.[7]

Moreover, Smith writes, "The expence of defending the society . . . of the administration of justice . . . of maintaining good roads and communications," as well as "institutions for education and religious instruction, [are] likewise, no doubt, beneficial to the whole society, and may, therefore, without injustice, be defrayed by the general contribution of the whole society."[8]

Adam Smith's regard for "the administration of justice," "protecting . . . every member of society," and measures that are "beneficial to the whole society" underlines another significant feature of liberalism, namely, the *public nature of political power*. Political power is not conceived of as a private power to be exercised for the benefit of those who can afford it or to benefit only members of certain religious, ethnic, or otherwise privileged groups. Rather, it is a public power that is held in trust by governments, to be impartially exercised and, as John Locke says, "only for the public good."[9] The public nature of political power as impartially exercisable only for the public good is integral to the liberal idea of the rule of law and is another feature of liberalism that distinguishes it from libertarianism. Libertarianism rejects the idea of the public good and regards political power as a private power, to be provided to people on the basis of private contracts and in proportion to their willingness and ability to pay for it.

I suggested that classical liberalism, like capitalism itself, has been closely associated with utilitarianism.[10] Utilitarianism provides an argument for each of the main features of classical liberalism, including its support for robust property and contract rights, conjoined with its emphasis on market efficiency and market distributions.[11] It should come as no surprise that nearly all the great classical liberal economists, including Adam Smith, David Ricardo, Thomas Malthus, John Stuart Mill, F. Y. Edgeworth, and Alfred Marshall, were utilitarians. Capitalism's association with utilitarianism also helps to explain the evolution of laissez-faire capitalism into contemporary welfare-state capitalism. Utilitarians since David Hume have noted that a poor person experiences greater utility from a fixed sum of money than does a rich person.[12] Most utilitarians conclude that we have good reason (other things being equal) to guarantee the most disadvantaged, or at least the disabled, a minimum income in order to raise them at least to the threshold of a minimally decent life. Though contemporary classical liberals often contest the extent of the welfare state and its limitations of economic freedoms, still they generally accept that it is the role of government to provide a "safety net" for persons who are incapable of providing for their own welfare. The disincentive to work that so-called welfare (or a negative income tax) can create must be taken into account, classical liberals insist, but nonetheless they generally have accepted government's duty to provide some kind of social minimum, at least in the form of "poor relief" to meet basic subsistence needs for those unable to provide for such needs themselves.[13]

Classical liberals generally contend that redressing destitution is not a claim-right that individuals have, but a matter of charity,[14] grounded in the fact that provision of everyone's subsistence needs is a public good. Thus, Milton Friedman writes, it is because of the insufficiency of private charity due to "a neighborhood effect" that he endorses "governmental action to alleviate poverty; to set, as it were, a floor under the standard of life of every person in the community."[15] Friedrich Hayek writes that, in order to avoid "great discontent and violent reaction" among those whose capacity to earn a living ceases,

> [t]he assurance of a certain minimum income for everyone, or a sort of floor below which no one need fall even when he is unable to provide for himself, appears not only to be a wholly legitimate protection against a risk common to all, but a necessary part of the Great Society.[16]

I have touched upon certain essential features of liberalism and shown how classical liberalism exhibits each of them. These features include equal basic and inalienable rights and liberties; freedom of occupation with equal opportunities to compete for open positions; free competitive markets; government's duty to respond to market breakdowns and provide public goods; a social minimum that is at least sufficient to meet the subsistence needs of those unable to provide for themselves; and the public fiduciary nature of political power. The libertarianism of Robert Nozick and others rejects each of these essential features of liberalism; libertarianism's apparent resemblance to classical liberalism is misleading. What leads many to conflate libertarianism and classical liberalism is that both endorse similar (if not the same) robust conceptions of economic rights and liberties, and therewith endorse market capitalism as the appropriate mechanism for determining the just distribution of income, wealth, and economic powers and responsibilities.[17] It is this robust conception of property rights and economic liberties that distinguishes classical liberalism from the high liberal tradition and gives rise to their different conceptions of distributive justice. Classical liberalism's conception of property rights and economic liberties also explains the theory's more conservative estimate of what is required to guarantee equal opportunities and satisfy the social minimum; the more limited extent it assigns to government's role in regulating markets; its more restricted range of public goods; and its formal or legalistic conception of equality of opportunity. I discuss these differences within liberalism in the following sections.

2. *The High Liberal Tradition*

Capitalism is essential to the classical liberal tradition. It is not essential to liberalism per se; for a primary feature of capitalism (as I use the term) is that the outcomes of free competitive market activity provide the fundamental basis for settling the distribution of income and wealth. Not all liberal conceptions endorse this important feature of capitalism.

By the "high liberal tradition" I mean the school of liberal thought that originates in the nineteenth century with the political and economic writings of John Stuart Mill; it includes T. H. Green and John Dewey in the late nineteenth and early twentieth centuries,[18] and its major representative in the second half of the twentieth century is John Rawls. Though Mill professes to be a utilitarian and Rawls a contractarian, there are close similarities in their conceptions of liberalism, democracy, and distributive justice. Rawls and Mill both affirm a principle of liberty that protects largely the same set of basic liberties, the primary exception being equal political liberties for all citizens.[19] Mill was an ardent defender of representative democracy and a universal franchise for all citizens, female as well as male; still he was prepared to allow for unequal voting rights, with plural voting rights for those with greater education.[20] Rawls, by contrast, argues that being respected by others as an equal person and enjoying the status of an equal citizen is essential to a person's good and self-respect. Primarily for these reasons, he argues, citizens in a democratic society ought to have equal rights to vote, hold office, and freely express themselves in the political and public domains.[21]

While classical liberals rejected a universal franchise until well into the early twentieth century, few classical liberals today would deny citizens formal equality of political rights to vote and hold office. The category of "passive citizens," which once included women, many free blacks, and other citizens who did not meet property qualifications, is now limited to children and others requiring legal guardians. Nonetheless, classical liberals generally do not accept efforts to neutralize the effects of wealth on political campaigns and procedures in order to mitigate inequality of political influence and promote political impartiality. High liberals, by contrast, contend that the liberal principle of maintaining the equal status of citizens requires that governments preserve the "fair value" (as Rawls says) of the political liberties regardless of people's economic position in society.[22] This is to be achieved primarily by the regulation of campaign spending and political contributions and by public financing of campaigns, so that private wealth does not distort or unfairly influence the democratic process. High liberals regard the dependence of legislators and other political officials upon private contributions for their political campaigns as a distortion of "public reason," since it tends to undermine impartial judgment and gives to the economically more advantaged an unfair influence in the political life of a democratic society. Classical liberals, including those who currently are a majority on the United States Supreme Court, disagree; they generally see restrictions on political contributions and campaign spending, not as a requirement of political equality, but as an unjustified restriction on freedom of political expression.[23] Money talks in classical liberal jurisprudence.

Again, the contrast here of classical liberalism with libertarianism is instructive. Notably, classical liberals do not normally regard campaign spending limitations as an unjust limitation on one's economic rights to spend one's money to buy whatever one pleases (within the limits set by basic rights and liberties). Classical liberals' justification for not limiting private campaign contributions does not stem from their conception of the economic rights that attend capitalism. The liberal idea that political power is a public power to be impartially exercised for the good of all citizens implies a rejection of the idea that government or its officials have the power to auction off political decisions or that citizens should have a right to buy political protection or decisions, as though they were a private economic good. The right to make campaign contributions is regarded, not as an economic right to purchase political services, but as a political right of free speech and expression.

While classical and high liberals differ in their interpretations of political equality, their main differences stem from their positions on the nature and scope of economic rights and liberties. This will be the primary focus of the remainder of this essay. I will regard Mill and Rawls as the paradigmatic representatives of the high liberal tradition. John Dewey is an important representative during the first half of the twentieth century, but since he had less to say about institutional arrangements than Rawls and Mill, I will not focus on his "new liberalism" here.[24]

There are four significant common features of Mill's and Rawls's views regarding economic justice. I focus on these in the following discussion since they are primarily the features that distinguish the classical and high liberal traditions. First, both Mill and Rawls deny that property rights and economic liberties are among the rights and liberties that are protected by their principles of liberty. They both reject what Mill calls "absolute property" in favor of a more "qualified property" system, with greater regulation of economic contracts than laissez-faire traditionally allows.[25] Second, with respect to free markets, both distinguish between and emphasize the dual functions that markets play in allocating productive forces (on the one hand) and distributing income and wealth (on the other). They argue that markets play their most crucial role in protecting freedom of occupation and choice of careers and in securing the efficient allocation of productive resources, and they do not fundamentally tie the final distribution of income and wealth to markets and the price system. Third, Mill and Rawls both endorse a conception of equality of (social and economic) opportunity that goes well beyond the classical liberal view of legal equality and careers open to talents. Finally, with respect to control over capital and productive resources and the distribution of income and wealth, both criticize capitalism for its tendency to concentrate wealth and control over the means of production in the hands of a relatively small class, and they advocate private property market systems that, unlike capitalism, do not have this tendency. I discuss each of the four ways that high liberalism differs from classical liberalism and capitalism in the next several sections.

3. Private Property and Economic Liberties

Mill says that economic liberties are not protected by the principle of liberty. His reasons are not compelling. He says that trade is a "social act" that is not "self-regarding" in the way that the basic liberties protected by his principle of liberty are supposed to be. Mill's distinction between individuals' "self-regarding" conduct and their social or "other-regarding" conduct with the potential for harm is, standing alone, hard to sustain. Many kinds of speech and association protected by the purportedly self-regarding freedoms of thought, expression, and association are "social" and "other-regarding" insofar as their main purpose is to influence political and cultural opinion and conduct (e.g., political speech, political parties, the Chamber of Commerce, labor unions). The real basis for Mill's distinction between the "self-regarding" liberties that are protected by his principle of liberty and the economic liberties that are not, must lie elsewhere. Though he says the principle of liberty is justified ultimately by the principle of utility, his list of basic liberties and his exclusion of economic liberties originates in considerations of "individuality" and an ideal of persons as "progressive beings" (discussed in section 4).[26]

Rawls relies upon similar considerations to argue that the economic liberties are not among the basic liberties protected by his first principle of justice. He says that "the right to hold personal property" is among the basic liberties. But "the right to own certain kinds of property (e.g., the means of production) and freedom of contract as understood by the doctrine of laissez-faire, are not basic [liberties]; and so they are not protected by the priority of the first principle."[27] Instead, for Rawls the specification, scope, and extent of economic rights and liberties are decided by his second principle of justice (including the difference principle), which states:

> Social and economic inequalities are to satisfy two conditions: first, they are to attach to offices and positions open to all under conditions of fair equality of opportunity; and second, they are to be to the greatest benefit of the least advantaged members of society (the difference principle).[28]

Rawls's distinction between personal property and non-personal property, including means of production, might seem hard to maintain for economists. (For example, many people buy houses in which to reside for a limited time, always intending to sell them for a profit.) But Rawls's distinction is not made within economics or the social sciences, nor does it track the legal distinction between personal and real property. Rather, it is a distinction made within a theory of social and economic justice, and is defined relative to Rawls's principles of justice. "Personal property" for Rawls thus consists of institutional rights and responsibilities regarding possessions that enable persons to effectively exercise their basic liberties (freedom of conscience, expression, association, etc.), take advantage of fair equality of opportunity, and achieve individual independence as they pursue a plan of life that is chosen from the wide range of permissible ways of living. Rawls implies that, while ownership or control of one's residence and personal belongings is necessary for individual independence and privacy, laissez-faire rights of ownership and control of means of production and near-absolute freedom of economic contract are not necessary for these general purposes—however much certain individuals might want to enjoy these rights given their specific life plans (e.g., to be wealthy). If laissez-faire rights of property and contract are to be justified at all on Rawls's terms, it must be shown that a laissez-faire economic system satisfies the difference principle and is, compared with other alternatives, to the greatest benefit of the least advantaged. That is an empirical question, which Rawls, like Mill, does not think can be decided in laissez-faire's favor.

The bases for Rawls's and Mill's liberalism and accounts of economic justice reside in ideals of persons and their relations. These ideals provide the ultimate explanation for these philosophers' refusals to include property rights and economic liberties among the basic rights and liberties as classical liberals do. This deeper explanation will be discussed in more detail in section 4. Here I will discuss the kinds of qualifications to property and economic liberties that Mill and Rawls endorse and some intermediate reasons they provide.

Mill famously distinguishes between absolute and qualified property:

> The laws of property have never yet conformed to the principles on which the justification of private property rests. They have made property of

things which never ought to be property and absolute property where only a qualified property ought to exist. They have not held the balance fairly between human beings, but have heaped impediments upon some, to give advantage to others; they have purposely fostered inequalities, and prevented all from starting fair in the race.[29]

For Mill, "property is only a means to an end, not itself the end."[30] The justification of private property in productive resources lies, in the first instance, in its "expediency" in facilitating production, and ultimately in "the permanent interests of the human race." He condemns absolute property rights in land for their inefficiency. "In the case of land, no exclusive right should be permitted . . . which cannot be shown to be productive of positive good."[31] Thus, ownership of land that is cultivated "does not imply an exclusive right to it for purposes of access." And if land is not intended to be cultivated, "no good reason can be given for its being private property at all"; anyone permitted to own it "holds it by sufferance of the community":[32]

> No man made the land. It is the original inheritance of the whole species. Its appropriation is wholly a question of general expediency. When private property in land is not expedient, it is unjust.[33]

With respect to bequests, Mill says that they are one of the attributes of property. An owner, for reasons of "expediency" and to encourage savings, should have the right to bequeath by will "his or her whole property, but not to lavish it enriching some one individual, beyond a certain maximum, which should be fixed sufficiently high to afford the means of comfortable independence":

> I see nothing objectionable in fixing a limit to what anyone may acquire by the mere favour of others, without any exercise of his faculties, and in requiring that if he desires any further accession of fortune, he shall work for it.[34]

Rawls, too, would regulate bequests and limit rights of inheritance. Even if it were assumed that certain rights of gift and bequest are implicit in property, these rights do not include the absolute right to transfer all and everything owned to whomever the owner chooses.[35] It is true that rights of gift and bequest encourage individuals not to squander their economic resources, but to save and reinvest them. For this reason, instead of taxing estates, both Rawls and Mill favor a tax on inheritances, thereby limiting rights of individuals on the receiving end of gifts and bequests to a specified amount. Inheritance taxes have the socially desirable effects of encouraging owners to spread their wealth around to more people and to charitable and other beneficial institutions, as well as limiting the adverse consequences of large individual accumulations of wealth on the equitable distribution of social and political power.

Both Mill and Rawls reject "natural property" and "natural rights" to property in possessions. They endorse versions of a conventional "bundle of rights and interests" view and contend that property is a social/legal institutional convention that can be designed in different ways, depending upon the specification of the incidents of property (including the many rights, powers, duties, and liabilities, to possess, use, transfer, and dispose of things, both tangible and intangible). Rawls and Mill are both influenced by Hume's account of property as a social convention. Hume says that property is not a quality of objects or a natural relation of persons to things, but an "internal" or "moral" relation among members of a society that exists by "convention."[36] Rawls, too, regards property as a conventional institution, the incidents of which can be specified and designed in multiple ways. One of the primary tasks for an account of distributive justice is to set forth and justify a principle for the specification and regulation of the rights and duties of possession, use, transfer, and disposal of the tangible and intangible things we ordinarily call "property." For Mill, this role was ultimately to be served by the principle of utility—for Rawls, by his second principle of justice, primarily the difference principle. On either account—and this is perhaps a central feature of the high liberal tradition—the rights and other incidents of property (what might be called its "ontology") are relativized or adjusted to meet the requirements of antecedent principles of justice, as these principles are applied to different social and historical circumstances.

The "ontological relativity" that Mill and Rawls see as implicit in property is not peculiar to the high liberal tradition. Hume was, after all, a (nascent) classical liberal. Similarly, Friedrich Hayek and Milton Friedman both endorse the Humean institutional conception of property. Friedman writes:

> The notion of property . . . has become so much a part of us that we tend to take it for granted, and fail to recognize the extent to which just what constitutes property and what rights the ownership of property confers are complex social creations rather than self-evident propositions.[37]

Friedman says that among the essential roles of governments is "the definition of the meaning of property rights"—by which he means its legislative and judicial specification. With respect to distributive justice, Friedman affirms the classical liberal principle of market distributions, but qualifies it:

> The ethical principle that would directly justify the distribution of income in a free market society is "to each according to what he and the instruments he owns produces." The operation of even this principle implicitly depends

on state action. *Property rights are matters of law and social conventions . . .* [Hence,] *[t]he final distribution of income and wealth under the full operation of this principle may well depend markedly on the rules of property adopted.*[38]

The implication is that we stand in need of some principle to specify the rules of property that underwrite the classical liberal precept "To each according to what he or she and the instruments he or she owns produces." The ideas of ownership and property rights are but placeholders until this principle is specified and justified.

As for other classical liberals within the Anglo-American tradition since Hume and Adam Smith, for Friedman the ultimate grounds for robust property rights, economic freedoms, and market distributions depend, not on claims of natural property rights regarded as "self-evident propositions,"[39] but on considerations of economic efficiency and, ultimately, social utility. Insofar as claims of natural property rights are made, as in the work of Adam Smith, they too ultimately are conceived instrumentally, as the incidents of property that achieve efficiency and the public benefit.

4. The Allocative Function versus the Distributive Function of Markets

The second important similarity between Mill and Rawls is their conception of the proper role of markets. This clarifies their attitudes toward capitalism and helps to explain why both reject capitalism as understood by classical liberals. Mill distinguishes between laws of economic production and laws of distribution. He contends that laws of production are of universal applicability, whereas laws of distribution are not and are guided by institutional arrangements that differ among societies. The laws of production, Mill writes, "partake of the character of physical truths," whereas "the Distribution of Wealth . . . is a matter of human institution solely. The things once there, mankind, individually or collectively, can do with them as they like."[40]

Similarly, Rawls distinguishes between the role of market prices in allocating productive resources and their role in the distribution of income and wealth. "The former [allocative function] is connected with their use to achieve economic efficiency, the latter [distributive function] with their determining the income to be received by individuals in return for what they contribute." In using the market to allocate productive factors, "prices are indicators for drawing up an efficient schedule of economic activities":

It does not follow however that there need be private persons who as owners of these assets receive the monetary equivalents of these evaluations.[41]

The general implication is the same point made by Mill, namely, that a society's use of markets to determine the distribution of wealth is separate and apart from its use of markets to allocate productive resources.[42] In general, the efficient allocation of productive resources does not require that the distribution of wealth that results be determined by market distributions that result from efficient production.

Liberals generally endorse free markets and the price system for at least two reasons. First, unlike planned economies, a market system is crucial to realizing the basic liberty of persons to freely choose their own careers and workplaces. Markets are, in this way, essential to realizing both freedom of the person and equality of opportunity to compete for open positions. Planned economies and traditional societies constrained by class customs restrict individuals' choices in these matters or give them none at all; a person's occupation and workplace are assigned either by someone in authority or by social class and custom—in the latter case, your profession and path in life is the same as your father's or mother's. The second reason liberals generally endorse markets is that the market allocations of productive resources and labor are believed to be more likely to result in an efficient allocation of these factors of production than is a non-market system. Competitive markets thereby normally minimize economic waste.[43] There are other justifications that may be emphasized by classical liberals but are not endorsed by high liberals (e.g., free markets are required by the basic liberty of freedom of economic contract, which is not recognized as a basic liberty by high liberals), but on these two grounds at least, liberals of both varieties can agree.

Significantly, both of these arguments—from freedom of occupation / equality of opportunity and from allocative efficiency—relate to production and the allocation of labor and resources for purposes of productive economic activity. In the absence of a particular conception of property, the arguments do not by themselves imply anything in particular about who has rights to the economic product that is the efficient outcome of the activities of freely associated producers and entrepreneurs. Assuming that the three traditional "factors of production"— land, labor, and capital—all contribute their share to the final product, the question is left open as to how the resulting income, profits, interest, and rent are to be distributed among those cooperating to produce them or among members of society as a whole.[44] The answer to this question is determined largely by a society's specification of property rights in productive resources and the rights of workers and owners of capital to income from the product created by their respective contributions. As Friedman says, "Property rights are matters of law and social convention . . . The final distribution of income and wealth . . . depend[s] markedly on the rules of property adopted."[45]

5. *The Argument from the Fairness of Market Distributions*

Here many classical liberals and libertarians have argued that economic agents—workers and those who own and control capital alike—should each receive the marginal value of the contribution that each makes to productive output. "Profits," as Malthus says, "are a fair remuneration for that part of the production contributed by the capitalist."[46] Drawing on the marginal productivity theory of income distribution, many classical liberals and libertarians contend that each participant in a joint economic enterprise contributes his or her share of factors of production (labor, land and raw materials, or capital, both real and liquid) toward the final product. According to standard microeconomic theory, we can measure the economic value of each of the inputs to production by determining its marginal contribution to the final product. The *marginal product* of each factor that each participant owns and controls is then (it is said) what he or she can be said to "contribute" toward the final output. Since each participant is responsible for what he or she contributes, it follows that in accordance with the precept of justice "To each according to his or her contribution," economic agents *morally ought* to share in the distribution of income and wealth in a manner proportionate to the value of their marginal product.[47]

This is a popular argument among many classical liberals and libertarians, and it normally appeals to a notion of fairness or fair desert in the distribution of the products of economic cooperation. Classical liberals and libertarians argue that owners of capital should have a right to the entire profits, interest, and rent that result from their investment of capital—exclusive of others, whether they also contribute or not—because profits, interest, and rent measure the marginal product of their contribution. Just as workers have a right to the fruits of their labor as measured by the wages representing the value of their contribution, so too owners of capital have a right to profits, interest, and rent that result from their investment of capital, since these measure the marginal product of *their* contribution as well.[48]

Here it should be first noted that it is somewhat misleading to claim that "the income each receives . . . is equal to the contribution she makes, or the marginal difference she adds to the value of the total product."[49] Instead, *all* units of a factor get paid the factor's equilibrium value of the marginal product—the additional value produced by the *last* unit of the factor employed.[50] Thus, in the case of labor, it is the *last* worker hired who receives the value of his or her marginal product, and since only one person can be the last hired, the rest of the workers must receive something less than the value of *their* marginal product on the way to equilibrium. Only if each worker is regarded as the last hired can each be said to receive his or her marginal product. This is evident from the fact that, when we divide the total amount of revenue generated by all similarly skilled workers in a firm by the number of workers, the average contribution by each exceeds the wage rate, as measured by the marginal product of the last worker.[51] Though the first worker hired may generate $35 of revenue per hour, he or she receives the same $15 in income and benefits that the last worker does. The added revenue created by workers above the value of the marginal product of the last worker that all workers are paid goes to the owner or entrepreneur. This clarifies the background to the potentially misleading claim that "[i]n the standard competitive labor market, a person's earnings equal the value of his or her marginal productivity."[52] Strictly speaking, it is less than that.

Setting this qualification aside, what are we to make of this argument from fairness, that economic agents' share in the final product should be proportionate to their (marginal) contribution? Assume for the sake of argument that workers have a right to the value of their contribution. Here we have to set aside the fact that in a market economy what an individual contributes depends on such contingencies as firms' demand for his or her skills, which varies with demand for firms' products, as well as how many other workers offer similar talents and skills, and a host of other contingencies (a point returned to later). Nonetheless, there is a genuine naturalistic sense in which workers can be said to contribute their labor toward productive output, as well as a naturalistic sense in which land, raw materials, and real capital make a contribution. It is a natural fact, regardless of the form taken by social conventions and institutions, that nothing could be produced in the absence of labor (which includes the exercise of knowledge), land, natural resources, and the instruments of production created by their combination. Under capitalism and other private property systems, owners of capital and other resources are also causal agents in the production process due to their ownership and control of means of production. But the sense in which *owners* of factors of production other than labor themselves make a "contribution" to productive output is different from the kind of contribution made by labor, land, and capital itself. The contribution of owners is notional when compared with the contribution made by the factors of production they own; their contribution is a manner of speaking that is dependent upon the rights of ownership and control that owners enjoy by virtue of legal and other conventional arrangements.

By way of example to clarify the point, consider a slave economy. While it is clear that the slaves on a sugar plantation make a substantial contribution to agricultural production, to say that the *owners* of the slaves also make their "contribution" of labor ("after all, they own it") is to use that word in a very different sense from the sense we use when we say "workers contribute their labor." Owners of slaves "contribute" the labor of those persons they own in this notional sense; their "contribution" is at best a "legal fiction" (to use Jeremy Bentham's term) based in the legal fact of ownership. This much seems obvious.

Generalizing, the same notional sense of "contribution" is at work when it is said that owners of land, real capital, liquid capital, and any other resources "contribute" to economic output. Their "contribution" or involvement may be causally necessary within the social context; production could not, under the circumstances, take place without the legal right to use certain resources they legally control under conventional norms of property. But this contribution is not on a par with the natural contribution made by labor, just as it is not on a par with the physical contribution that natural and artificial resources make to productive output. The contribution made by the owners of productive resources is not a natural fact of either kind. Unlike workers, owners, regarded purely in their capacity as owners, do not themselves actually produce anything.[53] Often they are not even aware of doing anything (e.g., owners of shares of mutual funds). Theirs is a legal contribution effected by virtue of the legal rights and powers that owners of capital resources are recognized as having by other members of a society. Legal rights and powers are institutional facts made possible by people's shared beliefs and other attitudes, collective intentions, general agreement on norms, and social activities. Property exists by virtue of a background of social rules that are generally accepted and recognized as authoritative by (most) members of society and by people conforming their conduct to and cooperating according to these rules. It is by virtue of the institutional facts of private property that owners of capital are deemed to make a "contribution" to production. Their contribution is not a "brute fact"; it is, rather, a matter of people's attitudes and linguistic descriptions formed against a background of institutional facts (property, money, government, and the legal system) that themselves exist only by virtue of collective agreement, intentions, and activities.[54]

My claim is not that owners make no contribution at all to productive output. They contribute their property, whether it be their rights in real capital, money, or some intangible. The institution of property is very important for production, because some persons or groups have to legally own and control means of production to enable efficient economic activity. But this "contribution" is itself a colloquial way of talking about certain legal transactions and economic activities (borrowing, lending, investing, etc.). This way of talking becomes a self-serving conjuring trick when the inference is drawn that owners, in contributing their property, also contribute the (marginal) product of the capital resources they own and therefore have a right to its entirety. Talking in this way sustains the widespread illusion that owners make contributions on a par with labor. In the end owners' "contributions" are simply a matter of people's attitudes and linguistic descriptions formed against a background of property rights and other institutional conventions (money, contract and commercial law, more generally government and the legal system) that themselves, while necessary for productive activity, exist by virtue of collective attitudes and agreements, as well as conformity to institutional rules.

My claims regarding the contributions made by owners due to the legal phenomenon of pure ownership apply also to such popular locutions as claims that owners or investors "create value" and "generate wealth." With some modification, they also apply to the claim that owners of wealth are "job creators."

At this point, some will object that many capitalists, like Bill Gates, Steve Jobs, Mark Zuckerberg, and other Silicon Valley virtuosos, use their imagination, creativity, and entrepreneurial skills to start their own companies and that their contributions in these respects are crucial to the production of new goods and services, as well as new technologies, and to job and wealth creation in an efficient market economy. Similarly, billionaires such as Warren Buffett, George Soros, and other financiers apply their knowledge and skills to investment decisions regarding the purchase of stock in companies they later come to control. I do not deny that people in these positions make contributions or that they "create jobs, wealth," and so on. But if they do so, it is in their capacity as entrepreneurs, applying their knowledge and skills, which is a form of labor. They could also perform these same services by working for someone else and getting paid a salary, as most of their employees do. The same is true in the case of investors who make their own decisions regarding their investments. Financiers could and normally do hire many people to help them make investment decisions, and at some point, they may pull back and allow others to make investment decisions for them entirely, paying them a salary or a commission or in some other way. The research and computations involved in making investment decisions are a form of labor, a service that businesses offer for a fee. It has a price, and the income earned from making investment decisions (by stockbrokers, etc.) is taxed as income at a rate that now is normally distinguishable from the (lower) rate that owners of capital pay on dividends and capital gains.

So the answer to the claim that creative masterminds like Steve Jobs, Mark Zuckerberg, and others "create jobs and wealth" and therewith make enormous, not merely fictional, contributions to productive output is "Yes, they do so in their capacity as entrepreneurs, computer programmers, managers," and the like, and these positions and roles involve exercising various forms of labor that make a substantial contribution to productive output. The marginal contribution made by their labor may be quite substantial, even enormous in its scope. Then the question is, how much of their marginal product from their labor are they entitled to as a matter of justice? But whatever the answer is to this question, the marginal contribution that these innovators make by applying their extraordinary creativity, technological imagination, and skills is different in kind from the contribution they make purely in their capacity as owners of shares or owners outright of the companies they work for. The contribution they make on the basis of their knowledge and skills is substantial; that based on the legal fact of pure ownership is notional. Similarly, the wealth and jobs they create by applying their knowledge and skills are substantial; the wealth and jobs created by their capital are just that— they are created by the real and liquid capital itself, not by the institutional fact of their ownership of it. That owners of capital "create jobs" or "create wealth" is a convenient social and political fiction.

The criticism of the marginal productivity theory of just distributions that I make here is not new. It is a modern development of a similar criticism made in the nineteenth century by socialist critics of capitalism, including Marx. In response, economists have said that capitalist owners do in fact make a substantial or natural contribution to production after all, not just a notional one; for they contribute their "abstinence," or their "waiting to consume" their wealth. Owners of wealth and capital *could* consume what they possess, but do not and instead invest their resources and undertake risks others are unwilling to take. By undergoing this sacrifice and assuming these risks, owners benefit society by capital formation. Had someone not abstained from consumption and saved wealth and resources, there would be no capital for workers to labor on. Mill himself relied on this so-called abstinence theory of interest when, in response to the socialist claim that labor is the source of all value, he argued that owners of capital contribute their abstinence and should have a right to a return on their investment too.[55]

I agree that owners of capital do serve a valuable function and have a right to *some* return on their investment because of the investment itself, their risk-taking, and their waiting to consume. Still, abstinence from consumption does not by itself imply that owners of capital should have *complete* rights to the monetary value of the *entire* marginal product of the resources they contribute. The fact that the capitalist *could* consume his or her capital instead cannot establish a right to the entire marginal product of capital itself. After all, a professional thief could consume it too, but this fact surely does not entitle the thief to any return, either for refraining from theft of productive resources or for abstaining from consuming and investing instead resources already stolen. The reason the capitalist (as opposed to the thief) can be said to contribute his or her "abstinence" is precisely that the capitalist is legally entitled and normally has a legal *right* to consume what he or she owns but decides to invest instead. From this it does not follow, without further argument, that the capitalist should have a right to the entire marginal product that is created by the resources contributed. Considerations of fairness alone are not sufficient to establish such a controversial conclusion.

A similar point applies to the claim that owners of capital assume risks that others do not and that this assumption of risk is their contribution to productive output. What owners risk is their legal rights to the capital and natural resources they invest in, including risking the economic value of their initial investment. Normally, except in the case of perishables, productive resources and consumer goods will survive even if a venture fails and owners lose their capital and resources to someone else (through bankruptcy) or have to sell their goods and resources at a loss. It is not so much the real capital or natural resources that are put at risk; rather it is entrepreneurs' legally recognized *property rights* that are put at risk, including their rights to the value of their initial investment. By itself, putting their rights to capital at risk does not imply anything in particular about how much of the marginal product owners should be entitled to in return for assuming this risk should their investment be successful. From the fact that they risk losing their rights to their entire investment, it does not follow that they should have a right to the entire value of the marginal product resulting from this contribution. (Suppose the value of their investment triples; they invest $1 million in a venture and after a short time gain a $3 million windfall.)[56] Investors are due surely something for taking risks, but more needs to be said to justify the conclusion that they have a right to the entire marginal product of the real or liquid capital they own.

The general point here is that the argument from marginal productivity theory for market distributions depends upon an ambiguity involved when we speak of someone's "contribution to" productive output. It is this ambiguity between the de facto and de jure sense of "contribution to" (or "worker's vs. owner's responsibility for") the final product that is played upon by the argument for market distributions according to the marginal product of each party's "contribution."[57]

None of this is meant to deny that private property in productive resources often serves an important *function*. Economists will argue that, without private ownership of productive resources, much of the productive surplus that is created by labor likely would be consumed if it were distributed to workers themselves and would not then be saved and reinvested. By allowing for private property in productive resources, a society creates the strategic position of *owners*, which provides an effective way to both shepherd resources and save and reinvest the productive surplus. Allowing private ownership and control of productive resources creates a group of people who are willing to save their surplus income (profits, interest, and rent) and take risks on investments that lead to the development of new products and services. If we did not allow people some kind of market return on the risks they undertake with their wealth, they would not undertake these risks, and new innovations and other benefits of undertaking market risks would not be realized within a society.

If this argument is sound, then it supports some kind of market economy with private ownership of productive resources and some degree of market returns for their use (as opposed to a socialist system, where the public owns the means of production and receives the return on their use). Still, the functional argument for private ownership just stated does not justify rewarding owners with the *entire* marginal product of the capital they contribute to production. Rather, the functional argument simply establishes the beneficial effects of private over public ownership and implies nothing in particular about individuals' rights to income, the rate of taxation, or what the returns to ownership should be. Nor does the beneficial function served by private ownership even justify capitalism in the traditional sense argued for by classical liberals, for not all private property market economies are capitalist.[58] I conclude, then, that whatever role marginal productivity theory plays in microeconomic explanations of the market price of labor and productive resources, that theory cannot be used to justify full market distributions of income and wealth going to the private persons who legally own productive resources. For once we go beyond the natural contribution made by workers' labor and productive resources, the idea of a particular person's "contribution" toward or "responsibility for" productive output cannot be specified independently of the legal institution of property. When it comes to productive resources other than labor, individuals' "contribution to" and "responsibility for" the social product are institutionally dependent, indefinable outside an institutional (and normally legal) context. Again, as Milton Friedman said (in endorsing the classical liberal precept of justice "To each according to his or her contribution"), "The final distribution of income and wealth under the full operation of this principle may well depend markedly on the rules of property adopted."[59]

There remains then the problem of justice that appeals to marginal productivity theory were supposed to resolve—namely, the problem of justifying market distributions of income and wealth that result from productive activity. Assuming that for any legal system that is in place we can specify the legal or de jure contribution that owners are conventionally regarded as making toward production, this cannot morally justify market distributions according to each party's legally recognized contributions. Since the contribution of capitalists is not a natural contribution (in the way that the contribution of workers and productive resources is) but is instead an institutional artifact, the question arises, why should owners receive the entire income or marginal product of the resources they legally own in the form of profits, interest, and rent? It begs the question to say, "They own it," since the very problem to be addressed is the justice of existing property relations and what the rights of return on ownership should be. Thus, the argument for market distributions of marginal product must depend upon something other than marginal productivity theory. Ultimately, it depends upon some version of a laissez-faire theory of property rights, such as a theory of natural property, which contends that people legally should be entitled to complete rights to income generated by the use of economic resources they own and control.[60] Some such argument is presupposed by the contention that individuals are due the full marginal product of resources they own.

Finally, in contrasting owners' notional contribution with the natural contributions of labor, my point is not that workers should have complete rights to their contributions or "the fruits of their labors" either. Nor am I arguing the traditional socialist position, that since only labor actually produces anything of value, workers should be entitled to the entire (marginal) product. As I said at the outset, in a market economy where the price of labor is set by demand, the value of what an individual contributes via his or her labor depends on contingencies totally unrelated to what that worker actually produces: these contingencies include factors such as firms' demand for workers' skills, which varies with demand for firms' products, as well as the labor supply and how many other workers in the region offer similar talents and skills, and the like. These contingencies in turn depend upon whether and to what degree a society educates its members and provides opportunities for them to develop their talents and skills, not to mention the current level of unemployment, the mobility of labor, geographical factors, and many other factors. Two workers in different societies with the same education and skill can devote the same amount of labor time and effort to producing the same product or service (e.g., a shirt, computer chip, or kidney transplant), and yet receive markedly different wages or salaries for their respective contributions and efforts.

Moreover, though labor's contribution is natural in a way that the contribution of owners of capital is not, our understanding of workers' "contribution," "product," and "the fruits of workers' labor" is also institutionally dependent. In a socialist economy without competitive markets, such as the former Soviet Union, the idea of the marginal contribution of labor makes little sense or at least means something quite different than in a market economy. In a command economy, the concepts of workers' contributions and the fruits of workers' labor are interpreted very differently than in a market economy. Instead of marginal product, measures of labor time and effort expended, and the relative dangers, unpleasantness, and arduousness of labor, might be relied upon to determine the contribution workers make to productive output.

This means that the sense in which labor's marginal contribution is "natural," and not simply de jure as owners' contributions are, does not settle the moral status of workers' contributions either. For the fact that a contribution is natural in the relevant sense does not imply that its market value is not contingent on many other factors that are independent of that natural contribution. Marginal contribution theory, whatever its legitimate explanatory role in economic theory, is not any more relevant to establishing the just returns to labor than it is to determining just returns to pure ownership. Nor am I arguing that we should seek to construct some idea of the value of workers' natural contribution independent of market contingencies and reward them accordingly, such as workers' capacities, knowledge, skills, efforts, and labor time. For these, too, will be influenced by arbitrary contingencies other than market luck—the "natural lottery," a person's social background and the family into which he or she is born, natural accidents and social misfortunes, and the like—and the effects of these on individuals' capacities, efforts, knowledge, skills, and other natural attributes.

I conclude that the question of the degree to which individuals should be rewarded according to their contributions to productive output cannot be settled independent of questions regarding the nature of institutional property relations and of the economic system that is in place, and the justice of these conventional arrangements. The commonsense adage "To each according to his or her contribution"—if it has any relevance to distributive justice at all—is at best a secondary precept whose meaning varies with the background institutional and economic conditions. Its moral relevance and weight presuppose more fundamental principles of economic justice. My own view is that—whatever relevance the adage of rewarding each according to contribution might have in determining the appropriate shares of workers, management, and owners *within* a firm when they decide among themselves the wage rate versus shares going to owners—the traditional adage is of little relevance socially in determining the distributive shares owed to economically productive agents and other members of society.

6. Equal Opportunity and Economic Liberty

The argument for equality within the liberal tradition is more an argument for social equality than one for political equality. When Alexis de Tocqueville published *Democracy in America* in 1835, the majority of American citizens were regarded as "passive" and did not have the right to vote; men who did not meet property qualifications were excluded from the franchise, as were, of course, women and African Americans. What made the United States democratic in de Tocqueville's sense was not so much democratic government as the absence of a nobility or other inherited class structure and legal barriers to positions and occupations. The idea of careers being open to talents, or "the natural liberty of exercising what industry they please" regardless of birth or lineage or (most) religious affiliations, was affirmed by classical liberals in the eighteenth century.[61] Only much later was the idea to be extended to race and gender. One argument for the equal opportunity to compete for open positions lies in the classical liberal view of economic liberties. Workers should be free to market their services, employers should be allowed to employ whomever they choose, and merchants and other businesses should be free to engage in the exchange of goods and services with whomever they please, without being burdened by the legal enforcement of others' religious, social, or racial biases. Moreover, opening positions purely on the basis of talents and skills increases economic efficiency. The classical liberal ideal of equal opportunity played a major role in democratizing society by breaking down the barriers of inherited class privilege and legal discrimination according to social position, religion, wealth, and (eventually) race and gender.

Still, the classical liberal view of economic liberties did little directly to mitigate social (as opposed to legal) discrimination. Owners and employees still had the right in theory and in practice to refuse goods, services, and employment by virtue of their robust property and contract rights. Racial discrimination in hotels, restaurants, real estate sales, businesses and employment, and many other areas of life was common in the United States, even in the absence of Jim Crow laws in the South and elsewhere that legally mandated it.[62] Segregation and racial discrimination by businesses were legally protected in most of the United States until the 1960s, even when not legally required. Of course, classical liberals do not endorse racial or other forms of discrimination. The vast majority reject such discrimination in theory as much as other liberals do. Classical liberals often contend that, because of freedom of contract, these sorts of problems will eventually sort themselves out. Businesses or entrepreneurs that discriminate on grounds not related to economic efficiency are at a disadvantage, since they are imposing higher costs on themselves. Free markets will tend to drive out of business those who discriminate on grounds other than economic efficiency.[63]

This is one of many examples of something being true in the economic theory of perfectly competitive markets but in fact not true in our social world of the "second best." Where there is widespread racial or ethnic bias, discrimination on these grounds is a precondition of economic success. Even if enlightened businesses wanted to serve disfavored minorities, their trade would soon suffer due to ingrained social customs and prejudices. Until relatively recently in most parts of the South and in many other areas of the United States, a hotel, restaurant, or business that freely served blacks would soon serve only blacks, since whites would cease doing business there (or worse). Only with the Civil Rights Act of 1964 in the United States, which banned racial discrimination by employers and "public accommodations," was this problem of social inequality addressed (to the extent that it could be addressed by law) and did things begin to change. All employers or businesses that do business with the public are now legally prohibited from discriminating among job applicants or customers "on the basis of race, color, religion, sex, or national origin." Economic contracts are no longer regarded as purely private transactions between willing parties; their legal recognition and enforcement involves the exercise of public political power with serious social consequences for third parties.

In response to such anti-discrimination measures and policies enacted by the Fair Employment Practices Commission (FEPC), Milton Friedman objected that measures such as the Civil Rights Act are serious violations of individuals' freedom:

> There is a strong case for using government to prevent one person from imposing positive harm, which is to say, to prevent coercion. There is no case whatsoever for using government to avoid the negative kind of

"harm." On the contrary, *such government intervention reduces freedom and limits voluntary cooperation.*

FEPC legislation involves the acceptance of a principle that proponents would find abhorrent in almost every other application. If it is appropriate for the state to say that individuals may not discriminate in employment because of color or race or religion, then it is equally appropriate for the state . . . to say that individuals must discriminate in employment on the basis of color, race or religion. The Hitler Nuremberg laws and the laws of the Southern states imposing special disabilities upon Negroes are both examples of laws similar in principle to FEPC.[64]

The laws are said to be similar in principle, and both are condemned on the grounds that in both cases government's coercive powers are used in a way that "reduces freedom and limits voluntary cooperation." The political injustice done to the entrepreneur, restauranteur, or hotel owner who is legally required under the Civil Rights Act to fairly consider black job applicants or to serve Jews and Hispanics is then put on the same plane with the injustice done, not only to businesses and employers, but also to blacks and Jews who are legally prohibited from entering employment positions or frequenting public places or businesses in the Jim Crow South and in Nazi Germany. In both cases, their freedom is limited and cooperative relations are no longer voluntary.

There appears to be a conflation here between the reasons that underlie freedom of economic contract and those that underlie freedom of association in one's personal life. Freedom of association is among the most fundamental of the liberal basic liberties. It is a precondition of freedom of conscience that we be able to personally associate with others of like mind and conscientious convictions, and also a precondition of our realizing such great values as personal relations of love, friendship, and intimacy. For Friedman, economic contracts between strangers are to be regarded as if they were on a par with such private relations—both are forms of voluntary cooperation, and, as such, freedom of contract should be given the same degree of protection as freedom of religious associations or of personal or intimate associative relations between friends or lovers. It is as if there would be no moral difference between my being legally required to sell goods to a black person that I offer for sale to the general public and my being legally required to invite black guests for dinner if I also chose to invite non-blacks.

One important difference between the liberal freedoms of association and contract is that contractual relations—unlike associative relations between friends, lovers, and members of private clubs, fraternities, or religious groups—are legally sanctioned and enforceable. We can enter into and break off friendships, intimate relationships, club memberships, and religious and other affiliations, and it is none of government's business. Government's lack of enforcement primarily distinguishes freedom of association from freedom of contract. Unlike freely associative relations, there is no right of exit from contractual relations without legal consequences; one either has to pay damages or restitution or has to execute one's contractual obligations in cases of specific performance. Contracts freely entered into thus have the imprimatur of government and are specifically designed to invoke the exercise of public political power.[65] There is no parallel to this in the case of freedom of association; instead, there is a presumption of a right of exit without legal consequences (unless, of course, one has made a contract explicitly invoking government's involvement, as in the case of civil marriages). For high liberals, it is in large part the exercise of public political power to define and enforce legally recognizable contracts that gives liberal governments the legitimate authority to specify certain terms and conditions that contractual relations must satisfy.

Of course, given liberals' endorsement of free-market relations, there has to be good reason for government to limit freedom of contract by requiring (as in the case of FEPC legislation and the Civil Rights Act) that merchants do business with certain customers they would rather avoid. Friedman contends that there is not good reason. Continuing the argument above, he says that since both laws coercively restrict voluntary cooperation, "[o]pponents of [the Hitler Nuremburg] laws who are in favor of FEPC cannot argue that there is anything wrong with them in principle"[66]—thus suggesting that there is no principled basis for limiting voluntary cooperation in one case but not the other. But for high liberals, the basic reasons that the Nuremburg laws are unjust are not that they limit voluntary cooperation. (As Friedman and other classical liberals recognize, there are often legitimate reasons for limiting voluntary cooperation—in cases of conspiracies to commit crimes, conspiracies in restraint of trade, price collusion, bribery, etc.) The main reasons Nuremburg, Jim Crow, and other racist laws are fundamentally unjust are that (1) they publicly deny the equal moral and civic status of racial and ethnic groups, and (2) they legally restrict group members' basic freedoms of occupation and choice of careers, as well as (3) their rights to equal opportunities to compete and take part in social and economic life. These are the selfsame reasons and principles for which high liberals also restrict freedom of economic contract (in the Civil Rights Act and elsewhere) in ways that many classical liberals will not countenance. Friedman is then mistaken; the principles that expose the obvious injustice of the Nuremburg and Jim Crow laws are the selfsame principles that justify compelling those who do business with the public not to engage in invidious discrimination in their economic transactions.

A more robust conception of social and civic equality and equality of opportunity is, then, the primary reason that high liberals restrict freedom of economic contract in ways that most classical liberals will not countenance. John Stuart Mill's argument for the equality of women in economic, political, and social life gives early expression to the high liberal position that civic equality and equality of opportunity are not simply to be regarded as formal requirements that forbid the legal exclusion of women and other classes of individuals from taking advantage of social, political, and economic opportunities.[67] Equality of opportunity is a social requirement that is regarded as necessary to secure and maintain the equal social and civic status of all citizens in the public domain and in one another's eyes.

The public funding of educational opportunities is explicable within the high liberal tradition on similar grounds. Already, early classical liberals such as Adam Smith saw the benefits of publicly funded education to a nation's efficient productive capacities.[68] Moreover, as Friedman notes, education involves "neighborhood effects," the costs of which cannot be charged to those who benefit and should thus be publicly assumed.[69] Thus, many classical liberals see general education of all children as among the public goods to be provided by government. Here again, for high liberals, classical liberals' primarily economic justification of equality of opportunity does not suffice or pinpoint the real reasons for a right to publicly funded education. As I will discuss in my concluding section, there is an ideal of persons and their relations as equals that underpins the high liberal view of the substantive requirements of equality of opportunity.

7. *Distributive Justice: Income, Wealth, and Economic Powers*

The idea of distributive justice does not find much favor among classical liberals or libertarians, since (as Nozick said) it suggests that there is some pattern or end-state that must be met if the distribution of income and wealth is to be justified.[70] Here I use the term "distributive justice" more broadly than this, to refer to the standards that should be relied upon in society for assessing whether people have just entitlements to the income, wealth, and economic powers that they legally own, control, or exercise. So understood, capitalist market distributions against a background of robust private property rights specify the fundamental standard of distributive justice for classical liberals—on the assumption that economic agents have paid their proportionate share to maintain the institutions of justice and provide for public goods. Thus, the marginal productivity theory of just distributions discussed earlier says that the share of income that is owed to workers and owners of resources is to be determined by the market value of their respective contributions, which are construed as the (marginal) product created by their labor or property. This market distribution is a fundamental feature of capitalism as a social and economic system. For classical liberals, it stands as *the* fundamental principle of distributive justice. It may not be the only principle— people acquire rights to gifts and bequests, gambling winnings, abandoned property, and so on—but markets still provide the fundamental determining principle of distribution of the income resulting from productive economic activity itself.

Advocates of the high liberal tradition generally reject predominantly market-driven theories of just distributions. While they regard market transfers as an efficient instrument for distributing a substantial portion of the distributive shares that members of society are due, they reject (free and efficient) market distribution itself as the fundamental principle of economic justice in the distribution of income and wealth. Thus, Rawls contends that the fair distribution of income and wealth is to be determined by the "pure procedural" outcome of a "social process" wherein economic institutions and property are designed and specified according to Rawls's second principle of justice, including the difference principle.[71] Markets play an instrumental role in achieving this distribution, but they are not themselves the standard for determining just entitlements. Nor is the market the only procedural mechanism for realizing the fair distribution of income and wealth for high liberals. Rawls envisions income supplements (such as earned-income tax credits in the United States) as among the instrumental means of distribution of income required by distributive justice.[72] The ultimate standard for determining just distributions is the difference principle set against a background of institutions satisfying fair equality of opportunity. Distributive shares are fully just when economic institutions work, over time, to make the class of least advantaged workers in society better off in terms of their share of relevant primary social goods (income, wealth, and economic powers) than they would be in any other economic system that is compatible with the basic liberties protected by Rawls's first principle. (As I shall explain momentarily, this does not mean that the least advantaged are to have more income and wealth than in any alternative economy.)

I do not mean to say that all high liberals reject capitalism or the standard of market distributions altogether. Some do not, but rather contend that market distributions, while essential, are not sufficient for establishing just distributions. Thus, welfare-state capitalists might affirm market distributions as one among the fundamental principles of economic justice. But they deny the classical liberal position that the economic liberties and property rights are nearly coequal with the basic personal liberties. For example, Ronald Dworkin's position, "equality of resources," justifies a form of welfare-state capitalism.[73] It says that once the consequences of arbitrary natural and social inequalities have been neutralized, entitlements to income and wealth are determined by our choices and how well we fare in market activity. Dworkin seeks to equalize starting positions in life and neutralize the effects of "brute luck," which include differences in natural talents, social position, and misfortunes for which people are not responsible. (Mill expresses a similar luck neutralizing position regarding remuneration of labor.)[74] Each person then has a duty to pay his or her fair share in taxes toward maintaining an economic system that meets this and other conditions. But

Dworkin does not try to neutralize market luck (a form of "option luck") or otherwise put restrictions on the inequalities that free and efficient market activities and distributions may cause. He believes that, once individuals have paid their share toward public goods, social insurance, and other conditions necessary for maintaining justice, they should be entitled to whatever they gain by market activity. Dworkin's example shows that high liberalism does not necessarily imply a rejection of capitalism. Rather, what it implies is a rejection of unqualified capitalist market distributions and of the reliance on (free and efficient) markets as the fundamental standard for the distribution of income and wealth.

The rejection of markets as the fundamental standard for just distributions of income and wealth is the most obvious respect in which high liberalism differs from the classical tradition. I want to focus, however, on a different characteristic of some (if not all) high liberal positions that suggests a more thorough rejection of capitalism as traditionally understood. This feature is implicit in Mill's and Rawls's (and John Dewey's) advocacy of institutions that enable workers' control of their work environment and ownership of productive resources. I shall approach this topic by noting a peculiar feature of Rawls's view. Rawls rejects welfare-state capitalism in favor of "property-owning democracy," a private property market system that involves widespread private ownership of means of production. How can he do this in a way that is consistent with the difference principle? Assuming, as classical liberals argue, that free-market capitalism is capable of producing greater economic output than any alternative economic system, how can Rawls avoid endorsing some form of welfare-state capitalism under the difference principle? For given efficient markets, increasing economic output, more reinvestment, and greater overall income and wealth, it seems that there will always be greater income and wealth created to redistribute to the less advantaged in a capitalist economy than in any alternative economic arrangement. Therefore, it would seem that the least advantaged should fare better under welfare-state capitalism than under any other economic system. How then can Rawls reject the capitalist welfare state?

The answer to this puzzle must be that Rawls's difference principle is the ultimate standard for distributing not only income and wealth but also the primary social goods that Rawls calls "powers and positions of responsibility," and also "the social bases of self respect." By "powers" he means legal and other institutional powers of various kinds, primarily those powers required to make economic decisions, including powers of control over productive resources. What primarily distinguishes property-owning democracy from welfare-state capitalism, Rawls says, is that the former involves less inequality in primary social goods—income and wealth, economic powers and positions, and the social bases of self-respect—and greater worker ownership and control over productive resources and over workplace conditions.[75]

Here again, Rawls's account resembles Mill's. In the third edition of his *Principles of Political Economy*, Mill revised his discussion "On the Probable Futurity of the Laboring Classes" (book 4, chap. 7). In the revised version, he states that, as opposed to laissez-faire, his own position is based on "equality" and that the desirable form of production is "association without dependence." The wage relationship is undesirable, Mill says, since it makes workers "servants," dependent on capitalists for their subsistence and well-being. Moreover, it puts workers and owners of capital in conflict and has a demoralizing effect on the working classes.[76] He optimistically predicts that eventually "the relations of masters and workpeople will be gradually superseded by partnership in one of two forms: "in some cases, association of the labourers with the capitalists; in others, and perhaps finally in all, association of labourers among themselves."[77] Mill goes on to discuss these two arrangements in some detail: first, the share arrangement between owners and laborers where profits are divided among them; and second, "the association of the laborers themselves on terms of equality."[78] Either arrangement would give workers an interest in production and in the success of the firm, and would work to cure workers' indifference toward their work and their hostility and conflict with owners. Mill's preferred arrangement is the second, which involves ownership and control of firms by workers themselves, where accumulations of capital "become in the end the joint property of all who participate in their productive employment. . . . [This] would be the nearest approach to social justice and the most beneficial ordering of industrial affairs for the universal good."[79]

These workers' "Associations" or "Co-operations" (as Mill calls them) are to take place within a framework of competitive markets for labor and productive resources. To be successful, he says, they must allow for incentives within the firm as well as worker-approved individual managers rather than collective management by workers themselves. Thus, unlike Marx and other socialists of his era, Mill affirmed a need for markets and competition among firms; he opposed a central and planned economy with public ownership; he endorsed some degree of inequality of income and wealth as necessary for incentives; and he opposed organized revolutionary activity by the working classes. But Mill still regarded it as essential to individual independence and the free development of "individuality" that employees not be subservient to their employers; that the wage relationship and the division between workers and capitalists be moderated if not dissolved; and that workers be given economic powers and ownership interests in their workplaces.[80]

Rawls refers to Mill's worker-managed cooperative firms as one among several possible economic arrangements within property-owning democracy.[81] Rawls shares with Mill a rejection of capitalism and the endorsement of a private-propertied competitive market system where ownership and control of productive resources and wealth are widely distributed among workers and citizens generally. What is revealing about Rawls's claim that distributive justice requires a property-owning democracy rather than a capitalist welfare state is that it shows that his primary concern with distributive justice is not simply, or even primarily, the distribution of income and wealth—if that were his concern, then the capitalist welfare state might do the job better than alternatives. Equally if not more important for Rawls is that workers maintain their sense of self-respect as equal citizens, and be able to own a share of productive wealth and have some control over their own productive activities:

> What men want is meaningful work in free association with others, these associations regulating their relations to one another within a framework of just basic institutions. To achieve this state of things, great wealth is not necessary.[82]

Having a share of economic powers while engaging in "meaningful work" is instrumental if not essential to fostering "perhaps the most important primary [social] good," the self-respect of free and equal democratic citizens.[83] This leads into my final topic, the conception of persons underlying the high liberal tradition.

8. Conclusion: The Bases of the High Liberal Tradition

I have discussed the main differences between the classical and high liberal traditions. While they both endorse personal liberties as fundamentally important, the classical tradition also gives priority to robust if not unqualified rights of private property in productive resources and other economic liberties, regarding them as of nearly equal significance with other basic liberties. Consequently, the just distribution of income, wealth, and economic powers is for classical liberals largely determined by property rights and the exercise of the economic liberties within a framework of free and efficient markets. Property and the economic liberties also largely determine the scope of the classical liberal requirement of equality of opportunity; it is regarded primarily in formal terms, as careers being legally open to talents with an absence of legal discrimination against disfavored groups. Finally, workers' private ownership and control of their means of production is regarded as hopelessly inefficient and hence undesirable. Moreover, the measures needed to put into place and maintain Mill's or Rawls's ideas of property-owning democracy would require the curtailing of many economic liberties and powers that classical liberals regard as fundamental.

What accounts for these differences between classical and high liberals regarding economic justice? Historically, utilitarianism has provided the main philosophical foundation for Anglo-American classical liberalism. Even among philosopher-economists who are part of (or influenced by) the Austrian tradition, such as von Mises and Hayek, a kind of indirect utilitarianism plays a significant role in the defense of their positions.[84] There are, of course, many philosophers who see themselves as classical liberals and nonetheless reject utilitarianism and welfarism generally in favor of a more Kantian or natural law grounding for their views. These views sometimes are hard to distinguish from libertarianism, and when they are, I would contend that they are not classical liberal views. But nothing rides on the honorific title "classical liberalism" or "liberalism." What is important are the central features of purportedly liberal views and the justifications provided for them.

Here I will conclude with some remarks on the primary kind of argument that underwrites the high liberal tradition and the main features I have gone over that distinguish it from classical liberalism. Once again I shall rely on Mill and Rawls. In the work of both, there is to be found an ideal of persons and their essential good that underlies these theorists' conceptions of the distinctive features of high liberalism. For Mill, this is a kind of perfectionist ideal, which he calls "individuality": "The free development of individuality is one of the leading essentials of well-being."[85] A person exercises individuality when he or she freely forms and lives according to a life plan that consists of activities involving the free exercise and full development of the "higher faculties" of reason, understanding, creative imagination, feeling and emotions, and moral sentiments. Individuality, Mill says, includes both the self-development of one's "higher faculties" and self-government according to "the rigid rules of justice."[86] While Mill says that his principle of liberty is grounded not in natural right but in utility, he famously qualifies this claim, saying that "it must be utility in the largest sense, grounded on the permanent interests of man as a progressive being."[87] Achieving individuality is primary among these "permanent interests" and is a large part of Mill's conception of utility.

It is helpful to understand not just Mill's principle of liberty but, more generally, his account of political and economic justice and the rights of property, as grounded in this ideal of individuality, which he incorporated into his utilitarianism. As the basic liberties protected by the principle of liberty are essential conditions of people realizing their individuality, so too this same ideal of a person's "permanent interests" justifies, for Mill, representative democracy, the social equality of women, and the "socialist" revisions to capitalism (as Mill calls them) that he advocates as a necessary corrective to laissez-faire if a market economy is to prove superior to communism. The reason that absolute property and freedom of economic contract are not basic liberties for Mill is not that (in his words) "trade is a social act"; rather, these economic rights and liberties are not essential conditions for citizens generally to realize their individuality and exercise and develop their distinctly human capacities. Indeed, as Mill suggests in some places, the traditional conception of laissez-faire tends to undermine the possibility that many people will realize these great goods. Under those circumstances, "the great social evil exists of a non-labouring class" that is able to work but subsists off the labor of others.[88] As a result, "the rich regard the poor as, by a kind of natural law, their servants and dependents," and the working classes are without "just pride" or self-respect; they "return as little in the shape of service as possible."[89] The future well-being of the laboring classes is primarily dependent on their own mental cultivation and their taking care of their own destiny.[90] This can occur only under working conditions of "association without dependence."

Rawls makes it explicit that an ideal of the person and a person's essential good grounds his principle of equal basic liberties and provides the standards for specifying which liberties are basic and have priority over other social values. The ideal of "free and equal moral persons" who have fundamental interests in the realization of their "moral powers" of practical reasoning and social cooperation combines with an ideal of a "well-ordered society" that is grounded in relations of reciprocity and mutual respect which are acceptable to all its citizens. These ideals of persons and society underwrite Rawls's second principle of justice, including the difference principle. Like Mill, Rawls holds that classical liberal property rights and the enforcement of the traditional doctrine of laissez-faire are not conditions of free and equal persons' adequate development and full exercise of their moral powers and their achievement of their rational autonomy, "and so are not an essential social basis of self-respect."[91] Nor are laissez-faire property rights and relations generally acceptable terms of social cooperation among free and equal persons who desire to cooperate on grounds of reciprocity and mutual respect. Instead, laissez-faire undermines the likelihood that many citizens will ever achieve these essential goods.

One of the main contributions Rawls makes to liberal and democratic theory is the idea that the liberties and procedures historically associated with liberalism and with constitutional democracy should be conceived as grounded, not upon utilitarianism or an a priori conception of natural law and natural rights, but upon an ideal conception of persons and of society. The freedom and equality of persons are fundamental liberal values. Liberals have different interpretations of these values, and these are embedded in different ideals of persons and their social relations. Rawls's conception of the person and of society, and Mill's idea of persons' "permanent interests" in the free development of their individuality, provide the foundations for these theorists' high liberal conceptions of fundamental liberties and social and economic justice. One or more alternative conceptions of persons and their social relations are implicitly relied upon by classical liberals too, to bolster their arguments for capitalism and market distributions. Many historical and contemporary classical liberals (such as David Gauthier and Richard Posner) see persons as rational utility-maximizers, who are willing to make trade-offs between all their desires and interests in pursuit of maximum individual utility. There are other classical liberals and libertarians who reject such welfarism and advocate laissez-faire capitalist freedoms and robust or absolute property rights on different grounds; they too rely, implicitly if not explicitly, upon a different conception of persons and their social relations than do Rawls, Mill, and others in the high liberal tradition.[92] If there is any progress to be made in debates about the importance for liberalism of capitalism, robust private property rights, and the essential role of markets in establishing economic justice, it will require awareness and discussion of the different and conflicting ideals of persons and their social relations that liberals implicitly rely upon in the positions they advocate. At issue in these debates is not simply the nature of our economic and social relations, but ultimately the kinds of persons we are and can come to be.[93]

Notes

1. Following Joseph Schumpeter, I associate classical liberalism with the economic liberalism of the classical economists, starting with Adam Smith in the eighteenth century and David Ricardo, Thomas Malthus, and other classical economists (including J. B. Say in France but excluding John Stuart Mill, for reasons to be discussed) in the nineteenth century. Classical liberalism in the nineteenth century is associated with the doctrine of laissez-faire, "the theory that the best way of promoting economic development and general welfare is to remove fetters from the private enterprise economy and to leave it alone" (Joseph A. Schumpeter, *History of Economic Analysis* [Oxford: Oxford University Press, 1954], 395). Friedrich Hayek and Milton Friedman are major twentieth-century representatives of classical liberalism, along with James Buchanan and the Virginia school of public choice theory, Gary Becker and other members of the Chicago school, Ludwig von Mises of the Austrian school of economics, David Gauthier among philosophers, and Richard Posner and Richard Epstein among legal scholars. While each of these thinkers may not strictly endorse each and every one of the features of liberalism I discuss that distinguish it from libertarianism, each does subscribe to a predominant majority of them. Some thinkers (Loren Lomasky perhaps) may not fit neatly into either category and might reject my distinction between classical liberalism and libertarianism. For a more extensive discussion of the primary differences between liberalism and libertarianism, see chapter 2.

2. By "libertarianism" I mean primarily the doctrine argued for by Robert Nozick, and also accounts by Jan Narveson, Murray Rothbard, John Hospers, and others (including perhaps Ayn Rand). There is also a school of thought known as "left

libertarianism." This position resembles libertarianism primarily in recognizing self-ownership and absolute freedom of contract. Otherwise, it bears little resemblance to traditional libertarianism, since it envisions qualified property rights along with extensive government redistribution to enforce egalitarian measures that (for example) neutralize the consequences of luck. See Peter Vallentyne and Hillel Steiner, eds., *Left-Libertarianism and Its Critics* (New York: Palgrave, 2000).

3. Michael Munger suggests that many classical liberals incline toward relying on restrictive covenants and the law of nuisances rather than municipal zoning laws. Still, unlike libertarians, classical liberals are willing to use zoning and eminent domain powers when restrictive covenants are ineffective or not available.

4. For example, Friedrich Hayek, in *The Constitution of Liberty* (Chicago: University of Chicago Press, 1960), discusses, among other legitimate government measures affecting economic liberty: the legitimacy of prohibitions on contracts in restraint of trade (230); regulation or prohibition of certain monopolies (265); regulations governing techniques in production (224–25); safety regulations in building codes (225); and certain restrictions on land use (229). Regarding property, he writes: "[T]he recognition of the right of private property does not determine what exactly should be the content of this right *in order that the market mechanism will work as effectively and beneficially as possible*" (229; emphasis added). Moreover, on freedom of economic contract, he writes: "The old formulae of laissez-faire or non-intervention do not provide us with an adequate criterion for distinguishing between what is and what is not admissible in a free system. There is ample room for experimentation and improvement within that permanent *legal framework which makes it possible for a free society to operate most efficiently*" (231; emphasis added).

5. Even major proponents of classical liberalism within the tradition of Austrian economics, such as Hayek and von Mises—while they may not put as much direct emphasis on economic efficiency and may emphasize instead the informational virtues of free markets (but why is this important if not for reasons of efficiency?)—should not find my characterization of capitalism at odds with their understanding. When Hayek rejects "utilitarianism," he in effect rejects rational planning and direct appeals to the principle of utility in regulating markets or assessing the distribution of income and wealth. Friedrich Hayek, *Law, Legislation, and Liberty*, vol. 2: *The Mirage of Social Justice* (Chicago: University of Chicago Press, 1976), 22–23. Still, like David Hume's, Hayek's arguments for the rules of justice and of capitalism are generally based in consequentialist considerations regarding their beneficial effects. (See, The Constitution of Liberty, 158–159, 158 n.18 endorsing "restricted utilitarianism" and Hume.) As John Gray contends, Hayek ultimately relied upon indirect utilitarian arguments as the justification for his account of the rules of justice and capitalism. John Gray, *Hayek on Liberty* (Oxford: Basil Blackwell, 1984), 59–60.

Moreover, as Alan Kors points out, Ludwig von Mises's argument for economic freedom also relies upon instrumental appeals to utility and economic efficiency. Von Mises writes: "We liberals do not assert that God or Nature meant all men to be free . . . What we maintain is that only a system based on freedom for all workers warrants the greatest productivity of human labor and is therefore in the interest of all the inhabitants of the earth . . . This is the fruit of free labor. It is able to create more wealth for everyone." Ludwig von Mises, *Liberalism in the Classical Tradition* (Indianapolis: Liberty Fund, 2005), chap. 1, sec. 2.

6. John Locke is generally regarded as the first great liberal. While Locke endorses each of the other features of liberalism I discuss, missing from his writings is a developed idea of the role of free markets in achieving economic efficiency. The idea was not sufficiently developed at the time he lived in the seventeenth century. Libertarians rely upon a Lockean account of natural property, but their account of absolute property rights is not Locke's view since, like liberals generally, he had no reservations about taxation and governmental regulation of property for important public purposes.

7. Adam Smith, *An Inquiry into the Nature and Causes of the Wealth of Nations* (Indianapolis: Liberty Fund, 1981), book 4, chap. 9, 687–88; see generally book 5, chap. 1, part 3, 723–816, "Of the Expence of Publick Works and Publick Institutions." Milton Friedman quotes approvingly and discusses the passage in the text, in Milton Friedman and Rose Friedman, *Free to Choose* (New York: Harcourt Brace Jovanovich, 1980), 19–25, adding a fourth duty of government, "to protect members of the community who cannot be regarded as 'responsible' individuals" (24).

8. Smith, *Wealth of Nations*, book 5, chap. 1, 814–15.

9. John Locke, *Second Treatise on Government*, ed. Peter Laslett (Cambridge: Cambridge University Press, 1988), sec. 3, 268.

10. I do not claim that all classical liberals are utilitarians, but only that in the eighteenth and nineteenth centuries the two schemes of thought developed in tandem and mutually influenced one another. Of course, the idea of natural rights associated with John Locke played a significant role in the development of liberalism, and Adam Smith appealed to natural rights, in spite of his utilitarianism and Hume's rejection of natural rights. Still, Smith, like Locke, endorsed a robust idea of the public or common good and saw property rights as subject to requirements of the public good. The idea endorsed by contemporary libertarians, that property rights and economic liberties are absolute and are not to be regulated according to the public good, seems to be a nineteenth-century development. On my interpretation, libertarians' rejection of the idea of the public or common good, like their rejection of the public nature of political power, marks a significant departure from classical liberalism.

11. Some contemporary welfarists (or "philosophical utilitarians," in T. M. Scanlon's sense) such as David Gauthier argue for capitalism and classical liberalism on Hobbesian contractarian grounds, but the argument is still driven mainly by

considerations of economic efficiency. See David Gauthier, *Morals by Agreement* (Oxford: Oxford University Press, 1986).

12. See David Hume, *An Enquiry Concerning the Principles of Morals*, 2nd ed. (Oxford: Clarendon Press, 1970), sec. 3, "On Justice," 193–94.

13. On classical liberal support for "poor relief," see Hayek, *The Constitution of Liberty*, 285–86. He provides historical background in *Law, Legislation, and Liberty*, 2: 190 n. 8, quoting such classical liberals as N. W. Senior and Moritz Mohl (writing in 1848). It is noteworthy that Adam Smith accepted the English Poor Laws, which, as he says, date back at least to the Elizabethan era (i.e., to the Parliamentary Acts of 1597–98 and 1601). Smith objected to the requirement that each local government be responsible for raising funds to pay for the support of its own poor, since this requirement discouraged the free movement of labor—therewith providing an argument for the centralization of governments' duty to maintain disabled, incompetent, and destitute people. See Smith, *Wealth of Nations*, book 1, chap. 10.c, 152–57. The Poor Law Reforms of 1834 finally centralized poor relief but—in part due to the influence of Bentham, Malthus, and Ricardo—made poor relief normally available only in the now infamous workhouses. Mill approves of "public charity" on classical liberal grounds, namely, that private charity is not adequate and that leaving the poor to private charity encourages them to commit crimes. See J. S. Mill, *Principles of Political Economy* (Indianapolis: Liberty Fund, 2006), book 5, chap. 11, sec. 13, 960–62. Mill's departures from classical liberalism rest not in his views regarding poor relief but in his conception of taxation (of estates especially), qualified property rights, remuneration of labor, and the organization of industry into workers' associations. On the Continent, there is adequate philosophical precedent in central European liberalism for governmental provisions for the poor. Immanuel Kant in the eighteenth century saw it to be the duty of governments to "require the wealthy to provide the means of sustenance to those who are unable to provide the most necessary needs of nature for themselves." See Kant, *The Metaphysical Elements of Justice*, trans. John Ladd (Indianapolis: Bobbs-Merrill, 1965), 93.

14. See Hayek, *The Constitution of Liberty*, 292.

15. Milton Friedman, *Capitalism and Freedom* (Chicago: University of Chicago Press, 1962), 191. Friedman's proposal for a negative income tax to replace in-kind welfare benefits follows on 191–95.

16. Friedrich Hayek, *Law, Legislation, and Liberty*, vol. 3: *The Political Order of a Free People* (Chicago: University of Chicago Press, 1979), 55. See also Hayek, *The Constitution of Liberty*, chap. 19, "Social Security." The problem with the modern welfare state, Hayek contends, is that "the doctrine of the safety net, to catch those who fall, has been made meaningless by the doctrine of fair shares for those of us who are quite able to stand" (285, quoting *The Economist*).

17. Libertarians differ from classical liberals in that they do not recognize (among other things) government's authority to regulate contracts to maintain the

fluidity of markets, or to restrict property rights for the public good, or to tax people to pay for public goods or poor relief.

18. See T. H. Green, *Lectures on the Principles of Political Obligation* (Cambridge: Cambridge University Press, 1986). For a discussion of Green's "new liberalism," see David Brink, *Perfectionism and the Common Good: Themes in the Philosophy of T. H. Green* (Oxford: Oxford University Press, 2003), 77–88.

19. Rawls's first principle of justice, the principle of equal basic liberties, states: "Each person is to have an equal right to the most extensive total system of equal basic liberties compatible with a similar system of liberty for all" (John Rawls, *A Theory of Justice*, rev. ed. [Cambridge, MA: Harvard University Press, 1999], 266; *TJ* in further citations of this work). In later work, Rawls substituted the phrase "a fully adequate scheme" for "the most extensive total system" (John Rawls, *Political Liberalism* [New York: Columbia University Press, 2005], 291; *PL* in further citations of this work). The basic liberties that Mill and Rawls jointly recognize include liberty of conscience, freedom of thought and expression, freedom of the person, including freedom of occupation (Mill says, "freedom of tastes and pursuits," which could be interpreted more broadly than Rawls's freedom of the person), and freedom of association. Rawls also includes among the equal basic liberties political rights of participation and the rights and liberties covered by the rule of law.

20. As opposed to classical liberals and the political practice of the time that denied voting rights to those who did not meet property qualifications (as well as to women), Mill argued that those with more education, not with more property, were in a better position to deliberate impartially and decide what measures best promoted the public good (which Mill understood in quasi-utilitarian terms). See J. S. Mill, *On Representative Government*, chap. 8, "Of the Extension of the Suffrage," in Mill, *"On Liberty" and Other Essays*, ed. John Gray (Oxford: Oxford University Press, 1991), 334–41. The only exception to a universal franchise that he endorsed was the exclusion of recipients of poor relief (333).

21. See *TJ*, §82, 477–478.

22. See *TJ*, 194–200; see also Ronald Dworkin, *Is Democracy Possible Here?* (Princeton, NJ: Princeton University Press, 2009), 128–29.

23. For example, recently the US Supreme Court in a 5–4 decision struck down a long-standing prohibition on corporate and union payment for broadcasts of campaign-related materials supporting or opposing specific candidates, on the grounds that it restricted corporations' rights to free expression and political influence. See *Citizens United v. Federal Elections Committee*, 558 U.S. 50 (2010).

24. Dewey's main works on liberalism and political philosophy are *Individualism: Old and New* (1930); *Liberalism and Social Action* (1935); and *Freedom and Culture* (1939). For an instructive account of Dewey's liberalism, see Alan Ryan, *John Dewey and the High Tide of American Liberalism* (New York: W. W. Norton, 1995), esp. chaps. 3 and 8.

25. Mill, *Principles of Political Economy*, book 2, chap. 1, sec. 3, 207. Jerry Gaus and Ellen Paul remind me that Mill's attitudes toward laissez-faire evolved through the several editions of *Principles*. Mill writes: "*Laisser-faire*, in short, should be the general practice: every departure from it, unless required by some great good, is a certain evil" (book 5, chap. 1, sec. 7, 945). But the next nine sections discuss "Large exceptions to laisser-faire," including "Cases in which the consumer is an incompetent judge of the commodity." Here Mill argues, among other things, for public support for elementary schools, making schooling free to children of the poor (950). Moreover, in his discussion of "socialism," Mill says that impoverished workers have no choice of whom to work for or on what terms and that freedom of contract is an absurdity, given the disparity of bargaining power that exists between owners and wage workers. If all that Mill means above by "laisser-faire" is a presumption in favor of markets in production, then Rawls accepts it in this limited sense. Historically, however, the term implies much more than this, including minimizing government economic regulation and the endorsement of near-absolute freedom of contract and nearly unqualified property rights in land and means of production, which Mill and Rawls clearly reject.

26. Thus, Mill says in *Principles of Political Economy*, book 5, chap. 11, sec. 3, 940, that in a democratic age, "[t]here never was more necessity for surrounding individual independence of thought, speech and conduct, with the most powerful defenses, in order to maintain that originality of mind and individuality of character, which are the only source of any real progress."

27. *TJ*, 53–54. This inclusion of a right to hold personal property among the basic liberties in the first (1971) edition of *A Theory of Justice* (61) led some critics to contend that a capitalist conception of robust property rights is protected by Rawls's first principle. They argued (on the assumption that a right to personal property must include nearly unqualified laissez-faire rights of use and transfer) that there is little space left for redistribution under Rawls's difference principle once Rawls assumes that a right to hold property is a basic liberty. In the 1999 revised edition of *A Theory of Justice* (54), Rawls added the sentence quoted above in the text, which makes clear that this interpretation is a misunderstanding. Later, on the basis of his second principle of justice (discussed here), Rawls explicitly rejects laissez-faire conceptions of property and contends that rights and other incidents of property are to be determined by the difference principle.

28. John Rawls, *Justice as Fairness: A Restatement*, ed. E. Kelly (Cambridge, MA: Harvard University Press, 2001), 42–43; *JF* in further citations of this work.

29. Mill, *Principles of Political Economy*, book 2, chap. 1, sec. 3, 207.

30. Mill, *Principles of Political Economy*, book 2, chap. 2, sec. 4, 223.

31. Mill, *Principles of Political Economy*, book 2, chap. 2, sec. 6, 231–32.

32. Mill, *Principles of Political Economy*, book 2, chap. 2, sec. 6, 232.

33. Mill, *Principles of Political Economy*, book 2, chap. 2, sec. 6, 230.

34. Mill, *Principles of Political Economy*, book 2, chap. 2, sec. 4, 223, 225.

35. Rawls explicitly excludes rights of acquisition and bequest from the basic right to hold personal property (*JF*, 114). The nature and extent of these rights instead are to be settled by the difference principle. Regarding rights of bequest, he says: "An estate need not be subject to tax, nor need the total given by bequest be limited. Rather the principle of progressive taxation is applied at the receiver's end . . . The aim is to encourage a wide and far more equal dispersion of real property and productive assets." Rawls adds that the aim is also "to prevent accumulations of wealth that are judged to be inimical to background justice, for example, to the fair value of the political liberties and to fair equality of opportunity" (160–61).

36. David Hume, *Treatise on Human Nature* (Oxford: Oxford University Press, 1960), 527, 491.

37. Friedman, *Capitalism and Freedom*, 26.

38. Friedman, *Capitalism and Freedom*, 161–162 (emphasis added).

39. Friedman, *Capitalism and Freedom*, 26.

40. Mill, *Principles of Political Economy*, book 2, chap. 1, sec. 1, 199. See Alan Kors's discussion of this aspect of Mill's position. Lionel Robbins, in his 1979–81 lectures, *A History of Economic Thought*, ed. Stephen Medema and Warren Samuels (Princeton, NJ: Princeton University Press, 1998), says, "I ran into my friend Friedrich Hayek in the summer, and he was saying that he thought that Mill had done great harm by his distinction between the laws of production and distribution" (224).

41. *TJ*, 241. Rawls indicates that he draws on the work of J. E. Meade for this distinction.

42. Rawls's more specific point here is that even a socialist society with public ownership of the means of production can use prices to allocate factors of production. This is what he calls "market socialism" or "liberal socialism."

43. This is normally, if not always, the case since markets often generate "irrational exuberance," causing speculative "bubbles" that eventually burst (e.g., the recent overbidding and oversupply in the housing market).

44. Mill says of wealth and productive output: "The things once there, mankind, individually or collectively, can do with them as they like. They can place them at the disposal of whomever they please, and on whatever terms. Further, in the social state . . . any disposal whatever of those can only take place by the consent of society, or rather of those who dispose of its active force." Mill, *Principles of Political Economy*, book 2, chap. 1, sec. 1, 199–200.

45. Friedman, *Capitalism and Freedom*, 162. The following argument in the text relies on an argument in my essay "Equality of Resources, Market Luck, and the Justification of Market Distributions," *Boston University Law Review* 90, no. 2 (2010): 921–48.

46. Thomas Robert Malthus, *Principles* (1st ed.); quoted in Schumpeter, *History of Economic Analysis*, 656.

47. Robert Nozick relies on marginal productivity theory for a similar argument: "People transfer their holdings or labor in free markets . . . If marginal productivity theory is reasonably adequate, people will be receiving, in these voluntary transfers of holdings, roughly *their* marginal products" (Robert Nozick, *Anarchy, State, and Utopia* [New York: Basic Books, 1974], 187-88, emphasis added; *ASU* in further citations of this work). See also *ASU*, 301–2, 304–5. In Nozick's utopia, "each person receives his marginal contribution to the world" (302). Similarly, David Gauthier maintains: "In the free exchanges of the market each may expect a return equal in value to her contribution. Thus the income each receives . . . is equal to the contribution she makes, or the marginal difference she adds to the value of the total product." See Gauthier's *Morals by Agreement*, 92–93. "The equation of income with marginal contribution ensures just this impartiality . . . [E]ach benefits from, and only from, the contribution she makes" (97).

48. Milton Friedman makes the argument both on grounds of fairness and equality of treatment and also on economic grounds. He says: "Payment in accordance with product may be necessary to achieve true equality of treatment." And later he says: "Payment in accordance with product is therefore necessary in order that resources be used most effectively" (Friedman, *Capitalism and Freedom*, 162, 166). Hayek also makes an economic argument based, he says, not in merit, but in order that people "achieve a maximum of usefulness": "If the remuneration did not correspond to the value that the product of a man's efforts has for his fellows, he would have no basis for deciding whether the pursuit of a given object is worth the effort or risk. He would necessarily have to be told what to do" (Hayek, *The Constitution of Liberty*, 96). A more recent argument by an economist is that of N. Gregory Mankiw, ' "Defending the One Percent," *Journal of Economic Perspectives* 27, no. 3, (2013): 30.

49. Gauthier, *Morals by Agreement*, 93.

50. See Paul Krugman and Robin Wells, *Microeconomics*, 2nd ed. (New York: Worth, 2009), 521.

51. The average contribution by each worker is then a good deal more than the marginal contribution of the last worker hired. According to Krugman and Wells, "The theory says that machinists will be paid the value of the marginal product of the *last machinist hired*, and due to diminishing returns to labor, that value will be lower than the average over all machinists currently employed" (*Microeconomics*, 2nd ed., 522). They continue, "In 2006 each skilled American machinist generated approximately $120,000 in yearly revenue. But there is a $50,000 difference between the salary paid to Hamill machinists and the revenue they generate" (522).

52. Mankiw, "Defending the One Percent," 17.

53. Of course, owners often manage or otherwise work in their own firms (particularly in smaller businesses); but then they are no longer acting purely in their capacity as owners, but are contributing their labor to production.

54. On the distinction between brute facts and institutional facts such as private property and money, and the constitution of institutional facts out of individuals' beliefs and other attitudes and their collective intentions and activities, see John Searle, *The Construction of Social Reality* (New York: Free Press, 1995), chaps. 2 and 3.

55. Mill, *Principles of Political Economy*, book 2, chap. 2, sec. 1, 215–16.

56. Some might think a rule of symmetry should apply here—if you risk losing the value of your *entire* investment, you should have a right to the *entire* value gained in return. But in fairness shouldn't symmetry entitle the investor of $1 million to at most a $1 million gain, not to the entire $3 million in the example in the text? Our intuitions of fairness are unreliable here in the absence of some guiding principle that takes into account other considerations, such as the effects on others of rewarding investments in this or some other way, the kind of investment it is (in solar energy or in coal mining), etc.

57. Marx, in effect, remarks on this conflation of different senses of "contribution" in a well-known passage on the "Trinity Formula," in *Capital*, book 3. See *Karl Marx: Selected Writings*, ed. David McClellan (Oxford: Oxford University Press, 1977), 500.

58. For example, a property-owning democracy, which Rawls contrasts with welfare-state capitalism, structures institutions to encourage workers' private ownership and control of their industries (*JF*, 135–40). Martin Weitzman advocates replacing the wage relationship with a system that ties workers' compensation to an index of a firm's performance, such as a share of revenue and profits. See Martin Weitzman, *The Share Economy* (Cambridge, MA: Harvard University Press, 1984). John Roemer advocates a model of profit-maximizing firms that distribute profits across society; all members of society are given an equal or fair share of corporate stock upon reaching maturity, with a right to dividends depending upon how their firms or mutual funds perform. See John Roemer, *A Future for Socialism* (Cambridge, MA: Harvard University Press, 1994).

59. Friedman, *Capitalism and Freedom*, 162.

60. Thus, Robert Nozick invokes the state of nature and a right of initial appropriation of "unowned" things, subject to a "Lockean Proviso" (*ASU*, 174–182).

61. Smith, *Wealth of Nations*, book 4, chap. 2, 470.

62. So-called Jim Crow laws arose in the South and elsewhere in the United States after the end of Reconstruction in the 1870s and continued until the 1950s and 1960s. They mandated, among other restrictions, de jure segregation of most public facilities and accommodations, including schools, public restrooms, buses and trains, and restaurants and hotels. In 1954, the U.S. Supreme Court,

in *Brown v. Board of Education*, declared segregation of public schools uncon-
stitutional. This case was a milestone in the eventual elimination of Jim Crow
laws by the Civil Rights Acts of 1957 and 1964 and the Voting Rights Act of
1965. See C. Vann Woodward's classic history, *The Strange Career of Jim Crow*
(New York: Oxford University Press, 1955), and Michael J. Klarman, *From
Jim Crow to Civil Rights: The Supreme Court and the Struggle for Racial Equality*
(Oxford: Oxford University Press, 2004).

63. See Friedman, *Capitalism and Freedom*, 109–10.

64. Friedman, *Capitalism and Freedom*, 113 (emphasis added).

65. This accords with the ruling by the US Supreme Court in *Shelley v. Kraemer*,
334 U.S. 1 (1948), which held that private restrictive covenants barring blacks
from ownership of real estate are unenforceable since they violate the equal
protection clause of the Fourteenth Amendment to the US Constitution. The
Court said it is illegal for the government, including the judiciary, to enforce
such covenants, since the state then plays an integral role in a policy of racial
discrimination in violation of the Fourteenth Amendment.

66. Friedman, *Capitalism and Freedom*, 113.

67. See J. S. Mill, *The Subjection of Women*, in *"On Liberty" and Other Essays*.

68. See Smith, *Wealth of Nations*, book 5, chap. 1, art. 2, on compulsory
education: "For a very small expence the public can facilitate, can encourage,
and can even impose upon almost the whole body of the people, the necessity of
acquiring these most essential parts of education" (785). Smith says that among
the benefits to the state of educating "the inferior ranks of people" is that they
are more disposed to work and be respectful of themselves, others, and their
superiors, and less prone to disorder, superstition, and sedition. "An instructed
and intelligent besides are always more decent and orderly than an ignorant and
stupid one." (788)).

69. "The education of my child contributes to your welfare by promoting a stable
and democratic society." Friedman, *Capitalism and Freedom*, 86. Friedman
argues for publicly issued vouchers to be used at privately run, for-profit or non-
profit schools (89).

70. *ASU*, 149–50. Hayek more generally condemns the idea of "social justice." The
title of the second volume of his *Law, Legislation, and Liberty* is *The Mirage of
Social Justice*.

71. Rawls's second principle of justice is set forth earlier in the chapter.

72. *TJ*, §43, esp. 242–45. On income supplements more generally, see Edmund
Phelps, *Rewarding Work* (Cambridge, MA: Harvard University Press, 1997; 2nd
ed., 2007). Earned-income tax credits in the United States are means-tested
income supplements paid primarily to low- and moderate-income workers
with children (workers earning $48,278, or less if they have fewer than three
children). In 2010, the Earned Income Tax Credit paid $3,050 for one child,
$5,036 for two, and a maximum of $5,666 ($457 is paid to workers with no

children earning less than \$13,460, or \$18,440 if married and filing jointly). See Publication 596 EIC at http://www.IRS.gov. Other countries, including Canada and the United Kingdom, have similar programs.

73. Ronald Dworkin's position on economic justice is set forth in his *Sovereign Virtue* (Cambridge, MA: Harvard University Press, 2000), esp. chaps. 1, 2, 7–9; and also in his *Justice for Hedgehogs* (Cambridge, MA: Harvard University Press, 2011).

74. Mill writes in *Principles of Political Economy*, book 2, chap. 1, sec. 4, 210: "The proportioning of remuneration to work done, is really just, only in so far as the more or less of work is a matter of choice: when it depends on natural difference of strength or capacity, this principle of remuneration is itself an injustice: it is giving to those who have: assigning most to those who are already favored most by nature."

75. *JF*, 135–40, 158–62, 176–78.

76. Mill says that the wage relationship divides "the producers into two parties with hostile interests, the many who do the work being mere servants under the command of the one who supplies the funds, and having no interest of their own in the enterprise except to earn their wages with as little labour as possible." Mill, *Principles of Political Economy*, book 4, chap. 7, sec. 4, 769.

77. Mill, *Principles of Political Economy*, book 4, chap. 7, sec. 4, 769.

78. Mill, *Principles of Political Economy*, book 4, chap. 7, sec. 4, 775.

79. Mill, *Principles of Political Economy*, book 4, chap. 7, sec. 4, 793–94.

80. John Dewey also advocated arrangements that democratize work without socializing the means of production. He wrote, "Democracy is not in reality what it is in name until it is industrial as well as civil and political." John Dewey, "The Ethics of Democracy," in *John Dewey, The Early Works*, vol. 1 (Carbondale: Southern Illinois University, 1969), 246. Later in the same work, Dewey writes, "That the economic and industrial life is *in itself* ethical, that it is to be made contributory to the realization of personality through the formation of a higher and more complete unity among men . . . such is the meaning of the statement that democracy must become industrial" (Dewey, "The Ethics of Democracy," 248). For a discussion of what he calls Dewey's "guild socialism," see Ryan, *John Dewey*, 111–17, 309–27.

81. *JF*, 176, 178.

82. *TJ*, 257.

83. *TJ*, 386–88, on the primary social good of self-respect; *TJ*, 477–78, on self-respect and equal citizenship; and *JF*, 114, on property rights, personal independence, and self-respect. The importance of the social bases of self-respect in Rawls's own argument for property-owning democracy is discussed here in chapter 4.

84. As discussed earlier.

85. Mill, *"On Liberty" and Other Essays*, 63. Mill continues: "It [individuality] is not only a co-ordinate element with all that is designated by the terms civilization,

instruction, education, culture, but is itself a necessary part and condition of all those things" (63).

86. Mill, *"On Liberty" and Other Essays*, chap. 3, 70.

87. Mill, *"On Liberty" and Other Essays*, chap. 1, 15.

88. Mill, *Principles of Political Economy*, book 4, chap. 7, sec. 1, 758: "I do not recognize as either just or salutary, a state of society in which there is any class which is not 'labouring'; any human being, exempt from bearing their share of the necessary labours of human life, except those unable to labour, or who have fairly earned rest by previous toil."

89. Mill, *Principles of Political Economy*, book 4, chap. 7, sec. 1, 767.

90. Mill, *Principles of Political Economy*, book 4, chap. 7, sec. 1, 763.

91. *JF*, 114.

92. Thus, libertarians such as Nozick might regard persons in the first instance as self-owners with absolute rights in their persons as well as their possessions, and society as a free association of such owners whose relations are contractually specified. The question then becomes, what capacities and features of persons justify our seeing ourselves and our relations primarily in this way?

93. For their helpful comments on a draft of this chapter, I am grateful to David Reidy and other members of the philosophy department at the University of Tennessee; to Frederick Rauscher and other members of the philosophy department at Michigan State University; to Charles Beitz, George Kateb, Alan Ryan, and other participants at a Princeton Center for Human Values colloquium; to members of the Philosophy Department at University of Wisconsin-Milwaukee; and to Ellen Paul for her many helpful suggestions and editorial remarks; and to many others for their criticisms and comments.

2

Illiberal Libertarians

WHY LIBERTARIANISM IS NOT A LIBERAL VIEW

1. Introduction

Liberalism as a philosophical doctrine can be distinguished from liberalism as a system of social and political institutions. Philosophical liberalism maintains that, first, there is a plurality of intrinsic goods and that no single way of life can encompass them all. There are then different ways of living worth affirming for their own sake. Second, whatever intrinsic goods are appropriate for individuals, their having the freedom to determine and pursue their *conceptions* of the good is essential to their living a good life. Finally, necessary for individuals' good is that their freely adopted conceptions of the good be consistent with justice. All have an interest in exercising their freedom so as to respect others' basic rights and other requirements of justice. While this does not mean that justice is necessarily an intrinsic good (although it can be), it does mean that observing justice's demands is a normal precondition of living a good life.

Kant, Mill, Rawls, Berlin, Dworkin, Raz, Nagel, Scanlon, Ackerman, Barry, and many others endorse some version of these claims. Philosophical liberalism is but one way to argue for liberal institutions, including a liberal constitution. Utilitarianism and other forms of welfarism historically have provided an alternative foundation for liberal institutions.[1] Utilitarianism is philosophically non-liberal: since it affirms one ultimate good—overall utility or welfare—as the source of all value, it rejects the plurality of intrinsic goods and subordinates to utility the goods of freedom and the virtue of justice.

My focus is not philosophical liberalism but liberal institutions and the primary features of a liberal constitution. My aim is to situate on the map of political conceptions three contemporary views, each of which is called "liberal": (1) classical liberalism, (2) what I call "high liberalism," and (3) libertarianism. Major proponents of classical liberalism include David Hume, Adam Smith and the classical economists (most of whom were utilitarians), and contemporary theorists such as David Gauthier, James Buchanan, and Friedrich Hayek. I use the term "classical liberalism" in the Continental sense to refer to a liberalism that endorses the doctrine of laissez-faire and accepts the justice of (efficient) market distributions but that allows for redistribution to preserve the institutions of market society. By "high liberalism" I mean the set of institutions and ideas associated with philosophical liberalism, which I take to be the high liberal tradition.[2] Its major philosophical advocates in each century from the eighteenth to the present are Kant, Mill, and Rawls. Locke, the original liberal in many regards, appears to accept philosophical liberalism as defined and thus also might be classified as a high liberal. But because of his account of property, he is often read as a classical liberal.[3] Locke's account of property has had a major influence on libertarianism too. By "libertarianism" I primarily mean the doctrine argued for by Robert Nozick and also in differing accounts by Jan Narveson, Ayn Rand, Murray Rothbard, John Hospers, Eric Mack, and others. These and other libertarians have particular differences, but there are certain basic principles and institutions that they all endorse (see sections 3 and 4).

It is commonly held that libertarianism is a liberal view.[4] Also, many who affirm classical liberalism call themselves libertarians and vice versa. I argue that libertarianism's resemblance to liberalism is superficial; in the end, libertarians reject essential liberal institutions. Correctly understood, libertarianism resembles a view that liberalism historically defined itself against, the doctrine of private political power that underlies feudalism. Like feudalism, libertarianism conceives of justified political power as based in a network of private contracts. It rejects the idea, essential to liberalism, that political power is a public power, to be impartially exercised for the common good.

To appreciate these claims requires some stage-setting. I begin with a discussion of primary liberal institutions. Section 3 turns to libertarianism and discusses its interpretation of liberty as a kind of property. Then, in section 4, I explain how libertarians' conception of liberty as a kind of property leads them to reject basic liberal institutions.[5]

2. *Institutional Features of a Liberal Constitution*
2.1. Equal Rights to Basic Liberties

The most characteristic feature of a liberal society is its tolerance of beliefs and diverse ways of life. Dissent, nonconformity, and an assured space of independence are accepted as normal in social life. Tolerance is institutionalized by the political recognition that certain liberties are more important than others. These basic liberties are designed to maintain, through the rule of law, the security and integrity of persons and their freedom to live as they choose, within prescribed limits. Basic liberties apply to all persons equally (or at least all citizens) without regard to social or economic status. The equality of basic liberties is the primary way that equality is recognized in liberal institutions.

Liberal philosophers offer different lists of basic liberties, but for all of them liberty of conscience is central. Liberty of conscience includes freedom of religious beliefs, which was critical to liberalism's origins in the seventeenth century.[6] In modern times it has come to include freedom to form philosophical views and ethical convictions about questions of ultimate value and life's meaning. Liberty of conscience is perhaps the most important liberal basic liberty since it secures tolerance and freedom of religious, ethical, and philosophical beliefs and allows for pluralism of conceptions of the good. But other liberties have come to be regarded as of equal political significance. The list of liberties that Mill maintains as part of his principle of liberty are liberty of conscience; freedom of thought and discussion (including freedom of speech, press, opinion, and inquiry into all subjects); "freedom of tastes and pursuits," or the freedom to pursue a "plan of life" to suit one's character; and freedom of association.[7] Rawls's list of basic liberties is similar.[8] In addition to liberty of conscience, freedom of thought, and freedom of association, Rawls includes equal political liberties (including the right to vote and hold office, freedom of assembly, and the right to organize and join political parties), the rights and liberties needed to maintain the freedom and physical and psychological integrity of the person (including freedom of occupation and of movement and the right to hold personal property),[9] and the rights and liberties needed to maintain the rule of law.[10]

In holding these rights *basic*, liberals mean that they are both fundamental and inalienable. To say certain rights or liberties are *fundamental* means that they have absolute priority over other political values; they cannot be sacrificed or weighed off against non-basic rights or other political values in ordinary political procedures. The basic liberties of citizens, then, are to be infringed upon neither for the sake of satisfying the preferences of democratic majorities, nor to improve economic efficiency, nor to achieve perfectionist values of cultural excellence. Liberal doctrine standardly holds that limits on the exercise of basic liberties are to be imposed only to protect and maintain others' basic liberties and the rights and duties of justice needed to sustain them.[11]

More important for our purposes, the idea of basic liberties also includes their *inalienability*: a person cannot contractually transfer basic liberties or give them up voluntarily. No liberal government would enforce a contract or agreement in which one or more persons tried to sell themselves into slavery or indentured servitude, or agreed to give up liberty of conscience and freedom of association by making themselves permanent members of some religious sect. Because people cannot voluntarily transfer basic liberties, such liberties are not like property rights in particular things.[12] People might involuntarily forfeit certain liberties upon committing a crime that violates others' rights, but involuntary forfeiture is not the same as voluntary alienation.[13]

Different arguments have been made for inalienability.[14] One argument stemming from Kant is that the inalienability restriction is needed to maintain the status of persons as beings with dignity. For Kant, our humanity consists in our capacities for freedom and reason. Having these capacities, persons have dignity, a kind of value "beyond all price." Having dignity, persons are due respect whatever their status or situation. Equal basic rights secure (because they partly constitute) equal respect for persons as moral beings with dignity. Since basic rights secure equal respect, they are without a moral exchange value; agents cannot bargain their rights and humanity away. To attempt to freely alienate one's capacity for freedom is morally void since it disrespects one's own humanity. By securing the status of each as an equal due respect, inalienability maintains the dignity of persons.

Some criticize the Kantian argument for inalienability for its "paternalism," defined as a restriction of the self-regarding free choices and agreements of competent and consenting adults to protect interests they may not endorse. Critics contend that respect for persons implies respect for their voluntary informed choices, even if their choices are not rational. If maintaining one's own dignity and capacities for freedom are not important enough to a person, why should that person be restricted from voluntarily entering binding agreements that limit freedom to further "individuality" or felt interests?[15] This objection raises the controversial issue, about which liberals differ, as to why people should enjoy basic rights and liberties to begin with: Is it because of persons' capacities for reason and freedom (as Kantians claim), or because of their capacities for happiness or desire (as liberal utilitarians may say), or because all are created equal by God (as Locke and natural law theorists contend), or for some other reason (e.g., everyone's having a capacity for self-realization or perfectibility)?

The liberal argument for inalienability can avoid this source of contention. For the issue of inalienability comes down to a question of the design of basic legal institutions, in particular the institutions of property and the use of government power to enforce personal agreements.[16] Nothing about liberalism's inalienability restriction prevents people from voluntarily assuming the roles of master and subordinate to nearly any degree they choose. If this is the kind of life a person wants to live in relationship with another who consents, so be it; it is protected by freedom of association. The inalienability restriction implies that a person has the right to exit this essentially private relationship at any time.[17] The problem comes with the contrary suggestion: that into this private relationship should be introduced the legal mechanism of contract and the institution of private property, with their provisions for coercive enforceability. Then the voluntary servitude arrangement is no longer merely a matter "between consenting adults"; it becomes a matter of civic law and a publicly recognized right. One party to the arrangement enters the public and political realms to demand, as a right, that others recognize and respect a private agreement bestowing ownership in another person. Society is called upon to adopt publicly a parallel attitude and to treat a person, not as a being with rights due moral consideration and respect, but as property, an owned thing. Alienation of basic rights, if politically recognized, imposes duties not just upon the transferor but also upon society and its members to respect and uphold such transactions. We are called upon to ignore the moral fate and political status of others as equals and to participate in their civic and moral debasement. Moral and legal duties of mutual respect, protection from unwanted harm, and mutual assistance of others in distress are suspended, and society's members are obligated to apply their collective force to compel another's "property" to comply with contractual obligations.[18] By embracing alienation agreements as matters of enforceable public right, we accept a mandate to coerce and harm certain people against their will and to regard and respond to them as if they were things. Moreover, in recognizing and enforcing these contracts, government and its agents are treating people accordingly.

Liberalism holds that consenting adults do not have the rights or powers to impose such extraordinary duties upon others as a result of their private agreements. Beneficiaries of servitude pacts and other bargains alienating basic rights cannot ask government to recognize and enforce them. It may be in an agent's interests at the time to alienate her basic rights; nonetheless, the private demand to publicly recognize this agreement as a binding contractual relationship conflicts with others' moral duties and interests (as liberals perceive them). Moreover, it conflicts with the public interest in maintaining the status of persons as free and equal and the moral quality of civic relations. Liberals refuse to use public laws to treat people as objects without rights, even if people want to be treated this way. There is no place within the liberal conceptual order for the political or legal recognition of people as property or as anything less than persons with basic rights.[19]

So, it is because contract and property are matters of publicly enforceable right imposing uniform duties upon everyone that liberals do not respect the outcome of just any given private agreement as a valid enforceable contract. This is related to the omission of rights of property and freedom of contract from the lists of liberal basic rights and liberties mentioned earlier. Some may see this omission as glaring. Locke, after all, is commonly said to have argued for a "natural right of property."[20] To many, his argument seems to place rights of property on a par with basic rights. But whatever Locke intended by his account of property in a state of nature, neither he nor any other major liberal philosopher argues that governments have no authority to regulate property and contractual agreements, and burden them when necessary for the public good.[21]

Here the formal right to own property needs to be distinguished from the right to particular properties, for instance, my right to my homestead. Like the right to enter binding contracts, the formal right of ownership—the capacity to have rights in things as they are defined by law and to have this capacity equally with other citizens—is arguably basic for liberals. (Or, if not basic in the defined sense, rights to property and to contract are necessary enabling rights since they are a precondition of the effective exercise of most basic liberties.) To be incapable of ownership and contracts, as these rights and powers are defined by law, is one of the marks of dependence and/or servitude (as with married women and children in common law). But the formal capacity of ownership implies little about the content of one's rights or the kinds of rights in things people ought to be allowed to have in any particular property system.

Liberals of the classical and high traditions can agree that legal capacities for ownership and contract are basic rights (or at least are essential to exercising basic rights). Having exclusive control over some personal property and a protected domicile are conditions of individual independence. But this does not mean that rights to particular things are themselves basic (or fundamental) rights.[22] On any liberal conception, government can regulate and proscribe uses of property (e.g., my use of my homestead for commercial purposes), and even appropriate property by eminent domain procedures if necessary for the public good (so long as fair compensation is made). This introduces an element of historical contingency into property: rights of property, as legally specified, must be revisable by law to meet changing conditions for the sake of efficiency, public safety or convenience, or some other social value. Rights of property are not in these regards fundamental: they can be regulated and revised for reasons other than protecting and maintaining basic rights and liberties.

One characteristic mark of libertarianism is the contrary claim that rights of property are both plenary and fundamental (as defined above): a person's rights to use and transfer particular possessions (e.g., an automobile or income) cannot be infringed upon or burdened for the sake of other social values. Instead one's use of property can be restricted only to protect others' (moral) rights. I shall call this conception of property "absolute."[23] Absolute property is perhaps *the* most significant right in a libertarian view (as discussed in section 3).

2.2. Equality of Opportunity

A second feature of a liberal constitution is the absence of political restrictions on entry into social and political positions. Positions are to be held open to everyone regardless of their racial, ethnic, or gender group, religious or philosophical views, or social or economic position. Equality of opportunity developed out of the rejection of the idea that people are assigned social positions by birth and cannot legally move out of their class into another. As Kant said, "Every member of the commonwealth must be permitted to attain any degree of status. . . to which his talent, his industry, and his luck may bring him; and his fellow subjects may not block his way by [appealing to] hereditary prerogatives."[24] The requirement of open positions is part of equality of opportunity. This is another way that liberals incorporate equality, in addition to equality of basic rights and liberties.

Liberals interpret equality of opportunity differently. At a basic level, it is formally construed as an absence of legal restrictions that bar socially disfavored groups access to social positions. Legal prohibitions against allocating positions regardless of race, gender, and other natural or social attributes unrelated to job performance are incompatible with legal equality of opportunity. The underlying idea is that careers should be at least legally "open to talents" (as Adam Smith said) or to "merit" (as others say); that is, positions should be legally accessible to all who are willing to compete for them and who are able to satisfy performance demands. The "system of natural liberty" affirmed by classical liberals incorporates this formal conception of equality of opportunity.[25] This reading fits well with classical liberals' emphasis on economic efficiency. A more robust version of "careers open to talents"—advocated by high liberals and some contemporary classical liberals—includes legal measures, such as the 1964 Civil Rights Act, that prohibit private employers from discriminating against job applicants on grounds of race, religion, ethnicity, sex, or other characteristics unrelated to job performance. But other classical liberals regard such laws as unjust restrictions on the basic freedom of economic contract.[26]

High liberals and most contemporary classical liberals also contend that merely eliminating restrictions on entry to positions does not take equality of opportunity seriously. The sense in which positions are open to the poor is nominal if not illusory under the formal conception, since the poor have no real opportunity (far less an equal or fair one) to compete for favorable positions without educational benefits. Society then has a duty to support an education system to even out class barriers so those with similar abilities can compete on a more equal footing. Others argue that fairness requires still more, namely, both adequate universal healthcare so that all may realize their capacities and perhaps even preventing excessive accumulations of property and wealth that undermine fair access to social positions.[27] These fuller conceptions of equality of opportunity are characteristic of the high liberal tradition and mark one major difference with classical liberalism.

It is sometimes said that equality of opportunity can never be achieved and that the idea is illusory.[28] But within liberalism, equal opportunity has never been interpreted to imply equal likelihood of success, an impossible aim under any system. Nor is it seen as a value that has absolute priority. In liberal thought, equal opportunity presupposes the priority of certain basic rights and liberties. We could perhaps better equalize people's chances if the family were radically altered or abolished, but that would infringe upon freedom of association. Liberal equal opportunity means that society should eliminate legal barriers and mitigate the effects of chance in allocating positions, consistent with freedom of association, freedom of occupation, and other basic liberties. Moreover, many liberals argue that preferential treatment or "affirmative action" for disadvantaged minority classes is necessary for equality of opportunity, at least temporarily, to alleviate the current ongoing effects of past injustices against disadvantaged minorities. Other liberals argue that these measures are incompatible with formal and perhaps even fair equality of opportunity.

2.3. Markets, Allocative Efficiency, and the Social Minimum

A third feature of liberalism is the significant role assigned to markets in economic relations. Liberals emphasize markets for different reasons, and this marks yet another difference between the classical and high liberal traditions. For such high liberals as Mill and Rawls, markets are seen primarily as a condition of freedom of occupation and association, and achieving fair equality of opportunity. Markets are also important for liberals generally since they normally provide for the effective allocation of productive resources, and so better promote the efficient production of goods than do non-market schemes. Markets then have an important function in the *allocation* of productive resources.

The allocative role of markets is important for all liberal views. But it does not commit liberalism to using markets as the exclusive mechanism for the *distribution* of income and wealth. The idea that people have a vested right to whatever income and wealth they can acquire by market exchange is rejected, at least by members of the high liberal tradition. A basic tenet of high liberalism is that all citizens, as a matter of right and justice, are to have an adequate share of material means so that they are suitably *independent*, capable of governing and controlling their lives and taking advantage of their basic liberties and fair opportunities. Without sufficient income and wealth, one's liberties and opportunities are worth little. For the destitute particularly, basic rights of free expression and the political liberties are virtually useless. To ensure that everyone's liberties are opportunities of significant value, the high liberal tradition envisions non-market transfers of income and wealth of some degree, to be arranged by political institutions.[29]

Classical liberals by contrast do not envision a non-market mechanism that ensures each person a *right* to income and wealth adequate for individual independence. This does not mean that classical liberals do not provide for a social minimum too; they normally do, but it is not recognized as a requirement of *justice* and what each person is entitled to. Instead, the social minimum is conceived as a matter of public charity so that people will not starve (Friedman), or it is depicted as an expedient required by some other political value, such as (in Hayek) the need to prevent social strife.[30] Characteristic of classical liberalism is the idea that market distributions realized under competitive conditions, or distributions that would be realized under perfect competition, are to provide the basic standard for just distributions. Since real markets are imperfect, government has a role in regulating markets and even redistributing income and wealth if needed to correct for market imperfections. Because classical liberals put great emphasis on market efficiency as providing the standard for just distribution, they also assign greater weight to rights of private property and freedom of contract.

By contrast, high liberals such as Mill, Rawls, and Dworkin maintain that property rights should be decided by asking which system of property laws and conventions best enables all citizens, including the less advantaged, to realize their freedom, independence, and individual good, by effectively exercising their basic rights and liberties and by taking advantage of equal opportunities. Here markets have an important but by no means exclusive role in arriving at just distributions. Moreover, there is no a priori assumption that mandates private property in the means of production. Liberal socialism, allowing for public ownership combined with market allocations of productive resources, is theoretically possible and, if feasible, may be called for under certain historical conditions to enable everyone to effectively exercise equal basic liberties.[31] The question of whether markets have a preponderant or subordinate role in defining and achieving distributive justice marks the major division within the liberal tradition.

2.4. Public Goods

Classical and high liberals alike envision a prominent role for government in the provision of (economic) public goods.[32] Markets break down with respect to the provision of certain goods (because of their "indivisibility"), and all liberals accept that one of government's primary roles is to exercise its powers of regulation and taxation to provide public goods (or at least to ensure their provision through private means). The provision of public goods is one standard argument liberals give for political authority and the need for government. Even when everyone respects others' rights and obeys the laws, there is still a need for political authority to coordinate people's activities so that public goods are provided. This argument goes back to Hume and is given prominence by Adam Smith.[33]

Classical liberalism is associated with the doctrine of laissez-faire. But it is important to see just what laissez-faire meant to the classical economists of the Scottish and English schools who advocated it. It did not mean rejection of government's redistributive powers and acceptance of the "night-watchman state."[34] The role of government in providing public goods and even in alleviating economic distress was affirmed by Smith and other classical economists.[35]

Instead, laissez-faire implied an absence of government intervention on the side of allocation of productive factors and non-interference with markets except to maintain their fluidity and prevent the concentration of market power. Something quite different (we will see) is involved in libertarian views.

2.5. The Public Nature of Law and Political Authority

The final primary feature of a liberal system is not expressed by any single institution but characterizes liberal political institutions generally—the principle that political power is a public power, to impartially issue and enforce uniform public rules that apply to everyone and that promote the common good. Political power is sometimes characterized as a monopoly on coercive force held by those who claim (unjustifiably, libertarians say) the authority to rule.[36] But liberalism conceives of legitimate political power differently. Society is possible only if people observe common rules, and for rules to be effective, they must be public and generally accepted. It may be that coercive sanctions are needed to enforce these rules (then again, they may not be);[37] but a monopoly on coercion is not what is most distinctive about a political system. What is essential is that necessary public rules be issued and uniformly applied by a commonly recognized authority. Political power is regarded as a *public power* by liberals. This means: (1) Political power is *institutional* and not personal; it is ultimately held not by a specific individual but by an artificial person, that is, a publicly recognized institution (the government and finally by the "Body Politic" according to Locke, Kant, and the liberal social contract tradition). (2) Political power is *continuous*; the public institution vested with political power appoints individuals to occupy offices of authority periodically and survives their demise. Certain commonly accepted rules of succession are needed to specify the steps for transferring power.[38] (3) Political power is held in trust, as a *fiduciary* power; those who occupy political offices act in a representative capacity, for others' benefit. Since it is held in trust, political power is not to be exercised for the benefit of the person who occupies political office. So far as political power is contractual, then, it is not based in a mutually beneficial bargain between ruler and ruled. Here a distinction is to be drawn between a *social contract* and a mutually beneficial *contract of government* between ruler and ruled. It is the former idea, not the latter, that plays such an important role in the history of liberal thought, providing an account of legitimate political power. The social contract is conceived as a (hypothetical) agreement among equals, by everyone with everyone else. Its purpose is to form political society (the Body Politic), then to establish a constitution and create on its basis a government that serves as *agent* for the People. This is very different from a private contract between (unequal) parties for mutual benefit, which is the economic model used for contracts of government. (4) As a fiduciary, government has political power *delegated* to it by the Body Politic; as the People's agent, government is to exercise power solely for the benefit of those represented. But since political power is public, it is to represent everyone and therefore is to be *impartially* exercised, and only for the *common good*. (5) Since government is to rule in a fiduciary capacity and solely for the common good, those who hold political power are recognized as having *authority* to rule, and their legal actions are conceived as possessing *legitimacy*. Its political legitimacy in turn supplies government with its basis for demanding allegiance and obedience to its laws.

This account accords with Locke's definition of political power as "the right of making laws . . . only for the Publick Good."[39] For Locke, the relevant contrast was the doctrine of divine right as argued for by Robert Filmer in support of absolute monarchy. According to this doctrine, political power is privately owned by particular persons or families and extends over a territory and all people within it. Political power is exercised according to its owner's will, without impediments or regulation by any worldly authority.[40] The liberal idea of the rule of law evolved to reject this claim that anyone's conduct can be beyond legal restriction. The rule of law, representative assemblies (elected and non-elected), separation of powers, and the convention that government acts solely as representative of the people are all institutional expressions of the public nature of political power. Democracy, or a universal franchise with equal rights of political participation, is a natural extension of this idea; for if what affects all concerns all, and assuming that adults are normally best situated to understand and advance their own interests, then it is natural to conclude that each person ought to have a share of political authority to better ensure that no one's basic rights are undermined or interests are neglected in political procedures. Characteristic of contemporary liberalism then is a further feature of the public nature of political power, namely (6) the requirement of *open democratic rule*. The combination of liberalism and democratic government is a nineteenth-century accomplishment, argued for by Mill. It is not found in Locke or Kant or in the classical liberalism of Hume, Smith, or Constant; Bentham and the classical utilitarians only gradually came to accept it.[41]

I have discussed six institutional features of liberal political systems: the public recognition and legal enforcement of basic rights and liberties equally provided for all citizens; some account of equality of opportunity with open careers and positions; a central role assigned to efficient markets in allocating productive resources; government's role in the provision of public goods; its duty to provide a social minimum; and the public nature of political authority. Assuming that these institutions are characteristic of liberal society and a liberal constitution, liberalism has to be distinguished from a view with which it is often confused.

3. Libertarianism's Formative Principles

Libertarianism is commonly referred to as a liberal view. This is understandable. After all, libertarians endorse individual rights, individual freedom, and the liberal idea that people ought to be free to determine their conduct and lives as they see fit, so long as they do not violate others' rights. But a great deal depends on how rights are specified within this liberal formula. My argument is that libertarians define people's rights so as to take the view outside the boundaries of a liberal conception. For it is not as if libertarians simply accept all the usual basic rights and liberties that liberals do, then go liberals one better by adding additional liberties, namely, freedom of contract and freedom to do with one's possessions as one pleases. Liberals already recognize that these rights, suitably construed, are important for the exercise of other basic liberties. But given the absolute terms in which libertarians define these additional liberties, they come to occupy a predominant position and in effect eliminate any need (in libertarians' minds) for basic rights and for liberal institutions.[42]

What are libertarianism's basic formative principles? Libertarians often depict their view as based in a moral injunction against coercion or aggression, or against forcing people to do what they do not choose to do. (Nozick, for example, emphasizes the "libertarian side constraint that prohibits aggression against another," and Rothbard says his anarchism "abolish[es] the regularized institution of aggressive coercion.")[43] But libertarians do not condemn all coercion or aggression, or hold that no one can be forced to act in ways she has not chosen to. Libertarians clearly endorse the coercive enforcement of personal and property rights and contractual agreements. The need for such enforcement provides the basis for libertarian arguments for a minimal state. Also, it is misleading to suggest that the coercion required to enforce the rules of a libertarian society will be any less than in other systems. Whether libertarianism requires less (or more) coercion depends upon its popular support and the degree to which members of a libertarian society see its principles as legitimate and accept the many restrictions that they imply.

Libertarians may reply that the enforcement of a person's rights is not coercive interference with others' rights. "Coercion" in their account is not just any use of force, but aggressive interference with another's rights. People are not coerced when prevented from carrying out actions (such as trespass and theft) they have no right to perform. This moralized definition of "coercion" may accord with common usage in some cases, but to extend this manner of speaking to all cases has peculiar consequences. Carried to its limit, the moralized definition of "coercion" implies that any justified use of force to enforce people's rights is non-coercive. Legitimate incarceration would not then be coercive according to the moralized definition, nor would the use of force to arrest a guilty suspect or to evict an interloper.[44]

The problem with the moralized definition of "coercion" is that it is stipulated; as such it does not advance the argument for libertarianism. But even if we accept libertarians' moralized definition, nothing of real consequence follows from their declarations against coercion and aggression. Any political conception prohibits the unjustified use of force against others, and this is what the libertarian constraint against aggression or coercion really amounts to. It is a prohibition against infringement of people's moral rights and entitlements. Arguments regarding the content of these rights and entitlements then must carry the burden of justification in libertarian argument, not claims about the prohibition of coercion and aggression.

Nor is the fundamental libertarian principle an injunction that people should be subject only to duties and constraints they have chosen or consented to. The non-consensual constraints on conduct recognized by libertarians are quite extensive. Our duties to respect the lives and the physical integrity of others' persons, as well as their freedom of action and extensive property claims, and our obligations to keep our contracts, avoid fraud, and make reparations for harms we cause are not based in free choice, consent, or any kind of agreement (actual or hypothetical). These are natural rights and duties, libertarians claim, that people have independent of social interaction. Despite their emphasis on consent, voluntariness, and contract, libertarians are averse to appeals to consent or social agreement to justify their preferred list of moral rights and duties. Freedom of contract plays a central role in defining the particular rights and obligations people have *within* a libertarian society and accounts for the origin of Nozick's minimal state. But the idea of a *social* contract has no role in justifying freedom of individual contract itself or in defining its scope; the same is true of the justification of any of the other moral rights and duties that form the basis of libertarians' view.[45]

What of libertarian declarations that "people *interfere* with each other's liberty as *little* as possible"?[46] This declaration cannot mean that libertarians seek to minimize the number of interfering *actions*. It is easy to imagine a libertarian society without popular support, where the majority of people do not accept (because they cannot afford to) its absolute property rules, are prone to forage for their subsistence, and meet with constant and regular interference because of legal trespass or theft. The point of libertarian arguments for minimizing interference is to keep to a minimum, not interfering actions, but the kinds of political duties we have, and in particular any enforceable obligations to transfer market-acquired holdings to benefit the disadvantaged. There is still a need for some deeper principle that justifies complete rights to the control and disposal of market distributions regardless of the resulting restrictions this places on people's freedom of action or opportunities.

Can it be found in some notion of liberty or freedom? Libertarians commonly announce their view with a claim such as "The only relevant consideration in political matters is individual liberty,"[47] or "Libertarians agree that liberty should be prized above all other political values,"[48] or "The idea of libertarianism is to maximize individual freedom."[49] Nozick, more cautiously, makes no such general claim. But he does contend that "liberty upsets patterns"[50] of distribution and argues as if anyone with a proper regard for liberty should see that patterned theories of distributive justice violate a commitment to freedom.[51]

These announcements account for much of libertarianism's popularity, for few would deny the political importance of individual freedom. But libertarianism does not endorse freedom to any greater degree than liberalism does. Indeed, libertarianism assigns far less importance than does liberalism to freedom as individual independence and autonomy, the degree to which people are self-sufficient and can control their options and important aspects of their lives. Libertarians have a different conception than liberals of the kinds of liberties that are important and of the kinds of constraints to be placed on people's conduct to protect others' liberties. It is a fundamental libertarian precept that people ought to have nearly unrestricted liberty to accumulate, control, and transfer *rights in things* (property), whatever the consequences or constraints may be for other people. To refine Nozick's claim—"liberty upsets patterns"—it is not liberty per se or any basic liberty that liberals recognize that upsets patterns of distribution. Rather, what upsets patterns is the unrestricted liberty to accumulate and to transfer to whomever one pleases absolute property rights. But why should this set of liberties be important, let alone fundamental? To support a claim for its significance, we first need an argument for libertarian property and transfer rights. Some more basic principle still must underlie the right to these absolute liberties.

I have suggested that the concepts libertarians normally appeal to—liberty, consent, non-coercion, non-aggression, non-interference—gain their force and content by reference to a deeper principle. What is this principle? Libertarianism is grounded in a certain conception of people's individual rights, and in particular their property rights, that is, the kinds of rights and powers that individuals may exercise in the possession, use, transfer, and disposal of things. The centrality of the concept of property is evident in Rothbard's and Narveson's views. Both conflate all specific liberties into a general right to liberty. Then they argue that the right to liberty, and all other rights, are in the end property rights, bolstered by an ultimate right, property in oneself. Narveson says, "Liberty is Property . . . the libertarian thesis is really the thesis that *a right to our persons as our property is the sole fundamental right there is.*"[52] And Rothbard writes:

> In the profoundest sense there *are* no rights but property rights. The *only* human rights, in short, are property rights . . . Each individual, as a natural

fact, is the owner of *himself*, the ruler of his own person. The "human" rights of the person . . . are, in effect, each man's *property right* in his own being, and from *this* property right stems his right to the material goods that he has produced.[53]

Nozick again is more cautious, avoiding such broad generalizations. Still he relies on what he calls the "classical liberal notion of self-ownership." The problem with all non-libertarian principles of distributive justice, Nozick argues, is that they involve "(partial) property rights in other people."[54] As for democracy, it too violates the absolute ownership rights each person has in himself, for it is nothing but "ownership of the people, by the people, for the people."[55]

Such claims and arguments as these that confirm the suspicion that libertarianism is not so much about liberty as about property. Libertarianism's regulative institutional principle is that individuals ought to have absolute rights to accumulate, use, control, and transfer rights in things. To ground these controversial institutions, libertarians extend the concept of property, via the notion of self-ownership, to each person's own person and powers. The fundamental libertarian claim is then that each person is absolute owner of herself, her body and powers.[56] Because we each have absolute property in our person, it is supposed to follow that we each have absolute power over what we own or acquire consistent with others' ownership rights. On this conception, a person's liberties are among the things owned by that person; in this sense "liberty is property."

G. A. Cohen says that "Nozick's political philosophy gains much of its polemical power from the attractive thought . . . that each person is the morally rightful owner of himself."[57] While it may have polemical appeal in contemporary American society, the idea of self-ownership is more confusing than attractive. If all that libertarians mean by "self-ownership" is that each person has certain exclusive rights with respect to his or her person and powers, then the claim of self-ownership dissolves into standard liberal accounts of basic rights and liberties: liberty of conscience, freedom of thought, freedom of association, freedom of movement and integrity of the person, freedom to act on a permissible conception of the good, and so on. But libertarians mean more than this; otherwise they could not extract their most controversial conclusions regarding individual control of economic resources and their distribution. Whatever more is meant by "self-ownership" and "property in oneself" is crucial at this fundamental stage of libertarian argument.

Libertarians often appear to take "property" to be an intuitively clear notion, involving the nearly unrestricted freedom to control and determine what is done with a thing.[58] But as a legal and moral category, property is more complicated than this. Property presupposes an elaborate system of institutional rules that specify the kinds of rights, powers, duties, and liabilities persons have with respect to the use, control, transfer, and disposal of things. Systems of property differ depending on how these rules are defined. Actions permitted under one property system (such as full rights to sell or bequeath one's estate) might be prohibited under others.[59] There are conceptually an indefinite number of property systems (though only some of these may be feasible, and far fewer are just). The concepts of ownership and property rights are definable by reference to this institutional background; these are formal and secondary notions, which are given content relative to one or another system of property rules. To say that a person (legally) owns something is to say that this person has certain key rights of possession and use and powers of control within a property system; the family of rights and powers constituting "ownership" often differ from one conventionally established property system to another.[60] By extension, moral claims regarding the right to property or rights of ownership commit one to specific claims about the kinds of rights, powers, duties, and liabilities people ought to have with respect to things within a just property system.[61]

If property is seen in this way, it is difficult to understand the familiar but complicated concepts of ownership and property outside of institutional contexts. Libertarians of course deny the institutional conception of property. Fundamental to their arguments are ideas of non-cooperative natural property and pre-social ownership. They assume the lucidity of these concepts and take it as self-evident that property involves unrestricted rights to use and dispose of things. What makes libertarians' notions of self-ownership and property in oneself doubly obscure is that they extend to a person's own capacities a normative relationship normally applied to things. Although one person may, within the legal institution of slavery, legally own another, what does it mean to say a person, legally or morally, owns itself? This is not to deny the conceptual coherence of "self-ownership"; perhaps several accounts can be given (just as there are several accounts of the reflexive notion of self-consciousness). Locke (for example) used "property in one's own person" to mean that no one is born politically subject to another but that each has upon reaching maturity rights of self-rule.[62] But I suspect that once we understand what libertarians mean by "self-ownership," the concept will lose whatever intuitive attraction it has for most people. For what it inevitably implies is something Locke and all subsequent liberals deny, namely, that a person has the moral capacity to make of himself a fungible thing.

4. *Why Libertarianism Is Not a Liberal View*
4.1. The Full Alienability of Basic Rights

I claimed that the most central liberal institution is protection of the basic rights and liberties needed to secure individual freedom and independence. Libertarians would have us believe that they accept all the basic rights liberals do and simply add more liberties, namely, absolute freedom of contract and of property. Libertarians then claim their view offers us even greater liberty, as if they were just improving upon liberalism, drawing its natural conclusion. The problem is that these added liberties, when combined with the libertarian account of self-ownership, undermine the idea of basic liberties. For what libertarian self-ownership ultimately means is that we stand toward our person, its capacities, and the rights of moral personality in the same normative relationship as we stand to our rights in things. All rights are conceived as property rights. Rights to liberties then become just one among several kinds of rights that persons own and have at their disposal. Basic liberties are of no greater moral or political significance than any other kind of property right. But given the crucial role of absolute freedom of contract—that all contractual agreements are to be publicly recognized and enforced—it follows that all liberties can be alienated, just like any economic good.

Consequently, there is no place in a libertarian scheme for inalienability, the idea that certain rights are so essential to maintaining the dignity and independence of persons that they cannot be given up by consent. So Nozick says, "My nonpaternalistic position holds that someone may choose (or permit another) to do to himself *anything*, unless he has acquired an obligation to some third party not to do or allow it."[63] Read within the context of a libertarian acceptance of absolute freedom of contract, permitting another to do "anything" to herself implies the capacity to give another the right to invoke the coercive powers of the state (or anyone else) to force you to comply with your earlier agreements, no matter what you have agreed to or how much you presently object to it. Not surprisingly then, Nozick later says a free system allows a person to sell herself into slavery.[64] Assuming the transaction is freely entered into, it is the role of the minimal state to enforce it against the unfortunate person who once consented to enslavement but who now, quite understandably, has had a change of mind. It should follow that there is nothing morally objectionable about owning slaves and treating people as objects against their will;[65] moreover, it is not unjust for the state, or any third party, to compel people to abide by their slavery or other servitude contracts.

Earlier I argued that it is a mistake to conceive of servitude agreements as simply private matters between consenting adults protected by freedom of association. If genuine freedom of association were involved, then either party could terminate the relationship freely. But here we have something very different: contractual transfers of rights in oneself, the result of which negates a person's freedom of association as well as other basic rights. Contracts by their nature are no longer simply private relationships that leave others' rights and duties unaffected; they become publicly enforceable agreements altering others' rights and obligations. Contracts impose upon others duties to recognize and respect contractual terms, and upon governments duties of coercive enforceability. These facts should not be obscured by the common locution of "private contracts." Libertarians describe *full alienability* of rights as if it were a matter of showing respect for people's freedom and voluntary choices. A better description of a social system that enforces complete or even partial dominion over human beings is that it is a perverse property system. For it is not as if libertarians put a premium upon *maintaining* individuals' freedom of action, much less so their independence or their capacities to exercise their rights and control significant aspects of their lives. Instead what is fundamentally important for libertarians is maintaining a system of historically generated property rights whatever the consequences for individuals' freedom, independence, or interests. Libertarianism is, in the end, not so much about liberty as it is about protecting and enforcing absolute property and contract rights. The liberties that libertarians provide are defined by reference to absolute property in persons and in things, and who has these rights in the end is not morally important, so long as their holdings come about by observing libertarian transfer procedures and side-constraints.

Libertarians will insist that the distribution of property rights in persons and things still must be generated by the free consent of rights owners. But this does not show that libertarians value each person's freedom any more than giving equal consideration to everyone's (equally intense) desires shows that utilitarians place a fundamental value on equality and maintaining each person's happiness. In both cases we are dealing with a feature of a decision procedure for distributing goods (happiness for utilitarianism, rights for libertarianism) without any check on the distributions this procedure generates. For libertarians, each person starts with ownership of his or her person and any possessions acquired by transfer. These property rights are deemed of equal significance, and each person is at complete liberty to transfer whatever rights he or she has. So far as any right is given priority, it is absolute liberty of contract and transfer, which determines the procedural mechanism for distributing rights and powers. But no attention is given to maintaining the basic rights, liberties, and powers that (according to liberals) are needed to institutionally define a person's freedom, independence, and status as an equal citizen. So we arrive at the peculiar possibility that the world and all within it can be someone's (or more likely some class's) property, with all but one (person or group) devoid of freedom and independence, and yet all is right and just since libertarian procedures and side-constraints have been satisfied.[66]

However unlikely, the example emphasizes libertarians' lack of concern with preserving basic rights and liberties or individual self-governance and independence.[67] This marks an essential difference with liberalism. No liberal regime would enforce or permit enforcement of an agreement against a person who has tried to alienate one or more of her constitutionally protected basic rights. For these are the rights that define a person's status as a free agent, capable of rationally deciding her good and taking responsibility for her actions. Liberalism affirms this ideal of free moral agency and seeks to secure it via the institutional recognition of basic rights. That rights are basic means they are not susceptible to being overridden by *anyone's* desires. Being fundamental, basic rights are secured against the (aggregate) wants of others. Being inalienable, they are secured against the wants of those who would dispossess themselves of their basic rights and abandon their freedom and independence.

Libertarians will object that liberals still show "less respect" for liberty, since they refuse to recognize all of a person's free decisions. But no view holds that all of a person's free decisions are to be respected; libertarians, like everyone else, require that free decisions not violate others' rights. The issue between liberalism and libertarianism then becomes whether all permissible liberties are on a par and are equally important or whether some liberties are more significant than others. Libertarians assign absolute priority to freedom of contract and to property rights. Liberals give priority to different rights and liberties: those that are crucial to maintaining a person's status as a free, responsible and independent agent. Given the priority of these liberties, liberals do not recognize decisions to contract away all one's liberties or respect the liberty to do so. If this is all libertarians mean when they say liberals give "less respect to liberty," it simply reasserts the main point: liberals deny complete alienability. Liberals can reply that recognition of rights to alienate freedom is not to respect freedom but to debase it; it makes freedom a fungible thing, tradable for something with a qualitatively different and lesser value.[68]

4.2. Absolute Property and Invidious Discrimination

Consider next libertarian attitudes toward liberal institutions affording equal opportunity. Even if narrowly construed, equal opportunity implies more than simply an absence of legal restrictions on entry into preferred social positions by members of salient social classes. Jim Crow laws were not the primary cause of segregation in the South.[69] In many places few laws, if any, explicitly restricted blacks from entry into desirable social positions, from purchasing property in white neighborhoods, from entering private schools and colleges, or from using hospitals, restaurants, hotels, and other private businesses frequented by whites.[70] Still, these events rarely occurred due to tacit (often explicit) agreement among whites. Because of privately imposed restrictive covenants, discriminatory business practices, and blacks' abject economic status, there was little need for laws imposing segregation and discrimination. It could be left up to the "invisible hand."

Libertarianism has no principles and allows for no laws or institutions that prohibit such invidious discrimination.[71] This is a consequence of the strict priority assigned to absolute property and contract rights. According to the libertarian conception of property, people may transfer their holdings to whomever they please and may allow holdings to be used only by others they choose. Moreover, other than prohibitions against fraud and duress, no legal restrictions can be placed on contractual agreements. It follows that there is nothing unjust about racial, ethnic, gender, or religious discrimination in employment, education, and the provision of goods and services. Libertarians may pay lip service to the classical liberal view of "careers open to talents," but nothing in their doctrine prohibits widespread violation of this idea. Nor do libertarians allow for institutions that prohibit the intentional imposition of racially segregated housing patterns. The same is true of the sale or provision of all other goods and services. Race, gender, and other forms of discrimination, while they may be uneconomical, unseemly, or imprudent, are still not unjust according to libertarianism. Libertarian property rights then come to provide cover for bigotry and invidious discrimination against what liberals see as the basic interests and rights of citizens, including the right to be treated as an equal person.

4.3. Markets and Monopolies

Under competitive conditions, markets normally allow for efficient allocations of productive resources and increased output of goods to meet (effective) demand. But if market activities are left unregulated, freely associating individuals can just as well enter agreements designed to restrict others' options, frustrating instead of promoting productive output. The right of unrestricted freedom of contract so central to libertarianism implies that markets are to be wholly self-regulating; government has no role to play in securing market fluidity. There is then no place for laws and institutions designed to promote competition and deter non-competitive agreements. Absolute contract rights, conjoined with rights of unlimited accumulation that inhere in libertarian property, can then readily lead to cartels, monopolies, price collusion, and hoarding to inflate prices. That someone may have acquired complete control over some scarce natural resource, such as timber, oil, or water supplies, and charges others whatever he pleases is wholly consistent with libertarian property rights. Such arrangements are not allocatively efficient. But because libertarians reject any interference with free economic transactions and individuals' complete control over resources, they must place subordinate value on the efficient allocation of productive resources. It is more important to maintain individuals' absolute property and contract rights.[72] In the absence of institutional arrangements enforced by government to prevent excessive accumulation of market power, the likely outcome of libertarian entitlements is a series of contracts establishing cartels' control in each industry. Once this stage is reached, nothing but goodwill can prevent libertarianism's progression into veritable economic serfdom.

To say that economic efficiency is of subordinate importance to libertarians does not mean that appeals to efficiency have no place in libertarian argument. My claim is that efficiency plays no significant role in establishing the basic principles of the system (i.e., absolute property and contract rights, and the distribution of income and wealth) and that efficiency considerations will be sacrificed to maintain libertarian rights of contract and property. In Nozick's account, efficiency is one of several considerations to take into account in refining property rights and resolving disputes;[73] moreover, a condition of initial appropriation in a state of nature is that others not be made worse off by an initial taking (the Lockean Proviso). But these appeals to efficiency are meant simply to put weak limits on what may be appropriated and to help specify the contours of property rights once appropriated. Once property rights are defined and acquired, there is no requirement that further uses, transfers, and disposals of property be efficient. One may accumulate, use, and dispose of property at will, so long as others' rights are not violated and they are not made worse off than they would be *in a state of nature*.[74] By contrast, efficient use (either Pareto or Kaldor-Hicks) is determined by reference to the status quo ante at the time of use, and not by reference to a (real or imagined) state of nature that existed in the distant past. In this regard, efficiency considerations are not fundamental or integral to Nozick's entitlement theory.[75]

4.4. The Libertarian Rejection of Public Goods and a Social Minimum

Libertarianism has no place for government to enforce the provision of public goods, those goods not adequately and effectively provided for by markets. The role of the libertarian state is exclusively to protect and maintain rights and entitlements against infringement, to enforce contractual agreements, and to resolve disputes. For governments to tax people to provide public goods is unjustly coercive, as it is for government to tax some and redistribute it to others (for purposes of healthcare, unemployment, emergency relief, etc.). The state has no role to play in distributing income and wealth (other than enforcing existing rights); distributions are to be decided entirely by owners' free decisions and voluntary transfers, regardless of the consequences for others. These matters require little discussion here, since libertarians emphasize them as central to their position.[76]

4.5. Political Power as a Private Power

Since Locke, liberals have conceived of political power mainly in terms of three primary functions of governments: political power is the authority (1) to legislate public rules and revise them to meet changing circumstances; (2) to adjudicate disputes arising under these rules; and (3) to enforce these rules when necessary against those who violate them or who resist adjudicative resolutions. For Locke these three powers are needed to remedy the "defects" of the state of nature.[77] These defects warrant the creation of political society (via a social contract, on Locke's account). This political society ("the Body Politic," "the People") has the authority to legislate a constitution and to place limited political power in a government, which is appointed as the People's fiduciary agent to fulfill these functions on behalf of the People.

One peculiar feature of strict libertarianism is the absence of legislative authority, a public institution with authority to introduce and amend rules and revise social conventions. The need for new or revised rules is to be satisfied through private transactions and the invisible hand, by the eventual convergence of many private choices. Libertarians generally accept that adjudicative and executive powers are necessary to maintain personal and property rights. But these functions are performed by private protection agencies and arbitration services (in Nozick's account, a "dominant protective agency," which is the minimal state). No public body, commonly recognized and accepted as possessing legitimate authority, is required to fairly and effectively fulfill these functions. Political power is privately exercised.[78]

The libertarian conception of private political power is evident from Nozick's account of the minimal state. Nozick's account is selectively Lockean, for he disregards Locke's duty to protect and maintain humanity and assist others in need and distress.[79] This enables Nozick to contend that it would be irrational for the inhabitants of a Lockean state of nature to overcome the inconveniences of their situation by a social contract.[80] Instead, they enter into separate private contracts with competing protection agencies to enforce their personal and property rights. Eventually, one protection agency achieves a natural monopoly in providing "protection services" for those willing and able to pay for them. (This "dominant protective agency" is the "ultra-minimal state.") Different "packages" of protection services are offered, depending on customers' wants, circumstances, and ability to pay. This dominant protective agency evolves into the minimal state when it provides a minimum level of protection services (the "least expensive protection policy") without charge to those unable to afford them. These services selectively protect non-members: they are guarded against aggression by paying members, but are not shielded from aggressive non-members.[81]

So conceived, the libertarian state originates in and is sustained by a network of private contracts.[82] This network of agreements continues into the present and is needed to maintain the minimal state. Clients of the minimal state must purchase their protection "policies," just as they purchase auto or medical insurance. They contract for different services depending on their willingness and ability to pay; and if they cannot pay, then they receive minimal protection against the minimal state's clients. They do not receive protection from the aggression of its non-clients (others equally unable to afford protection services).

How are we to assess this conception of political power? How does it compare with liberalism? Begin with the minimal state's lack of legislative authority. H. L. A. Hart has argued that any society is bound to be static and primitive if it relies entirely on custom and people's uncoordinated responses to new situations, and is without a commonly recognized and accepted procedure that identifies the kinds of rights and duties people have and that issues public rules to promptly respond to changing conditions.[83] One challenge to libertarianism is to show that this is not its inevitable fate. No matter how knowledgeable and informative the invisible hand, libertarian agents are invariably going to be unsure of and will disagree about the application of their abstract rights and duties. The absence of a public institution that refines libertarian principles and authoritatively issues public rules to apply to historical conditions and specific circumstances will result in (as Locke says) great "inconvenience." Without institutions to publicly identify the principles of libertarian natural law and to specify their rules under existing circumstances, it is difficult to see how the countless sophisticated rules that make up the modern institutions of property, contract, securities, negotiable instruments, patents and copyrights, and so on could effectively evolve simply by the invisible hand. Even if these institutions were to evolve without legislative power, once in place there would be no legal person with the authority to revise rules to meet changing conditions, eliminating ineffective rules and introducing new ones in their stead. No institution exists for changing norms to adapt to new circumstances except for the gradual process through which all libertarian rules and institutions evolve.

Political power is then truncated under libertarianism since there is no commonly recognized legislative authority. Moreover, the judicial and enforcement powers that do exist remain in private hands. One of the most characteristic features of libertarianism is that the protection and enforcement of people's rights are treated as economic goods, to be provided for by private market interactions.[84] Initially held by each individual, these private political powers are transferred by each through separate contractual agreements to other private persons who compete on the market to provide protection, arbitration, and enforcement services. Different arrangements are made depending on the political services people want and can afford. In Nozick's version, a single dominant protection agency eventually acquires a de facto monopoly on political power; its competitors go out of business. In Rothbard's and other anarchical versions, no such monopoly need exist; presumably, competing protection agencies can peaceably coexist. In both accounts, political power is privately exercised for the benefit of those who can afford it and according to whatever favorable terms each person can bargain for.[85]

The distribution of political "services" depends, then, on a person's wealth and relative bargaining position.

Is this a just and feasible arrangement? Libertarians place in private hands the role of identifying, interpreting, and coercively enforcing the conditions of social cooperation, including the most basic claims for restraint, protection, and assistance that are a condition of social life. Political power is privately exercised and is distributed like any other private economic good. Recall the features of public political authority as conceived by liberals, discussed in section 2: (1) its non-personal, institutional nature; (2) its institutional continuity: political power is maintained over time, by generally accepted rules of succession; (3) political power is recognized as authoritatively held and as legitimate; (4) because of its fiduciary nature, political power is to be exercised in trust, for the benefit of those represented; and (5) the impartiality of political power: it is to be exercised equitably for the public good and for the good of each citizen or subject.

Can libertarianism meet these liberal conditions on public political authority? Assume, for purposes of argument, that libertarianism can satisfy (1) and (2). We can imagine the libertarian state as a kind of corporate body (not simply the power of an individual or family) with settled procedures; it exists continuously due to its corporate rules for selecting and replacing officers, and it survives individuals' retirement or demise.[86] Does this institution meet the remaining conditions for public political power? Beginning with condition (3), does the libertarian minimal state enjoy political legitimacy?

Libertarian political power is based in private bilateral contractual agreements. So far as there is a monopoly on coercive power, it is a natural, not a de jure monopoly.[87] Indeed, it is essential to libertarian political power that it not claim a de jure monopoly on political power or any *right* to political rule. So, the effectiveness of libertarian political power is made to depend on its de facto exercise against persons who have not consented to its exercise against them (which is true even of clients of Nozick's dominant protection agency). What is there to maintain the effectiveness and stability of libertarian political power other than its de facto monopoly? Do people have reason to respect this power, or do they comply with its judgments, orders, and decrees simply out of fear? If political power is based simply in a natural monopoly, then in what sense can it be seen as the exercise of political *authority* as opposed to simply the employment of brute force? That some private body monopolizes political power is no reason to respect it (although it might be reason to fear it). There is then likely to be no general recognition of the moral or legal authority of the private state in libertarian society. But without the public's sense of its authority, libertarian political power lacks one of the most effective means for enforcing rules and judicial judgments, namely, the sense of allegiance and political obligation to public authority. Moreover, the exercise of effective judicial power depends on such concepts as *jurisdiction* over parties and particular grievances and disputes, as well as the *validity* of judicial judgments based in an authorized body of laws. The mere exercise of mock judicial powers and making and enforcing judgments would seem to be insufficient to give rise to these normative concepts.[88]

These three attributes—recognition of a government's rightful *authority* to rule (accompanied by a corresponding sense of allegiance and political obligation), governments' *jurisdiction* over persons and disputes, and issuing *valid and binding legal judgments*—are central features of governments as enduring political and legal systems. They are all part of the idea of *political legitimacy*. It is doubtful whether the de facto monopoly on force possessed by the libertarian minimal state can ever give rise to political legitimacy in this sense (and even more doubtful that the competing protection agencies that anarchical libertarians defend can achieve it). This raises questions regarding libertarianism's feasibility and stability. It also implies questions of justice, for what gives political power its legitimacy ultimately is its fiduciary nature, its impartial exercise, and its primary objective, the common good.[89]

What then of the fiduciary nature (4) of libertarian political power? Libertarian political power is exercised pursuant to the terms of economic contract: it is individually bargained for, is sold for a profit at the going market (or more likely monopoly) rate, and is normally distributed only to those who pay for it.[90] Economic contractual relations normally are driven by private interest; parties are indifferent about the good of each other and negotiations are conducted at arm's length. Economic contractual relations are not fiduciary relations, which by their nature require acting for another party's interests even at the expense of one's own. Moreover, a peculiar feature of the minimal state, and of competing protection agencies under anarchical libertarianism, is that political power becomes a sort of (private) corporate power. As a for-profit enterprise, the protection agency's primary duties extend to its owners or shareholders. While the manager–shareholder relationship may be conceived as fiduciary (as a matter of public law), this is very different from the fiduciary capacity of governments, where the beneficiaries of political authority are supposed to be those who are governed, not those who exercise and control political power.

Here a libertarian might reply: "Its basis in private contract does not by itself make libertarian political power non-fiduciary, for lawyers and bank trustees are deemed fiduciaries. This is just the product they have to sell: they contract out their fiduciary services (as guardians, trustees, agents, etc.) to represent and act in the interests of their clients." But they do so within the structured setting of a system of public laws and political institutions, which regulates their contracts to be fiduciaries and prescribes specific duties upon them above and beyond those specifically contracted for. Lawyers would not be allowed to reach agreements with their clients that relieve them of the fiduciary duties imposed on them by law or absolve them of liability for their negligence or intentional wrongs. Moreover, lawyers are deemed to act as "officers of the courts": they stand in a fiduciary relationship not just to their clients but to the public as well and cannot pursue their own or their clients' interests contrary to the public interest (as conventionally defined). Lawyers are sanctioned when they breach these responsibilities. Within libertarianism, however, there is no structure of publicly recognized principles and institutions that impose general duties on protection agencies to act in a fiduciary capacity for their members' interests or for the public interest. Insofar as it is exercised for the benefit of another, libertarian political power is guided only by the obligations fixed by many bilateral contractual bargains.[91]

Consider finally condition (5)—political power is to be exercised impartially and for the public good—and the sense in which libertarian political power is most conspicuously non-public: (a) Libertarian political services are not uniformly supplied but are provided in proportion to a person's willingness and ability to pay. People receive only those protection, arbitration, and procedural rights they can afford to pay for. Political power is not then *impartially* administered. This holds true even for Nozick, who (unlike other libertarians) provides minimal protection benefits to non-members without charge: the level of protection provided is not equal to that of others (e.g., no arbitration services are provided); moreover, minimal protection is not provided against the people most likely to attack non-members, namely, other non-members. (b) Further, in acting from private economic motives and for the private benefit of its paying customers (ultimately its owner-shareholders), there is no objective or understanding that the minimal state acts for *public benefit*, for the good of society and all of its members. As it eschews public goods in the economic sense, libertarianism eschews the public good in the moral sense. Political power is not exercised for the sake of justice (even as libertarians define it), but for self-interested private ends, including maximization of the private state's profits.

What is striking about libertarians' conception of political power is its resemblance to feudalism. By "feudalism" I mean a particular conception of *political* power. I do not mean the manorial system, or the economic system that relies on the institution of serfdom (as in European medieval feudalism).[92] Feudalism is a system of personal political dependence that is based in a network of private contractual agreements. Under feudalism the elements of political authority are powers that are held personally by individuals, not by enduring political institutions. These powers are held as a matter of private contractual right. Individuals gradually acquire the power to make, apply, and enforce rules by forging a series of private contracts with particular individuals or families. Oaths of fealty or service are sworn in exchange for similar or compensating benefits. Those who exercise political power wield it on behalf of others pursuant to their private contractual relation, and only so long as their contract is in force. Since different services are provided to people, there is no notion of a uniform public law that is to be impartially applied to all individuals. Instead, "custom and verbal agreement take the place of written law."[93] Moreover, subjects' political obligations and allegiances are voluntary and personal: they arise out of private contractual obligations and are owed to particular persons, families, or other private groups. Political obligation and allegiance are not seen as moral imperatives that are based in a duty of justice or in duties to humanity or to members of any national or ethnic group.[94]

Of course, under feudalism proper in Europe, personal loyalty between liege and vassal was seen as a moral duty arising out of contract. Loyalty was an important political motivation, and a complicated system of loyalty norms cemented personal allegiances. Loyalty motives and norms are, of course, absent from libertarianism; it relies on self-interest and the obligation to keep one's contracts as sufficient incentives to keep one's political obligations (e.g., to provide protection services). But in all other respects mentioned, libertarianism resembles feudalism. This resemblance stems from both doctrines' conception of political power as a system of personal political dependence grounded in a network of private contractual relations. Like the provision of any other individual service, contracting for protection and arbitration services is simply the way people defend themselves and secure their interests from others' aggression.[95]

Liberalism evolved in great part by rejecting the idea of privately exercised political power, whether it stemmed from a network of private contracts under feudalism or whether it was conceived as owned and exercised by divine right under royal absolutism.[96] Libertarianism resembles feudalism in that it establishes political power in a web of bilateral individual contracts. Consequently, it has no conception of legitimate public political authority or any place for political society, a "body politic" that political authority represents in a fiduciary capacity. Having no conception of public political authority, libertarians have no place for the impartial administration of justice. People's rights are selectively protected only to the extent that they can afford protection and depending on which services they pay for.[97] Having no conception of a political society, libertarians have no conception of the common good, those basic interests of each individual that, according to liberals, are to be maintained for the sake of justice by the impartial exercise of public political power.[98]

5. Concluding Remarks

My purpose has been to show that the primary institutions endorsed by the liberal political tradition are incompatible with libertarianism. I have assumed that liberal institutions can have different philosophical justifications and can be accepted from different points of view. This is to be expected given the reasonable pluralism (as Rawls calls it) that will exist in a well-ordered liberal society. Libertarianism will no doubt be advocated by some in any liberal society, but they will not endorse basic liberal institutions. Whether libertarianism will gain sufficient adherents to undermine a well-order liberal society is a question of the stability of liberal institutions. No matter how coherent its justification, classical liberal institutions may be prone to disintegrate into libertarianism. Instability would most likely result from the extensive significance that classical liberalism assigns to private property and the desirability of market distributions. If people are led to believe in the inherent justice of market distributions and the "sanctity" of private property as defined by existing law, then regardless of classical liberalism's theoretical justification (overall utility, market efficiency, a Lockean argument, or the Hobbism of Gauthier and Buchanan), citizens will likely come to believe that they have a fundamental moral right to whatever they acquire by market exchange, gift, and bequest. If so, then liberal institutions will periodically be jeopardized. Those better off will resent taxation to pay for public goods, social security and healthcare for the elderly and handicapped, and minimum income supports and other assistance for the poor. Moreover, democratic government's very legitimacy may be questioned. These are familiar and recurring events in US history.[99]

Among nations, the United States is distinctive in that it celebrates as part of its national consciousness the Lockean model (some would say "myth") of the creation of political society by original agreement among free (and freeholding) persons, all equally endowed with certain natural rights. Modify this national story slightly (mainly by substituting a web of bilateral contracts for the social contract and eliminating the duties it entails) and we have the essential makings of libertarianism. Perhaps this explains why libertarianism is such a popular and peculiarly American view. However slight these modifications may seem, their effects are far-reaching, for what we have in libertarianism is no longer liberalism, but its undoing.[100]

Notes

1. Mill says he is a utilitarian, but he understands that doctrine differently than classical or contemporary utilitarians. For Mill "individuality" and the exercise and development of higher capacities, including a sense of justice, form the larger part of individual well-being (see chap. 2 of *Utilitarianism*, and chap. 3 of *On Liberty* in *"On Liberty" and Other Essays*, ed. John Gray [Oxford: Oxford University Press, 1991]). See also Rawls's suggestion that Mill endorses a "liberalism of freedom" rather than a "liberalism of happiness" that is based in utilitarianism or welfarism. John Rawls, *Lectures in Moral Philosophy* (Cambridge, MA: Harvard University Press, 2000), 330, 340, 366.

2. Some may object that the term "high liberalism" is tendentious, but it no more implies moral superiority to classical liberalism than "High Renaissance" implies that Raphael's art is superior to Botticelli's. To call it "welfare liberalism" wrongly suggests that classical liberals do not support public assistance for the poor; it also puts the emphasis in the wrong place (especially given Rawls's denial that he is arguing for the welfare state). See *TJ*, xiv–xvi.

3. Locke's writings allow him to be interpreted either way. Because Locke antedated classical price theory and the classical economists' emphasis on the efficiency of free markets, and did not foresee the conditions of a modern market economy, the dispute concerning whether Locke is a classical or high liberal may have no definite resolution. For instructive accounts of Locke on property and economic justice, see A. John Simmons, *The Lockean Theory of Rights* (Princeton, NJ: Princeton University Press, 1992), chaps. 5 and 6; Jeremy Waldron, *The Right to Private Property* (Oxford: Oxford University Press, 1988), chap. 6; and James Tully, *A Discourse on Property* (Cambridge: Cambridge University Press, 1980).

4. Jeffrey Paul, for example, refers to Nozick's libertarianism as the "recent successor of Lockean liberalism" (Paul, ed., *Reading Nozick* [Totowa, NJ: Rowman & Littlefield, 1981], 4. T. M. Scanlon says Nozick's book is "liberal in the nineteenth century sense of the term" ("Nozick on Rights, Liberty, and Property," in Paul, *Reading Nozick*, 107). Nozick himself claims he relies on a "classical liberal notion of self-ownership" (*ASU*, 172).

5. My purpose is not to establish "bragging rights" to the honorific term "liberal," but rather to point to a fundamental difference in principles and institutions and to locate the principles that libertarians really endorse that lead to this difference. If anyone wants to continue calling libertarianism a "liberal" conception, this is fine so long as its qualitative differences with other liberal views are understood as significant. But to categorize libertarianism as a form of liberalism obscures what is really distinctive about both views.

6. After nearly two centuries of religious strife and civil war, enlightened opinion gradually began to accept that a religious confession was no longer capable of providing a basis for political unity and allegiance. It was seen that inevitably people will have conflicting religious views and that for governments to try to enforce one faith is a recipe for perpetual strife. On the origin of liberalism in the wars of religion, see *PL* xxiv–xxvi; see also John Gray, *Two Faces of Liberalism* (Oxford: Blackwell, 2000), chap. 1.

7. See Mill, *"On Liberty" and Other Essays*, chap. 1, 16–17.

8. See *PL*, lecture 8, 291, for Rawls's list of basic liberties, which simplifies the initial definition of basic liberties given in *A Theory of Justice* (Cambridge, MA: Harvard University Press, 1971), 61 (*TJ* orig. in further citations of this work); *TJ*, 53.

9. See *PL*, 335, where Rawls says that denial of freedom of movement and occupation violates the liberty and integrity of the person. In *TJ* org., 61, *TJ*, 53, and *PL*, 298, Rawls says that the right to hold personal property is part of freedom of the person.

10. The rule of law involves several requirements, including similar cases treated similarly, no offense without a law, public promulgation of laws, no ex post facto laws, fair and open trials, rules of evidence ensuring rational inquiry, and a number of other rights associated with the idea of due process. See *TJ*, §38.

11. For example, a person's freedom of speech can be limited if it causes imminent violence or fear thereof (e.g., threats, conspiracies, or inciting to riot), or deceptions regarding property (prohibitions against fraud or false advertising), or unjustifiable injury to personal integrity (restrictions against private libel or breach of privacy). These are examples of what Rawls means by "liberty can be restricted only for the sake of liberty." See *TJ*, 214, and *PL*, 295.

12. Some legal scholars argue that exclusive employment contracts are on a par with slavery and indentured servitude, differing only in degree. But this misconceives the nature of exclusive employment contracts. They do not involve the alienation of freedom of occupation and control over one's person. At any time, a person may quit and take up another career (although usually not the same career for the period covered by an exclusive services contract). For example, a professional athlete can retire and take up another line of work but cannot compete in the same sport for another team during the term of his contract.

13. A prisoner obviously surrenders some of his basic liberties—freedom of association, freedom to pursue his good, freedom of movement, and normally the right to vote, but not liberty of conscience or all freedom of thought and expression.

14. See Mill, *"On Liberty" and Other Essays*, chap. 5, 113–15; Rousseau, *Social Contract*, book 1, chap. 4, "On Slavery," in Rousseau, *The Basic Political Writings*, trans. David A. Cress (Indianapolis: Hackett, 1987), 144–47. In *The Metaphysical Elements of Justice*, trans. John Ladd (New York: Library of Liberal Arts, 1965), 98 (Akademie edition 6: 330), Kant says, "No one can bind himself by a contract to the kind of dependency through which he ceases to be a person, for he can make a contract only insofar as he is a person." In "On the Proverb: That May Be True in Theory but Is of No Practical Use" (Akademie edition 8: 293, quoted in *Perpetual Peace and Other Essays*, trans. Ted Humphrey [Indianapolis: Hackett, 1983], 75), where Kant says that no person can lose his equality as a person except through transgression; equality cannot be alienated "through a contract . . . for there is no act (neither his own nor that of another) that conforms with right whereby he can terminate his possession of himself and enter into the class of domestic animals."

15. See Joel Feinberg, *Harm to Self* (Oxford: Oxford University Press, 1986), 94–97.

16. The argument that follows in the text assumes that one does not have to be a Kantian to recognize the following: duties of mutual respect and mutual aid; that inflicting harm upon others against their will and for one's own personal benefit is wrong; that slavery is wrong since it involves treating others as things;

and that failure to respect others as persons with rights is wrong. Utilitarian and natural law theories can accept all of these as legitimate reasons.

17. Brian Barry emphasizes that a right of exit is essential to freedom of association. See his *Culture and Equality* (Cambridge, MA: Harvard University Press, 2001), 148–62.

18. As an illustration of this problem, suppose slave contracts are accepted as legally and morally binding. I agree to grant refuge to an abused runaway who is contractually bound to slavery due to youthful exuberance, indiscretion, or desperation. Am I under a legal and moral duty to turn her in? Wouldn't I be guilty of more than one crime if I did not: not simply aiding and abetting, but also crimes of property such as conversion and receiving stolen goods? How can I fulfill my legal and moral duties in this society without harming this person, and treating her according to rules appropriate for things? The example can be developed in other disturbing directions. Suppose the slave's owner is a pimp. Does this mean that forcing the slave to engage in involuntary intercourse is not rape so long as her owner consents? Or, if it is still rape, do johns nonetheless have a right to rape with the owner's permission? Whatever the case, if slavery agreements are permissible, we have to assume it would be wrong, morally as well as legally, for third parties to interfere to prevent coerced sex.

19. The public recognition of all as civic equals and as free is crucial here. This means that the liberal case for inalienability does not depend simply on the idea that liberal government and its citizens are not to be made complicit in the enforcement of servitude contracts. Suppose the defender of servitude contracts were to say, "Okay, so do not exercise the coercive powers of the state to enforce servitude contracts. All we ask is that beneficiaries have immunity from criminal laws when they seek self-enforcement (perhaps with the help of their henchmen). No one else need dirty their hands." The liberal position is that servitude contracts are absolutely void, not deserving any legal recognition. The fact that the beneficiary of an involuntary servitude contract seeks to coercively enforce the contract himself is reason enough for government to intervene. (After all, it is a violent assault on a person.) As explained below, liberals see the exercise of coercive power ultimately as a public power. Individuals are authorized in certain instances to use coercive power (most commonly in self-defense), but then it may not be exercised excessively or to undermine the public good. Central to the liberal public good is maintaining the civic status of persons as free and as equals. Basic rights are the primary means for securing this status. As citizens have a duty to respect one another's basic rights (even when some are willing to abandon them), governments have a duty to protect these rights and maintain conditions appropriate for their exercise. For this reason, a government cannot sit idly by while one person seeks self-enforcement of a servitude contract.

20. This is not a term Locke uses; indeed, he rarely referred to "natural rights" at all. Cf. his reference to "that *equal Right* that every man hath, *to his natural Freedom*" (*Second Treatise*, para. 54, in John Locke, *Two Treatises of Government*, ed. Peter Laslett [Cambridge: Cambridge University Press, 1960], 304).

21. See John Locke, *Second Treatise on Government*, ed. Peter Laslett (Cambridge: Cambridge University Press, 1988), paras. 73, 120, 138, and 139, for clear indications that government has the authority to regulate property, tax it, and burden it for the public good.

22. Of course, they could not be basic in the defined sense implying inalienability, if particular property rights are to retain their status are freely transferable.

23. The term "absolute property" derives from J. S. Mill's *Principles of Political Economy*, "Of Property," book 3, chap. 1, sec. 3. Mill distinguishes absolute from "qualified property." Absolute property does not imply no restrictions whatsoever on property. For Nozick, "The central core of the notion of a property right in X . . . is the right to determine what shall be done with X," but one's options are constrained. "My property rights in my knife allow me to leave it where I will, but not in your chest" (*ASU*, 171). "Constrained options" designed to protect others' rights are compatible with absolute property.

24. Kant, "On the Proverb: That May Be True in Theory but Is of No Practical Use," in *Perpetual Peace and Other Essays*, trans. Ted Humphrey (Indianapolis: Hackett, 1983), 74.

25. The phrase "system of natural liberty" derives from Adam Smith's *The Wealth of Nations* (New York: Random House Modern Library, 1937), book 4, chap. 9, 651. David Gauthier approvingly quotes the relevant passage in *Morals by Agreement* (Oxford: Oxford University Press, 1986), 83.

26. See Milton Friedman, *Capitalism and Freedom* (Chicago: Chicago University Press, 1962), 113.

27. See Rawls's account of "fair equality of opportunity" (*TJ* orig., 73f.; *TJ*, 63f., §§14 and 46; also *PL*, 184, 248, 363f.). On the relevance of adequate healthcare to Rawls's principle of fair equality of opportunity, see Norman Daniels, *Just Health Care* (Cambridge: Cambridge University Press, 1987).

28. Nozick makes this argument in *ASU*, 235–39.

29. This may be true of Locke even in his day. See Locke, *First Treatise*, para. 42, in *Two Treatises of Government*, 170, where he says that God "has given no one of his Children such a Property, in his peculiar Portion of the things of this World, but that he has given his needy Brother a Right to the Surplusage of his Goods, so that it cannot justly be denied him, when his pressing Wants call for it." For Kant, see *Metaphysics of Justice*, Akademie 6:326 (in Ladd, *Metaphysical Elements of Justice*, 93): By "the General Will of the people . . . government is authorized to require the wealthy to provide the means of sustenance to those who are unable to provide the most necessary needs of nature for themselves."

For a discussion of the Locke quotation and his views on justice and the duty of charity, see Simmons, *The Lockean Theory of Rights*, 227–36.

30. Friedrich Hayek, *The Constitution of Liberty* (Chicago: University of Chicago Press, 1960), 285–86, makes the Hobbesian argument that "poor relief" is instrumental in preventing widespread theft and disorder. Hayek endorses society's "duty of preventing destitution and providing a minimum level of welfare," but rejects the "welfare state" since it aims at "egalitarian distribution" (289). Hayek also endorses social insurance measures such as compulsory payment for health insurance and old age pensions (298). See also Friedrich Hayek, *Law, Legislation, and Liberty*, vol. 2: *The Mirage of Social Justice* (Chicago: University of Chicago Press, 1976), 87, on society's interest or duty to provide "an assured minimum income, or a floor below which nobody needs to descend Milton Friedman seems to advocate a public charity position based in beneficence; he states a need to "assure a safety net for every person in the country, so that no one need suffer dire distress." See Milton Friedman and Rose Friedman, *Free to Choose*, 110; see 110–17 on the negative income tax as the way to provide this "safety net."

31. See *TJ* orig., 270–74, 280–82, *TJ*, 239–42, 247–49, on the compatibility of the difference principle with both liberal socialism and a "property-owning democracy."

32. Commonly mentioned among public goods are national defense, public health and sanitation, police and fire protection, highways, street lighting, ports and canals, water and sewer works, and education, none of which are adequately provided for by markets. For a discussion of public goods, see *TJ*, §42.

33. Smith, *The Wealth of Nations*, book 4, chap. 9, 651; book 5, chap. 1, part 3, 681ff.

34. On this, see John Gray, *Liberalism* (Milton Keynes: Open University Press, 1986), 27; and Stephen Holmes, *Passions and Constraints* (Chicago: University of Chicago Press, 1995), chap. 1. See also Friedrich Hayek, *Law, Legislation, and Liberty*, vol. 3: *The Political Order of a Free People* (Chicago: University of Chicago Press, 1979), 55, 187, n. 13.

35. On Smith's concern for the poor, see Holmes, *Passions and Constraints*. It is noteworthy that Smith takes the English Poor Laws for granted and does not object to public charity (Smith, *The Wealth of Nations*, 135ff.). He objects rather to the "settlement" requirement (that for one to be eligible for poor relief, it must be publicly known that one is a resident for at least forty days), since it discourages the "free circulation of labor" and freedom of movement and freedom to choose one's place of residence ("an evident violation of natural liberty and justice") (141).

36. Even for Nozick, where the minimal state legitimately acquires a natural monopoly on political power, it has no right to claim political authority or a right to monopoly rule (*ASU*, 108).

37. In *The Concept of Law* (Oxford: Oxford University Press, 1961), chap. 10, H. L. A. Hart, argues against the position that coercive sanctions are a precondition for law and a legal system.

38. Continuity of rule does not mean that the form of government or political constitution itself is necessarily permanent. Locke, for example, envisions the possibility that the Body Politic might "set Limits to the Duration" of a form of government; still, he indicates that the Body Politic itself, as a legal body, is permanent. See Locke, *Second Treatise*, para. 243, in *Two Treatises of Government*. Here I take Locke to envision the permissibility of periodic constitutional conventions, where the form of government is reconsidered by the People. Thomas Jefferson went further and argued for a need for periodic constitutional conventions, so that the Body Politic could reconsider and recommit itself to the Constitution with each successive generation of its members. Thanks to an anonymous editor of *Philosophy & Public Affairs* for drawing my attention to Locke's position.

39. See Locke, *Second Treatise*, para. 3, in *Two Treatises of Government*; see also para. 171.

40. The doctrine of divine right held that the Crown was responsible to God in exercising private power, but that the Crown was beholden to no one on earth. Political power remained unlimited de facto and by positive law, if not by moral right.

41. See Joshua Cohen, "Structure, Choice, and Legitimacy: Locke's Theory of the State," *Philosophy & Public Affairs* 15, no. 4 (1986): 301–24, on Locke's argument against a universal franchise and for a "property owners' state."

42. Here it should be noted that there is much disagreement among libertarianism's major proponents. Nozick argues, contrary to anarchical libertarianism, that a minimal state's monopoly on political power is legitimate and necessary to protect rights and entitlements. There are also disagreements over the philosophical foundations of libertarianism (contrast Nozick's Kantian and Lockean foundations with Narveson's Hobbism). I pass over these disputes. My concern is with the basic normative principles and institutions held in common by these views that distinguish them from liberalism. I also recognize that political philosophers cannot always be neatly categorized as liberal or libertarian. Some avowedly classical liberals endorse certain aspects of libertarianism, such as the absence of a social minimum. Even some non-classical liberals, such as Joel Feinberg, reject the inalienability of basic liberties. Whether these mixed views are coherent and have no unreasonable justifications would require separate discussion.

43. *ASU*, 33–35; Murray Rothbard, "Society without a State," in *The Libertarian Reader*, ed. Tibor Machan (Totowa, NJ: Rowman & Littlefield, 1982), 54.

44. See G. A. Cohen's discussion of libertarians' moralized concept of freedom: "Capitalism, Freedom, and the Proletariat," in *Liberty*, ed. David Miller

(New York: Oxford University Press, 1991), chap. 8; also Cohen's "The Structure of Proletarian Unfreedom," in his *History, Labor, and Freedom* (Oxford: Oxford University Press, 1988), 256.

45. This is also true of Jan Narveson's use of David Gauthier's version of contractarianism to argue for libertarianism. Following Gauthier, Narveson appeals to a "Lockean Proviso" to moralize the Hobbesian state-of-nature baseline from which agreement takes place by bestowing a right to liberty and exclusive ownership rights on all involved prior to the social contract. Jan Narveson, *The Libertarian Idea* (Philadelphia: Temple University Press, 1987), 175–77.

46. Narveson, *The Libertarian Idea*, 32.

47. Narveson, *The Libertarian Idea*, 7.

48. Tibor Machan, ed., Preface to *The Libertarian Reader* (Totowa, NJ: Rowman & Littlefield, 1982), vii.

49. Narveson, *The Libertarian Idea*, 175.

50. *ASU*, 160.

51. See *ASU*, 160–64, containing Nozick's famous Wilt Chamberlain example and claim that income tax "is on a par with forced labor." See Jonathan Wolff, *Robert Nozick*, 83–92, for a valuable discussion.

52. Narveson, *The Libertarian Idea*, 66. "The idea of libertarianism is to maximize individual freedom by accounting each person's *person* as that person's own *property*" (175).

53. Murray Rothbard, *Power and Market* (Kansas City, MO: Sheed Andrews and McMeel, 1977), 238. See also John Hospers's definition of libertarianism as "the doctrine that each person is the owner of his own life, and that no person is the owner of anyone else's life." "What Libertarianism Is," in *The Libertarian Alternative*, ed. Tibor Machan (n.p.: Nelson-Hall, 1974).

54. *ASU*, 172; see also 281–83.

55. *ASU*, 290.

56. Others have made similar but more detailed observations about the centrality of property and self-ownership to libertarianism. Most notably see G. A. Cohen, "Self-Ownership, World-Ownership, and Equality" and other papers in his *Self-Ownership, Freedom, and Equality* (Cambridge: Cambridge University Press, 1995); see also Wolff, *Robert Nozick*, 7ff., 29.

57. See the original version of Cohen's "Self-Ownership, World-Ownership, and Equality," in *Justice and Equality Here and Now*, ed. Frank Lucash (Ithaca, NY: Cornell University Press, 1986).

58. The idea seems to be that, because persons have absolute ownership rights in themselves, they acquire absolute property in unowned resources they appropriate, in the products of their labor made from them, and in whatever is freely exchanged for these products. See Murray Rothbard, *Power and Market* (New York: New York University Press, 1981), 1. Nozick again is more

nuanced: "People do not conceive of ownership as having a thing, but as possessing rights . . . which are theoretically separable" (*ASU*, 281). Still, he assumes that initial appropriation of unowned things bestows plenary property rights.

59. For example, in early common law, the "fee entailment" prohibited owners from alienating their estates; landed estates passed by law to the eldest surviving male issue. Entailments were abolished with the predominance of the market system.

60. US law rarely utilizes the concept of ownership. The most common concept used is "property interest," of which there are different kinds, each of which is distinguished by various rights and duties.

61. Libertarians and other proponents of self-ownership commonly claim that private ownership of one's person and powers implies ownership of the *product* of one's labors and, hence, ownership of the product of one's property. But the problem is that a person's "product" or "contribution" cannot be established independent of an institutional context. Libertarians usually assume, without much argument, that absolute plenary property rights follow from appropriation in a state of nature. For a fuller statement of the institutional conception of property relied on here see my "Property as an Institutional Convention in Hume's Account of Justice, *Archiv für Geschichte der Philosophie* 73, no. 1 (1991): 20–49; and "Morals by Appropriation," *Pacific Philosophical Quarterly* 71, no. 4 (1990): 279–309.

62. Locke seems to mean, by the archaic sense of "property" in oneself, that each person has certain rights in his or her own person and is not politically subordinate to anyone else. Locke did not endorse the libertarian idea that persons stand to their person in the same relationship that they stand to property in things. His social contract doctrine relies on the law of nature that persons do not have the right to alienate or dispose of their person, since all have a duty to maintain themselves exclusively as *God's* property. See Locke, *Second Treatise*, sec. 6. On Locke's use of "property" see Simmons, *The Lockean Theory of Rights*, 226 ff., and Tully, *A Discourse on Property*, 116.

63. *ASU*, 58.

64. *ASU*, 331; see also 283.

65. The libertarian may object that it is question-begging to say that enforcement of slave contracts is against purported slaves' will. "After all, they agreed to it! Free informed consent is binding precisely because it expresses (or represents, or even constitutes) the will." I assume that it is against a person's will to coerce her to act in ways she does not want to act. The fact that earlier she committed herself to act as she now is forced to act does not negate the fact that she is now being forced to act against her will.

66. Nozick's Lockean Proviso (that no one can be made worse off than in a state of nature) would not prevent such an eventuality, since individual or class ownership of everybody else is possible in a state of nature. The Proviso's purpose is to

put limits on initial appropriations of unowned things, and not on transfers of original rights in oneself. See *ASU*, 175–82.

67. Libertarians may object that the same can be said of democracy, understood as bare majoritarianism. "Just because democracy *could* result in totalitarianism does not mean that anything is necessarily wrong with democracy." I disagree, for the conceptual possibility shows the moral limitations of majoritarian democracy. Pure majoritarianism—the view that whatever the majority wills is fair, just, or even legitimate—is unreasonable. To define the legitimate scope of majority rule and restrict the kinds of laws majorities can agree to, it is necessary to subsume majority rule within some larger democratic conception of justice. For this reason, few people (if any) advocate pure majoritarianism as an adequate account of justice, but people *do* advocate libertarianism as adequate, even though it puts no restrictions on permissible distributions.

68. Here further consideration needs to be given to the libertarian's insistence (mentioned earlier) that ordinary contractual agreements are binding because they express, or represent, or constitute the will. This provides the main support for their argument that to deny authority to the will by not enforcing alienation contracts undermines the moral basis for enforcing even routine contracts. But if invalidating alienation contracts jeopardizes the authority of routine contracts because it negates the will, then it should also be the case that invalidating contracts to kill third parties or to commit other criminal conspiracies also jeopardizes the authority of more routine contracts. The libertarian will reply that in the case of criminal contracts there is sufficient reason to override the will and freedom of contract (namely, to protect third parties' rights). But then, according to the liberal argument for inalienability, there is likewise sufficient reason to void alienation agreements and not allow their enforcement, namely to protect the status of persons as free and equals. This returns the argument to the real source of disagreement between liberals and libertarians, namely the basis for individual rights. Thanks to a reviewer for *Philosophy & Public Affairs* for raising this objection on libertarians' behalf.

69. See the seminal work of C. Vann Woodward, *The Strange Career of Jim Crow*, 102.

70. See, on each point, Woodward, *The Strange Career of Jim Crow*, 98, 101, 99.

71. Narveson is quite open about this: see *The Libertarian Idea*, 313–18. "But if a business is really private, that means it is the property of its owners. They can do as they wish with it" (315).

72. See Narveson, for example, who says the idea of monopoly is undefinable in a rigorous way and that "the use of one's resources for whatever purposes one will is the hallmark of liberal [*sic*] freedom" (*The Libertarian Idea*, 203).

73. See, e.g., *ASU*, 280, where Nozick suggests that "perhaps the precise contour of the bundle or property rights is shaped by considerations about how externalities may be most efficiently internalized." The idea is at least worth further examination, he says.

74. See *ASU*, 178–82, on the Proviso.
75. Contrast Gauthier's superficially similar argument for natural appropriation, according to which property rights in a state of nature are always revisable in the interests of efficient use. See his *Morals by Agreement*, 293–94. Gauthier's classical liberal account is designed to accommodate considerations of economic efficiency at each crucial point. There is nothing comparable to Gauthier's provisional account of property rights in Nozick's state of nature. For Nozick, individuals acquire absolute property immediately upon appropriation of unheld resources, due to their natural rights and liberties and considerations of individual autonomy and self-ownership.
76. See, e.g., *ASU*, ix.
77. See Locke, *Second Treatise*, secs. s 124–26, on the three "inconveniences" or "defects" (sec. 131) of the state of nature that give rise to a need for government, and secs. 136 and 137 on the need for legislative power to publicly specify the laws of nature and for an impartial judge to decide disputes. The three defects are the lack of "an established, settled, known Law," of a "known and indifferent Judge," and of a "Power . . . to give [law and sentences] due Execution." Locke does not advocate separation of powers (in the US sense) but (as under the British Constitution) appears to subsume judicial power under the executive and holds that legislative power is "supreme" (sec. 132). In chap. 13 Locke distinguishes the "Legislative, Executive, and Federative Power of the Commonwealth," the last being in charge of foreign policy and war and peace (sec. 146).
78. Nozick does recognize the need for a decision mechanism to determine the level of risk that individuals may impose on others. "But the precise mechanism to accomplish this has yet to be described; and it would also have to be shown how such a mechanism would arise in a state of nature." The implication is that such a procedure would have to be "reached by the operation of some invisible-hand mechanism" (*ASU*, 74). Some may disagree with my claim that libertarianism has no place for legislative authority. But focus again on Nozick's view (which I take as the paradigm). Why couldn't Nozick's minimal state simply create a committee with the task of making rules that decide disputed and indeterminate matters of natural law? Take, for example, the problem of defining riparian rights. The committee could issue a set of rules saying, among other things, that riverbed owners have no right to pollute, or to dam water flow, beyond certain limits. Would this decision have the status of legitimate law? Recall that Nozick's minimal state is in effect a joint stock company with a natural monopoly on force. While it may have de facto power to make and enforce rules, it does not have any right or authority to do so, nor does it claim any (see *ASU*, 108–10). Any rights or powers the minimal state has must derive from its members. As no person or group has the right to unilaterally issue rules applying to everyone, the same is true of the minimal state. "There is no right the dominant protection

agency claims uniquely to possess" (*ASU*, 109), including, I assume, the authority to legislate.

79. See sec. 159 of Locke's *Second Treatise*, where Locke refers to "the Fundamental Law of Nature and Government, viz. That . . . *all* the Members of the Society are to be *preserved*" (referred to also in secs. 6, 16, 18, 134, 135, and 183). Because of the fundamental law, every person has a duty "to preserve himself" as well as "to preserve the rest of Mankind" (sec. 6). It is consistent with Locke, if not explicitly required, to infer a duty to join political society and recognize public political authority, since governments justified by the social contract are necessary background conditions for the effective exercise of each person's duty to preserve himself and all of mankind.

80. "Anything an individual can gain through such unanimous agreement he can gain through separate bilateral agreements" (*ASU*, 90).

81. Protection services against members are provided to non-members without charge in compensation for requiring them to resolve disputes with the agency's paying clients within the agency's arbitration procedures, thereby losing their rights of private enforcement of their rights. See *ASU*, chaps. 2 and 5, esp. 101–19.

82. This claim and the ensuing argument in this section—that libertarianism resembles feudalism—applies to the minimal libertarian state and to the competing protection agencies envisioned by anarchical libertarianism. Though Nozick says that the minimal state is "the only morally legitimate state" (*ASU*, 333) and that "any state more extensive violates people's rights" (*ASU*, 149), he still leaves open the theoretical possibility that a "more extensive state" could arise legitimately out of the minimal state, so long as it is unanimously agreed to. Nozick has a long discussion of how (something purportedly resembling) democracy might arise out of a minimal state. His account of democracy is a caricature, since it involves all persons making themselves slaves to one another. He says this "tale" of how a more extensive state might arise is "designed to make such a state quite unattractive" (*ASU*, xii). In any case, as he says, "it is highly unlikely that in a society containing many persons" a more than minimal state could survive, precisely because unanimous consent is required. In light of these remarks, I see Nozick as contending that the minimal state, even if it may not be the only conceptually possible legitimate state, is nonetheless the only realistically possible legitimate state. This would explain his explicit statement that it is "the only morally legitimate state." I am grateful to an editor of *Philosophy & Public Affairs* for calling this feature of Nozick's view to my attention.

83. Hart, *The Concept of Law*, 89–96.

84. See *ASU*, 24: "Protection and enforcement of people's rights is treated as an economic good to be provided by the market, as are other important goods such as food and clothing."

85. It remains true on Nozick's account that political power is exercised mainly for the benefit of those who pay for it even when non-clients are provided protection services against clients' aggression. The protection agency provides non-clients with these minimal services only to compensate them for being prevented from apprehending and punishing clients for alleged wrongs. Providing non-clients minimal services is just one of the costs incurred in providing protection services for paying clients. See *ASU*, 110–13.

86. Strictly speaking, corporations are products of public law, existing by virtue of statutes that prescribe their conditions, powers, and governing procedures. The minimal state can at most be a non-legal institution, with private rules resulting from contractual agreements among its owners, without legal or constitutional sanction or authority.

87. See *ASU*, 108–10. The phrase "monopoly on coercive power" or "monopoly on force" (whether de jure or de facto) does not mean that no one but the state actually exercises such power—obviously violent criminals do, as do people acting in self-defense—but that anyone exercising force must answer to the state as monopoly holder and show that the exercise is justified or excused.

88. See again Hart, *The Concept of Law*, 94–96.

89. It may be objected here that libertarians such as Nozick already have an account of political legitimacy that I simply ignore: that is, the dominant protection agency is politically legitimate insofar as it has a larger (or monopoly) share of the jointly held right to punish (and therewith interpret and enforce natural law) than any competing agency. But Nozick is explicit that the dominant protection agency does not enjoy a de jure monopoly; it simply exercises a de facto monopoly (*ASU*, 108–10). (Indeed, it is crucial to Nozick's response to the anarchist that the minimal state does not claim a de jure monopoly.) Also, Nozick nowhere says that the dominant protection agency possesses political legitimacy (which is different from moral legitimacy, which he does claim exclusively for the minimal state) (*ASU*, 333). Political legitimacy does not seem to be a concept that Nozick employs or even sees as significant.

90. The exception, again, is the minimal protection services provided to non-clients in Nozick's minimal state.

91. I do not mean to say that the private libertarian state does not act *at all* for the interests of its clients. If it did not, no one would buy its services. The point rather is that it does not act as a fiduciary but performs only those services that are specifically contracted for by each individual, and when there is a dispute about services to be provided, it is resolved by considerations of the "bottom line." A good analogy is patients' relations with for-profit HMOs. Even in a competitive climate, for-profit HMOs provide only enough services to keep a client's business, and only then if it pays to do so. (So, without public regulation HMOs seek to clear the rolls of people who require a lot of medical treatment.) Imagine now that a for-profit HMO has acquired a monopoly over medical services and

does not need to fear the entry of a competing HMO into the market (e.g. it has made exclusive employment contracts with all the local physicians). Knowing how for-profit HMOs operate even under competitive conditions, it is not hard to imagine how the monopoly HMO will respond to claims for services in the event of inevitable contractual ambiguities. In this regard (and others) the minimal state, like the monopoly HMO, does not act in a fiduciary capacity for the interests of its clients, but seeks to maximize profits for the owners of the minimal state.

92. As G. G. Coulton notes, feudalism "is proverbially difficult to define" (*Medieval Panorama* [Cambridge: Cambridge University Press, 1955], 45). For my purposes "feudalism" is construed as a conception of political power exercised as a private prerogative and is grounded in a network of private agreements. Neither Aquinas (who saw politics as ideally grounded in a conception of the common good) nor any of the Scholastics endorsed feudalism in this sense; they endorsed a limited monarchy subject to clerical power in matters affecting religion (see *St. Thomas Aquinas: On Politics and Ethics*, ed. Paul Sigmund [New York: Norton, 1988], xxii–xxiii). Feudalism and kingship are then different and opposed systems. Feudalism historically arose out of the breakup of the monarchical system in both Japan and Europe (after 800 c.e. and the end of Charlemagne's reign). Under feudalism "in its most developed form—that is in eleventh century France—the national system [had] become obliterated" (Coulton, *Medieval Panorama*, 49). "Political authority and private property were merged together into the new feudal relation" (Christopher Dawson, *The Making of Europe* [New York: Meridian, 1956], 227). Around 1100, monarchy began reasserting its powers in the Franken lands where feudalism was most prevalent. Feudalism and monarchism gradually melded into one system as monarchies slowly regained political power, and feudal lords still retained a good deal of their private political power. It was during this syncretic period (not during the high era of feudalism, from ca. 850–1100) that so-called feudal law appeared, regulating among other things contractual relations between lieges and lords.

I emphasize that feudalism is intended here as a doctrine about *political* power. It does not imply serfdom or the manorial system. Feudalism in Japan had nothing resembling the serfdom of European feudalism. Much less so should feudalism be identified with serfdom, for serfdom also occurred in non-feudal societies whose political basis lay not in contract but in ties of kinship (see Peter Duus, *Feudalism in Japan* [New York: Knopf, 1969], 9, 15–16, 77). The tradition that identifies feudalism with serfdom and the manorial economy stems from Marx's use of "feudalism" and receives its classic expression in Marc Bloch, *Feudal Society* (Chicago: University of Chicago Press, 1964). If feudalism is understood in Marx's sense, then of course libertarianism differs from medieval feudalism since libertarianism rejects hereditary serfdom.

Finally, I use "feudalism" to denote an idealized *conception* of political power. It may be that no historically existing political arrangement ever fully satisfied all the features of the conception set forth in the text. (For example, even in what is now France, where feudalism was most prevalent, at least lip-service was paid to the monarchy.) But in this sense, feudalism does not differ from liberalism or libertarianism as idealized political conceptions.

For helpful discussions of the history of feudalism in Europe and Japan, see Coulton, *Medieval Panorama*, 45–56; the books by Duus and Bloch cited earlier in this note; Norbert Elias, *Power and Civility* (Oxford: Basil Blackwell, 1982), 57–66; and Jean Pierre Poly and Eric Bournazel, *The Feudal Transformation: 900–1200* (New York: Holmes & Meier, 1991).

93. Coulton, *Medieval Panorama*, 47.

94. See Duus, *Feudalism in Japan*, 73, 94. Contrast nationalism, where political loyalty is non-voluntary, non-personal in that it extends to the nation-state, and based in a non-contractual duty of allegiance.

95. See Elias, *Power and Civility*, 57–65, on feudalism. Note here that the coronation oaths establishing relations between feudal lords and their vassals were explicitly referred to as "compacts." Moreover, the term "feudalism" derives from the Latin *foedus*, which according to one interpretation means "a contract, covenant, agreement between individuals." See *Cassell's New Latin Dictionary* (New York: Funk & Wagnalls, 1969), 252, under "foedus." See also Poly and Bournazel, *The Feudal Transformation*, chap. 2, on the feudal contract.

96. Divine right absolutism and feudalism differ, of course, in that the former recognizes institutionally unconstrained political power, whereas under feudalism (as under libertarianism) political power extends no further than what is contracted for. Pure feudalism in effect recognizes no state, just a network of private contractual relations. In Europe, absolutism was a reaction to the quasi-anarchy brought about by feudalism. But absolutism retained feudalism's idea of political power as something privately held (no longer based in contract but now purportedly in divine right).

97. Even in Nozick's account, where non-clients are minimally protected for "free" from clients' (but not other non-clients') aggression, they are still selectively, not impartially, protected.

98. Why couldn't Nozick's minimal libertarian state govern for the common good, understood as protecting people's libertarian rights? Since the minimal state is just a private for-profit business that happens to have a de facto monopoly on power, it cannot be said that it governs with any *intention* of promoting and maintaining a common good. It may be that the common good, understood as protecting libertarian rights, in fact is promoted (as a kind of positive externality) by minimal state action; but this does not really differ from the way in which any private firm, in seeking private benefit, incidentally promotes a common good. So if the libertarian state promotes the common good, it does

so in the same way as does Microsoft, General Electric, or Pinkerton Private Security Services. I assume, however, that the idea of the common good has more structure than this in liberal political thought. It is an operative idea in liberal theory, not an incidental side effect, and government is instituted and designed with the intention of securing the common good. Securing the common good, even if understood in libertarian terms, is not an aim of the libertarian minimal state, as argued in the text. (For Nozick's explicit rejection of the idea of the social good, see *ASU*, 32–33.)

99. High liberalism should not be prone to the same instability, for it distinguishes personal property that is part of or essential to basic liberty from economic rights to control means of production, and construes the freedoms implicit in the latter rights in terms of what is needed to secure each person's individual independence. See *JF*, 114–15, 177. This complicated topic warrants further discussion since it goes to the fundamental difference between the classical and high liberal traditions.

100. I am grateful to Amy Gutmann, Frances Kamm, Arthur Kuflick, Rex Martin, Douglas McLean, Joseph Raz, Andrews Reath, Henry Richardson, Samuel Scheffler, Russ Shafer-Landau, John Tomasi, Jay Wallace, Gary Watson, and Susan Wolf for their helpful remarks and to audiences at Columbia University, New York University, Swarthmore College, Temple University, the University of California at Berkeley, the University of California at Irvine, the University of Geneva, and the University of Kansas. I am also grateful to the Princeton Center for Human Values for its support in 1992–93, when an early draft of this chapter was written and presented. An anonymous reviewer for *Philosophy & Public Affairs*, where this chapter originally appeared, made many helpful suggestions regarding needed clarifications. Finally, special thanks are due to John Rawls.

PART II

Distributive Justice and the Difference Principle

3

Rawls on Distributive Justice and the Difference Principle

1. Introduction: Distributive justice

Justice is associated with equality: equal treatment, equal distribution, equal social status, or the formal requirement to treat similar cases similarly. But equality is not the only value of justice. A democracy that denies all citizens personal freedoms of conscience, association, and expression is oppressive, hence unjust. An egalitarian society is also unjust if it is able but unwilling to provide educational, cultural, and diverse career opportunities, enabling citizens to develop their capacities and skills and choose from a wide range of activities and life plans.

John Rawls said early on that his principles of justice express a complex of three ideas: liberty, equality, and rewarding contributions that promote the common good.[1] He also said that justice as fairness incorporates and reconciles two different conceptions of equality: equality of distributions and equality of respect for persons (*TJ*, 447). Equality regarding distributions, Rawls says, is incorporated into the difference principle's reciprocity requirement—that departures from equality must benefit everyone starting with the least advantaged. Equality of respect for persons is, however, more fundamental; it is owed to humans as moral persons and is grounded in their possessing the moral powers of rationality and justice. Equality of respect for moral persons, Rawls suggests, is exhibited by the equal basic liberties and their priority, fair equality of opportunities, and such natural duties as mutual respect. Rawls also appeals to the ideal of free and equal moral persons cooperating on grounds of reciprocity and mutual respect to explain why inequalities of economic distributions are justified to guarantee the worth of the basic liberties and fair opportunities for all citizens.

G. A. Cohen, Rawls's most trenchant egalitarian critic, contends that Rawls's account of distributive justice is a confused amalgam of egalitarian and welfarist/prioritarian considerations that sacrifices justice-as-equality for the sake of efficiency.[2] But if we take seriously Rawls's position that justice is based in equality of respect for free and equal moral persons and accordingly must guarantee equal liberties and their worth for all, fair equality of diverse opportunities, and also promote the common good, then Cohen's interpretation of Rawls seems shortsighted. The several values of justice incorporated into Rawls's principles put into perspective the complexities of Rawls's account of distributive justice.

Rawls's account of distributive justice has several key components. I begin by clarifying the role of the basic structure (section 2) and then discuss the distributive role of the basic liberties and fair equality of opportunity (section 3). I next clarify the broad and narrow requirements of the difference principle (section 4) and discuss whether inequalities are permissible or mandatory under it (section 5). In section 6, I discuss the scope of the maximizing provision and why the difference principle is not a consequentialist prioritarian principle. In section 7, I set forth principles for applying the difference principle to ideal and non-ideal conditions. I conclude with a discussion of why the difference principle justifies property-owning democracy rather than welfare-state capitalism (section 8).

2. The Basic Structure as the Primary Subject of Justice

Social cooperation and reciprocity are for Rawls fundamental to distributive justice. It is the role of principles of social justice to specify the standards for the fair distribution of primary social goods that attend and result from social cooperation in any functioning society. The primary goods include basic rights and liberties; diverse opportunities, powers and prerogatives of office and positions of authority and responsibility in political and economic institutions; income and wealth; and the social bases of self-respect.[3]

Rawls assumes that certain basic social institutions are necessary to sustain social life in any modern society and to guarantee the creation, distribution, and secure possession and enjoyment of these primary social goods. Basic social institutions include the political constitution, whose role is to make and enforce laws and adjudicate disputes; the legal institution of property, broadly conceived as rights and powers with respect to the possession, use, and disposal of tangible and intangible things; the economic system of production, transfer, and distribution of goods and services; and the family, which is the primary institution for reproducing society from one generation to the next. How these institutions are designed into a social system constitutes a society's "basic structure." The "primary subject" to which principles of social justice apply is the design of basic institutions into the basic structure of society (TJ, 6–7).

One reason Rawls gives for focusing on the basic structure is its profound and pervasive effects on individuals' life prospects, including its effects in shaping their primary aims and aspirations, their characters, and their self-conceptions.[4] The effect of the political constitution and the rights it guarantees on our prospects and aspirations is readily apparent by comparing liberal political systems that protect basic liberties with non-liberal ones that deny them. Also, differences in natural endowments, the social class one is born into, and accidental misfortune during one's lifetime (illness, accident, unemployment, economic crises) profoundly affect inequalities of life prospects. How the institutions of the basic structure respond to and use these three arbitrary contingencies to meet social purposes is a fundamental question of social and economic justice.

The second reason for the primacy of the basic structure is that a correctly designed basic structure is necessary to maintain "background justice" in a liberal economic system that relies on a "social process" of "pure procedural justice" to determine fair distributions. Rawls contrasts background justice in his social process view with Locke's and Nozick's "historical process view," where just distributions are regarded as the accumulated outcome of free and purportedly fair agreements and consensual transfers among private owners (*JF*, §15). Historical process views do not correct for the three arbitrary contingencies that cause inequalities in life prospects. As a result, "the invisible hand guides things in the wrong direction and favors an oligopolistic configuration of accumulations."[5] The normal tendency of unregulated market transactions is increasing inequality and concentration of wealth in fewer hands.[6] The background conditions necessary for fair exchange, fair equality of opportunities, and the fair value of political liberties are then increasingly undermined. In order to maintain a fair background for the economic system and a just distribution of income and wealth, the accumulation of property and market power must be regulated by taxation, laws governing inheritance, gifts, and other means for acquiring market power, income, and wealth.

3. Basic Liberties and Fair Equality of Opportunities: Distributive Effects

Rawls's two principles of justice are as follows: (1) Each person is to have the same indefeasible claim to a fully adequate scheme of *equal basic liberties*, which scheme is compatible with the same scheme of liberties for all. (2) Social and economic inequalities are to satisfy two conditions: first they are to be attached to offices and positions open to all under conditions of *fair equality of opportunity*; and second, they are to be to the greatest benefit of the least advantaged members of society (the *difference principle*) (*JF*, 42).

Rawls uses the term "distributive justice" "in the narrow sense" (*JF*, 61) to refer to the difference principle and the economic distribution of income, wealth, and economic powers. Still, he emphasizes that the other principles have significant distributive effects. Indeed, Rawls says the difference principle cannot be taken seriously apart from the first principle and fair equality of opportunity (*JF*, 46n.). He says this partly in response to the frequent challenge that the difference principle puts no restrictions on overall inequalities. For example, G. A. Cohen argues that the difference principle permits the enormous inequalities typical of capitalism so long as inequalities marginally increase the share going to the least advantaged class.[7] But there are restrictions on inequalities imposed by both the first principle and fair equality of opportunities. Inequalities in income and wealth are unjust if they dilute the "fair value" of equal rights of political participation or if they undermine the adequacy of educational, professional, and cultural opportunities and citizens' ability to take advantage of formally equal opportunities and compete on fair terms with others.[8]

Inequalities in wealth then cannot be so great that they seriously dilute the "full and equally effective voice" and political influence of the less advantaged or distort the political process and its agenda to favor the interests of the more advantaged (*PL*, 361). The less advantaged should be in a position to participate in politics and influence public life on a par with the more advantaged. For them to do so, Rawls says, "property and wealth must be kept widely distributed" (*TJ*, 198). He provides no specific formula or threshold to determine the limits on economic inequalities needed to preserve political equality.[9] There may be no specific answer to the question of limits on economic inequality needed to preserve political equality; the question may depend on a society's political culture. There are considerable inequalities in Germany, Sweden, and other European countries, but they do not have the decisive influence on politics that wealth has in the United States. Because of the "curse of money," Rawls suggests, our politics is dominated by corporate and other organized interests that distort if not preclude public discussion and deliberation (*CP*, 580).

Regarding fair equality of opportunity, Rawls again says that economic inequalities are to be restricted when they reach a point that subverts the fair distribution of (formally) equal opportunities to compete for open educational and career positions and take advantage of the benefits of culture.

> Fair equality of opportunity means a certain set of institutions that assures similar chances of education and culture for persons similarly motivated and keeps positions and offices open to all . . . It is these institutions that are put in jeopardy when inequalities of wealth exceed a certain limit . . . The taxes and enactments of the distribution branch are to prevent this limit from being exceeded. (*TJ*, 245–46)

Again, Rawls provides no formula to decide limits on inequalities needed to maintain fair equal opportunities. He discusses progressive income, estate, inheritance, and gift taxes as means to prevent excessive concentrations of wealth and private power (*TJ*, 245–46; *JF*, 51, 53, 64, 161). Perhaps Rawls is less specific on these matters because he assumes that the economic system justified by the principles of justice is not capitalism but a property-owning democracy, "a democratic regime in which land and capital are widely though not presumably equally held" (*TJ*, 247). An essential feature of property-owning democracy is that, unlike what prevails in capitalism, the preponderance of productive resources is not controlled by a small sector of society. The absence of extreme inequalities in ownership of capital in property-owning democracy eliminates the primary impediment to fair equality of opportunity that exists in a capitalist society.

Rawls says that equality of opportunity is not the authorization to leave the less fortunate behind (*TJ*, 91). This is a problem with formal equality of opportunity and "careers open to talents," where access to social positions is governed by the principle of efficiency (*TJ*, 73, 91). Fair equality of opportunity (FEO) addresses this problem to some degree since it requires that the economically less advantaged be afforded generous educational opportunities, enabling them to compete fairly for positions with those equally talented regardless of social class. But on its "liberal interpretation," when combined with the principle of efficiency, fair equality of opportunity also leads to a meritocracy that leaves the less talented behind. For then resources for educational development are allotted mainly according to talents and the return on productive abilities and skills (*TJ*, 73, 91).

Rawls says that on its democratic interpretation, FEO does not lead to a meritocratic society, for then it is combined with the difference principle. Fair equality of opportunity then requires that the less talented and less favored have ongoing educational, career, and cultural opportunities from early on and throughout their lifetimes, so that they can develop their capacities and take advantage of the benefits of culture (*TJ*, 92, 265). This is especially important in view of the "essential primary good of self-respect" (*TJ*, 91).

> Resources for education are not to be allotted solely or necessarily mainly according to their return as estimated in productive trained abilities, but also according to their worth in enriching the personal and social life of citizens, including here the less favored. As a society progresses the latter consideration becomes increasingly more important. (*TJ*, 92)

The redistributive demands of fair equality of opportunity on its democratic interpretation can potentially be quite extensive. For example, consider evidence that children in upper-middle-class families acquire educational and cultural advantages well before their formal schooling, due to constant attention lavished upon them by their parents.[10] T. M. Scanlon has suggested that to achieve fair equality of opportunity, considerable efforts must be made to bestow similar advantages upon poorer children whose parents are not in a position to provide such educational and cultural benefits.[11] This would support, for example, publicly funded day care for all children soon after infancy, designed to stimulate their capacities and develop their mental abilities and social skills. Also, family allowances may be required by FEO as well as the difference principle, so that families can afford to expose children to social and cultural experiences otherwise reserved for parents who can afford such advantages (cf. *TJ*, 243). There are many other options that might be applied to lessen inequalities in fair opportunities that stem from family circumstances. The point is that, if the aim of fair equality of opportunity is to both extend the benefits of culture to all and neutralize the effects of social class as much as is reasonably possible consistent with equal basic liberties and preserving the benefits of the institution of the family, it requires much more than simply supplying talented children born to poorer parents with educational advantages so that they can compete for desirable positions in a meritocratic system. As Rawls says, fair equality of opportunity applies to all citizens, whatever their degree of talent, to enable them to develop their capacities, take advantage of cultural opportunities, and enrich their personal and social lives. The distributive demands of FEO, so conceived, can be quite extensive, independent of considerations of the reciprocity claims of the less advantaged under the difference principle.[12]

Finally, regarding inequality of opportunity for women due to childbearing and their assuming the predominant burden of childrearing, Rawls says that childrearing within the family is "socially necessary labor" and that either women's (or men's) share of childrearing should be equalized or they should be compensated for it (*CP*, 600). This would be personal compensation in addition to family allowances intended to benefit children and required by FEO and the difference principle (*TJ*, 243).

4. The Difference Principle: Its Broad and Narrow Requirements

Though Rawls says it is a principle of "distributive justice," the difference principle is more generally a principle of economic justice that regulates the design of economic systems. For the difference principle applies to institutions other than those directly affecting the distribution of income and wealth. It is the fundamental standard to assess and reform a wide range of economic institutions necessary for economic production, commerce, and consumption. Many of these institutions concern the fair and efficient functioning of the economic system and only indirectly bear on economic distributions of income and wealth: the law of contracts, securities, bank and finance regulations, business corporations and partnerships, commercial law, labor law, liability and remedies in economic torts, and so on. For example, the difference principle applies to the restriction of predatory "payday" loans and the regulation of interest rates, late payment penalties, and other terms of consumer credit loans; or to the regulation of the terms of mortgages and the restriction of banks' investment of customers' deposits in risky derivatives, mortgage securities, and other speculative ventures behind the 2007 financial crisis.[13]

Distributive justice is often depicted as the problem of dividing preexisting accumulations of goods or of income and wealth, and allocating them to individuals who need not stand in cooperative relationships. Rawls calls such approaches "allocative" accounts of distributive justice (*TJ*, 56, 77; *JF*, 50) Familiar examples are: to each equally, or according to need or merit, or to maximize welfare (aggregate, average, or weighted in favor of the less advantaged). The difference principle is not an allocative principle. It applies "at the front end," to assess and reform economic institutions (property, contracts, and others mentioned above) that make possible the production and transfer as well as the distribution of income and wealth. Distributions of income and wealth are just when they result from individuals' actual compliance with the institutions of an "ideal social process" structured by the difference principle (*JF*, 54). Individuals' shares are then decided according to "pure background procedural justice," by the outcomes of the workings of just background institutions (*JF*, 57).

Since the difference principle applies to institutions "at the front end" of this process, it also determines the justice of distributions of ownership and control of means of production. This includes ownership of productive capital as well as rights to exercise "powers and prerogatives of offices and positions of responsibility" (*PL*, 181). This is essential to Rawls's argument for property-owning democracy (discussed in section 8). Since the difference principle has multiple roles, it is not simply an allocative principle of distributive justice. It is the fundamental standard of economic justice for a democratic society.

Rawls regards the difference principle as a "principle for institutions" that directly applies *only* to the institutions of the basic structure. It "is not meant to apply to small-scale situations [but] is a macro, not a micro principle" (*CP*, 226). The difference principle is not then an individual rule of conduct that we observe in making economic decisions; there is no natural duty to choose to maximize the circumstances of the least advantaged. Instead it applies to the economic framework and the policies, laws, and other norms that regulate economic transactions. Rawls has been widely criticized for restricting the application of the difference principle to the basic structure.[14] His reasons are complex;[15] they connect with Rawls's liberalism, which guarantees individuals' special commitments and freedom to pursue their conception of the good, and with the difference principle's being a principle of reciprocity rather than consequentialist or "end-state" (discussed in section 7).[16]

By "greatest benefit to the least advantaged" Rawls means that "inevitable inequalities"—in income, wealth, and powers and positions—are to be arranged to make the least advantaged class *better off than they would be under any alternative social and economic scheme of cooperation* (*JF*, 59–60, 63). A fundamental role of the difference principle then is the comparison and assessment of the justice of different economic systems. Rawls says justice as fairness "is a conception for ranking social forms viewed as closed systems" (*TJ*, 229). Existing economic systems are to be critically assessed according to how closely they approximate the ideal of a "well-ordered society." The second principle of justice is then to be used as the ultimate standard to make and reform laws, regulations, and other economic norms in order to eventually realize the economic system the second principle prescribes. This raises the complex question of how the difference principle is to apply in ideal and non-ideal circumstances (see section 7).

Rawls says, "In appraising institutions we may view them in a wider or a narrower context," either assessing the justice of institutions separately, one by one, or assessing the justice of the social system of institutions as a whole (*TJ*, 50). This suggests two separate but complementary requirements of the difference principle. First, there is a narrower *local requirement*: for any alternative economic measure (laws, conventions, regulations, or economic policies), its justice depends upon the degree to which it maximally advances the position of the least advantaged members of society, given the existing background of laws and institutions of which it is to be made a part. As a practical matter this requires that in deliberating, for example, upon the rate of taxation, a legislative body should choose the tax program that makes the least advantaged better off in the near and intermediate future than other alternatives. Similar critical assessments apply with respect to regulations of securities and financial institutions, the specification of property rights, corporate law and labor relations, and all other significant measures bearing on economic production, transfer, exchange, and consumption.

Most discussion or criticism of the difference principle has focused on this local requirement and the narrow application of the difference principle. This makes sense practically, from our perspective now since legislative and other institutional changes normally proceed in piecemeal fashion, one step at a time. The narrow application of the difference principle and gradual reform of the status quo in the direction of greater economic justice are perhaps as much as we can realistically hope for under current circumstances. But this can obscure the second and even more fundamental requirement of the difference principle. This is the *broad systemic requirement* presupposed by its narrower local application. Strictly applied, the difference principle says that a society has the duty to put into place the *economic system* of basic institutions that makes the least advantaged members of society as well off as they can be, consistent with preserving the equal basic liberties and fair equality of opportunity. This means that the difference principle requires, in the first instance, that societies take steps to reform their institutions and enact measures that put into place that organized combination of institutions (laws, conventions, regulations) that maximally benefits the least advantaged members of their society over their lifetimes.

Imagine "a rough continuum of basic structures" (*JF*, 70), each of which is an efficient arrangement that specifies a particular division of social advantages. "The problem is to choose between them, to find a conception of justice that singles out one of these efficient distributions as just" (*TJ*, 61). Simplifying, there is a range of feasible economic systems, each discussed by Rawls at some point (cf. *JF*, 136) except the social democratic welfare state (table 3.1).

On the far right of the table is the ideal libertarianism of Robert Nozick and others, which provides for absolute property rights and unfettered freedom of contract. Income, wealth, and all property rights are then distributed solely by consensual transfers through market exchanges, gifts, bequests, and gambling. Next is the laissez-faire "System of Natural Liberty" (*TJ*, 57, 62) of the classical economists. Unlike libertarianism, it allows for some regulation of negative externalities (price collusion, etc.) and taxation for essential public goods; but otherwise income, wealth, and rights in things are distributed as libertarians profess. Next is the system of "Liberal Equality," (*TJ*, 57, 63), which, by incorporating a degree of fair equality of opportunity, funds education, a social "safety net," and other measures intended to neutralize the effects of social class on starting positions and life chances. This is endorsed by Friedrich Hayek and moderate classical liberals, and to a lesser degree by Milton Friedman (whose proposed negative income tax supplies a social minimum at the upper end of the poverty level).[17] Then comes the capitalist welfare state, which puts in place a more robust social minimum, universal healthcare, and perhaps (as in Ronald Dworkin's "equality of resources") a compensatory social insurance system that addresses individual misfortune and disadvantage, but otherwise allows income and wealth to be distributed by

Table 3.1 Feasible Economic Systems

Command Economy State Socialism	Market Socialism	Property-Owning Democracy	Social Democratic Welfare State	Welfare-State Capitalism	"Liberal Equality," Fair Equality of Opportunity, and Safety Net	Classical Liberal Laissez-Faire "System of Natural Liberty"	Libertarian Laissez-Faire

market and other consensual transfers.[18] Rawls contrasts the capitalist welfare state not with a social democratic welfare state, but with "property-owning democracy" (POD). POD largely dissolves the capitalist distinction between the owning and laboring classes by widely distributing economic wealth among all society's members. Also, it allows a wider distribution of economic powers among society's members and generally requires that economic distributions satisfy some more egalitarian principle than the capitalist welfare state. Next is liberal socialism, which provides for market allocations of publicly owned means of production and normally enforces an egalitarian principle of distributive justice.[19] Finally, there are command economy arrangements as Marx envisioned, which dispense with private economic ownership and with markets in allocating factors of production, including labor.

The difference principle's wide systemic requirement is that a society put into place the economic system that makes its least advantaged class better off than other alternative economic schemes (JF, 59–60). Next, society is to fulfill the difference principle's narrow requirement and continually make local adjustments and economic reforms needed to improve and maintain the position of the least advantaged. The *crucial point* is that the difference principle is not satisfied in non-ideal conditions such as our own simply by making local adjustments to particular institutions that marginally improve the position of the least advantaged—especially not if inequality is increased. It requires instead widespread across-the-board revision of any economic system that is not designed to maximally benefit the least advantaged—taking the necessary measures of reform to guarantee that "the least advantaged are better off than they are under any other scheme" (JF, 60).

This addresses G. A. Cohen's criticism that the difference principle is compatible with the enormous inequalities typical of capitalism and requires exaggerating these inequalities if they benefit the least advantaged.[20] Cohen assumes the status quo of the capitalist welfare or safety-net state in the United States and argues that many of capitalism's gross inequalities are justified by the difference principle, for they make the least advantaged better off than they otherwise would be in the absence of those inequalities. This overlooks Rawls's contention that the inequalities resulting from our capitalist system are unjust and that the difference principle requires instead a property-owning democracy or a liberal socialist system.[21] The difference principle necessitates systemic reforms to capitalism, and these reforms are not advanced by the Pareto measures Cohen assumes that only reinforce and increase gross inequalities.

For example, assume (as conservatives argue) that the least advantaged in the United States would enjoy less (employment, earned-income tax credits, public assistance, healthcare, etc.) were it not for lower tax rates imposed under the Reagan and Bush Jr. presidencies, with ensuing extraordinary rewards going to corporate executives, "high-flying" financiers, and other extremely wealthy persons. Even if true, this does not mean that Rawls's difference principle sanctions these tax measures or the activities and gross inequalities that result. For the position of the least advantaged surely could have been improved far more by *some* degree of increased taxation of capital gains and extreme salaries and bonuses, using increased tax income for public goods and transfers to those much less advantaged. But more important, according to the difference principle's systemic requirement, the current economic system wherein people are allowed to engage in such "high-flying" practices and reap extreme benefits from pure ownership is itself unjust and should be reformed in the direction of a property-owning democracy or at least an equitable welfare state. These inequalities are unjust, not simply because the rate of taxation on the wealthy and benefits to the least advantaged are set far too low, but because an economic system that encourages this sort of economic activity and the attitudes or "ethos" that sustain it, and that allows such extremely unequal distributions of income, wealth, and economic powers, is unjust according to the difference principle. Our capitalist economic system currently is one where few conscientious efforts are being made to advance, far less maximize, the position of the least advantaged. The "trickle-down" economics institutionalized since the Reagan–Thatcher era is directly at odds with the difference principle.

It is not true then that local improvements for the least advantaged that allow increasing inequalities of the kind Cohen envisions are sanctioned by the difference principle. Not just any improvement of the position of the least advantaged is justified; strictly speaking only very few are. The difference principle is not to be confused with a Pareto-like principle that says that *any* measure that improves the position of the least advantaged is permissible, regardless how much it increases inequality.[22] Strictly applied, the difference principle requires taking those measures that, among existing alternatives, *maximally* benefit the least advantaged, *"other things being equal"* (*JF*, 63). "Other things" are not equal under our non-ideal conditions, when policies involve narrow measures that may benefit the least advantaged in the short run but nonetheless increase and reinforce enormous inequalities; for narrow measures are not designed to modify the economic system in the direction of a more just basic structure, whether it be property-owning democracy, liberal socialism, or even an equitable welfare state.

5. Is Maximin Optional?

Consider now in more detail how the difference principle applies in different circumstances of justice. Rawls says a system is "perfectly just" when the expectations of the least advantaged group (LAG) are maximized; this is the "best arrangement." A system is "just throughout" when the expectations of the least advantaged would diminish if those of the most advantaged groups (MAG) were lessened, but would improve still further if the expectations of the MAG also were to improve. And a system is unjust when worsening the expectations of the most advantaged could improve those of the least advantaged (*TJ*, 68; *CP*, 138).

The United States (unsurprisingly) is unjust according to Rawls's definition. For there are multiple ways to improve the position of the least advantaged group that would also diminish inequality. Instead of adopting these measures, the usual approach involves, at best, measures that increase benefits to the most advantaged and further increase inequality, in the hope that modest benefits will "trickle down" to the less advantaged. Which if any of these (alleged) Pareto improvements are just? Congress in 2017 enacted further tax cuts for the wealthiest, claiming this would benefit everyone.[23] Such purportedly Pareto measures cannot be said to be *required* by justice under unjust conditions since there are many other measures that would benefit the less advantaged more (e.g., income supplements and family allowances) and would also reduce inequality and the excessive economic expectations of the most advantaged. Are Pareto improvements then at least permissible? If under unjust conditions Pareto improvements further increase substantial inequalities, they will be permissible only if they are a necessary short-term feature of a program that substantially improves the LAG's position and reduces inequality in the longer run. Generally, under unjust circumstances where there are ways to improve the LAG while reducing inequalities, Pareto improvements that increase inequality are not justifiable under the difference principle. *Only* measures that decrease inequality while raising the level of the least advantaged are authorized by the difference principle. Pareto measures that do not increase inequality may be permissible so long as they are not part of a policy designed to avoid reducing inequalities. But in unjust conditions of substantial inequality, Pareto measures are unjust when they further increase permanent inequalities. Justice is always prior to (Pareto) efficiency and is consistent with it only in a "perfectly just" economic system where the least advantaged position is maximized (*TJ*, 69).

A more difficult question: Assume no further improvements can be made for the LAG by reducing inequality through transfers or other measures. Are local *maximin* measures, those that given existing alternatives maximally improve the LAG under the circumstances, then optional or required by the difference principle? What if maximin measures substantially increase inequality for the indefinite future? Under these circumstances, normally there should be several alternative courses of institutional action that over time would result in less inequality and still make the LAG better off than it is under the existing economic system. Does the difference principle nonetheless require taking *only* those measures that maximally benefit the least advantaged, even when other alternatives result in less inequality and leave the less advantaged only marginally worse off than the maximin alternative? Could a society simply forgo any further measures that increase inequality, even if they are needed to improve the LAG's position? Finally, are maximin measures even permitted under circumstances when they permanently increase substantial inequalities?

Answers to these questions depend on whether the basic structure is more or less just or unjust according to justice as fairness. Suppose there were a fairly adequate social minimum in the United States (e.g., a $35,000 guaranteed income supplement plus child allowances for the LAG) and that further redistribution would worsen the LAG's position. Only by reducing the capital gains tax on wealth from 20 percent to 15 percent (its level during the Bush Jr. era) could we further increase the social minimum; but this would create substantially greater discrepancies between the most and least advantaged. In an unjust basic structure where there is a fairly adequate social minimum, *surely* the difference principle does not *require* the tax reduction on capital gains when it further increases substantial inequalities indefinitely. One reason is the potentially bad effects of increased inequality on the self-respect of the least advantaged, which outweighs the benefits of marginal increases in their income. But let's assume self-respect does not decide the issue (the increased inequality would not further decrease the LAG's self-respect).

Rawls suggests that in making decisions that increase the social minimum, a society may choose suboptimal measures involving less inequality. For example, referring to his diagram of the difference principle curve (see figure 3.1), he says that when the difference principle is satisfied, "[s]ociety would always be on the upward-rising part or at the top of the OP curve" (*JF*, 64). The OP curve is the production curve.

This might explain his ceteris paribus qualification: "Other things being equal, the difference principle directs society to aim at the highest point [D] of the OP curve of the most effectively designed system of cooperation" (*JF*, 63). Other things are *not* equal when a society is an unjust system and local measures that optimize the position of the least advantaged *within that system* require substantial increases to inequality. The requirement to strive to be at the highest point, D, on the curve strictly applies only within "the most effectively designed system"—presumably a property-owning democracy. In unjust circumstances typified by gross inequalities, it is at least optional, and sometimes may be required, for a society to forgo local measures that optimally improve the least advantaged position when they also increase existing inequalities. Thus, in the example above, where the LAG has a fairly adequate social minimum ($35,000) and the maximin measure (reducing the capital gains tax) would substantially increase existing inequality, society should take alternative measures to reform the system in the direction of a property-owning democracy, even if this comes at the expense of delaying

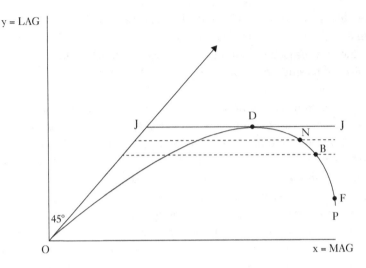

LAG = Least Advantaged Group
MAG = Most Advantaged Group
OP = Production Curve
D = Difference Principle: Efficient Point nearest Equality
B = Bentham point where sum of utilities is maximized
N = Nash point where product of utilities is maximized
F = Feudal point where OP curve becomes vertical
45° line = Equality
JJ = Highest Equal Justice line

FIGURE 3.1. Rawls's illustration of the difference principle. Key: LAG, least advantaged group; MAG, most advantaged group; OP, production curve; D, difference principle: efficient point nearest equality; B, Bentham point where sum of utilities is maximized; N, Nash point where product of utilities is maximized; F, feudal point where OP curve becomes vertical; 45° line, equality; JJ, highest equal justice line.

Source: Rawls, *Justice as Fairness: A Restatement* (Cambridge, MA: Harvard University Press, 2001, 62. Reprinted with permission from Harvard University Press.

immediate increases to the social minimum. Moreover, local short-term maximin measures would not even be permitted if they not only increased but cemented extreme inequalities, thereby impeding the transition to a more just basic structure. When conditions of extreme inequality obtain, even local maximin measures can sometimes be unjust.

I return to these difficult questions regarding the application of the difference principle in non-ideal or unjust conditions in section 7. But first, consider more ideal circumstances and a system that is not as unjust and beset with such gross inequalities as is United States. Consider an "effectively designed" economic system, a property-owning democracy that is "just throughout" in Rawls's sense: the prospects of the least advantaged would decline if those of the most advantaged group declined, but would improve if the expectations of the most advantaged also improved.

I'll call "Optional Inequality" the interpretation of the difference principle which says that (further) increases in inequality that (maximally) benefit the least advantaged are *not required* by the difference principle, but are *optional and to be left to democratic decisions*. At the limit, Optional Inequality suggests that a society does not have to institute *any* inequalities; democratic citizens might instead choose strict equality. Strict equality might seem an option, given the difference principle's wording. Rather than mandating inequalities, it addresses "permissible inequalities in the basic structure" and specifies how "social and economic inequalities are to be arranged" (*TJ*, 56, 72).

Still, the strict equality option is not supported by Rawls's suggestion that society is to be on the upwardly rising incline of the OP curve.[24] It also conflicts with Rawls's clear assertions that "[t]he basic structure of society is perfectly just when the prospects of the least fortunate are as great as they can be" (*CP*, 138; see also *TJ*, 68); also, "the difference principle directs society to aim at the highest point on the OP curve of the most effectively designed scheme of cooperation" (*JF*, 63). This parallels Rawls's statement: "Taking the two principles together, the basic structure is to be arranged to maximize the worth to the least advantaged of the complete scheme of equal liberty shared by all. This defines the end of social justice" (*TJ*, 179). I'll call this the "Mandatory Maximizing" interpretation; it says that inequalities are not optional but required whenever they benefit the least advantaged and that given the feasible alternatives a society must enact those measures that maximally improve the position of the least advantaged.[25]

Rawls says various things that can seem to support both the Optional Inequality and Mandatory Maximizing readings of the second principle. The truth appears to lie somewhere in between. Taken by itself and independent of prior principles, the difference principle alone may indeed imply that economic inequalities are optional. But Rawls says the difference principle's "meaning is not given by taking it in isolation" (*JF*, 158n.); it must be considered in conjunction with the demands of prior principles and the need to guarantee the worth of the basic liberties and fair equal opportunity.[26]

For example, suppose a well-ordered democratic society legally mandated and sustained an egalitarian agrarian/artisan society, much like the one the Amish voluntarily reside in, assiduously avoiding modern infrastructure needed for higher education, cultural achievements, and the benefits of modern technology. This would have adverse consequences for the diversity of career and cultural opportunities available to society's members, depriving them of the conditions needed to fully educate themselves and take advantage of careers and pursuits enabling them to develop their talents and capacities and pursue a wide range of experiences and conceptions of the good. The worth of citizens' equal basic liberties and fair equality of opportunities would be significantly diminished in this stubbornly agrarian egalitarian society, to the point of injustice. This is implied by Rawls's statement that the "end of social justice" is to maximize the worth of the basic liberties to the least advantaged.[27]

The crucial point is that justice, including distributive justice, cannot simply be a matter of instituting equality of social goods—of liberties, opportunities, income, wealth, and economic powers—or equality of welfare. Justice also requires that a society provide *fully adequate resources and diverse opportunities* to enable citizens to develop their capacities, effectively exercise their basic liberties, and pursue a wide range of conceptions of the good. This requires substantial public investment in public goods, including infrastructure, education at all levels, public health and universal healthcare, and so on. This is a crucial difference between Rawls's *liberal* egalitarian position and strictly egalitarian accounts of distribution. Justice for Rawls requires, not equality of (access to) resources, opportunities, or welfare regardless of material and social conditions, but fair equality of access to a wide range of career and cultural opportunities, and economic resources sufficient to give fully adequate, if not maximum, worth to all citizens' equal basic liberties. This distribution and the social circumstances and institutions needed to effect it are for Rawls the "end of social justice," not strict equality or equalizing the consequences of good and bad luck.

The Optional Inequality interpretation of the difference principle must then be significantly qualified. It can apply only under conditions where the least advantaged citizens have sufficiently adequate career and cultural options and economic resources to enable them to take full advantage of their basic liberties and fair opportunities and therewith develop their capacities and pursue a wide range of life plans. Otherwise strict equality of income, wealth, and economic powers would not be just.

6. Mandatory Maximizing and the Scope of the Difference Principle

What about the Mandatory Maximizing interpretation, suggested by Rawls's remark that "the end of social justice" is to maximize the worth of basic liberties to the least advantaged"? (*TJ*, 179). The extreme version of this interpretation would impose a strict requirement that *all* social policies not regulated by prior principles be assessed by the difference principle and designed to maximally benefit the least advantaged. Maximizing the position of the LAG would then be a kind of constrained dominant end guiding all social policies (except those covered by prior principles), much like a "mixed conception" with a similarly constrained principle of utility (*TJ*, §49). Call this the "Strict Mandatory Maximizing" interpretation: *all* social policies not covered by prior principles are to maximally benefit the least advantaged.

There are many social policies for which the difference principle does not appear to be the appropriate standard of assessment: foreign policy and non-trade treaties; many decisions about public goods, such as highways and other infrastructure; public investments in scientific research and technological innovation (e.g., NASA or computing and the internet); support for public museums and parks or fine arts and athletic programs in schools; most family, child custody, and marriage law; ordinary negligence and determinations of fault and remedies in non-economic torts and other areas of law not integral to economic cooperation; redressing disabilities and care for the severely handicapped; preserving the environment for aesthetic reasons; and many other policies. In designing these and other policies, legislators should avoid creating adverse consequences for the least advantaged; but this does not mean these policies should be tailored to *maximally* benefit them, for the difference principle does not respond to the nature of the issues raised by these policies.

Of course, when these and other non-economic measures do result in significant inequalities, such as divorce laws that result in poverty for women, there is a problem of unjust inequality. But the difference principle is no more appropriate to questions of the fair division of assets in divorce proceedings than it is to ascertaining fault and equitable remedies in auto negligence cases. Regarding divorce Rawls endorses giving spouses an equal share in income and the increased value of family assets acquired during marriage (*CP*, 600), but this measure does not rely on the difference principle but on other considerations of fairness. Like determinations of fault and remedies in negligence cases, it would be unfair to require that assets between divorced spouses be divided so as to maximally benefit the least advantaged class, since they are normally entirely unrelated individuals. The difference principle responds to a different set of issues than family and marriage law and most negligence and other tort law. What are these issues?

In any society, there is the problem of designing the social institutions that make economic production and commerce possible and fairly dividing the social product among those who contribute to productive activity. These institutions include property and legal control of means of production, markets and other conventions of transfer, and economic contracts and other commercial transactions. Utilitarianism in large part originated in Hume's argument that these "conventions of justice" should be designed to promote public utility.[28] Rawls is addressing a similar problem but offers a different solution: the basic institutions necessary for productive economic cooperation should be designed so as to achieve *economic reciprocity*, or fairness in the division of the social product among "normal and fully cooperating members of society" (*JF*, 8). By "normal and fully cooperating citizens" Rawls means those who are actively engaged in economic cooperation and who do their fair share in contributing to social and economic life. Or, as Rawls says, "This assumption implies that *all are willing to work and do their part in sharing the burdens of social life*" (*JF*, 179: emphasis added).

This explains why Rawls comes to define the least advantaged as the lowest paid, least skilled workers, and not as the severely disabled or even the poorest citizens.[29] The difference principle is designed to address the question of the fair and efficient distribution of economic powers and responsibilities in production and the equitable distribution of ensuing income and wealth among members of society engaged in productive social and economic activity. It is not conceived as a principle of redress or assistance to meet the basic or special needs of citizens. Their circumstances require principles that are specifically tailored to their conditions. Thus, Rawls says that the two principles of justice presuppose a principle of basic needs, ensuring that citizens' basic needs are met so that they are able to "understand and to be able fruitfully to exercise [basic] rights and liberties" (*PL*, 7). Meeting *all* citizens' basic needs is a "constitutional essential" in any liberal society and in "decent societies" as well (*PL*, 166, 228ff.). Rawls does not enumerate such principles of basic needs or assistance for those severely handicapped over their lifetimes; these are to be decided at the constitutional and legislative stages according to principles yet to be specified (*JF*, 176n.). The important point is that the difference principle has a different role than such principles of redress: namely, to maintain *democratic reciprocity*, or "reciprocity at the deepest level" among citizens who are "normally and fully cooperating" and thus engage in socially productive activity "over a complete life" (*JF*, 49).

This distinct role of the difference principle provides further reasons to reject the strict mandatory maximizing reading of the difference principle. For what could be the justification for requiring that *all* laws and social policies maximally promote the position of least paid workers when this would come at the expense of other equally if not more important social needs and interests, such as meeting the basic needs of all citizens and the special needs of the disabled?

Assuming then that the difference principle does not provide the proper standard of assessment for all laws and social policies, the question remains whether, with respect to the basic institutions and economic measures to which it *does* apply, it mandates maximizing the least advantaged position. The difference principle is often regarded as an aggregative consequentialist principle that requires maximizing the sum of advantages for the least advantaged class. "Prioritarianism" is such a position sometimes attributed to Rawls's difference principle.[30] On the prioritarian interpretation the difference principle would require maximizing the absolute level of the least advantaged regardless of their position relative to those better off or the resulting degree of inequality.

The "Qualified Optional" interpretation implies that the difference principle is not prioritarian; for it says that a society may forgo further increases in inequality if the least advantaged already have an adequate share of relevant primary social goods that enables them to effectively exercise their basic liberties and take advantage of diverse opportunities. This parallels Rawls's assertion that the difference principle does not require that society strive for ever-increasing growth over generations in order to maximize the expectations of the least advantaged indefinitely. "That would not be a reasonable conception of justice" (*JF*, 63–64, 159).

Also against the prioritarian reading is Rawls's assertion that, "even if it uses the idea of maximizing the expectations of the least advantaged, the difference principle is essentially a principle of reciprocity" (*JF*, 64). This suggests that the difference principle has a different purpose than maximizing the absolute sum of benefits for the LAG—namely *economic reciprocity*, or fairness in the division of the social product. Unlike consequentialist principles, as a principle of reciprocity the difference principle determines distributive shares *relationally*, not in absolute terms: the fairness of each person's entitlements is ascertained relative to those of others, with the justice of distributions to the least advantaged decided by how well off they are compared with the most advantaged. If the absolute position of the least advantaged were all that mattered, then any distribution where the least advantaged were better off would be more just than distributions where they had less. But this is clearly not the case under the difference principle. A distribution affording less to the least advantaged quite often can be more just than alternatives affording more. For example, assume that a moderately unequal society is "just throughout" (on the upwardly rising slope of the OP curve) with a $40,000 social minimum. The same society could have adopted policies (or might yet still) resulting in a $42,000 social minimum but with substantial inequalities that are unjust since, were they diminished, the social minimum could be improved further (to $44,000). Society when it is "just throughout" with a $40,000 minimum is more just than if it had aimed for a $42,000 minimum with substantial unjust inequalities.

Moreover, under ideal conditions of a just society with a fully adequate social minimum, a society with a lesser minimum might even be *as just* as it would be if it adopted policies with a greater minimum requiring greater inequalities. Under ideal conditions, when society is just throughout, the difference principle requires that, from among alternative measures that increase inequality, they must choose those that make the least advantaged better off at that point than other alternatives. But this does not mean a society continually has to adopt measures that increase inequality in order to maximize the absolute sum going to the LAG. Referring again to the OP curve (*JF*, 62), a society is not always required to aim for and achieve that distribution (point D) that maximally benefits the least advantaged; instead it can permissibly decide on a point on the upwardly rising incline of the OP curve that improves their position but involves less inequality. Even if not "perfectly just" (*TJ*, 68) such a point can be said to be "sufficiently just," since at any point on the upwardly rising curve, the position of the LAG is still maximized relative to the MAG's share at that point. This is compatible with the wording of the difference principle, since inequalities have been "arranged so that they are to the greatest benefit of the least advantaged" (TJ, 266). The difference principle's strong reciprocity condition is satisfied, even when the position of the LAG is not maximized absolutely by increasing inequality further and moving to point D. In this regard, too, Rawls's difference principle is not prioritarian.[31]

Thus, under ideal conditions of a just, well-ordered society where the worth of the basic liberties and fair opportunities is fully adequate for all, a society may democratically decide not to increase inequality further to maximize the absolute sum going to the least advantaged. Return to Rawls's claim that the difference principle does not require ever-increasing growth to maximize the expectations of the least advantaged indefinitely (JF, 63–64, 159). He says this to not rule out "Mill's idea of a just stationary state where real capital accumulation may cease" (JF, 159).[32] Suppose the ideal case, a property-owning democracy where all citizens own a fair share of productive capital and the least advantaged have incomes of $150,000 per year. Assume these resources are fully adequate and enable them to effectively exercise their basic liberties and take full advantage of a wide range of professional and cultural opportunities. Then surely justice would not require that this society take measures to increase the social minimum still further, especially if this would increase existing inequalities. "That would not be a reasonable conception of justice" (JF, 159). This may even apply to further economic growth that does not increase inequalities. In either case important social values—such as limiting adverse effects on the environment, or creating a shorter workday to increase everyone's leisure time—can justify limits on economic growth and the social minimum.

7. Ideal versus Non-Ideal Theory and the Difference Principle

Rawls's argument for the difference principle does not ultimately rely on the maximin rule of choice observed by rational parties in the original position (JF, 94–95). Instead his argument is contractualist in that it appeals to the perspective of reasonable persons in a well-ordered society: the difference principle is justifiable and generally acceptable to free and equal moral persons morally motivated by a sense of justice and self-respect. Rawls's arguments for the difference principle are based mainly in considerations of democratic reciprocity, the strains of commitment, and the conditions needed to maintain the self-respect of free and equal citizens.

The ideal of a well-ordered society grounds ideal theory for Rawls, including his assumption of full compliance: it is a society where all reasonable persons willingly endorse and normally comply with demands of justice. Critics claim that Rawls's ideal theory means that the principles of justice apply only to a "perfectly just" society, not to non-ideal circumstances of injustice.[33] But justice as fairness would have no point if the principles of justice did not apply to assessing the injustices of non-ideal circumstances. Clearly the equal basic liberties and fair equality of opportunity apply to our circumstances, for Rawls discusses their application at length.[34] Moreover, he is explicit that ideal theory guides the application of the principles of justice to non-ideal situations (*TJ*, 267). "Until the ideal is identified . . . nonideal theory lacks an objective, an aim, by reference to which its queries can be answered" (*LP*, 90; see also, *JF*, 13).

The relevant question then is, how should the difference principle be applied to assessing non-ideal circumstances and guiding reform under unjust conditions where a just basic structure is not in place. Questions of reforms needed to bring about a just basic structure are largely empirical and strategic, especially given entrenched interests that benefit from injustice, but certain rules of application still apply. Here in broad outline is a proposed summary of rules for applying Rawls's difference principle in ideal and non-ideal circumstances. These suggestions need further elaboration and refinement.

7.1. Application of the Difference Principle under Ideal Conditions of a Well-Ordered Society

Assume that the difference principle's broad requirement is satisfied: "The most effectively designed system" is in place, and the least advantaged are better off than in any other system. The alternatives Rawls proposes, property-owning democracy and liberal socialism, do not by nature involve the substantial inequalities typical of capitalism. There is no privileged class of persons who own and control the preponderance of productive wealth. Economic markets are regulated to prevent taking unfair advantage of citizens and undermining economic efficiency. Moderate inequalities exist, but since there is fair equality of opportunities and an adequate social minimum, with income, wealth, and economic powers being widely distributed, these inequalities are both necessary and fair: inequalities realize "reciprocity at the deepest level" since society is on the upwardly rising slope of the OP curve. Consequently, the self-respect of the less advantaged is not adversely affected by these moderate inequalities.

Under these ideal conditions, first, a well-ordered society is normally to adopt in its economic policies local measures regarding basic social institutions that maximally benefit the least advantaged. The exception would be the rare case where maximin measures involve a substantial increase in inequality; if so, then a society may choose alternative measures that improve the position of the LAG but that involve less inequality.

Second, a well-ordered society is to continue to improve the position of the least advantaged in its economic policies up to a point where further increases in the social minimum would not substantially add to the effective exercise of the basic liberties of the least advantaged (and presumably other income groups) or their ability to take full advantage of a wide range of educational, career, and cultural opportunities. *At this point* a society may decide the social minimum is fully adequate and devote further increases in social wealth entirely to improving infrastructure and other public goods; increasing benefits and services for the handicapped and disabled; providing assistance to poorer societies beyond what is already required by justice (*LP*, 106–107); setting aside additional savings for future generations; and promoting other democratically legitimated public values compatible with public reason (exploring space, preserving nature and improving the environment, promoting cultural values, etc.). Alternatively, assuming all its duties of social and political justice are satisfied (to the disabled, burdened societies, and future generations), a society may choose to maintain the economic status quo and its fully adequate social minimum and forgo increasing national wealth any further. This is Mill's stationary state, where further increments to real capital accumulation have ceased (*JF*, 64). Under these conditions a society should replenish existing capital and maintain its infrastructure and public goods for future generations.

7.2. Application of the Difference Principle under Non-Ideal Conditions

Non-ideal conditions, such as those in the capitalist-welfare or "safety-net" state, or in a libertarian society with no safety net, entail many complexities; in addition to strategic problems involved in applying the principle of justice (because many citizens reject them), a society has to weigh off narrow measures that (maximally) improve the position of the least advantaged now with broader measures needed to bring about "the most effectively designed economic system" (a property-owning democracy). How strong is society's duty to promote a just basic structure compared with its duty to maximally benefit the least advantaged in the short run? Clearly the difference principle does not allow society to sacrifice the basic liberties or well-being of the least advantaged for the sake of maximally promoting the greater well-being of increased numbers of the least advantaged in future generations (*TJ*, 263–64). But can it forgo local maximin measures and adopt alternatives that benefit existing generations somewhat less in order to enact broader economic reforms? This does not seem unreasonable if it is the only way to realize needed reforms of an unjust basic structure. And yet we saw earlier that non-maximin Pareto-improving measures that benefit the least advantaged are not authorized by the difference principle if this increases inequality, since there are alternative measures that decrease inequality and benefit the least advantaged still more. But if these inequality-increasing Pareto measures are because of political realities the *only* way to achieve necessary reforms of an unjust system (as they often are in a capitalist society such as the US), then things are different: such unjust measures might still be an improvement on an even more unjust status quo. Finally, we saw that not only Pareto measures but even measures that *maximally* benefit the least advantaged in the short run sometimes can be unjust when they also substantially increase and solidify gross inequality and/or delay indefinitely the achievement of reforms that would move society in the direction of less inequality and a just basic structure.

The following principles address these and other complexities in broad outline, though they may raise as many questions as they resolve. The first two can result in conflicting demands, but many of these can be resolved by an added qualification. (1) A society is normally to adopt those local economic policies that reduce inequalities and/or maximally benefit the least advantaged, if not in the short run, then intermediately and during a substantial portion of their lifetimes. The exception, just noted, is maximin measures that aggravate and solidify substantial inequalities and impede reform in the direction of a more just economic system. (2) A society *also* has a duty to reform the economy by adopting broad measures that are *most effective* or (the qualification) at least *moderately effective* in bringing about a just basic structure, *so long as* these measures eventually improve the position of the least advantaged of current generations. Of course, not all local measures in (1) that maximally benefit the LAG now or in the near future are also broad measures that *most* effectively bring about the "most effectively designed system" of justice and vice versa. Hence, (2) allows for local maximin measures that are less than maximally effective in promoting a just society if they significantly improve the position of the least advantaged now (e.g., immediate income tax credits for the LAG); but still it excludes local maximin measures that considerably delay or make a just basic structure much less likely in the future. Thus ruled out are further tax cuts for the wealthy that maximally benefit the LAG in the short run but solidify substantial inequalities and impede a transition to a just basic structure, such as a property-owning democracy (POD).

(3) If measures that both maximally benefit the least advantaged in the short run and also promote a future POD would *substantially* increase existing inequalities, a society *may* choose alternative measures causing less inequality that improve the position of the less advantaged (so long as society remains on the upwardly rising part of the OP curve [*JF*, 64]) and still are consistent with advancing just institutions in the future. This might be justifiable on grounds of maintaining the self-respect of the less advantaged—substantial increases in economic inequality must always be carefully assessed for these reasons. But even when measures have no detrimental effects on self-respect, still a society is not required by justice

to adopt local maximizing measures that substantially increase inequalities when there are alternatives causing less inequality that also benefit the LAG. The latter measures causing less inequality may even be required by justice if they are more likely to advance a just basic structure.

(4) This is the most difficult case: What about broad reforms that are *necessary* to eventually institute a just basic structure (POD) but that temporarily *worsen* the condition of the least advantaged? For example, the difference principle requires at some point a (gradual) restructuring of the property system with redistribution of economic wealth so all (working) citizens own a fair share (e.g., of shares in firms, or in mutual funds). This likely will result in an economic downturn, increased unemployment, and considerable loss of market value of shares (similar, e.g., to the 50 percent decline in the US stock market from October 2007 to March 2009).[35] Such measures are permissible, if not required, when their short-term effects on the less advantaged are not too severe and long-lasting; otherwise more gradual measures should be devised. Moreover, such measures must eventually benefit existing members of less advantaged classes, *and* they must reduce existing inequality, hence involve sacrifices to the most advantaged as well. This "one step backward, two steps forward" approach seems inevitable if serious economic reform of an unjust economic system is to be possible. It is a complex matter requiring far more discussion than can be given here.

8. Property-Owning Democracy versus the Welfare State

According to the difference principle, the least advantaged class is the one whose distributive shares, or "index" of primary social goods, are the least. In addition to having less income and wealth, the least advantaged have the fewest social and economic powers and responsibilities. Rawls says that, for the sake of simplicity in making interpersonal comparisons, we should rely on representative persons' share of income and wealth, since one's share of powers, responsibilities, and social bases of self-respect normally track one's share of income and wealth. He assumes the LAG is the "class of unskilled laborers" (*TJ*, 67).

A question Rawls does not adequately address is, how is the index that determines representative persons' share of primary goods to be composed? How much (what percentage) is assigned to social and economic powers and responsibilities and self-respect compared with income and wealth? (Rawls suggestively says that self-respect is perhaps the most important primary social good [*TJ*, 386].) Normally this issue is of little consequence, assuming income and wealth are a reliable indicator of one's relative position with respect to other primary social goods (*JF*, 65). But it may be important in assessing Rawls's arguments for property-owning democracy versus welfare-state capitalism

(WSC). He argues that one of the decisive factors in favor of POD is that it affirms the self-respect of citizens who are least advantaged, since they own a share of capital or total productive wealth in society (*JF*, §42). I assume, too, that part of the argument for property-owning democracy relies on all citizens also having at least some share of economic rights, powers, and responsibilities in their workplace (co-determination rights, rights to periodically alter their daily tasks to reduce monotony, move around freely in the workplace, take periodic breaks, etc.).[36]

These questions are especially relevant in the hypothetical case of a capitalist welfare state where the least advantaged have no economic wealth, powers, or responsibilities but the social minimum of income and wealth to meet basic needs may be generous so that it potentially exceeds the income and wealth of the least advantaged in a property-owning democracy where the least advantaged own capital (e.g., shares of firms) and have some degree of economic power. Though the index of primary goods is greater in POD, those in WSC have, let's assume, greater income. What is the argument for POD in this case? Why shouldn't there be a permissible trade-off of economic wealth and powers for a greater share of income for the LAG? The best way to address this problem, however unrealistic it might be, is to examine Rawls's reasons for arguing in favor of POD and against WSC. He relies primarily upon economic reciprocity and the primary good of self-respect, as he did in arguing for the difference principle.

Rawls argues that one of the major reasons that POD satisfies the difference principle is that, unlike WSC, it maintains reciprocity "at the deepest level." Such democratic reciprocity exists when increasing benefits are shared by all members of society and maximally benefit the least advantaged (hence society is on the rising slope of the OP curve). This affirms the self-respect of the least advantaged, since they know that their interests are not being sacrificed for the sake of greater gains to the more advantaged or the general welfare, as in WSC. A problem with WSC is that, once basic needs are met, there are no guaranteed further gains for the least advantaged, even though they continue to contribute to the social product. The least advantaged are thus put in a position where they justifiably believe they are left behind by society and are not fully members of it. This is partly because in WSC the social minimum is a conventional assessment of basic needs, a vague idea inevitably subject to disagreement, giving rise to political conflict between the more advantaged and least advantaged members of society. The least advantaged are a minority, and in the absence of a public understanding and agreement that democratic reciprocity requires that their position be maximized, arguments that the social minimum should be increased or sustained are likely to be met with the reply that the least advantaged are a drag on society's productivity, do not deserve the share they now have, and if anything it should be reduced. (Such disputes are familiar in the United States, where one party now argues that food stamps and other benefits for the poor, 40 percent of whom are children, should be decreased, if not eliminated, allegedly in order to maintain the self-respect of the poor.)

But what if the least advantaged in a POD are *willing* to sacrifice the economic powers and modest share of wealth they enjoy for the sake of a marginally greater social minimum of income? Suppose their share of total income in wages and dividends in a POD is $40,000, while were they to agree to surrender their shares of stock and economic powers to their employers and other entrepreneurs, their wages plus income supplements eventually would rise 10 percent, to $44,000. Why shouldn't the least advantaged be allowed to make this decision?

One reason not to sacrifice the wealth and economic powers of the least advantaged is that it reinstitutes the separation and conflict between economic classes of capitalists versus laborers. There may be income classes in a POD too, but unlike what occurs in capitalism, there is not a division of social classes between owners who control most real and liquid capital, who exercise predominant economic and most likely political power as well, and whose interests conflict with the class of productive laborers who have neither wealth nor economic control with its attendant powers. The hypothetical assumes that in such a class-divided society of capitalists versus labor, less advantaged workers can maintain their economic agency and self-respect, in spite of the fact that they have been deprived of any economic powers or any share of capital wealth.

Why wouldn't giving up their share of wealth and economic powers eventually have adverse effects on the self-respect of the least advantaged that were similar to those of property qualifications on the franchise, where the least advantaged are deprived of political rights? Many of the poor today are so politically despondent that they would sell their right to vote, but this does not justify such alienability. Similarly, it would not be justified if the least advantaged were given greater income supplements and in return alienated their rights to fair equal opportunities to develop their capacities. Rawls assumes that *social equality and self-respect* of citizens depend upon a fair and widespread distribution of *all* primary goods to *all* social classes. This includes not just equal basic liberties, fair opportunities, and income, but also ownership and some degree of control of economic wealth, as well as exercise of economic powers and responsibilities in the workplace.[37] Welfare-state capitalism effectively bars the least advantaged from access to a share of economic wealth, powers, and responsibilities, and this undermines social equality and their sense of self-respect. The argument for property-owning democracy over welfare-state capitalism is in this regard an extension of the fundamental significance assigned to social equality, democratic reciprocity, and the social bases of self-respect that informs Rawls's arguments for equality of political and other basic liberties, fair equality of opportunity, and the difference principle.

9. Conclusion

The difference principle is but one part, even if the most significant, of Rawls's account of distributive justice. In addition to distributive measures that guarantee the fair value of the political liberties and fair equality of opportunities, there is the right to healthcare guaranteed by FEO, the just savings principle applying to future generations, the duty of assistance owed to burdened peoples in the Law of Peoples, the duty of assistance owed to those with significant disabilities who are unable to make economic contributions, and finally, presupposed by both principles of justice, the fundamental requirement of basic justice that society meet the basic needs of all citizens so they can effectively exercise their basic rights and liberties. All of these requirements have priority over the difference principle, and their claims must be satisfied before the social minimum required by the difference principle can be fully settled. A more complete account of Rawls's complex conception of distributive justice would include discussion of them.[38]

Notes

1. John Rawls, "Justice as Fairness," *Collected Papers*, ed. Samuel Freeman (Cambridge, MA: Harvard University Press, 1999), 48; *CP* in further citations of this work. On the difference principle and the common good, see Rawls, "Distributive Justice," *CP*, 153.

2. G. A. Cohen, *Rescuing Justice and Equality* (Cambridge MA: Harvard University Press, 2008).

3. *PL*, 181; *JF*, 58–9. This is Rawls's final and (I will assume) authoritative list of primary social goods. In *TJ* orig. he says simply "rights and liberties, powers and opportunities, income and wealth" and adds "the primary good of self respect." (*TJ* orig., 62; see also 92, 93, 94). In the revised edition he drops "powers" and simply says "rights, liberties, and opportunities, and income and wealth [and] self-respect" (*TJ*, 54, see also 79). In "Kantian Constructivism in Moral Theory" (1980), he restored "powers" and set forth the authoritative list cited above. See *CP*, 313–4; see also 362–3.

4. See *TJ*, 6–7; see also *CP*, 138, and *JF*, 55–57.

5. John Rawls, *Political Liberalism*, expanded ed. (New York: Columbia University Press, 2005), 267; *PL* in further citations of this work.

6. Thomas Piketty, *Capital in the Twenty-First Century* (Cambridge MA: Harvard University Press, 2013).

7. Cohen, *Rescuing Justice and Equality*, 138.

8. Rawls says, "Background institutions must work to keep property and wealth evenly enough shared over time to preserve the fair value of the political liberties and fair equality of opportunity over generations" (*JF*, 51).

9. Instead Rawls discusses public funding of forums for free public discussion and of political parties and campaigns, as well as strict limits on private contributions, to neutralize the corrupting effects of money on politics (*TJ*, 198–99; *PL*, 328, 357; *JF*, 149–50).

10. Annette Lareau, *Unequal Childhood*, rev. edition (Berkeley: University of California Press, 2011).

11. T. M. Scanlon, "Substantive Opportunity," chap. 5 in *Why Does Inequality Matter?*, Oxford: Oxford University Press, 2018) sees FEO as imposing a strong egalitarian requirement.

12. Phillipe van Parijs also discusses the significant demands of FEO and suggests a paradox: the resources needed to fully satisfy basic liberties and FEO may leave no resources for the difference principle (Phillippe van Parijs, "Difference Principles," in *The Cambridge Companion to Rawls*, ed. Samuel Freeman [Cambridge: Cambridge University Press, 2003], 225–26). However, as the first principle does not require maximizing equal basic liberties but instead a scheme "fully adequate" to exercise the moral powers, FEO also is not a maximizing principle requiring "perfect equality of opportunity," or perfectly equal chances in life (*TJ*, 265, 448). Rather, it requires that all should have a "fair chance" to attain offices and social positions with educational and training opportunities adequate for enabling the less advantaged to fully develop and exercise their capacities so they can fairly compete for open positions and take full advantage of cultural and social life (*JF*, 43).

13. See Alan Blinder, *After the Music Stopped: The Financial Crisis, the Response, and the Work Ahead* (New York: Penguin, 2013), on such practices and measures needed to avoid them.

14. Cohen, *Rescuing Justice and Equality*; Liam Murphy, "Institutions and the Demands of Justice," *Philosophy & Public Affairs* 27, no. 4, (1999): 251–91.

15. For discussion see chapter 4.

16. Robert Nozick says the difference principle is an "end-state" "patterned" principle. See *ASU*, 209. Rawls said in conversation that he did not understand how Nozick could say it is end-state. Rawls also denies it is patterned. See *CP*, 229.

17. See Milton Friedman, *Capitalism and Freedom* (Chicago: University of Chicago Press, 1962), 191–194, on the negative income tax. Friedrich Hayek similarly endorses a "minimum income" as "a necessary part of the Great Society," in *Law, Legislation, and Liberty*, vol. 3: *The Political Order of a Free People* (Chicago: University of Chicago Press, 1979), 55, 187 n. 13.

18. Ronald Dworkin, *Sovereign Virtue* (Cambridge, MA: Harvard University Press, 2002). For an assessment of Dworkin's account, see Samuel Freeman, "Equality of Resources, Market Luck, and the Justification of Adjusted Market Distributions," *Boston University Law Review* 90, no. 2, (2010): 921–48.

19. See John Roemer, *A Future for Socialism* (Cambridge MA: Harvard University Press, 1994), who advocates equality of opportunity for welfare and "coupon

socialism," wherein all individuals own rights to receive dividends from publicly held shares that they can trade on markets but cannot bequeath or sell to others.

20. Cohen contends the difference principle is consistent with "a maximizing ethos [that] will produce severe inequalities and a meager level of provision for the worst off" (*Rescuing Justice and Equality*, 138). He argues that the difference principle can even sanction distributions like those in the United States, where the least advantaged are worse off than they are in a society where people have a more egalitarian ethos, like Germany (143). This conflicts with Rawls's claim that the least advantaged are to be better off than in all other systems. If a more egalitarian ethos would make the least advantaged better off, then the difference principle would require institutions, consistent with freedom of conscience, that encourage people to develop such an ethos. See Samuel Freeman, *Justice and the Social Contract* (New York: Oxford University Press, 2007), 121; see also Joshua Cohen, "Taking People as They Are," *Philosophy & Public Affairs* 30, no. 4 (2001): 363–86.

21. *TJ*, xiv–xvi; *JF*, 8n., 135–40. That the local application of the difference principle assumes in the ideal case the background institutions of property-owning democracy, see *TJ*, 67–68, 242.

22. G. A. Cohen says the "lexical difference principle" is the "canonical version" (*Rescuing Justice and Equality*, 17, 156–161, 164f., 320). Rawls, citing Sen's suggestion, briefly mentions the lexical principle if close-knitness fails, but in the revised edition of *A Theory of Justice* he dismisses it as irrelevant: "[W]hen the greater potential benefits to the more advantaged are significant, there will surely be some way to improve the situation of the less advantaged as well. The general laws governing the institutions of the basic structure insure that cases requiring the lexical principle will not arise" (*TJ*, 72). Accordingly, I forgo discussion of the lexical principle. Cohen's criticisms heavily rely on it. He argues that Rawls's difference principle is a "strong Pareto Principle" that justifies benefiting the more advantaged but not the less advantaged (*Rescuing Justice and Equality*, 29–30n., 158). This conflicts with Rawls's statement, "[T]he difference principle is a strongly egalitarian conception in the sense that unless there is a distribution that makes both persons better off . . . an equal distribution is to be preferred" (*TJ*, 65–66).

23. Congress reduced the top rate from 39.5% to 37% and the corporate tax rate from 35% to 21%.

24. Rawls says that strict equality is irrational (*JF*,151).

25. Further support for Mandatory Maximizing lies in the "equal justice" lines JJ (*JF*, 62, fig. 1; *TJ*, 66, fig. 6), which suggest that any distribution higher on the OP curve provides the least advantaged with greater benefits and is more just than one lower that provides them with less, since it is on or closer to a higher equal justice line.

26. "[T]he parts of the two principles are designed to work in tandem and apply as a unit" (*JF*, 46n.). Moreover, "the meaning of the difference principle is

determined in part by its ranking as subordinate to the first principle of justice. That meaning is not given by taking it in isolation" (*JF*, 158n.).

27. Rawls also says that "the priority of fair opportunity" over the difference principle means "that we must appeal to the chances given to those with lesser opportunity [and] hold that a wider range of opportunity is open to them than would otherwise be the case" (*TJ*, 265).

28. David Hume, *Enquiries Concerning Human Understanding and Concerning the Principles of Morals*, 3rd ed. (Oxford: Oxford University Press, 1975), 183–204.

29. On unskilled workers as the least advantaged class, see *TJ*, 67–68, 83–84. On the presumption that the least advantaged work, see *CP*, 455 n. 7, and *PL*, 182 n. 9: "Those who are unwilling to work . . . must find a way to support themselves." On society's duties to the severely handicapped, see *JF*, 176n.

30. See Derek Parfit, "Equality or Priority? The Lindley Lecture," University of Kansas, 1991, and Derek Parfit, "Equality and Priority," *Ratio* 10, no. 3 (1997): 202–21. "On the Priority View, we are concerned only with people's absolute levels" (214).

31. I believe this interpretation is compatible with Rawls's intentions, even if it does not fully conform to all he says, such as his claim that the difference principle directs society to be on highest point on the OP curve of the most effectively designed scheme of cooperation) (*JF*, 63).

32. Mill argued that society would finally be able to direct its energies toward social ends more worthwhile than the incessant pursuit of material wealth.

33. See Amartya Sen, *The Idea of Justice* (Cambridge MA: Harvard University Press, 2009), 16, 100, arguing that Rawls's "transcendental principles" apply only within a "perfectly just society" and are irrelevant to our non-ideal circumstances. See also chapter 8, this volume.

34. See *PL*, lecture 8.

35. Blinder, *After the Music Stopped*.

36. Freeman, *Justice and the Social Contract*, 133–36.

37. Samuel Freeman, "Assessing G. A. Cohen's Critique of the Difference Principle," *Harvard Review of Philosophy* 19 (2013): 23–45.

38. For their helpful comments I am grateful to T. M. Scanlon, Joshua Cohen, Samuel Scheffler, Philippe van Parijs, Thomas Christiano, Christine Korsgaard, Arthur Kuflick, Kok-Chor Tan, Justin Bernstein, Pierce Randall, as well as to members of the Department of Philosophy and Law School at the University of Arizona, the Philosophy Department at the University of Vermont, the Global Justice Program at Yale University, and to participants at the conference on the heritage of Rawls at the Ignatium Academy in Krakow, Poland, June 2014. I am especially grateful to Serena Olsaretti for her extensive comments and helpful suggestions.

4

Property-Owning Democracy and the Difference Principle

1. Introduction: The Choice of a Social System

John Rawls says, "The main problem of distributive justice is the choice of a social system" (*TJ*, 242). Discussions of distributive justice normally are narrowly focused on the distribution of income and wealth, whether equally or according to effort, contribution, need, utility, free-market outcomes, and so on. Rawls transforms this narrow understanding of distributive justice into a complex inquiry regarding the organization of productive relations among democratic citizens, including their ownership and control of productive resources and the distribution of economic powers and responsibilities as well as income and wealth.

Rawls says the difference principle is not a "micro" or "allocative principle" that applies directly to "small-scale situations" to divide up preexisting sums of income and wealth. Rather, it is a "macro principle" for organizing economies and "for ranking social forms viewed as closed systems" (*TJ*, 229). The point here is not simply that the difference principle applies to "the basic structure of society" to specify a "social process" by which distributive claims are determined by "pure procedural justice." Rawls is often accused of endorsing the severe inequalities typical of capitalism.[1] According to G. A. Cohen, because it applies to institutions rather than directly to the assessment of individual entitlements and conduct, Rawls's difference principle justifies the practices of "high-flying" Wall Street "buccaneers" that may improve the least advantaged position but also result in vast inequalities typical of capitalism.

Cohen's objection assumes that the difference principle narrowly applies to existing institutions within a capitalist society and authorizes piecemeal changes in the status quo to benefit the least advantaged, no matter how much inequality results. There are two problems with this assumption. First, there is a limit to the degree of inequality allowable by the difference principle. Rawls says that the difference principle cannot be taken seriously apart from its setting within prior principles and that "[t]he requirements of the prior principles have important distributive effects" (JF, 46 n. 10). The principles of equal basic liberties and fair equality of opportunity restrict permissible inequalities of income and wealth that might otherwise be allowed by the difference principle. Moreover, in saying that the problem of distributive justice is the "choice of a social system" Rawls means that the principles of justice impose a broad systemic requirement on the economy. Societies are to take comprehensive measures to put into place the economic system that makes the least advantaged members better off than they would be under any alternative economic system (consistent with prior principles). This broad requirement contrasts markedly with Cohen's narrow interpretation of the difference principle, namely, that it authorizes almost any measure that alters the status quo in a capitalist society so long as it improves the position of the least advantaged. Only when society's basic structure *already* satisfies the systemic requirement, and the least advantaged are better off than in any alternative system, is it appropriate to apply the difference principle in the piecemeal fashion envisioned by Cohen's objection, to make marginal improvements to the position of the least advantaged.

The broad interpretation of the difference principle leaves open many practical questions about its application to non-ideal circumstances like those in the United States. These are complex issues, but clearly the difference principle does not under non-ideal circumstances justify just any measures that (maximally) benefit the least advantaged in the short run, when that closes off future options that bring about the appropriate social systems under which the difference principle ideally applies. Thus, measures that benefit the least advantaged while cementing and exacerbating the already existing severe inequalities in our capitalist system violate the difference principle (as well as the first principle and fair equality of opportunity) since they take the wrong path to reform. Such measures make it more difficult to reform fundamentally unjust background institutions and take effective measures toward approximating a social system that maximally benefits the least advantaged.

Rawls argues that, correctly applied to the choice of a social system, the principles of justice do not justify any form of capitalism. The two economic systems that meet these principles' requirements are property-owning democracy and liberal socialism. Since neither is capitalist, and both limit inequalities and broadly disseminate ownership and control of productive capital, high-flying Wall Street buccaneers and other sources of capitalist inequalities will not exist in these societies.

2. *Capitalism, Socialism, and Property-Owning Democracy*

Rawls says in the preface to the revised edition of *A Theory of Justice* that were he to write the book again, he would sharply distinguish between property-owning democracy and the welfare state (*TJ*, xiv).[2] In *Justice as Fairness: A Restatement* he explains this distinction. He interprets property-owning democracy and welfare-state capitalism in terms of the degree to which they embody the main features of his principles of justice. A property-owning democracy (POD) he characterizes as a democratic society in which land and capital are privately owned and widely (though not equally) held. Concentrations of wealth have been dissolved or mitigated so that "[s]ociety is not so divided that one fairly small sector controls the preponderance of productive resources." With the wide dispersion of property in income and wealth, there are no longer distortions of democratic government typical of capitalist democracies. Rawls says, "When this is achieved and distributive shares satisfy the principles of justice, many socialist criticisms of the market economy are met" (*TJ* orig., 280).

Rawls's advocacy of POD parallels his response to socialist arguments against markets and capitalism. In *Restatement*, §52, "Addressing Marx's Critiques of Liberalism," Rawls contends that a POD informed by the principles of justice would permit all citizens a right in property in productive assets; give adequate protections to the positive liberties; largely overcome the demeaning features of the division of labor; and ensure all "a fair opportunity to exert political influence." Moreover, since POD provides for both worker-managed firms and greater democracy within capitalist firms, it addresses Marx's concern for democracy in the workplace and in shaping the general course of the economy (*JF*, 177–78).

In distinguishing property-owning democracy from welfare-state capitalism, Rawls depicts capitalism as a particular kind of private property market system. Like Marx, Rawls sees capitalism as a social and political as well as an economic system. Private ownership and control of means of production are concentrated to a great extent in the hands of a privileged minority. Consequently, there are large inequalities, not only in the distribution of income, wealth, and economic powers and positions of responsibility, but also in the exercise of effective political powers and social prerogatives, as well as in access to social and economic opportunities. This privileged class exercises a preponderance of political power, and capitalists' wealth and social and economic powers put them in a strategic position to exert a dominant influence over the political agenda. Unlike Marx, Rawls does not see open class conflict as an inevitable feature of capitalism, but he does think there are structural conflicts of interest normally decided in favor of the most advantaged.

Rawls distinguishes between laissez-faire and welfare-state capitalism. He regards these and other economic systems he compares—property-owning democracy, liberal socialism, and state socialism—as "ideal institutional descriptions" approximated by real-world societies. When working well, he says, social institutions meet the public aims and principles of design of these idealized societies (JF, 137). Rawls elaborates on the primary features of these economic systems, discussing the degree to which they approximate or depart from his own principles of justice.

Laissez-faire capitalism strongly resembles the position Rawls calls "the system of natural liberty" (TJ, 57). Laissez-faire constitutionally guarantees certain personal liberties, such as freedom of conscience and association, together with extensive economic rights, including private ownership and control of the means of production and full freedom of economic contract. Laissez-faire also guarantees formal equality of opportunity, which bars government-imposed discrimination in awarding educational and employment opportunities on grounds of race, religion, gender, and so on. But there is no prohibition of private discrimination in education and employment, nor are there guaranteed rights to publicly funded education or healthcare. Finally, laissez-faire recognizes government's duty to provide certain public goods (highways, canals, etc.); to maintain the efficiency of markets (by preventing price fixing and regulating monopolies); and to guarantee a "rather low" social minimum (for the disabled, orphans, etc.).[3] Otherwise income and wealth are distributed according to competitive market relations or by gift, bequest, and other voluntary transfers.

Though laissez-faire still has many advocates (especially in the United States), welfare-state capitalism now has become the norm in democratic capitalist societies. Unlike laissez-faire, welfare-state capitalism does not constitutionally guarantee extensive private economic liberties; instead property and contract rights are regulated and restrained for the public good, including economic efficiency, promoting the general welfare, and providing a social minimum. Welfare-state capitalism achieves some degree of fair equality of opportunity (TJ, xv), mainly by providing a publicly funded universal education system and prohibiting private discrimination on grounds of race, ethnicity, religion, and gender in education and employment. Finally, welfare-state capitalism guarantees a sizable social minimum that includes old-age pensions, unemployment benefits, welfare payments to meet basic needs, and universal healthcare.

By "socialism" Rawls means an economy with public ownership of the means of production. "State socialism" involves a command economy and state planning. In "liberal socialism," economic power is decentralized and markets allocate productive resources, including labor. Publicly owned capital is leased to worker-managed and -controlled firms at a market rate of interest. Democratic decisions under the constitution determine general features of the economy, such as the rate of savings, the portion of the social product to be devoted to public goods, and the direction of certain investments (*TJ*, 248).

In defining socialism institutionally, in terms of public ownership, Rawls differs from others who associate socialism with economic egalitarianism (G. A. Cohen, John Roemer, et al.). In Roemer's so-called coupon socialism, government provides all citizens with coupons to purchase stock in firms and/or mutual funds of their choice, and they receive income from profits in the form of dividends, with rights to trade for shares in other firms/funds, but not to sell their shares or transfer ownership interest to others by gift or bequest.[4] Whether this form of ownership is to be regarded as public, private, or a hybrid, it meets a primary aspiration of property-owning democracy: to break up concentrations of private capital and disperse ownership, or at least rights to profits, widely among citizens.

Regarding socialism, Rawls suggests that public ownership is independent of how much of society's wealth is devoted to public goods (*TJ*, 235). The same would apply to social welfare programs. Like laissez-faire capitalism, a socialist society (such as China) may choose to provide little in the way of social welfare benefits and other public goods (public health, a clean environment, parks, etc.) and instead impose a high rate of savings and reinvestment of its productive wealth to further build up society's capital. This suggests that Rawls need not conceive of the welfare state as peculiar to capitalism; one could as well speak of "welfare-state socialism" in contrast to other socialisms that are not as concerned with maintaining the individual welfare of all its members.

3. Ideal Institutional Designs

In his discussion of property-owning democracy, Rawls discusses the five "ideal" institutional arrangements: laissez-faire capitalism, welfare-state capitalism, state socialism, liberal socialism, and property-owning democracy. The first three, he argues, violate the principles of justice in several ways (*JF*, 137–38).

Laissez-faire capitalism infringes upon three main provisions of Rawls's principles: first, even when it provides formal equality of political rights, laissez-faire does not guarantee the fair value of the political liberties. Moreover, it ensures formal but not fair equality of opportunity. Finally, since laissez-faire primarily aims for economic efficiency, its social minimum, when it exists, is fixed "rather low."

Rawls says that while *welfare-state capitalism* (WSC) mitigates many inequalities of laissez-faire, it still allows for great inequalities in ownership of productive resources; consequently, "the control of the economy and much of political life rests in few hands" (*JF*, 138). As a result, it fails to guarantee the fair value of the political liberties and does not fully achieve fair equality of opportunity. Finally, even though welfare provisions and the social minimum may be quite generous, "a principle of reciprocity to regulate economic and social inequalities is not recognized" (*JF*, 138).

State socialism with a command economy and one-party rule are said to violate the basic liberties, including equal political liberties and their fair value. Rawls suggests in *A Theory of Justice* that freedom of occupation and choice of workplace and careers (among the rights securing integrity and freedom of the person) are jeopardized in a command economy (*TJ*, 241). Not much more is said about state socialism, except that it uses markets, if at all, only for purposes of rationing consumer goods.

Rawls contends that only *property-owning democracy* and *liberal socialism* realize his two principles of justice. Both provide for institutions that guarantee the fair value of the political liberties. Here Rawls mentions four institutions: publicly funded campaigns; restrictions on contributions to candidates; assurance of an even access to public media; time, place, and manner regulations of speech and the press during campaigns. These and other measures are to achieve "fair and equal access to the political process as a public facility" and prevent the more advantaged from dominating "the limited space of the public political forum" (*JF*, 149–50). Also, both POD and liberal socialism, unlike WSC, conceive of political democracy as deliberative, involving public reasoning on the common good. Democracy is then more than a procedural mechanism for satisfying the greater sum of interests, or a majoritarian competition among conflicting interests, which Rawls sees as typical of capitalist democracies. POD and liberal socialism endorse constitutional limits on majority rule that protect "constitutional essentials," including the basic liberties, equality of opportunity, and a "social minimum providing for the basic needs of all citizens" (*JF*, 48). Rawls says that the first principle requires that inheritance and income be taxed at progressive rates and that property rights be specified "to secure the institutions of equal liberty in a property-owning democracy and the fair value of the rights they establish" (*TJ* orig., 279). This suggests that, to achieve and maintain the fair value of the political liberties, it may be necessary to reduce inequalities of income and wealth, and modify ownership of property, more than the difference principle requires. Rawls from early on envisioned the basic liberties as having significant distributive effects.

Next, to meet fair equality of opportunity, both POD and liberal socialism provide for extensive universal educational benefits and job training, childcare allowances for working parents, as well as universal healthcare, which may also be provided by WSC. But in POD, unlike the welfare state, estate and inheritance taxes widely redistribute individuals' assets upon death to break up concentrations of wealth. In *A Theory of Justice*, Rawls suggests that steeply progressive income and wealth taxes might be necessary "to forestall accumulations of property and power likely to undermine the corresponding institutions" that maintain both fair equality of opportunity and the basic liberties (*TJ* orig., 279). Rawls also says that it is the duty of governments to bring about reasonably full employment so that those who want work can find it. This notably includes government assuming responsibility for being the "employer of last resort."[5] Finally, in POD the economic system is organized to achieve reciprocity among free and equal persons rather than maximum efficiency or aggregate wealth or welfare. Unlike WSC this requires a more equal distribution of income and wealth and a greater social minimum that goes beyond meeting the basic needs of the least advantaged. Rawls mentions here "graded income supplements (a so-called negative income tax)" and family allowances, which add to the market income the less advantaged receive from their work (*TJ*, 243). Also, POD seeks the widespread distribution of productive wealth, as well as economic powers and positions of responsibility among those actively engaged in production. Here Rawls says POD encourages either worker-owned and -managed firms or cooperatives (*JF*, 176, 178), or "share economy" arrangements, with workers' partial ownership of firms with rights to share in profits (*JF*, 72). Finally, though he says there is no basic right that workers own and control the means of production, Rawls mentions the importance of democracy in the workplace and in shaping the general course of the economy (*JF*, 114, 178). Given these and other claims, property-owning democracy for Rawls seems to include some degree of worker prerogatives and responsibilities, if not worker control, as well as workers' participation in firms' governance, for example by voting for management and having representatives on boards that make major decisions (such as *Mitbestimmung*, or co-determination rights).[6]

Rawls did not say anything further about the institutions of a POD informed by the principles of justice. It would seem open to him to endorse a wide range of measures, such as substantial initial property endowments for all citizens (Ackerman, Dworkin), widespread dispersal of stock ownership and firms' profits among all citizens (Roemer), and limits on inheritance of wealth that equalize starting positions enough to ensure that people could not live too comfortably without working (Meade).[7] Rawls seems to have had a rather flexible conception of POD, allowing for mixed arrangements that include both worker-owned and -managed firms together with more traditional joint-stock firms where ownership is widely dispersed throughout society. What seems important to Rawls is not so much specifying the combination of institutions that should constitute a POD as clarifying the reasons and elucidating the principles of justice that should inform decisions of institutional design.

Rather than discussing further the institutions of POD or their feasibility, I will now discuss how Rawls's commitment to POD clarifies his understanding of the principles of justice and their application to social systems. Rawls regards the five social and economic systems he discusses as ideal institutional descriptions that incorporate certain public aims and principles of design (*JF*, 137). The public aims and principles incorporated by property-owning democracy and liberal socialism on Rawls's account are his own principles of justice. What are the aims and principles of welfare-state capitalism for Rawls?

Martin O'Neill, Ben Jackson, and others have questioned whether the welfare state is as different from POD as Rawls contends.[8] They correctly observe that many policies of a POD (universal healthcare, old age pensions, unemployment insurance, a social minimum, etc.) are also integral to the welfare state. O'Neill contends that it is unclear why the welfare state could not guarantee the fair value of the political liberties or fair equality of opportunity by the institutions that Rawls mentions. The real difference between WSC and POD, he says, is that POD involves the widespread distribution of wealth, including ownership of real capital or productive resources.

It is true that Ronald Dworkin, Bruce Ackerman, and Jeremy Waldron, among others, defend versions of WSC that incorporate many institutions Rawls says are needed to guarantee the fair value of political liberties (publicly funded campaigns, etc.), as well as institutions that further fair equality of opportunity (extensive educational benefits, universal healthcare, steep estate taxes). Rawls does not take these more moderate forms of WSC into account, and many of his criticisms may not apply to them. Rawls seems primarily concerned with an idealization of the *capitalist* welfare state that only partly resembles these accounts and the Northern European welfare states that moderate capitalism with social democratic measures giving workers certain economic powers. Rawls seems to regard welfare-state capitalism, in its pure form, as embodying the "aims and principles" characteristic of some form of utilitarianism. I'll return to this momentarily.

But first, questions remain as to whether the fair value of the political liberties and fair equality of opportunity can be genuinely guaranteed in a capitalist welfare state that enacts campaign finance and other specific measures Rawls discusses. O'Neill correctly says that these are complicated issues of political sociology that philosophers cannot answer. But it is not unreasonable to conjecture that, so long as severe inequalities of income and wealth are allowed to endure in welfare-state capitalism, these inequalities will still "indirectly" affect election outcomes, equal access to the public political forum, and the political agenda (*JF*, 139). The less advantaged are not organized like the wealthy and cannot afford specialists and lobbyists to influence or draft legislation as corporations and business-friendly non-profits do today. Nor can they afford to employ "experts" or fund institutes that relentlessly promote the economic interests of the more advantaged on political talk shows and elsewhere. (That the least advantaged do not own and control newspapers, TV and radio stations, or entire communications networks that explicitly advocate their political and economic positions goes without saying.) These inequalities enable the more advantaged to "control the course of public debate" (*TJ* orig., 225). The campaign finance measures Rawls, Dworkin, and others support address only part of the problem of the deleterious effects of vast wealth inequalities on citizens' equal access to the public political forum. *A Theory of Justice* emphasizes that reducing inequalities is necessary to combat the deleterious effects of wealth on the basic liberties (*TJ* orig., 279) and to prevent concentrations of power detrimental to the fair value of political liberty. "The wide dispersal of property. . . is a necessary condition, it seems, if the fair value of the political liberties is to be maintained" (*TJ* orig., 277).

Moreover, given continual conflicts between capital and labor that typify capitalism, it is questionable whether WSC can sustain the procedures of public reasoning about justice and the common good essential to Rawls's account of POD. For example, even though a social minimum and welfare benefits (healthcare, unemployment insurance, etc.) may be widely accepted in WSC, class differences between capital and labor can lead to more frequent disputes over how these benefits are to be determined and responsibilities shared than in a POD governed by a conception of reciprocity.

Similar problems stem from the influence of large wealth inequalities in connection with fair equality of opportunity. The wealthy and more advantaged who control employment have closed social networks and do not associate with the less advantaged. Moreover, in spite of efforts to equalize opportunities, there are class differences in childrearing and socialization practices that provide enormous advantages to the more favored.[9] Even if (as Rawls says) these differences are inevitable given the institution of the family, the effects of familial sources of inequality of opportunity are only aggravated by increasing discrepancies in income and wealth. It is a sobering fact that in the United States, which instituted measures forty years ago enabling the less advantaged to attend college (Pell Grants, subsidized loans, etc.), still only 3 percent of children in the top 150 colleges come from the bottom income quartile.[10] These and other class-based differences provide social, educational, and employment opportunities to the more advantaged that are unavailable to the less advantaged. These inequalities of opportunity can be mitigated only by reducing the extensive inequalities of income, wealth, and economic powers that typify welfare-state capitalism.

Considerations such as these may underlie Rawls's claims in *A Theory of Justice*, §43, that the institutions protecting fair equality of opportunity "are put in jeopardy when inequalities of wealth exceed a certain limit; and political liberty likewise tends to lose its value, and representative government to become such in appearance only" (*TJ* orig., 278). The institutional measures he discusses to support the fair value of the political liberties and fair equality of opportunity should not be assumed exhaustive or sufficient to neutralize the effects of capitalist inequalities of wealth and guarantee these basic rights. The mitigation of economic inequality even beyond what is required by the difference principle may be required.

Still, let's assume that there are forms of welfare-state capitalism that can effectively incorporate many of the institutional measures Rawls associates with property-owning democracy. Rawls was surely aware of these arrangements; indeed, some of the measures he mentions, though increasingly under attack since the 1980s, characterize the capitalist welfare state in the United States (campaign finance reforms, widespread education and job training programs, a once highly progressive tax rate on income, etc.). The reason that Rawls nonetheless presents WSC and POD as conflicting ideal institutional designs is that he regards them as incorporating different "public aims and principles of design" (JF, 137). Welfare-state capitalism is for Rawls a "liberalism of happiness," the public aim of which is promoting individuals' happiness or welfare. Its principle of design he sees as some form of utilitarianism. Rawls often said it's not a coincidence that the great classical economists of the nineteenth century, the primary advocates of laissez-faire, were all utilitarians.[11] Once the adverse effects of laissez-faire market distributions on the welfare of the poor, elderly, and disabled are taken into account, it is understandable why many twentieth-century utilitarians, including welfare economists, would advocate WSC.

To see capitalism as grounded in utilitarianism, or some form of welfarism that extolls economic efficiency, is not unreasonable.[12] Generally arguments in support of capitalism assume that the best life for individuals is one of consumption and that consumption is to be valued since it promotes individuals' welfare. What gets consumed must first be produced, and production depends upon economic incentives for individuals to expend efforts and take risks with the wealth at their disposal. Economic theory tells us that the motivational and informational benefits of free markets and private property in means of production outstrip any alternative system of ownership in productive efficiency and economic output. Economic output for purposes of consumption should then be maximized in a capitalist economy.[13] Add to this the preferences individuals have for freedom of contract, the liberty to use their property as they choose, and other economic freedoms, and the utilitarian/welfarist case for capitalism seems very convincing.

Rawls's contrast between POD and WSC is intended to be a comparison of the institutional embodiments of two different kinds of philosophical conceptions of justice. POD and WSC may have many of the same elements, but there remains an important difference in the way these rights and benefits are interpreted and determined by the "aims and principles" implicit in the different conceptions of justice underlying these political and economic systems. The measures taken in WSC governed by utilitarianism to maintain the value of political liberties and guarantee equal opportunity and a social minimum differ in important respects from those taken in a POD governed by Rawls's two principles of justice. For example, a primary consideration in the welfare state in determining a social minimum that meets basic needs will be maximizing (restricted or weighted) welfare, whereas in property-owning democracy, it is considerations of reciprocity.[14] That is the crucial comparison Rawls is setting up with his outline of these "ideal institutional designs."

For the remainder of this chapter I'll discuss the primary contrasts Rawls sees between property-owning democracy and welfare-state capitalism, focusing on the "aims and principles" he sees as embodied in each—justice as fairness with the difference principle, versus restricted utilitarianism. By "restricted utilitarianism" Rawls means a "mixed conception" that restricts the pursuit of social utility by recognizing equal basic liberties, equal opportunities, and a social minimum designed to meet basic needs.[15] While non-utilitarian advocates of the welfare state, and utilitarians who support positions to the left (or right) of it, may find Rawls's utilitarian welfare state to be a strawman, his exercise in comparison is still useful.[16] For it highlights a significant difference between welfare-state capitalism and property-owning democracy by focusing on a historically influential version of the welfare state—that of liberal economists, the vast majority of whom are utilitarians. The parallel between the development of the welfare state in the United States (perhaps the United Kingdom also) and welfare economics is too obvious to ignore. From this perspective, the role of the welfare state within capitalism is that of increasing the overall level of welfare in society by redistributions that mitigate poverty and provide all with adequate healthcare and other services needed for a decent life. The welfare capitalist focus on maximizing welfare while meeting basic needs provides a very different understanding of society and what it owes the less advantaged than does the idea of democratic reciprocity that informs Rawls's difference principle and his account of property-owning democracy.

4. The Difference Principle
and Property-Owning Democracy

Rawls contends that welfare-state capitalism fails to achieve reciprocity in economic relations; also, it marginalizes the least advantaged, who regard themselves as outsiders, and it undermines their sense of self-respect. In arguing for the difference principle, Rawls makes similar arguments against utilitarianism. In this section I discuss three main arguments Rawls makes for the difference principle and how they support property-owning democracy.

4.1. Democratic Reciprocity

Rawls relies on several ideas of reciprocity throughout his works. He says social cooperation, unlike socially coordinated behavior, involves reciprocity: all who do their part are to benefit (*PL*, 16–17). Reciprocity, Rawls also says, is a "deep psychological fact" (*TJ*, 433), for the sense of justice is regulated by three "reciprocity principles" that are "psychological laws" (*TJ* orig., 499–501; *TJ*, 437–39). Moreover, public reason involves a "criterion of reciprocity," requiring citizens to propose only those fair terms of cooperation they reasonably believe are reasonable for others to accept as free and equal citizens (*PL*, 446). Finally, important for our purposes, the difference principle is said to involve "a deeper idea of reciprocity" than alternatives, or "reciprocity at the deepest level" (*JF*, 124, 49). I call this deeper idea "democratic reciprocity."

Rawls provides two clues to what he means by "reciprocity at the deepest level." First, there is Rawls's familiar graph (see the preceding chapter, figure 3.1) comparing the relative positions of the most and least advantaged groups (MAG and LAG, respectively) under the difference principle (point D) versus the principle of (average) utility (B, the Bentham point) (*JF*, 62).[17]

Rawls claims that reciprocity is realized when society is on the upwardly rising slope of the OP efficient production curve (O = equality; P = production); for at any point on the upwardly rising slope, increases in the share of primary goods going to the MAG correspond with increases for the LAG, and increases in the share of the LAG correspond with increases for the MAG. Societies should always aspire to be on the upwardly rising slope of this curve, Rawls says. Democratic reciprocity is fully achieved when society is at point D, the highest point on the efficient production curve; at this point the share going to the LAG is maximized, given current levels of technology, resources, and so on. Any points to the right of D, on the downwardly sloping curve, involve further increases in the share going to the MAG that come at the expense of the less advantaged.

Rawls gives a second clue to what he means by "reciprocity at the deepest level":

> The deeper idea of reciprocity implicit in [the difference principle] is that social institutions are not to take advantage of contingencies of native endowment, or of initial social position, or of good or bad luck over the course of a life, except in ways that benefit everyone, including the least favored . . . This idea of reciprocity is implicit in the idea of regarding the distributions of native endowments as a common asset. Parallel but not identical considerations hold for the contingencies of social position and good and bad luck. (*JF*, 124)

Why should democratic reciprocity required by the difference principle matter to the parties in the original position and to the free and equal moral persons they represent in a well-ordered society? The problem of distributive justice as Rawls defines it is the appropriate division of a social product that is the consequence not only of citizens' cooperative efforts but also of morally arbitrary facts. These include the distribution of natural talents by the "natural lottery," the social class people are born into, and accidents of fortune and misfortune that people experience during their lives. All of these arbitrary contingencies contribute to market luck, or the economic contingencies of markets, which include the availability of productive resources, the size of the labor pool and the number of people with similar skills, the level of unemployment, and many other accidents of supply and demand affecting prices and market distributions. Given all these contingencies, free and equal moral persons with a sense of justice would find it unfair and unreasonable to depart from the deeper reciprocity realized by the difference principle in distributing the benefits of economic cooperation. Rawls's argument from democratic reciprocity resembles a contractualist argument which says that, among reasonable citizens in a well-ordered society, it would be unreasonable to reject the difference principle, since that would require that we distribute the result of arbitrary contingencies (including market luck) in ways that make those with greater income and wealth better off at the expense of the least advantaged members of society. Since free and equal citizens in a well-ordered society would find this an unreasonable demand, it is not rational for the parties in the original position to prefer the principle of restricted utility or other principles to the difference principle.

Here, it is noteworthy that Rawls recognizes that there may be some other reciprocity condition that supplies appropriate standards of distribution. "We haven't shown there is no other such condition, but it is hard to imagine what it might be" (*JF*, 124). Some have raised the question, why should departures from equality on grounds of arbitrary contingencies be permitted at all? For Rawls, inequalities are permissible if not required by justice to call forth citizens' greater efforts, contributions, and willingness to undertake economic risks, on the assumption that we are not impartially benevolent but have special ties and commitments, and endorse a plurality of values and different conceptions of our good, and for these reasons we respond to incentives and the expectation of added advantages.

After Rawls wrote the *Restatement* (in the early 1990s) at least two other prominent accounts of distributive justice, by Ronald Dworkin and G. A. Cohen, were developed that might be seen as raising the question, why wouldn't a still *deeper* level of reciprocity be achieved if the consequences of arbitrary contingencies were strictly treated as a common asset and were equally distributed, and differences in income and wealth were permitted only as a result of individuals' free choices? I cannot discuss these accounts here except to raise the question of whether these and other so-called luck-egalitarian accounts are really about reciprocity at all. They seem to interpret distributive justice more as a matter of *redress* or *compensation* for misfortune than as one of reciprocity among equal citizens who contribute their fair share to the social product and share in the division of social benefits and burdens. Because luck egalitarians focus, not on reciprocity among socially productive citizens, but on redressing arbitrary contingencies and compensating those disadvantaged by arbitrary inequalities, they are open to the claim that distributive justice should not be contingent upon social cooperation and contributing one's fair share but instead should be global in reach. Global egalitarianism, as some proponents contend, is a natural extension of luck-egalitarian views.[18]

Return now to the question, why does Rawls think that justice as fairness requires property-owning democracy rather than welfare-state capitalism? A distinctive feature of Rawls's difference principle is that it determines not simply how the social product is distributed among productive agents, but also how society is to structure ownership and divide up control of productive resources.[19] This directly bears on Rawls's argument for property-owning democracy over welfare-state capitalism. The capitalist welfare state concentrates social and economic powers and positions of authority and responsibility largely in the hands of a privileged class and regards claims of the less advantaged primarily as a matter of *compensating* them for their misfortunes and lack of income and other resources needed to satisfy their basic needs. Having a share of productive wealth and exercising economic powers and positions of responsibility are not among the basic needs of citizens in the capitalist welfare state.

In this connection, Rawls says that WSC focuses on "the redistribution of income at the end of each period," whereas POD "ensures the widespread ownership of productive assets and human capital (that is, education and trained skills) at the beginning of each period" (JF, 139; TJ, xv).

> The intent is not simply to assist those who lose out through accident or misfortune (although that must be done), but rather to put all citizens in a position to manage their own affairs on a footing of a suitable degree of social and economic equality . . . The least advantaged are not, if all goes well, the unfortunate and unlucky objects of our charity and compassion, much less our pity but those to whom reciprocity is owed as a matter of political justice . . . Although they control fewer resources, they are doing their full share on terms recognized by all as mutually advantageous and consistent with everyone's self-respect. (JF, 139)

The clear implication here is that, for purposes of the difference principle, Rawls conceives of the least advantaged as *working members* of society, or the lowest paid and least skilled workers. The difference principle is not a principle of redress that responds to the basic needs of those who are disabled and unable or unwilling to work. Addressing individuals' basic needs for living a decent life—the driving impetus behind welfare-state capitalism—is important, a "constitutional essential," Rawls says. But he does not see addressing basic needs as a requirement of *distributive justice*. Distributive justice addresses the question of the fair distribution of the cooperatively produced social product among those who are "fully cooperative" citizens and actively engage in productive activity and contribute their "full share." This clarifies a further respect in which the difference principle realizes "reciprocity at the deepest level": it presupposes *productive reciprocity*,[20] that members of society contribute their full and fair share as a condition of their making distributive claims on the social product. "We are not to gain from the cooperative efforts of others without doing our fair share" (*TJ*, 301).

Rawls believed that all able-bodied persons should be encouraged to work or otherwise make legitimate economic contributions. Though he endorsed income subsidies and family allowances to supplement workers' market wage, he did not regard it as appropriate to provide people with "welfare" payments if they were able but unwilling to work (*CP*, 455n.; Rawls then rejects the idea of a universal basic income).[21] By providing a social minimum for all, whether they are able and willing to work or not, the welfare state can encourage dependence among the worst off and a feeling of being left out of society. Rawls thinks that part of being an independent person is to be in a position to provide for oneself while working in a way that is not demeaning or that otherwise undermines one's self-respect.

This is an appropriate place to emphasize what I take to be one of the main reasons for Rawls's support for POD and liberal socialism over the welfare state. It is easy to forget that among the primary goods whose distribution is determined by the difference principle are not only income and wealth, but also powers and positions as well as the social bases of self-respect. By powers and positions Rawls means in large part economic powers and prerogatives, and offices and positions of responsibility in production. A common criticism of the capitalist wage relationship is that it leaves workers powerless in their relationships with ownership and management. Workers do not own capital in the firm they work for or in other firms, receive none of their firm's profits, and have no economic powers or responsibilities in deciding the direction or policies of the firm or often even in taking initiatives in fulfilling their day-to-day responsibilities of employment. They must accept the market wage they are offered and the conditions of labor imposed upon them, however unpleasant and demeaning their work conditions might be.

To be in such a subservient position has serious consequences for worker's self- respect and their image of themselves as social equals. This is particularly true for the least advantaged, who are the least skilled and those most prone to being manipulated, if not dominated, and subject to duress and arbitrary treatment. One of the primary ways that property-owning democracy differs from welfare-state capitalism is that POD provides workers a share of productive capital in firms, as well as some degree of economic power, if not responsibility, within the firm they work in. This explains to a large extent why Rawls can argue that POD makes the least advantaged workers (the least paid and least skilled) better off than does WSC, in spite of potentially greater income supplements that WSC occasionally might provide the least advantaged. More on this later.

4.2. The Argument from Stability

The second ground for the difference principle Rawls discusses in comparing it with (average and restricted) utility is the greater stability of a well-ordered society governed by the difference principle. Stability is also one of the main grounds Rawls later mentions in favor of property-owning democracy over the capitalist welfare state. One conception of justice is more "stable" than another when it engages citizens' sense of justice and they are more prone to comply with its demands. Rawls in later works uses the term "stability for the right reasons."[22] This phrase suggests that people generally accept terms of social cooperation *because* they find them reasonable and morally justifiable, and not because of a modus vivendi based in a contingent balance of forces. A conception of justice is stable for the right reasons when free and equal citizens all endorse it and want to comply because it seems reasonable in light of relevant moral/political reasons, it engages their sense of justice, *and* it is "congruent" with their good and their reasonable comprehensive views.

Rawls's arguments for the stability of a well-ordered society are largely arguments about the reasonableness of conceptions of justice from the perspective of free and equal persons in a well-ordered society who are morally motivated and want to justify themselves to one another on terms that everyone can reasonably accept.[23] Moral persons with a sense of justice in a well-ordered democratic society will not generally accept principles of justice if they find that these principles place unreasonable demands on themselves or on others. According to the reciprocity argument discussed above, it would be unreasonable for free and equal moral persons to reject the difference principle in favor of restricted utility since that would require that they distribute the result of arbitrary contingencies (including the consequences of market luck) in ways that made those with greater income and wealth better off at the expense of the least advantaged members of society. Rawls's arguments from stability are not then simply arguments about human nature or what is rational for the interested parties to agree to in the original position to promote their good. What makes it rational (or not) to agree to a conception of justice in the original position turns in large part on whether the demands it imposes in society engage reasonable persons' sense of justice; and the answer to this question turns on whether the conception places reasonable or unreasonable demands on citizens in a well-ordered society who seek to justify their social relations with one another on terms that respect them as free and equal citizens and as rational moral persons.

Rawls makes several arguments for the greater relative stability of the difference principle over restricted utility and other "mixed conceptions" that guarantee a social minimum. The difference principle encourages the cooperative virtues and mutual trust among citizens since it is publicly understood that the three main kinds of contingencies (natural talents, social class, and accidents of fortune, including market luck) will be dealt with only in ways that are to the advantage of each person. Moreover, shifts in relative bargaining positions are much less likely to be exploited for self- or group-interested ends if all accept and are assured that the difference principle applies (*JF*, 126). Also, the difference principle relies upon easily accessible information (the least advantaged are identifiable by their share of income and wealth) and can be applied relatively straightforwardly in order to determine which policies are to their greatest advantage (*CP*, 229). The difference principle then resists temptations among the more advantaged to employ manipulation and instills greater mutual trust among citizens. Contrast this with the principle of utility: "[I]t is much more difficult to know what maximizes average utility" (*CP*, 229). There are competing conceptions of utility, none of which are likely to attain general acceptance; moreover, all are complex and difficult to apply in ways that elicit widespread assent. Ongoing disputes over these matters increase mistrust among individuals and groups. Moreover, "the principle of utility asks more of the less advantaged than the difference principle asks of the more advantaged" (*JF*, 127), and asking that the less advantaged accept fewer social and economic advantages for the sake of greater benefits to the more advantaged is an extreme and unreasonable demand. The extreme and pervasive inequalities permitted by the principle of utility are hard to accept and put excessive "strains of commitment" on the willingness of the least advantaged to accept society's principles of justice (*JF*, 127).

Given disagreements over the interpretation and application of the principle of utility, restricted utility provides no clear public criterion for determining the social minimum. Most likely it will rely upon an idea of basic needs essential for leading a decent human life. This and other intuitive ideas in societies regulated by restricted utility will be a constant source of political dispute between the more and less advantaged, with those better off taking advantage of their greater social and political powers to manipulate public opinion and limit the social minimum. A seemingly enduring feature of capitalist societies is that the more advantaged seek to manipulate opinion and reduce the social minimum since they feel they are saddled with the burden of paying for it, and with their superior political resources they often emerge victorious. This is a familiar feature of the welfare capitalist system in the United States, where social programs for the poor are constantly disparaged and liable to be defunded or eliminated, and the welfare state is subject to forces that drive it back toward the laissez-faire capitalism in place before the Great Depression.

The result of continuing uncertainty and ongoing disputes about the social minimum is that the less advantaged become resentful and feel left out of sharing in society's achievements of greater benefits. They become withdrawn and cynical about public life; rather than seeing themselves as full members of society, they regard themselves as outsiders who are not relevant to it. As a result they cannot wholly affirm, if they do so at all, society's principles of justice (*JF*, 128–30).

This last argument, which Rawls makes against the stability of restricted utility, is much the same argument he makes against welfare-state capitalism. Rawls says that "the concept of a minimum as covering the needs essential for a decent human life is a concept for a capitalist welfare state" (*JF*, 129). Rawls does not reject the idea of basic needs or a decent minimum; one of the essential criteria of any liberal (if not decent) society is that it meets the basic needs of all persons in society, particularly the disabled. But satisfaction of the basic needs of the disabled is different from the reciprocity requirements of distributive justice among "fully cooperative" citizens. In effect, Rawls's objection to welfare-state capitalism is that it treats the poorest members of the working classes as if they were disabled, for it applies to them the same standard of meeting their basic needs. If fully cooperative free and equal moral persons

> are not to withdraw from their public world but are to consider themselves fully members of it, *the social minimum, whatever it may provide beyond essential human needs, must derive from an ideal of reciprocity* appropriate to political society so conceived. While a social minimum covering only those essential needs may suit the requirements of a capitalist welfare state, it is not sufficient for . . . a property-owning democracy in which the principles of justice are realized. (*JF*, 130; emphasis added)

4.3. Publicity and Self-Respect

Rawls's claim that the least advantaged in WSC are prone to withdrawing from society relates to a third argument for the difference principle, from the primary social good of self-respect. The argument from publicity and self-respect is one of the main grounds Rawls gives in *A Theory of Justice*, §29, for the parties' choice of the principles of justice over average and classical utility. He argues that equal basic liberties and fair opportunities are the main social bases of self-respect, for they are institutional expressions of the freedom and equality of moral persons. Moreover, the reciprocity guaranteed by the difference principle is a public expression of persons' "respect for one another in the very constitution of their society. In this way they insure their self-respect" (*TJ*, 156). Rawls's claim then is that democratic reciprocity embodied in the difference principle is an expression of persons' respect for one another, which in turn is among the bases of their self-respect. This appeal to respect for persons leads into Rawls's Kantian interpretation of the difference principle:

> [T]he difference principle interprets the distinction between treating men as means only and *treating them also as ends in themselves*. To regard persons as ends in themselves in the basic design of society is to agree to forgo those gains that do not contribute to everyone's expectations. By contrast, to regard persons as means is to be prepared to impose on *those already less favored* still lower prospects of life for the sake of the higher expectations of others. (*TJ*, 157, emphasis added)

The principle of utility requires the less fortunate to accept lower life prospects for the sake of others who are more advantaged. "In a public utilitarian society men, particularly the least advantaged, will find it more difficult to be confident of their own worth" (*TJ*, 158).

Though framed to apply to a utilitarian society, this Kantian argument from respect and self-respect retains much of its force when applied to a liberal welfare state governed by restricted utility. Even though a social minimum is guaranteed, it is determined not by appeal to mutual respect and reciprocity but by a conception of basic needs, weighted utilities, and greater overall welfare. In such a welfare capitalist society, citizens are more likely to regard the least advantaged as imposing social costs and burdens on others for not pulling their own weight; there is ongoing public disagreement about basic needs and the level of a decent minimum required to meet them. The least advantaged are less likely to see themselves as economically independent and as deserving of others' respect. This aggravates their tendencies to alienate themselves from public life due to what they might see (justifiably) as public shaming by others. The damage to their self-respect, though not as severe as that caused by invidious discrimination and denial of equal liberties or fair opportunities, is serious.[24] This argument from self-respect favoring the difference principle over restricted utility readily applies to the comparison between POD and WSC.

The social basis of self-respect is a primary justification for POD over WSC.[25] In a welfare capitalist society, where the social minimum is determined by a conventional understanding of basic needs that are to be met by ex post welfare payments, the least advantaged are thought of and see themselves as dependent on others' largesse. This contrasts with POD, where all citizens have a share of society's capital ex ante, receive income from it, and (if all goes well) have no need of income supports. Productive members of the least advantaged class then have more reason to see themselves as contributing their fair share to society and as not dependent on others for income or meeting their wants and needs.

Moreover, since POD also gives all productive citizens a share of economic powers and responsibilities in their employment, workers are not put in the subservient wage relationship typical of capitalism. They have a say in decisions regarding their day-to-day work activities and have representatives with a significant role in managing or policing the management of the firm. In these respects, citizens in a POD have the opportunity to exercise economic agency in addition to the political agency guaranteed by equal political rights. Both are among the social bases of self-respect.[26]

5. *Fair Equality of Opportunity in Property-Owning Democracy versus the Welfare State*

The basic aim of fair equality of opportunity (FEO) is twofold: first, to give everyone with the same talents and abilities, regardless of social background, a fair chance to compete for and achieve educational and employment positions; second, to maintain "roughly the same prospects of culture and achievement for those similarly motivated and endowed" (*JF*, 44). This second aspect, the prospects of culture and achievement, does not have to be tied to the first, that is, to fair competition for employment (so I will argue).

The primary measures Rawls discusses for achieving fair equality of opportunity include widespread educational opportunities for all (including job retraining), universal healthcare,[27] and the adjustment of long-term trends of a market economy to prevent excessive accumulations of property and wealth that would undermine fair opportunities and lead to political domination (*JF*, 44). FEO calls for limiting inequalities in income by progressive income taxes (*TJ* orig., 279) and restricting intergenerational transfers of wealth by progressive estate taxes or by inheritance taxes at the receiver's end to encourage the wide dispersal of wealth. Also, FEO justifies restrictions on "private" discrimination on grounds of race, gender, religion, and so on by employers and non-public educational institutions, through such measures as the 1964 Civil Rights Act in the United States.[28]

Rawls claims POD differs from WSC in requiring fair equality of opportunity. While WSC goes beyond laissez-faire in requiring more than merely formal equal opportunities by publicly funded education and health care for all, for example, Rawls says it does not go far enough. Martin O'Neill questions this argument, saying that WSC is capable of providing FEO, as Rawls defines it.[29] And indeed, Rawls himself earlier says that the system of "Liberal Equality" guarantees a form of fair equality of opportunity (*TJ*, 12). Liberal Equality resembles WSC since both endorse market efficiencies and distributions while providing a social minimum meeting the basic needs of the least advantaged.[30] Moreover, many of the institutions Rawls mentions as necessary for FEO are to some degree found in existing WSC societies. Also, many welfare states, even the United States before the 1980s, have steeply progressive income and estate taxes (more than 75 percent for the top bracket in the United States in 1970).[31] In what sense then is it *not* open to a capitalist welfare state to take its duties to the less advantaged more seriously and realize fair equality of opportunity?

There are perhaps two features of Rawls's understanding of WSC that prevent it from realizing FEO in the broad sense in which he understands that idea. First, there is an egalitarian aspect of FEO that conflicts with WSC, especially when interpreted in terms of (restricted) utilitarianism or where the principle of efficiency predominates. Second, there is Rawls's association of capitalism with "meritocratic" societies.

There is a narrow interpretation of FEO that fits with WSC, where its primary purpose is to educate individuals so that they maximize the development of their productive capacities. Individuals are to be educated commensurate with their talents and motivations so that they are prepared for fair competition for employment in the open positions arising within a free-market capitalist economy. On this understanding of FEO, education benefits will be unequally distributed largely in favor of those who are naturally more talented than others, on the assumption that their talents are more worthwhile to society and justify the expense of lengthier education and training.[32] The implication of this narrow reading is that (as Rawls says of Liberal Equality), it corrects for inequalities of social class in the competition for social positions by providing the talented similar educational opportunities regardless of social class. This does nothing, however, to compensate for the consequences of natural inequalities. Indeed, FEO narrowly construed may even aggravate the effects of unequal natural talents by generating greater social inequalities between the more and less talented.[33]

When Rawls discusses FEO combined with the difference principle in the position he calls "Democratic Equality," he construes it more broadly than the narrow understanding initially set forth in conjunction with Liberal Equality. He sees FEO as imposing more direct limitations on the degree of inequality in income and wealth than would otherwise be allowed by WSC, or even by the difference principle (*TJ* orig., 278–79). The institutions protected by FEO "are put in jeopardy when inequalities of wealth exceed a certain limit" (*TJ* orig., 278).

Moreover, in Democratic Equality realized in POD, fair equality of opportunity should not result in pronounced inequalities of educational benefits that favor the more talented. Because of the reciprocity requirements of justice as fairness, "the priority of fair opportunity . . . means that we must appeal to the chances given to those with the lesser opportunity" (*TJ* orig., 301). Unlike the narrow role it has within Liberal Equality and WSC, fair equality of opportunity in POD is not part of a meritocratic social system that rewards talent in order to promote economic efficiency over other social values (*TJ* orig., 84; *TJ*, 73). "Equality of opportunity does not mean the opportunity to leave the less fortunate behind in the personal quest for influence and social position" (*TJ* orig., 106). Instead it requires that all citizens be given greater educational and cultural benefits, regardless of their talents, so that they are able to fully develop their capacities, in order to effectively take advantage of the full range of opportunities available in society and to instill a sense of their self-worth.

> We must when necessary take into account the primary good of self-respect . . . The confident sense of their own self-worth should be sought for the least favored and this limits the forms of hierarchy and the degrees of inequality that justice permits. Thus, for example, resources for education are not to be allotted solely or necessarily mainly according to their return as estimated in productive trained abilities, but also according to their worth in enriching the personal and social lives of citizens, including here the least favored. As a society progresses the latter consideration becomes increasingly more important. (*TJ* orig., 107; *TJ*, 91–92).

Unlike its narrow role in Liberal Equality and welfare-state capitalism, the primary aim of fair equality of opportunity in Democratic Equality and property-owning democracy is not technological advancement or encouraging a meritocracy to achieve greater productive efficiency and maximum national wealth. It is rather the egalitarian aim of guaranteeing an important social basis of self-respect for all citizens without regard to their natural abilities. When citizens are rendered unable to fully develop their capacities, those excluded are "debarred from experiencing the realization of self which comes from a skillful and devoted exercise of social duties. They would be deprived of one of the main forms of human good" (*TJ* orig., 84; *TJ*, 73).

Here again, it is notable that Rawls does not mention, in connection with Liberal Equality, that FEO requires mitigating inequalities of wealth. It is hard to see how FEO's egalitarian requirements could apply with much force within a capitalist welfare state where distributive justice is determined by the principles of utility or efficiency with a social minimum, or even by a prioritarian account of utility that gives greater weight to the utility of the less advantaged.

To sum up, Rawls says WSC realizes fair equality of opportunity to some degree, and even suggests a version of WSC, Liberal Equality, that incorporates FEO along with the principle of efficiency. But the "guiding aims and principles" of WSC do not seek to limit inequalities in the primary social goods that are necessary for achieving FEO in its full democratic sense. Just as reciprocity is not a "guiding aim" of WSC, so too restricting inequalities in relevant primary social goods—income, wealth, and social and economic powers—in order to guarantee fair equality of opportunity and the fair value of the political liberties is not a guiding aim of welfare-state capitalism either. Fair equality of opportunity in a property-owning democracy, unlike a capitalist welfare state, is understood in light of the ideals of persons as free and equal and of society as grounded in democratic reciprocity and mutual respect. Having fair opportunities that put citizens in a position to develop and exercise their talents and abilities, however modest they may be, is required to maintain citizens' equal status and self-respect as free and equal citizens who are capable of being fully cooperative over a complete lifetime. This broader reading of FEO fits with Rawls's emphasis on the role of the Aristotelian Principle in informing individuals' rational good—his contention that it is rational for free and equal moral persons to normally prefer activities and ways of life that exercise and develop their human capacities (*TJ* orig., §65; *TJ*, §65).

6. *Fair Equality of Opportunity to Exercise Economic Powers*

Rawls says the idea of fair equality of opportunity "is a difficult and not altogether clear idea" (*JF*, 43). Now I will suggest that its lack of clarity may be a virtue, since it leaves room for a still broader interpretation of FEO that allows for a third aspect, which is needed to fill a gap in Rawls's arguments for property-owning democracy. I argue in this section that, if economic agency is to have anywhere near the importance that political agency does in Rawls's account of property-owning democracy, then exercise of economic powers must be given greater weight than the difference principle allows (due to their potential trade-offs with greater income and wealth). Rawls says there is no basic liberty for individuals to exercise control over means of production. So, unlike the rights of political agency, economic powers necessary for economic agency cannot be guaranteed by Rawls's first principle. The only alternative is to see economic agency as part of the fair equality of opportunity principle.

The problem is this: we might conjecture the feasibility of a capitalist welfare state like Liberal Equality that enacts measures to promote to some degree fair value of the political liberties and fair equality of opportunity but without constraining inequalities of wealth. Because of wealth inequalities and incentives for the more advantaged, this capitalist welfare state is able to supply the least advantaged with income supplements and other welfare benefits that exceed the index of primary goods achievable within a property-owning democracy that provides the least advantaged with less income but a share of real capital and greater economic powers. One of the features of capitalism often cited in its favor is that it is capable of producing greater overall wealth and income than any other economic system, leaving more to redistribute in the form of welfare benefits to the less advantaged.

Imagine then a welfare capitalist society that provides income supplements to the least advantaged so that their hourly wage with benefits is $22 (= $44,000 yearly income). Were the same society's economy restructured as a POD, the least advantaged workers would receive $15 per hour plus dividends from a share of society's productive wealth, for an annual income of $36,000. It is not difficult to imagine least skilled workers in the capitalist society preferring a WSC yearly pay package of $44,000 to the $36,000 plus greater economic powers than they would achieve in POD. Since they are guaranteed equal basic liberties and fair opportunities anyway, the marginal damage to their self-respect that comes from receiving greater ex post income supplements instead of ex ante ownership of productive wealth and economic powers in their workplace might seem insignificant to them—not worth the loss of $8,000 per year in income to many of them. On these grounds, it has been argued that Rawls's contention that, under ideal conditions of a well-ordered society, POD satisfies the difference principle while WSC does not must be mistaken. It is at least as likely that WSC will satisfy the difference principle too under ideal but feasible conditions of a well-ordered society.[34]

One way to deal with this scenario is to assign greater weight to economic powers and the social bases of self-respect in constructing the index of primary social goods. This may seem ad hoc and unconvincing to advocates of capitalism who value increased income and consumption over exercising economic powers and having a share of productive wealth. In response to a similar objection, I have argued that a way to avoid this problem that fits with Rawls's emphasis on economic agency is to regard the possession of continual opportunities to exercise economic powers and responsibilities in one's work as among the conditions of fair equality of opportunity.[35] Then the lexical priority of FEO over the difference principle would insulate POD from the objection above. Even if workers might receive greater income in WSC and many prefer it to the combined index of primary goods that includes economic powers and positions of responsibility they would have in a POD, still the priority of fair equality of opportunity over the difference principle requires that they not alienate their fair opportunities to exercise economic powers and responsibilities. Like the rights and powers of political agency, free and equal citizens do not have a right to alienate the powers and responsibilities of economic agency.

The suggestion then is that the principle of fair equality of opportunity requires not simply (as Rawls says) fair opportunities to compete for open positions and ongoing opportunities to take advantage of educational and cultural resources; it also requires ongoing opportunities for citizens to exercise economic powers and some degree of freedom and control in their work, thereby assuming a degree of initiative and responsibility. There are then several noteworthy differences between POD and WSC on this democratic interpretation of Rawls's fair equality of opportunity principle. First, as mentioned earlier, in POD, unlike Liberal Equality, ongoing educational and cultural opportunities are available to all without regard to their natural talents or considerations of economic efficiency. Second, the kinds of open employment positions that individuals have opportunities to compete for in POD will not be the same as those in a WSC society, like Liberal Equality, which is oriented toward economic efficiency and technocratic values. Within WSC the occupations and open positions available to members of society are largely determined by market considerations of economic efficiency and maximizing overall wealth in society. As in the United States currently, the positions occupied by Wall Street financiers are among the most coveted by our most talented college students. In a POD, I've argued, these positions, if they exist at all, will have a different status and rewards attached to them. The same holds for many of the other essential occupational positions that sustain the severe inequalities of a capitalist economy. Finally, unlike (welfare-state) capitalism, where for reasons of maximum economic efficiency perhaps there is no opportunity for the less advantaged to exercise economic powers and responsibilities or even to own productive wealth, the ongoing accessibility of these primary goods to everyone, including the less advantaged, is an essential, perhaps the most distinctive, feature of a property-owning democracy.

What grounds are there for making this friendly amendment to Rawls's account? To begin with, for the least advantaged, like everyone else, it strengthens the social bases of self-respect to have ongoing opportunities to play an active role and take initiatives in their workplace, and not be subject to potentially rigid work restrictions and performing the same monotonous tasks all day. Having such powers and added responsibilities mitigates the harsher aspects of the division of labor for the least advantaged in low-skilled positions. Add to this the effects of having political powers within the firm to vote for management and/or representatives on boards of directors and to participate in making decisions regarding work rules, and even opportunities to participate through their representatives in making decisions regarding the firm's policies. Having these and other economic powers in the workplace are additional bases for self-respect that supplement those Rawls already alludes to in support of fair equality of opportunity, namely, continuing opportunities for educational and cultural resources to develop their capacities, including their "human capital" (*JF*, 139). The opportunity for less skilled workers to exercise developed capacities not just in their leisure time but in their workplace as well, by overcoming the subservience of the wage relationship through the assumption of economic powers and responsibilities, can play a crucial role in providing social bases of self-respect for free and equal citizens.

Finally, there are several passages in *A Theory of Justice* and *The Law of Peoples* where Rawls addresses "meaningful" work and the division of labor. Meaningful work is said to be among the "human goods" according to the Aristotelian Principle (*TJ*, 373), and the opportunity for meaningful work and occupation is a condition of "citizens' self-respect [and] their sense that they are members of society and not simply caught in it" (*LP*, 50). Also, in addressing a technocratic (presumably capitalist) society that requires ever-increasing wealth from one generation to the next, Rawls says: "What men want is *meaningful work in free association with others*, these associations regulating their relations to one another within a framework of just basic institutions. To achieve these states of things great wealth is not necessary" (*TJ* orig., 290; *TJ*, 257–58; emphasis added). Finally, in his discussion of the good of social union, Rawls says:

> A well-ordered society does not do away with the division of labor in the most general sense. To be sure, the worst aspects of this division can be surmounted: no one need be servilely dependent on others and made to choose between monotonous and routine occupations which are deadening to human thought and sensibility. Each can be offered a variety of tasks so that the different elements of his nature find a suitable expression. But even when work is meaningful for all, we cannot overcome, nor should we wish to, our dependence on others . . . The division of labor is overcome not by each becoming complete in himself, but by *willing and meaningful work within a just social union of social unions in which all can freely participate* as they so incline. (*TJ* orig., 529; *TJ*, 463; emphasis added)

These passages suggest that exercising one's capacities in work in a variety of meaningful tasks, and having the necessary economic powers enabling us to do so, are among the social bases of self-respect and an aspect of good of free and equal rational persons. There is room for arguing within Rawls's position that the fair equality of opportunity principle provides citizens with ongoing opportunities throughout their lifetime, not only to cultivate and exercise their powers through their work, but to have the necessary economic powers enabling them to engage in meaningful work in a variety of activities.

Does this interpretation transform the fair equality of opportunity principle into a perfectionist principle? I do not think so. Rawls is not saying that meaningful work or exercising our socially productive capacities "in free association with others" is necessary for self-realization and the human good. He is rather making an empirical claim supported by a "psychological law," the Aristotelian Principle, about the rational life plans that would be chosen by free and equal persons in deliberative rationality. This supports the further claim that for the vast majority of individuals, meaningful work, or at least non-subservience in work, is part of their rational good, if not essential to it. This is sufficient on a liberal view to justify giving everyone ongoing opportunities in their work situation to exercise economic powers and responsibilities enabling them to achieve their essential good, including their self-respect as equal persons. Those who have no interest in exercising economic powers and for whom their work means little—who would rather just tend to their simplified assigned tasks, avoid work whenever possible, draw their pay, and afterward go out and enjoy it—are not required to exercise economic powers or to participate in workers' decisions. But even for them, not being subject to conditions of "wage slavery," where their every action is monitored and regulated and they are liable to be dismissed for arbitrary reasons, is almost surely part of anyone's rational good. Especially for the least advantaged workers who have few if any employment options, having some degree of latitude and freedom on the job without fear of being dismissed is important and might be sufficient to make their work meaningful from their own perspective. Perhaps this is already taken care of by grounds relating to social bases of self-respect in the difference principle, but it warrants reinforcement. I'm suggesting that there may be room within Rawls's liberal principle of fair opportunities to appeal to such values as "meaningful work in free association with others" in order to guarantee citizens continuing opportunities throughout their lives to exercise economic powers and responsibilities. These values are realizable for *all* citizens in a property-owning democracy but not in welfare-state capitalism.

7. *Conclusion*

Though it was touched upon earlier, I have not discussed in detail the role of the fair value of the political liberties in Rawls's argument for property-owning democracy and against welfare-state capitalism. This is necessary to fully appreciate Rawls's predilection for POD over WSC. I've noted that liberal advocates of the welfare state, such as Dworkin, endorse many of the measures Rawls advocates, such as campaign finance restrictions, to achieve political equality. Still, there are two aspects of Rawls's conception of democratic government that may not be endorsable by proponents of the capitalist welfare state, particularly the utilitarian version Rawls focuses on.

First, there are restrictions on inequalities of income, wealth, and economic powers that are required in order to achieve the fair value of the political liberties. It is not clear how extensive these restrictions would have to be. Rawls says little about this crucial issue. It may be that their requirements are so stringent that any social and economic system that realized them could no longer be regarded as a form of capitalism.

Second, there is Rawls's claim that a POD based in the principles of justice will be a deliberative democracy, which involves public reasoning about laws designed to promote the common good and the fundamental interests of free and equal citizens. Rawls understood citizens' common good in terms of such values of justice as freedom, equality, the moral powers, fair opportunities, and economic reciprocity. He associated democratic capitalism with majoritarian democracy and a conflict of class interests, with little public reasoning about requirements of justice and the common good. Even if it be argued, in defense of the utilitarian capitalist welfare state, that maximizing restricted (average) utility weighted in favor of the least advantaged is the common good that democratic legislators should promote, this sort of prioritarianism is still geared toward maximizing welfare and does not guarantee democratic reciprocity and mutual respect among free and equal citizens, the fundamental grounds of Rawls's conception of a just and well-ordered property-owning democracy.[36]

Notes

1. G. A. Cohen, *Rescuing Justice and Equality* (Cambridge MA: Harvard University Press, 2008), 138.
2. Rawls uses the term "property-owning democracy" but five times in the original edition of *A Theory of Justice* (78, 274, 279); he does not mention the welfare state or welfare-state capitalism at all.
3. In these three, and other, respects laissez-faire capitalism differs from Nozick's libertarianism, which rejects public goods, a social minimum, and contract restrictions.
4. John Roemer, *A Future for Socialism* (Cambridge MA: Harvard University Press, 1994).
5. John Rawls, *The Law of Peoples* (Cambridge, MA: Harvard University Press, 1999), 50; *LP* in further citations of this work.
6. See Waheed Hussain, "Nurturing the Sense of Justice: The Rawlsian Argument for Democratic Corporatism," in *Property Owning Democracy: Rawls and Beyond*, ed. Martin O'Neill and Thad Williamson (Oxford: Wiley-Blackwell, 2012), 180–200, who argues that within Rawls's framework, workers' co-determination rights should be just as significant as equal political liberties.
7. Rawls refers to James E. Meade, *Efficiency, Equality, and the Ownership of Property* (London: George Allen & Unwin, 1964) in *A Theory of Justice* in discussing POD (*TJ*, 241–42). Meade assumed that the typical arrangement would be the corporation where workers might have some ownership interest in firms they worked for but also would own stock in many other firms.
8. Martin O'Neill, "Free and Fair Markets without Capitalism," in O'Neill and Williamson, *Property Owning Democracy* (75–100); Ben Jackson, "Property Owning Democracy: A Short History," in O'Neill and Williamson, *Property Owning Democracy* (33–52).
9. Annette Lareau, *Unequal Childhood*, rev. ed. (Berkeley: University of California Press, 2011).
10. Andrew DelBlanco, *College: What It Was, Is, and Should Be* (Princeton, NJ: Princeton University Press, 2012).

11. John Rawls, *Lectures on the History of Political Philosophy*, ed. Samuel Freeman (Cambridge, MA: Harvard University Press, 2007), 162; *LHPP* in further references to this work.

12. David Gauthier's social contract doctrine, while not utilitarian, is still a form of welfarism with the principle of Pareto efficiency playing a predominant role.

13. Jon Elster, "Self-Realization in Work and Politics: The Marxist Conception of the Good Life," in *Alternatives to Capitalism*, ed. Jon Elster and Karl O. Moane (Cambridge: Cambridge University Press, 1989), 127–58.

14. In *A Theory of Justice* Rawls also discusses "mixed conceptions" that determine a social minimum by intuitive balancing of the principle of utility with an equality principle. See *TJ*, 279.

15. John Roemer said in discussion that, rather than utilitarianism, it is better to see the welfare state as grounded in a kind of prioritarianism that maximizes weighted utilities, giving greater weight to basic needs. Rawls probably would have regarded prioritarianism as a form of what he called "restricted utilitarianism."

16. Ben Jackson noted in discussion that Rawls relied upon James Meade's account of POD and that Meade himself was a utilitarian. Being an economist, Meade's utilitarianism comes as no surprise. Also, unlike today, there were few readily available philosophical alternatives to utilitarianism before the 1971 publication of *A Theory of Justice*.

17. See also *TJ*, §13, fig. 6.

18. For example, Kok-Chor Tan, *Justice, Institutions, and Luck* (Oxford: Oxford University Press, 2012).

19. "A scheme of cooperation is given in large part by how its public rules organize productive activity, specify the division of labor, assign various roles to those engaged in it, and so on. These schemes include schedules of wages and salaries to be paid out of output" (*JF*, 63).

20. Stuart White uses this term in "Property-Owning Democracy and Republican Citizenship," in O'Neill and Williamson, *Property Owning Democracy*, 129–46.

21. See Phillippe Van Parijs, *Real Freedom for All: What (if Anything) Can Justify Capitalism?* (Oxford: Oxford University Press, 1998).

22. *PL*, xli, 390, 392.

23. This parallels T. M. Scanlon's claim that, except for maximin, Rawls's other arguments for the principles of justice can be "interpreted as arguments within the form of contractualism which I have been proposing." See Scanlon, "Contractualism and Utilitarianism," in *Utilitarianism and Beyond*, ed. Amartya Sen and Bernard Williams (Cambridge: Cambridge University Press, 1982), 127.

24. Joshua Cohen ("Democratic Equality," *Ethics* 99 [1989]: 727–51) emphasizes the central role of the social bases of self-respect in justifying the difference principle over "mixed conceptions" that guarantee a social minimum. Rawls cites Cohen's article, saying it is a "very full and accurate account of the difference principle" (*JF*, 43 n. 3).

25. Martin O'Neill ("Free and Fair Markets without Capitalism") contends that the social basis of self-respect is the primary reason for Rawls's arguments for POD over WSC.

26. Waheed Hussain ("Nurturing the Sense of Justice") and Nien-hê Hsieh ("Work, Ownership, and Productive Enfranchisement," in O'Neill and Williamson, *Property Owning Democracy*, 149–62) both emphasize the central role of economic agency and workers' enfranchisement in Rawls's account of POD.

27. *PL*, 184.

28. Rawls neither explicitly endorsed nor objected to "affirmative action," or preferential treatment for disadvantaged minorities. In conversation he did say that it would be appropriate as a provisional measure in non-ideal conditions, to address the ongoing effects of racial and other forms of discrimination against underrepresented minorities.

29. O'Neill, "Free and Fair Markets without Capitalism," 84.

30. Liberal Equality's provision of a social minimum is not suggested in *A Theory of Justice*, but is implicit in Rawls's later claim that a constitutional essential of any liberal society is a social minimum, or "adequate all-purpose means" to exercise freedoms (*PL*, xlviii, 228; *LP*, 15, 49–50: JF, 48).

31. *New York Times*, Sunday Review, April 15, 2012.

32. See Thomas Nagel, *Concealment and Exposure: And Other Essays* (Oxford: Oxford University Press, 2004), 127, who seems to interpret FEO this way.

33. James Meade remarks on this effect, in *Efficiency, Equality, and the Ownership of Property* (London: George Allen & Unwin, 1964).

34. See John Tomasi, *Free Market Fairness* (Princeton, NJ: Princeton University Press, 2012), 226–37; see also Jason Brennan, "Rawls's Paradox," *Constitutional Political Economy* 18 (2007): 287–99. One response to their scenario is that, because of the inequalities it allows, no form of capitalism can provide for the fair value of political liberties and fair equality of opportunity. Tomasi denies this.

35. Samuel Freeman, *Justice and the Social Contract* (New York: Oxford University Press, 2007), 135–36.

36. I am grateful for comments from participants in a political philosophy workshop at NYU in 2012, including Charles Beitz, Liam Murphy, Thomas Nagel, John Roemer, Seana Schiffrin, T.M. Scanlon, and Samuel Scheffler; also to the participants at a conference on property owning democracy at the University of Zurich in 2012, including Francis Cheneval, Martin O'Neill, Christian Schemmel, and Thad Williamson; and to participants at a conference on "Unpacking Rawls," at Centro Einaudi, Turin, Italy in 2012.

5

Private Law and Rawls's
Principles of Justice

1. Introduction

John Rawls never mentions "private law." This is not surprising since this term is characteristic of civil law systems and was not prevalent in the Anglo-American common law system he was familiar with. But then Rawls did not have much more to say about the specific application of his principles of justice to specific areas covered by private law either, including the law of contract, torts, real and personal property, restitution and unjust enrichment, private trusts, wills and estates, and other areas. When Rawls discusses law, it is mainly public law, including taxation and constitutional law, and especially the constitutional guarantee of the basic liberties and equal opportunity, both of which are, he says, "constitutional essentials."[1] Rawls says the second principle, including *fair* equality of opportunity and the difference principle, is not a constitutional essential and applies at the legislative stage to social and economic legislation.[2] But in his discussion of property-owning democracy, which primarily addresses public law, he does not say much about what sort of private law system this would involve.

Commentators differ on the question of whether private law is part of the basic structure of society in Rawls's view, and especially whether the second principle applies to private law at all. Anthony Kronman wrote an early article contending that the difference principle should be applied directly to contract law, even though Rawls purportedly suggests it does not so apply.[3] Liam Murphy also suggests that Rawls's application of the second principle to the basic structure means that the difference principle is purely a matter of public law, especially taxation for purposes of the redistribution of income and wealth that results from free-market transactions. But otherwise for Rawls individuals should be left free to enter into economic contracts and transactions unconstrained by requirements of distributive justice set forth in the second principle.[4] Arthur Ripstein agrees with this interpretation of Rawls and endorses it; private law "has a certain kind of independence" and should lie outside the basic structure and governed by something other than the two principles of justice.[5] By contrast, Kevin Kordana and David Blankfein-Tabachnick argue that the principles of justice, including the difference principle, do apply to private law, not only the law of property and the law of contract, but also tort law.[6] Recently Samuel Scheffler contends that the difference principle applies to the law of contract as well as property.[7]

My position is that Rawls conceived the principles of justice as applying directly to the regulation of laws in terms of contractual agreements and individuals' use, control, and disposal of possessions in which they claim property. Moreover, the first principle of justice and the principle of fairness are relevant to tort law since tortious conduct can undermine the effective exercise of the basic liberties and the capacity to take advantage of fair opportunities. But the difference principle itself does not apply to most if not all tort law. In this respect at least, the role of the difference principle differs from the role assigned to the principle of efficiency in law and economics, which by its terms applies to all of private law, including contract, tort, and property law and other domains.

I begin in section 2 with the easiest case, the application of the principles of justice to the private law of property, which Rawls explicitly says is part of the basic structure. Here I distinguish between personal property, which is a basic right according to the first principle, and property rights in economic resources used in the course of production, commercial transfer, and distribution of economic goods and services, which is covered by the difference principle. Sections 3 and 4 address the application of the principles of justice to contract law. I contend that both the first and second principles have their range of application to rules of contract, with the first principle applying to the solidification of personal associations protected by the first principle (section 3) and fair equality of opportunity and the difference principle applying to the regulation of business law, including contracts involving production and commerce in goods and services (sections 4 and 5). The question of whether the principles of justice apply to tort law is addressed in section 6, where I contend that the first principle requires at least a right of compensation for civil wrongs (even if not traditional tort law of responsibility and fault) to "make whole" individuals' losses; but the difference principle does not apply to the determination of rules of responsibility and liability, certainly not in personal torts. I leave open the possibility that the difference principle and the principle of fairness may be relevant to some degree in deciding compensation for certain economic losses to others that regularly transpire in the course of doing business.

2. *The Principles of Justice and the Private Law of Property*

There are several passages in Rawls's works that suggest that the principles of justice would apply to determinations of private law. Rawls clearly thought that the principles of justice applied to the legal institution of property since, as he says repeatedly, property is one of the primary institutions constituting the basic structure of society. To begin with, the basic rights and liberties of freedom and integrity of the person require a right to hold and exclusively use personal property, since it is necessary for personal security, independence, and assuming control over one's life, and therewith is one of the institutional bases for self-respect.[8] Rawls regards the formal right to hold personal property (including the use of real property for personal purposes) as among the equal basic liberties that are necessary to give effect and value to core basic liberties of freedom of conscience, thought, association, and security and to freedom of the person. By extension, the formal right to hold personal property would have to include freedom of certain sorts of contracts. Without rights to acquire, use, control, and exchange the goods and possessions that are needed to give a person a sense of security and enable him or her to go out into the world to carry out primary purposes, a person is not able to effectively pursue a plan of life and establish worthwhile relationships with others. Perhaps the most fundamental justification of a system of property rules that guarantees secure and exclusive possession, use, and control over things is that individuals can then have a safe place to reside in and meet their basic needs and those of their loved ones, move about freely in the world, pursue their occupations and other purposes, and establish and nurture valuable relationships. Regardless of the economic system a person lives in, the right to hold personal property is a fundamental aspect of freedom of the person and hence the "rights and liberties guaranteeing the security and independence of citizens" (*PL*, 232).[9]

The first principle's guarantee of property rights in one's possessions is also necessary to give effect to the distributive shares guaranteed by the difference principle. If individuals did not have a secure right to possess, use, consume, transfer, and dispose of at least the social minimum guaranteed by the difference principle, then it could not be used by individuals to effectively exercise their basic liberties—one of the primary justifications of the difference principle—or to pursue their life plans and primary purposes.

This has important implications for the specification of rights of use and control of personal property, including real property rights in one's living accommodations: individuals should have those rights and powers in personal possession that are sufficient to protect their person and their privacy and enable them to maintain personal relationships, effectively exercise their basic liberties, take advantage of society's opportunities, and pursue a wide range of permissible conceptions of the good. This understanding of the essential role of personal property in safeguarding the security, freedom, and independence of the person is compatible with economic systems with different personal and real property arrangements, whether they be modern ("fee simple absolute") ownership, life estates, or even more restricted arrangements of rights and claims in real property used for personal purposes, such as leaseholds and terms for years. This is to say that, given Rawls's justification of the right to hold personal property, it does not imply our system of robust private ownership rights in one's home; a market socialist system that gave one exclusive and renewable leasehold rights for a definite term for years would seem adequate.

Rawls's justification of the right to hold personal property also clarifies why the first principle does not justify extensive laissez-faire property or contract rights in economic relations, any more than it justifies common ownership and democratic control of means of production (*TJ*, 54). Neither of these economic arrangements is *necessary* for the freedom, independence, and integrity of the person (as Rawls defines it) or to the effective exercise of other basic liberties in enabling individuals to form and pursue a rational life plan. Indeed, the doctrine of laissez-faire potentially conflicts with this justification of the right to hold personal property, for the laissez-faire social system, certainly in the absence of a social "safety net," carries no guarantee that the least advantaged will have adequate resources to enable them to afford a secure and exclusive living space and adequate means to freely pursue their purposes. (Compare the large number of homeless individuals in the United States, which has no guaranteed social minimum.) It is a misunderstanding of Rawls's position to contend that the principle of equal basic liberties does or should put laissez-faire economic freedoms on a par with the basic liberties and assign them the same degree of protection. This position conflicts with Rawls's understanding of the essential role of personal property in enabling the security, freedom, and independence of all citizens in society.[10]

For this reason, Rawls distinguishes between personal property and property in means of production, as he distinguishes between the personal freedoms protected by the first principle and economic freedoms that are to be regulated by the difference principle. Ownership and control of economic resources for commercial purposes of production, trade, and exchange are to be determined, not by the principle of equal basic liberties, but by the difference principle. This is true even if democratic majorities, exercising their basic political liberties, vote for a laissez-faire or a communist economic system: the priority of the basic liberties, including equal political rights of participation, over the difference principle does not mean that democratic majorities can vote for just any economic system they choose, especially if it bears on the requirements of fair equality of opportunity and the difference principle. The justice of democratic political decisions is always subject to guidance and assessment by the second principle of justice; otherwise that principle would have no point. It is a misunderstanding of the priority of liberty to think that the basic liberties may be exercised in ways that defeat fair equality of opportunity or the difference principle.[11]

A final point bearing on the basic right to hold property is that it does not guarantee a right to adequate resources enabling a person to effectively exercise this basic liberty. Like the other basic liberties (except equal political liberties), taken by itself it is a formal right that guarantees no specific amount of resources to give it value, but only the right or legal permission to securely hold possessions, assuming that one acquires and uses them in ways recognized by law. Still, even if the first principle does not on its face guarantee the value of this basic liberty, Rawls says in *Political Liberalism* that this principle presupposes a principle that the basic needs of all members of society are met.[12] That individuals' basic needs are met is a precondition, he contends, of the effective exercise of the basic liberties; for without adequate resources to meet one's basic needs, the basic liberties are virtually worthless. A similar guarantee of basic needs seems implicit in Rawls's general conception of justice in *A Theory of Justice*—that all primary social goods, including income and wealth, be distributed so that "any, or all, of these values are to everyone's advantage" (*TJ*, 54)—which is presupposed by Rawls's special conception with the two principles in order of priority.

Here Rawls differs considerably from Hayek and other classical liberals, who argue that the right to liberty and freedom from coercion by others does not include or require a right to any resources.[13] So long as a person is free to sell his services to others, Hayek claims, he is a free person, even if he is destitute. (This assumes someone will hire a destitute person for legitimate purposes.) Rawls and high liberals generally, unlike classical liberals and libertarians, regard the complete lack of options due to unfortunate circumstance to be nearly as bad and as coercive as coercion by other persons. The fact that no particular person willfully denies one the freedom to make choices and act on them does not mean that one's freedom to act and pursue one's purposes is not restricted or frustrated.

I conclude that the first principle of justice's guarantee of a basic right to hold property is highly relevant to the private law of property, at least insofar as it might tend to restrict or otherwise impede the security of persons and the effective exercise of their basic liberties. This applies also to the principle of fair equality of opportunity: individuals' abilities to take advantage of the fair opportunities available in a liberal society should not be compromised by private property rules. Accordingly, the Civil Rights Act of 1964, Title II, qualified the right to exclude from one's property, so that it does not include the right of owners of "public accommodations," including hotels, restaurants, theaters, retail stores and all other businesses engaged in interstate commerce, to exclude or deny equal access to their premises of persons on grounds of race, color, religion, or national origin (though not sex, which is included in Title VII, prohibiting discrimination in employment).

The relevant standard here is not that the rules of property must be specified in such a way as to *maximize* the effective exercise of basic liberties or the right to fair equal opportunities; nor is it that property rules must enable individuals to maximally exercise and develop the moral powers. Rawls rules out the idea of maximizing liberty, the effective exercise of liberty, and the moral powers in his discussion of the application of the first principle (e.g., *PL*, 333–34). This should also apply to property rules that specify the right to personal property. The correct standard here is best understood as an adequacy or threshold requirement: property rules should not be specified in a way that impedes the effective exercise of basic liberties and fair opportunities to an adequate degree. Of course, what that relatively vague standard means in practice is something to be worked out by courts subject to democratically determined guidelines.

What now of the relationship of Rawls's difference principle to the law of property? Rawls says again that the law of property along with the economic system is one of the primary institutions that make up the basic structure of society. As I've emphasized in earlier chapters, the primary role of the difference principle is to determine the appropriate economic system for the fair and efficient allocation of productive resources and the fair distribution of income and wealth among those who are engaged in and make contributions to economic cooperation. One of the difference principle's roles is then to provide the standard for specifying rights of ownership and control over economic resources that are to be used in the production and distribution of goods. In this connection, Rawls discusses property in chapter 5 of *A Theory of Justice*, in his discussion of distributive justice and the application of the second principle in the legislative stage of the four-stage sequence. There, for example, Rawls says the role of the allocation branch of government is to prevent concentration of market power and maintain efficient and competitive markets by suitable taxes and subsidies "and by changes in the definition of property rights" (*TJ*, 244). Moreover, the distribution branch of government preserves justice in distributive shares both by taxation and by "the necessary adjustments in the rights of property" to encourage "the wide dispersal of property." These include, he says, restrictions on rights of transfer and bequest, and inheritance and gift taxes (*TJ*, 245). Here Rawls clearly envisions restrictions on the size of estates, to further fair equality of opportunity. Rawls's discussion of property-owning democracy also suggests property arrangements that regulate or limit rights of ownership, use, control, and transfer that attend property in economic resources.[14]

There should be little question then that Rawls's difference principle applies to the specification of property rules, rights, and powers insofar as they bear on the economic system and its role in the production, transfer, and distribution of income and wealth in society. Rawls discusses the role of the difference principle primarily in connection with the third or legislative stage of his four-stage hypothetical contract.[15] He does not discuss the role of judge-made common law in specifying property rules or the attendant economic rights and powers of property that accompany them, but rather says that at the "final stage" of the four-stage sequence, "the constitution and laws are interpreted by members of the judiciary" (*JF*, 48). But the legislative stage of the four-stage sequence refers to the *use* of legislative power in making laws, and not simply to the legislative body. Whether legislators or judges at common law, they both exercise legislative power in setting forth and modifying property rules, and their decisions are subject to assessment by the difference principle. And in any case judges' judicial interpretations of property rules and their decisions in resolving legal disputes are also subject to assessment (from the perspective of the final stage of the four-stage sequence) to determine if they correctly apply property rules that are or should be based in the difference principle. Thus, with respect to the decisions of judges who apply the principle of efficiency to their interpretation of property rules or prior cases, though they are not necessarily in conflict with outcomes reachable via the difference principle, they very well could be if they suggest a pattern of sacrificing the interests of the less advantaged for greater overall economic gain to society as a whole. That would be a proper case for legislative correction guided by the difference principle or for judicial review in those terms.[16]

3. The Principles of Justice and the Law of Contract: The First Principle and the Principle of Fairness

I mentioned earlier papers by Kronman and Murphy, who contend that Rawls seems to say that the difference principle does not apply to contract law, and that it should. Arthur Ripstein more recently has argued that neither of Rawls's principles of justice should apply to private law, not just contract and tort law but also property. I discuss in the appendix to this chapter (section 8) the passage that Kronman and Murphy rely on to make their argument. But here I build the positive case for the application of both principles of justice and also the principle of fairness to the law of contract. The question is not *whether* the principles of justice are relevant to assessing and determining the rules of contract law—they rather clearly are given what Rawls says—but to what degree they should apply, and in particular whether the difference principle is to play a preponderant if not dominant role in determining contract law or whether there are limits to its application. I argue the latter.

Since Rawls says the right to hold personal property is a basic liberty, and property is among the most fundamental institutions of the basic structure, there should be little question that Rawls's principles of justice apply directly to the assessment and determination of rights of private property for both personal and economic uses. It would be peculiar if Rawls did not likewise regard freedom of contract for personal reasons as part of the basic right to hold property and also envision the use of the principles of justice to assess and determine the law of contract for both personal and economic purposes; for contractual relations are integrally involved in the acquisition, transfer, use, and disposal of property rights. There would be little point in having a basic right to hold personal property in the income one earns and in one's savings, for example, without equally basic rights to acquire and transfer it by contractual exchange (e.g., through contracts for the acquisition of a living space or sale of one's labor time). Moreover, the security and effective use of property rights and interests, whether for personal or productive economic purposes, depend to a large degree on the enforcement of contractual agreements.

That Rawls regards the principles of justice as applying to the law of contract, and freedom of contract as being protected to some degree by the first principle, is pretty clearly suggested in his discussion of the principle of fairness. In one of the only two places in *A Theory of Justice* where Rawls mentions legal contracts (he mentions social contract doctrine many times) he says, "There are many variations of promising just as there are of the law of contracts. Whether the particular practice as it is understood by a person, or group of persons, is just remains to be determined by the principles of justice" (*TJ*, 304).[17]

This section (*TJ*, §52, also §18 on the principle of fairness) addresses the conditions under which one is obligated to keep "promises and agreements" (*TJ*, 97). Rawls contends that people have a duty to do their fair share in cooperative practices and institutions, including promises and agreements, in which they have voluntarily accepted the benefits, *provided that* the practice or institution is itself just or fair, or at least not (too) unjust as assessed by the two principles of justice.[18] The principle of fairness imposes upon people an obligation to normally comply with their promises and agreements, *including their contractual agreements*, so long as their agreements respect the requirements of the principles of justice and other legally valid requirements. People rely upon one another's promises and upon the exchange of promises underlying binding contracts. The "obligation of fidelity" (*TJ*, 94) implicit in the principle of fairness is a condition of social cooperation since it is necessary to establish trust in others with whom we have personal and economic relationships. Rawls says that so long as the practice of promising and rules of contracts are themselves just, the principle of fairness imposes an obligation of fidelity to comply with the terms of promises and agreements.

Whether the rules specifying the form and content of contracts are legally valid thus depends in large part on whether the institution of the law of contracts itself satisfies the principles of justice. Some familiar examples here that would violate the principles of justice would be clearly unconscionable contracts or agreements, such as those that violate basic liberties (e.g., a contract to never change one's religion or marry again if one sues for divorce, or clearly involuntary servitude) or contracts that contravene fair equality of opportunity (e.g., contracts not to hire, do business with, or even associate with racial minorities or sell them real estate, as discussed below). These contracts are void and unenforceable and impose no moral or legal obligation under the principle of fairness because they violate the principles of justice.[19] Nor would contracts involving price fixing, restraints on trade, or other forms of collusion by firms be enforceable, or contracts that encourage monopolistic practices, since these agreements violate requirements of fair competition and economic efficiency that are implicit in the difference principle (discussed below).

Here it is revealing that the principle of justice that Rawls specifically mentions as applying to promises—and by implication the exchange of promises to establish binding agreements—is not the second principle, but the principle of equal liberty. Rawls says, "In general, the circumstances giving rise to a promise and the excusing conditions must be defined so as to preserve the equal liberty of the parties and to make the practice a rational means whereby men can enter into and stabilize cooperative agreements for mutual advantage" (*TJ*, 303–304). The relationship between the equal liberty principle and the principle of fairness seems to be that the practices of promising and agreements, including making legally binding contracts, are necessary for engaging in social cooperation and individuals' free pursuit of their (rational) conceptions of the good. As such, the freedom to make agreements is, like the right to hold personal property, essential to the exercise of the basic liberty of freedom of the person as well as freedom of association and other basic liberties. The capacity to make promises and agreements is intrinsic to freedom of association since it enables individuals to establish bonds of friendship, affection, trust, and cooperation with others and to stabilize and solidify these relationships and associations by legally binding contracts when appropriate. And promises and agreements play an instrumental role also in enabling individuals to freely act to pursue their purposes, so that they may rationally pursue their conceptions of the good.

Contractual relations are then essential to the formation and participation in many kinds of legally recognized relationships and free associations of persons for personal and other non-economic reasons and are in this regard essential to the effective exercise of freedom of association as well as other basic rights and liberties. The most familiar examples here are marriage contracts and prenuptial agreements, also agreements made upon divorce, including child custody agreements, and others within family law. The freedom to enter binding agreements to incorporate or otherwise form and join religious associations (churches, mosques, synagogues, etc.) or ethical and charitable associations (non-profit hospitals, Oxfam, or the Red Cross) is essential to the effective exercise of such basic liberties as freedom of conscience, enabling people to jointly act upon their conscientious religious and ethical convictions. Also, contractual agreements to form, incorporate, and join educational institutions (schools and universities) and cultural institutions (art museums and opera companies), or to associate with others for scientific or literary purposes, or to publish academic and literary journals and manuscripts, are crucial to freedom of thought, expression, and inquiry. Legal powers to form and join learned societies, clubs and amateur sports teams, fraternities and sororities, and other non-profit associations are also necessary for the cohesiveness of these forms of association. So even without taking into account the crucial domain of economic contracts for the purpose of production, trade, and exchange, the freedom to enter binding legal agreements to form associations and relationships of many kinds is essential to the effective exercise of many basic liberties and should be guaranteed for that reason.

There is for Rawls no requirement that the contours and interpretation of such associational contracts are to be designed to maximally promote anything, such as the exercise and development of the moral powers, or individual autonomy, or moral agency, just as it is not a requirement of the difference principle that all rules of economic contract maximize the position of the least advantaged (as discussed in section 5). In discussing the role of the moral powers in specifying the basic liberties, Rawls remarks that even if we could make sense of the idea of maximizing the moral powers, what would be the point of so perfecting these capacities for practical reasoning and social cooperation at the expense of other equally important values and capacities (our aesthetic or creative capacities, for example)? [20] Moreover, to adopt the maximization of autonomy, moral agency, or the moral powers in specifying the basic liberties or rules of contract law would suggest a Kantian comprehensive doctrine that is ruled out by political liberalism. There is no assumption then that the exercise of the moral powers is the supreme or sole form of the good. "Rather, the role and exercise of these powers . . . is a condition of the good," (PL, 334)which is why the specification of the basic liberties is "so as to allow the adequate development and the full and informed exercise of both moral powers" (PL, 333).

Since freedom of personal and other non-economic contracts is, like the right to hold personal property, justified by Rawls as instrumental to the exercise of the basic liberties and forming meaningful personal associations, the rules and interpretation of terms of legally enforceable contracts for non-economic purposes should be oriented toward two things: first, enabling individuals to effectively exercise their basic liberties, taking into account the purposes of forms of association for which contracts are made; and second, enabling associations to effectively carry out their purposes as these are commonly understood and/or as freely specified or conceived by their members—whether these be marital, religious, cultural, educational, charitable, recreational, fraternal/sororal, or other forms of association.[21] The question of the ultimate standards to which appeal is to be made to specify and assess rules of various forms of contract is a complicated one and will be taken up again (without fully resolving the question) in section 6.

Because of freedom of the person, freedom of association, and other basic liberties, promises and agreements made pursuant to maintaining personal and other non-economic relationships would seem to be given wide leeway in Rawls's account. Assuming they meet standard conditions for legally binding contracts (lack of fraud, misrepresentation duress, undue influence, and unreasonable differences in bargaining power), they would be normally enforceable unless they violate in some way individuals' basic liberties or otherwise involve morally unconscionable terms (e.g., agreements of involuntary servitude or agreements to never divorce a person or never cease being someone's constant companion, all of which infringe on basic liberties of the person). It is because the right to exit almost any association[22] is part of freedom of association that agreements regarding the terms of free associations (e.g., religious rules regarding who exercises authority and the scope of their authority or rules governing an association's procedures or use of property or funds) may be legally enforceable even if these rules otherwise seem unreasonable or unfair (such as membership terms in a private club excluding all atheists, non-nationals, or racial minorities from membership, or an agreement that one party in a non-marital relationship or commune will do all the housework, failing which she forfeits her share of commonly held property to the other(s)). Membership terms that exclude people on the basis of race or gender from certain private communal associations, such as country clubs or fraternal clubs like the Lions Club, are more complex, since they can have a significant bearing on fair equality of opportunity (discussed next in section 4).

4. Freedom of Contract and the Second Principle—Fair Equality of Opportunity

How does Rawls's second principle of justice apply to freedom of contract? Begin with the fair equality of opportunity provision of the second principle. In discussing the application of the principles of justice to legislation, Rawls says in *TJ*, §43, "Institutions for Distributive Justice," that fair equality of opportunity enforces and underwrites equality of opportunity in economic activities and in the free choice of occupation. This is achieved by policing the conduct of firms and private associations and preventing monopolies and barriers to desirable social positions (*TJ*, 243). Here again we have an implied limitation on (laissez-faire) freedom of contract, in this case for purposes of realizing fair equality of opportunity for all persons in economic activities and choice of occupation.

In general, for Rawls freedom of economic contract cannot be used in ways that undermine the fair equality of opportunity of persons and groups to compete for open positions, to take advantage of educational, cultural, and other opportunities, or to take advantage of economic or social opportunities open to other members of society. The implication is that, whereas freedom of association often leaves us free to enter into personal agreements and relationships that exclude people on grounds of race, religion, nationality, gender, and sexual preference, or just because we do not like their appearance, this protection does not apply to economic contracts and business relationships with the public at large, because of fair equality of opportunity. A person or firm that puts itself forth as doing business for economic gain cannot choose to discriminate against persons due to prejudice and bigotry against a class of persons, or even for capricious reasons unrelated to some legitimate business purposes. (For example, excluding boisterous or otherwise unruly customers who put off other customers is normally permissible, as are dress codes in restaurants requiring men to wear a jacket, trousers, and a tie; but excluding a customer simply because the maître d' dislikes his tie or the color combination of his clothes would not be.)

One example Rawls might have in mind here (by preventing "barriers to desirable social positions") is fair employment laws and anti-discrimination measures in the US Civil Rights Act of 1964 and 1968, which prohibits private discrimination in education and employment, and in the sale, rental, and financing of housing, and which requires commercial businesses, hotels, and restaurants to serve racial, ethnic, national, and religious minorities and groups. This measure was much lamented by Milton Friedman at the time, and still is by most libertarians, since it restricts economic liberties and compels businesses to economically cooperate and enter into contractual relations with classes of people whom they'd rather avoid.[23]

Another restriction that fair equality of opportunity would impose on contracts and transfers of property is represented by the US Supreme Court decision in *Shelley v. Kramer*, 334 U.S. 1 (1948), where the Court refused to give legal effect to racially based restrictive covenants in contracts and deeds of sale of real property that contained terms prohibiting the sale or lease of real estate to blacks. This again is a case of a private contract or transaction that is void and unenforceable because it requires state action that limits the economic and social opportunities of racial and other minorities against whom there has been a history of discrimination.

Finally, here it is noteworthy that Rawls mentions above not only "policing" firms and their business practices that tend to undermine the purposes of fair equality of opportunity, but policing the practices of "private associations" as well (*TJ*, 243). This suggests that freedom of association is not so robust as to undermine fair equality of educational and career opportunities. If this seems to conflict with the priority Rawls assigns to the first principle and freedom of association over fair equality of opportunity, one solution to the apparent conflict is to regard free choice of occupation itself as an equal basic liberty. Though Rawls normally and frequently says that free choice of occupation is part of or a condition of fair equality of opportunity (*TJ*, 243; *PL*, 228), he suggests a few times that it is also protected as a basic liberty as part of the liberty and integrity of the person.[24]

An example here would be private clubs that exclude racial minorities or men's clubs and fraternal organizations that exclude women, where business ties are cultivated and transactions often arranged (on the golf course, etc.). This is a difficult issue when it affects more intimate associations or smaller groups' freedom to control their membership and religious associations or associations to further First Amendment expressive rights. But with respect to large associations of several hundred or more people, it is noteworthy that, while the Supreme Court upheld racial discrimination by a Moose lodge in 1962,[25] more recently the Court affirmed (for different reasons) lower courts' decisions that prohibited the Jaycees, Rotary Club, and other larger associations from excluding women, on grounds that this violated various states' civil rights acts.[26]

5. *Contract Law and the Difference Principle*

Turn now to the difference principle and its bearing on economic contracts necessary for production and commercial activity. Here it is relevant that Rawls's second principle, and especially the difference principle, address a general problem that occupied philosophers as diverse as Hume, Adam Smith, and Mill, as well as Marx and others critical of capitalism: namely, how is a society to fairly design and efficiently organize the social institutions that make economic cooperation possible among free and equal persons who are actively engaged in productive activity, in such a way as to make possible the just and efficient allocation of productive resources and the fair distribution of income and wealth? Certain legal institutions—those Hume termed "the conventions of justice," including property, economic contracts, market transactions and other consensual transfers—are among the institutions necessary for fair and efficient economic cooperation in a modern economy.

Rawls says that "the structure of the economy" is part of the basic structure, which includes, "for example, as a system of competitive markets with private property in the means of production" (*JF*, 10). Economic contracts play an essential role in enabling and sustaining a system of competitive markets. In large part, the law of contract is specified so as to enable economic activity, by setting forth the terms and conditions of valid and enforceable agreements and other transactions that make fair and efficient economic cooperation possible. Since contracts and related legal transactions are the major means by which to effect market transfers that result from market competition, contract law must be part of the basic structure governed by Rawls's difference principle.

One of the primary reasons that Rawls distinguishes between the principles and rules for institutions that maintain "background justice," as well as the rules for individuals that directly regulate their conduct, is to free individuals from the moral demands of having to constantly pursue the moral requirements and ends implicit in the principles of justice, so that they can be left free to maintain personal commitments and pursue their conceptions of the good. In *Political Liberalism*, though Rawls denies a "right to liberty as such," he also recognizes, like most liberals, a "general presumption against imposing restrictions on conduct without sufficient reason" (*PL*, 292). Such a presumption should apply to individuals' ability to freely enter into legitimate contracts of various kinds to further their lawful purposes. But unlike agreements that specify the terms of associations for personal, religious, educational, and other non-economic reasons, freedom of economic contract and other economic liberties are not protected to the same degree as are personal contracts that support and solidify the many free associations protected by the personal and political liberties of the first principle. In only the second place in *A Theory of Justice* where Rawls mentions legal contracts, he denies that laissez-faire freedom of contract is among the basic liberties. He says: "Of course, liberties not on the list, for example the right to own certain kinds of property (e.g., means of production) and freedom of contract as understood by the doctrine of laissez-faire, are not basic; and so they are not protected by the priority of the first principle" (*TJ*, 54).

Earlier I mentioned the restrictions imposed on freedom of contract by the basic liberties and fair equality of opportunity. What if any additional restrictions are imposed by the difference principle? To argue that there are none would suggest that the least advantaged fare better with laissez-faire contracts (that do not violate basic liberties and fair opportunities) than they would in any alternative economic system. This is extremely unlikely, even assuming taxation and redistribution of market outcomes to maximize the share of income and wealth going to the least advantaged. Here it is relevant that, in his discussion of economic systems and his argument for property-owning democracy, Rawls explicitly rejects both laissez-faire and welfare-state capitalism on grounds that they do not satisfy the difference principle or other principles of justice (*JF*, 137).[27] The economic system in which the system of laissez-faire contracts could effectively function (most likely one that includes laissez-faire property rights too) is not the kind of economic system that can satisfy the difference principle's broad requirement that the position of the least advantaged is to be maximized within the economic system where their prospects are greater than they would be in any other economic arrangement. It would be poor consolation for the least advantaged in a laissez-faire economy with caveat emptor contract rules to tell them that they are still protected by the safety net, after they have just lost all equity in their home for failure to read the fine print in a mortgage contract that says they forfeit everything if they miss a monthly payment.

Traditional contract law, including the laissez-faire common law doctrine of caveat emptor, guarantees certain standard defenses against enforcement of contracts on grounds of fraud, duress, misrepresentation, and undue influence. These defenses are, of course, justifiable by both the first and second principles as well. But the difference principle also would not permit the laissez-faire doctrine of caveat emptor, especially in sales of goods, services, and real property to ordinary consumers who are not in a position to acquire information about the quality of goods and services or the trustworthiness of those from whom they make purchases. Certain implied warranties in contracts regarding the safety and reliability of goods, and other protections for consumers, would then also be justifiable on grounds of the difference principle. Gross differences in economic bargaining power might provide added grounds for judging contracts unconscionable or voidable where it is clear that a party has taken unfair advantage of another's ignorance, desperation, or poverty. Also, gross mistakes regarding the value of assets, or due to a failure to understand or even read long and complex documents written in legal jargon that are very difficult for a layperson to understand, may make contracts voidable. Unreasonable provisions in mortgage and other lending contracts (e.g., loss of equity in event of default) regarding foreclosures and debt collections might be deemed void under the difference principle. And predatory lending contracts to the less advantaged should be at least voidable under the difference principle, and subject to repayment of loans at a reasonable rate. These are some examples of rules consistent with the difference principle that should be incorporated into the law of contract.

These examples raise the question, to what degree is the difference principle to be applied to the governance of contract law? In his discussion of how the difference principle is to apply to contract law, Samuel Scheffler distinguishes "weak distributivism" from "strong distributivism." The former states a kind of Pareto condition, which says that contract law must not violate the basic liberties or fair equality of opportunity and that it "should be designed so as to avoid worsening the economic position of the least advantaged members of society."[28] "Provided all three of these constraints have been satisfied, weak distributivism asserts that the remaining content of contract law is not dictated by the principles of justice, and may be fixed in other ways."[29] Strong distributivism withdraws this option and holds that "the content of contract law should be entirely determined by the difference principle."[30] This means that contract law should be organized, not simply to avoid worsening, but to maximize the position of the least advantaged members of society. The problem with strong distributivism, as Scheffler notes, is that it violates the "division of moral labor" and occupies too much evaluative space, requiring that contracts of all kinds regardless of their purposes be formally oriented toward economic ends of maximizing the least advantaged position. But this means that individuals, in entering contracts to pursue their own purposes, are (unwittingly) also promoting the position of the least advantaged (as if they had to pay a fee to the least advantaged in order to contractually pursue their own ends). For such reasons, Scheffler says that Rawls, given his concern with not interfering with individuals' pursuit of other values, would choose weak distributivism. But the problem is that it is difficult to see how to avoid weak distributivism from collapsing into strong distributivism and thus requiring that all contracts formally comply with rules that maximize the worst-off position.[31]

Strong distributivism is an example of the mandatory maximizing interpretation of the difference principle (discussed in chapter 3, section 6), which says that the principle applies to the shaping of all political measures that do not otherwise come under equal basic liberties and fair equality of opportunity. One of the many problems with this interpretation is that the "least advantaged" class includes only those who make a real contribution to economic production, namely the least paid, least skilled workers, and does not include those voluntarily unemployed or involuntarily unemployed due to disabilities. Given the legitimate claims of so many others on the economic resources of society—the unemployed disabled, future generations, burdened societies in the Law of Peoples—it seems unreasonable to assign least paid workers exclusive priority over all other persons and social values in determining the structure and rules of contract law, especially when so many contracts that would be affected have nothing to do with economic production, trade, and distribution.

The problem Scheffler raises is not, I believe, as serious as it might seem once it is recognized that the difference principle is to apply only to the class of what I have called "economic contracts," those affecting the production, trade, and consumption of economic resources and goods. It does not apply to the many kinds of personal and associational agreements protected by freedom of association and other basic liberties discussed in the preceding sections. Clearly it would make no sense to design the rules of marriage, divorce, and child custody contracts, or contracts of incorporation and association for religious, charitable, cultural, educational, and other non-profit associations, so that they maximally promote the economic position of the least advantaged members of the working class. The dangers that the difference principle, even on the strong distributivism reading, will assume such a preponderant role in contract law and undermine the division of moral labor is substantially diminished if it is applied only to that part of contract law that bears on economic cooperation and the production, distribution, and consumption of economic goods and services.[32]

Scheffler rightly asks, if not always the difference principle, what other principles for the basic structure would appeal be made to specify rules of non-economic contracts? Here I think that weak distributivism should be strengthened so that it is a more moderate distributivism, whereby not only should the law of contracts not violate the basic liberties and fair equality of opportunity, but the rules of personal and non-economic contracts should be formally designed to enable individuals to adequately and effectively exercise their basic liberties in free association with others and take advantage of fair opportunities. This amendment ties rules for forming personal and non-economic contracts more closely to the conditions for enabling the basic liberty of the integrity and freedom of the person, freedom of association, and other basic liberties that Rawls cites in justification of the right to hold personal property (and therewith freedom of [non-economic] contract). This goes a substantial way, I believe, toward maintaining the division of moral labor that Scheffler believes is threatened by strong distributivism governed by the difference principle.

This amendment may not, however, be sufficient to entirely solve the more general problem of distributivism that Scheffler raises. For Rawls's first principle and fair equality of opportunity are distributive principles too, in the broad sense, requiring equality of certain primary goods (basic liberties and fair opportunities); and Scheffler's more general claim is that there should be principles that are part of the basic structure that are non-distributive or that affirm values other than distributive values. (One example he alludes to is the purposes of punishment in the criminal law.) Here it should be noted that, although equality of these primary goods is a distributive value, individual freedom and opportunities (to develop one's capacities and take advantage of the benefits of culture) guaranteed by these principles are not themselves distributive values.[33] Also Rawls sees civic friendship as a (non-distributive) value that is cultivated by adherence to the principles of justice and the duty of civility (*PL*, 253, 465). The example of civic friendship suggests how Rawls might address Scheffler's challenge—namely, by appealing to non-distributive values and principles (such as civic friendship) that either enable the effective exercise of rights and liberties guaranteed by his principles of justice or stabilize a reasonably just society. (The natural duties are non-distributive values too that are instrumental to justice in this sense.) Again, this may not be satisfactory for Scheffler, since this solution still makes non-distributive values instrumental to Rawls's distributive principles. But insofar as Rawls is concerned with principles of *justice* for the basic structure, the focus on the distributive principle is difficult to avoid, since distribution broadly construed is what the concept of justice involves. (See, e.g., Mill's formal characterization of concepts of justice: to give each his or her due; to treat people equally and treat similar cases similarly; to respect individuals' rights; and so on.)[34]

Finally, it is relevant here that, beginning with *Political Liberalism* Rawls made clear that the principles of justice and especially the difference principle did not apply to the determination or shaping of all laws but mainly "constitutional essentials and matters of basic justice" and the fairness and reciprocity of economic institutions. There are many laws and regulations regarding public goods and the distribution of government benefits that do not fall within these areas, and the difference principle would not apply to their content, including contractual rules specifically relating to them. The decision to set aside land and natural resources for a national park system for aesthetic purposes of preserving the beauty and sublimity of nature is an example. By the time of *Political Liberalism*, Rawls held that the democratic pursuit of aesthetic and, by implication, perfectionist values is permissible so long as it is not inconsistent with the principles of justice. (*A Theory of Justice*, by contrast, seemed to suggest that taxing people for such purposes is inconsistent with the difference principle.)[35] What point could there be in appealing to the difference principle to decide national park charters or regulations, or parking regulations and fees for violations? Instead, these questions are to be left up to democratic decision-making and based in values that are not values of justice but are democratically decided in ways that are not inconsistent with the principles of justice. This again is further evidence that Rawls did not conceive of the difference principle as governing all aspects of public life not covered by prior principles of justice.

Finally, something should be said about the controversial passage in *Political Liberalism* (lecture 8) on the basic structure that has led to the (mistaken) view that Rawls denies that contract law is part of the basic structure that is subject to assessment by the difference principle. Since this debate is, I believe, a diversion based on a seemingly infelicitous statement by Rawls, I address it briefly in the appendix (section 8). Scheffler, however, provides an extensive and, to my mind, definitive refutation of this misunderstanding.[36]

6. Tort Law and the Principles of Justice

The question remains whether Rawls's justice as fairness does or should apply to the law of torts. The law of torts is not a matter of distributive justice but rather of corrective justice, for it addresses civil wrongs against individuals that infringe upon their rights or otherwise cause harm. As Rawls says of retributive justice, tort law sanctions "are not simply a scheme of taxes and burdens designed to put a price on certain kinds of conduct and in this way to guide conduct" in mutually advantageous ways. Like the criminal law, it would be better if the acts sanctioned by tort law never occurred (*TJ*, 276–77).

This gives us some idea about how Rawls might respond to suggestions that the difference principle should be applied to tort law as an alternative to the principle of efficiency applied in law and economics. The purpose of tort law is to hold individuals responsible for intentional or negligent infringement upon others' rights, making them liable for the losses they cause and requiring them to compensate or "make whole" their losses. In this way, tort law reinstates what is regarded (whether rightly or wrongly) as a just distribution prior to the wrong, rather than modifying the status quo ante to create a just distribution anew. If that is the case, why should the difference principle be applied anew to remedy rather than restore a just status quo? This makes sense perhaps if one regards the difference principle as a maximizing consequentialist principle like the principle of utility or Kaldor-Hicks efficiency. But (as argued earlier and to be clarified anew) this is mistaken.

As a matter of corrective justice, any question of the application of Rawls's justice as fairness arises within non-ideal theory since it involves a question of non-compliance with individuals' rights and duties. There are two separate questions here: First, can the principles of justice be directly or indirectly used to determine the law of tort? Second, without regard to the principles themselves, should the original position (OP) and the subsequent stages of the four-stage sequence be used to determine rules of care and liability within tort law?

With respect to the second question, several legal philosophers have argued that Rawls's contractarian framework should be applied in order to clarify property and the Takings clause (Michelman), the best understanding of the rules of contract (Kronman), and tort law (Keating).[37] Arthur Ripstein, however, has argued that Rawls's original position provides an inappropriate perspective from which to determine the details of private law, and especially the rules of tort law. The reason, he says, is that argument from the original position leads parties to be concerned with consequences and states of affairs, and costs and benefits to themselves, and as such it tends toward consequentialist outcomes. "The parties in the original position attach value only to states of affairs."[38] They cannot then distinguish between nonfeasance and misfeasance, or a duty to aid versus a duty not to harm.[39] Tort law, by contrast, Ripstein says, is a deontological enterprise that rests on considerations of responsibility and fault of individuals. And reasoning from the original position only addresses questions of the distribution of benefits and compares states of affairs that result from alternative principles; it does not accommodate itself to deontological principles or generate principles of individuals' responsibility.[40] The deontological structure of tort law, he claims, "will always be invisible from the point of view of the contract argument."[41]

Ripstein here follows Thomas Pogge's consequentialist interpretation of reasoning in Rawls's original position (and of the difference principle). The methodology of the original position is unavoidably consequentialist and aggregative in character, Pogge claims, since it focuses only on outcomes. The self-interest of the parties leads them to compare alternative principles and the states of affairs they result in, and to choose the one that best guarantees a maximum share of primary goods and conditions that enable them to most effectively pursue their conceptions of the good. By trying to do the best for themselves, they are engaged in aggregative reasoning. There is no concern given to how these states of affairs are brought about. For this reason, Ripstein says, "the contractarian/consequentialist approach had no room for the distinction between nonfeasance and misfeasance," or duties to aid and duties not to harm, that are so essential to tort law and holding people responsible for their conduct.[42]

One problem with Pogge's consequentialist interpretation of the argument from Rawls's hypothetical contract is that it might seem to suggest (as it does to Ripstein) that the principles of justice themselves are consequentialist in their application, designed to bring about certain states of affairs that are to be maximized or otherwise efficiently promoted without moral or procedural constraints. But the principles of equal basic liberties and fair equality of opportunity clearly are not consequentialist in this or any other sense, but are equality principles that guarantee the protection of equal liberties and fair opportunities in procedures and in individual treatment under the law;[43] moreover, the difference principle (as I've argued in chapters 3 and 4) is a principle of reciprocity, not a maximizing consequentialist principle either.

More to the point, the consequentialist interpretation of the original position ignores the natural duties and obligations of individuals that are agreed to in the original position and that are necessary to give effect to the principles of justice: these include the duties to uphold justice, of mutual respect, to not injure others or harm the innocent, mutual aid, and obligations of fairness and fidelity to one's promises and commitments (*TJ*, 94). Clearly these are deontological duties, and their application by individuals does not involve their reasoning about costs and benefits or promoting states of affairs. Indeed, the natural duties are drawn from Kant, and Rawls's argument for them in the original position parallels Kant's own argument from the categorical imperative procedure for rules requiring individuals to keep their promises, not harm others, and assist individuals in need.

The natural duties and obligations of fairness and fidelity are rules for which individuals can be held responsible and assigned blame if they are violated. Moreover, the violation of some of these moral duties (the duty not to injure and the duty to respect others' property implicit in the duty of justice) provides the basis for actions that lie in tort. If these deontological rules for individuals can be agreed to by the parties in the OP, then what structural feature of Rawls's hypothetical contract and its application in the four-stage sequence prevents the parties from agreeing to rules of responsibility and fault that might be applied within tort law? It cannot be the fact that the parties engage in means–end—or, as Pogge calls it, "consequentialist"—reasoning. In general, it is a mistake to conclude that, because the parties in the OP engage in means–end reasoning and compare principles and the social worlds they realize on the basis of their consequences for the rational interests of the parties, this implies that the principles that result from their agreement must themselves be consequentialist principles. Even if we accept that the methodology of the contract argument *only* involves means–end reasoning, it is still not clear why the deontological content of tort cannot be derived by applying Rawls's hypothetical contractual reasoning.[44] This is especially so once it is recognized that, in deciding on principles, the parties reasoning in the OP and later stages do not engage only in instrumental reasoning about consequences; instead they must also take into account and mimic the reasoning of morally motivated persons who are members of a well-ordered society and who themselves reason in deontological terms and hold one another responsible for their actions and the consequences of their actions. A condition of the parties' agreement on the principles of justice is that they be found stable, which means they are not simply rational for parties in the OP, but also reasonable according to the sense of justice of free and equal moral persons who must abide by these principles and rules in a well-ordered society.

Add to this, finally, the fact that any reasoning about rules of tort from within Rawls's hypothetical contract would surely transpire, not in the original position itself, but at the later constitutional, legislative, or judicial stages of the four-stage sequence after the principles of justice are in place and where the parties are motivated by their sense of justice and are no longer concerned only with their interests and share of primary goods. Given this understanding of Rawls's hypothetical contract, there seems to be no obstacle to the parties converging on deontological rules of care and standards of fault, and making the requisite distinctions between misfeasance and nonfeasance that Ripstein contends is invisible to the parties in the original position.

Still, I think Ripstein is on the right track when he argues that the law of tort (or at least public rights of compensation, which he opposes) is essential to maintaining a Rawlsian society, by protecting the rights and claims of free and equal moral persons that enable them to form, revise, and effectively pursue their conceptions of the good. In order for individuals to freely decide and pursue their conceptions of the good, the rights, liberties, and distributive claims guaranteed by law must be secured from infringement by others. "If what is mine is not subject to my choice, but to yours . . . then it is not mine to use in setting and pursuing my own conception of the good."[45] This requires not only a public system of retributive justice, but, Ripstein claims, also a private law of tort that holds individuals responsible for their civil wrongs and liable for the damages they cause to others. Here it is not entirely clear why Ripstein rejects, and claims Rawlsian justice does too, a system of public compensation as in New Zealand. It would not seem to be for retributive reasons, since he concedes that a society can legitimately require everyone to carry liability insurance and might for administrative reasons dispense with any requirement of proof of negligence, which would seem to have the same effect.[46] Perhaps there are reasons of deterrence and avoiding moral hazards that would favor a system of tort law over public compensation: individuals would not fully assume or even admit responsibility for the injuries caused by their conduct if they did not have to assume liability for these losses. Or it may be that the wrongs done to a person by tortious conduct would not be adequately recognized by others as wrongs in a system of public compensation, especially if there is no prosecution, trial, or punishment for minor intentional wrongs (the many acts of petty theft and other misdemeanors that are not prosecuted). My view is that a Rawlsian understanding of tort law could go either way on this issue, depending on how these and other questions are resolved.

Now to turn to the other issue raised above: assuming there is nothing about impartial hypothetical contractual reasoning that would prevent its application to reasoning about questions of private law, including tort, the question remains whether tort law is also covered by Rawls's principles of justice in the same way, as I've argued earlier, that the laws of property and contract are. Here especially we must consider the role, if any, of the difference principle. The principles of justice are designed to determine the rules for institutions that are part of the basic structure, which institutions in turn decide the laws and rules that apply to individual conduct and that shape, among other things, the rules for individuals within private law. Is the law of tort and compensation for fault part of the basic structure that is covered by the principles of justice? It is clearly part of the legal system, and it might be argued that as such it is part of the basic structure. But this would not resolve the issue of whether the principles of justice apply to tort law. City parking laws are part of the legal system too, as are provisions for public swimming pools and laws regulating national parks; but this does not mean they are part of the basic structure that is covered by the principles of justice. Parking laws, public pools, and park regulations are not constitutional essentials, requirements of basic justice, or part of the economic system, so we cannot appeal to the principles of justice to determine their content. Again, as in the case of non-economic contract law, what point could there be in appealing to the difference principle to decide national park regulations or parking regulations and fees for violations? These questions are to be decided by democratic means, in ways and according to values of public recreation and convenience or aesthetic decisions that are not inconsistent with the principles of justice.

Since tort law, or at least a right of compensation, is essential for protecting the rights, liberties, and opportunities that are among (what Rawls calls) the constitutional essentials and requirements of basic justice, then tort law can in that regard at least be considered to be among the institutions of the basic structure. Any legal system that made injuries to persons only public wrongs and a matter of retributive justice but failed to provide remedies, whether public or private, for injuries and damages inflicted on persons would seriously undermine individuals' freedom to determine and pursue their rational life plans. It would seriously diminish the value of the equal basic liberties and fair opportunities not to provide remedies for private wrongs, since individuals could not be secure in their sense that they would be compensated for damages done to their person and property by violations of their rights and opportunities. Though a criminal justice system might protect individuals' rights and opportunities to some degree, it does not provide compensation for damages and harms needed to give one the sense of the security and permanency of the rights, liberties, and opportunities guaranteed by Rawls's principles of justice. Indeed, an argument can be made that a right to compensation for private wrongs (if not the tort law of fault and personal liability) is among those basic rights necessary to protect the security and independence of citizens (*PL*, 232), or (as Rawls normally says) the freedom and integrity of the person (*TJ*, 53; *PL*, 291; *JF*, 44).

Accordingly, unlike Ripstein, I think that more direct engagement with and application of the principles of justice, especially the first principle, as well as the hypothetical contract at an appropriate stage of reasoning to apply relevant principles and the rules they require (at the legislative and then judicial stages) is suitable for applying Rawls's theory of justice to the details of a Rawlsian tort theory. The first principle already embodies the most basic rights and liberties that are necessary to realize the ideal of moral persons that Ripstein advocates, enabling them to make plans and commitments and effectively pursue their ends and conceptions of the good. And the difference principle guarantees the economic resources that are necessary for the effective exercise of the basic liberties and fair opportunities. Standing alone, apart from the structure and content given to it by the original position and the principles of justice, the Kantian ideal of free and equal persons that Ripstein relies upon to ground tort law and theory is (like the idea of moral agency) rather inchoate and does not tell us much about what justice requires. Many different kinds of incompatible principles and tort rules might be argued for on grounds that they effectively promote the exercise of the moral powers and individuals' pursuit of their good (including libertarian rules) in the absence of the structure and content provided by the original position and the principles of justice. In this regard, I think that any Rawlsian theory of tort would need to take into account the rights and powers protected by the principles of justice, as well as later stages of reasoning within the hypothetical contract situation for their application, whether directly or indirectly, to tort law.

The difference principle is a different issue. In one respect the difference principle (together with the principle of basic needs) provides the standard for the distribution of income and wealth among society's members. Individuals come into possession of their distributive shares once they comply with the system of rules regulated by the difference principle (or have a right to have their basic needs met if they are unable to make economic contributions and do not otherwise have adequate income). Their shares are then guaranteed and protected as exclusive rights of property by the first principle's right to hold personal property. Still, it is a misunderstanding of the difference principle to apply its standard for the distribution of income and wealth (maximizing the share of the least advantaged) to the content of all laws; this qualification includes the determination of rules of compensation and standards of care in tort law. For example, in deciding on the standards of care and compensation in negligence cases, it surely would be inappropriate, if not unjust, to choose standards that tend to maximally promote the share of income and wealth going to the least advantaged. Why, rather than being "made whole," should the compensation due an accident victim depend on the difference principle, which seems irrelevant to the circumstances of compensating a victim of another's negligence? Clearly in a just society where distributive shares have been arrived at by rules that satisfy the difference principle, it would not be appropriate for courts to recalculate holdings by directly applying the difference principle to determine compensation. And even in non-ideal circumstances the difference principle is the wrong kind of principle to apply. It is not a principle of redress nor designed to address questions of compensatory justice (cf. *TJ*, 86, 8), but rather a principle for designing rules of property and other background institutions necessary for economic cooperation, in order to achieve a fair distribution that reflects each citizen's contribution to the social product.

In this respect, the difference principle differs from the principle of utility, which is an all-purpose principle designed to have universal application to all social and political norms, and all circumstances and transactions. For example, in law and economics, a kind of utilitarianism—the principle of Kaldor–Hicks efficiency—is applied to tort law just as it is applied to contract law and the law of property (and most everything else if one accepts a purely utilitarian perspective). By analogy one might think that Rawls's difference principle should have the same application. Kevin Kordana and David Blankfein-Tabachnick have argued (again, following Pogge) that the difference principle is a maximizing consequentialist principle; as such it applies to tort law and implies the rejection of corrective justice in favor of "an ex ante consequentialist (or deterrence based) approach" to tort law.[47] On this interpretation the difference principle serves as an alternative to the principle of (Kaldor–Hicks) efficiency that governs law and economics.

The difference principle is not (I've argued) a maximizing consequentialist principle, but rather a non-consequentialist principle of reciprocity that applies to the structuring of economic relations among economic agents who contribute their fair share to economic cooperation. Consequently, its applications have a limited scope in tort law. It normally should be of no more relevance to determining fault and assigning personal damages in intentional torts and most personal negligence cases than it is relevant to deciding fault and/or the division of assets following upon a divorce in family law. An exception here may be what can be called "economic torts," which involve damages to property, trespass, or nuisances, caused within the course of economic activities involving the production, transfer, and sale of goods and services normally regulated by rules assessable according to the difference principle. If determinations of liability and damages are unclear or indeterminate and there are significant economic consequences, then the difference principle would be preferable to the principle of efficiency, especially if the latter tends to reward those already more advantaged or who are not entitled to wealth to begin with. This is especially so under the non-ideal circumstances in the United States, where for political reasons a combination of classical liberal utilitarianism and increasingly libertarian principles largely structures the economic system. In an unjust economic system designed to maximally benefit those who are more rather than less advantaged, the application of the difference principle to distinctively economic torts might be a corrective to vast inequality and widespread economic injustice that originate in classical liberal utilitarian and libertarian economic practices and laws.[48] This would not be the case in a just and well-ordered society, where the task of tort law should be limited to restoring an already just status quo.

Finally, Gregory Keating has provided a Rawlsian account of "Strict Enterprise Liability," which involves non-negligent injuries and losses that occur in the course of doing business within an enterprise where such non-negligent injuries are statistically predictable. For example, in the trucking and shipping industries, there is a predictable percentage of non-negligent accidents in which innocent parties are injured and killed and property is destroyed in the course of firms' doing business on a large scale. If rules of negligence and fault were applied, businesses would not be liable for the damages they cause non-negligently. The costs would then be imposed on the unfortunate victims of such accidents, which would in effect shift the costs of firms' doing business to innocent victims harmed by statistically predictable accidents. Keating rightly argues that it is perfectly compatible with the Rawlsian account of fairness to hold businesses that engage in large enterprises strictly liable for these accidents, since they financially benefit from the enterprise, and the accident costs that the industry or enterprise impose on victims are statistically predictable. A similar argument applies to strict liability for accidents on the job in workman's compensation programs or in products liability. A comparable justification of strict liability in these cases involving injuries to persons also might be obtained by appeal to the first principle and the basic liberty of security and independence of the person.[49]

7. *Conclusion*

I have argued that Rawls's principles of justice apply to the assessment and determination of the rules of the private law of property, contract, and, to a lesser degree, torts. The first principle of equal basic liberties and the principle of fair equality of opportunity are relevant to private law in that they impose restrictions upon or negate any rules that might tend to infringe upon or excessively burden the exercise of the basic liberties and the achievement of fair equality of opportunity. This should be uncontroversial, since these principles apply to this degree to all laws, regulations, and decrees made by government officials. I have argued, however, that the basic liberties of the first principle, and to some degree fair equality of opportunity, should be applied in a more innovative manner: rules of property, contract, and tort should be formulated to enable citizens to effectively exercise the basic liberties and take advantage of fair opportunities, at least to an adequate (not maximum) degree.

I have also argued that the difference principle applies to the assessment and determination of the rules of private law of property and contract. This fits with Rawls's claim that "[t]he second principle applies at the legislative stage and it bears on all kinds of social and economic legislation."[50] Whether it is legislators, or judges in a common law system, who set forth the rules of property and contract law, they both occupy the legislative stage of the four-stage sequence, and the difference principle is relevant to at least the assessment of their rule-making and its interpretation, even if they do not directly appeal to this principle to guide their decisions.

But the difference principle does not apply to most tort law, with the exception perhaps of certain economic torts in non-ideal conditions of an unjust economic system. To this degree, I agree with Arthur Ripstein when he argues against "instrumental theories of private law [that] take private disputes as sort of a windfall opportunity for achieving such broader social purposes as economic redistribution or the fine tuning of optimal economic incentives."[51]

Finally, there remains the question concerning the extent to which the judiciary itself is to make direct appeals to the difference principle in interpreting rules of property and contract when deciding disputes in private law, especially in the absence of legislative intent that it do so. Though Rawls says (above) that the second principle "bears on all kinds of social and economic legislation," he later expresses caution about even legislators' assiduous application of the difference principle to economic legislation. He addresses a worry others express, that the difference principle "requires us, on every policy matter, to consider how it affects the prospects of the least advantaged." He suggests a "useful reply" that "frees us from having to consider the difference principle on every question of policy" (*JF*, 162):

We are to proceed by selecting a few instruments . . . that can be adjusted so as to meet the difference principle, once the whole family of policies is in place. As indicated above, given the equal basic liberties (with the fair value of the political liberties), fair equality of opportunity, and the like, perhaps the difference principle can be roughly satisfied by adjusting upward or downward the level of income exempt from the proportional income tax. (*JF*, 161–62)

Though this might seem to confirm objections that the difference principle applies only to public law of taxation and not private contract, it is fairly clear that this conjecture is part of ideal theory; it applies to a well-ordered society—a property-owning democracy, where the difference principle already informs the laws, including contract law, "once the whole family of policies is in place." It would not make sense in non-ideal unjust circumstances like ours to relieve political representatives of any duty to apply the difference principle to the alteration and reform of all other laws in our political system that promote such vast inequalities and adversely affect the poor. Whether or not citizens and their representatives recognize or agree with it, the principles and duties of justice impose upon society a duty to promote justice and reform its social and economic institutions so that they conform to the difference principle's requirements. The fact that government officials and members of society reject or ignore this principle does not absolve them or their laws and institutions from judgment according to the difference principle.

8. Appendix

I said earlier that Rawls mentions the law of contract in three locations, and thus far I have discussed only two of them. Here I will briefly comment on the third passage, the most controversial, which is in *Political Liberalism*, lecture 7, "The Basic Structure as Subject." This is the passage that leads to the interpretation that the law of contract is not among the laws or institutions that are part of the basic structure.[52]

In this passage Rawls says that, in addition to the rules for institutions that maintain background justice,

[t]his [basic] structure also enforces through the legal system another set of rules that govern the transactions and agreements between individuals and associations (the law of contract, and so on). The rules relating to fraud and duress, and the like, belong to these rules, and satisfy the requirements of simplicity and practicality. They are framed to leave individuals and associations free to act effectively in pursuit of their ends and without excessive constraints. (*PL*, 268)

Now, on the face of it, this passage does *not* suggest that the law of contract is not part of the basic structure; on the contrary, it says that the basic "structure enforces through the legal system" a set of rules for individuals that include the law of contract and that these rules for individuals are different from the rules for institutions that maintain background justice. There is no suggestion here that *either* set of rules, whether for institutions or for individuals, is not to be determined or assessed by the principles of justice that apply to the basic structure. In this sense, the difference principle applies to determine and assess the justice of legal rules that both guide the conduct and procedures of institutions and guide individual conduct. It applies then just as much to the rights and duties that guide the conduct of individuals in property and contract law as it applies to legislation or judicial decisions regarding taxation, public goods, income supplements, and the social minimum.

The suggestion that contract law is not part of the basic structure derives from the following paragraph, where Rawls says, perhaps infelicitously: "What we look for, in effect, is an *institutional division of labor between the basic structure and the rules applying directly to individuals and associations* and to be followed by them in particular transactions" (*PL*, 268, emphasis added). This has been read to suggest that rules of contract applying to individuals are not part of the basic structure. It would have been better had Rawls added to this infelicitous expression the term "rules for institutions" so that the entire phrase would read: "What we look for, in effect, is an institutional division of labor between the basic structure's rules for institutions and its rules applying directly to individuals and associations." This slight change makes the sentence consistent with the assertion in the preceding paragraph (and more generally with Rawls's discussion in *A Theory of Justice* and the *Restatement*) that the principles of justice governing the basic structure's institutional rules *also* specify the rules for individuals that govern their individual transactions and agreements. These rules for individuals, including the rules set forth in the law of contract, are governed by the principles of justice, including the difference principle when appropriate, as discussed above.[53]

Notes

1. See especially *PL*, lecture 8, "The Basic Liberties and their Priority."
2. See *JF*, 48–49, 162.
3. Anthony Kronman, "Contract Law and Distributive Justice," *Yale Law Journal* 89 (1980): 472–511.
4. Liam Murphy, "Institutions and the Demands of Justice," *Philosophy & Public Affairs* 27, no. 4 (1999): 251–91, sec. 2.
5. "Justice requires that private law—tort, contract, property, and unjust enrichment— have a certain kind of independence . . . We must also avoid being sucked

into the idea that relations between private individuals must be subordinated to distributive concerns." Arthur Ripstein, "The Division of Responsibility and the Law of Tort," *Fordham Law Review* 72, no. 5 (2004): 1811–44, esp. 1811, 1813, 1815–16. See also Arthur Ripstein, *Private Wrongs* (Cambridge, MA: Harvard University Press, 2016).

6. "The manner in which the rules of tort law function may have dramatic effects on the position of the least advantaged. To the extent that tort law is one of the means through which accidents are deterred and accident victims are compensated, it seems that it (in addition to tax) can be harnessed to meet the demands of the difference principle." Kevin A. Kordana and David Blankfein-Tabachnick, "Rawls and Contract Law," *George Washington Law Review* 73, no. 3 (2005): 598–632.

7. Samuel Scheffler, "Distributive Justice, the Basic Structure and the Place of Private Law," *Oxford Journal of Legal Studies* 35, no. 2 (2015): 213–35. My own position is closest to Scheffler's.

8. *JF*, 114; *PL*, 298; *TJ*, 53.

9. Freedom of the person also includes "freedom of movement and occupation" and is sometimes referred to as part of "the liberty and integrity of the person," (*PL*, 335; *JF*, 44).

10. The most prominent recent argument contending that Rawls's first principle makes extensive economic freedoms basic liberties is John Tomasi's contention that Rawls's criterion for identifying basic rights and liberties—primarily the rights and liberties necessary for the effective exercise of the moral powers—justifies moderate if not full laissez-faire property and contract rights. See John Tomasi, *Free Market Fairness* (Princeton, NJ: Princeton University Press, 2012). The moral powers are capacities for practical reasoning and social cooperation. Why should rights of unlimited accumulation of private wealth or laissez-faire freedom of contract be a condition for the effective exercise and full development of *those* capacities? Laissez-faire rights and liberties may be conditions for the full exercise of capacities for freewheeling entrepreneurship and extravagant living, but these and similar ways of living surely are not necessary to realize the moral powers, however important they may be to persons who hold those conceptions of a good life. A more difficult question is whether some scaled-back basic economic freedoms with private ownership of the means of production are justified by Rawls's criteria and should be protected by the first principle. This could rule out market socialism as a legitimate economic system, but not property-owning democracy, which is more than Tomasi wants to concede. Thanks to John Oberdiek for this point.

11. Here I basically agree with Kevin Kordana and David Blackfein-Tabachnick, who say that the priority of basic liberties, including equal political liberties, does not mean that democratic majorities can justifiably exercise that liberty to vote for measures incompatible with the difference principle. Having any formal basic right

or liberty does not mean one can exercise it in ways that are unjust. Thomas Pogge, they contend, suggested otherwise; if so, this is a misinterpretation of Rawls. Kordana and Blackfein-Tabachnick, "Rawls and Contract Law."

12. See *PL*, 7; also 166, 228–30 on meeting basic needs and constitutional essentials. In *JF*, 47–48, Rawls distinguishes the social minimum, a constitutional essential in any legitimate liberal society, from the difference principle.

13. "Freedom may be enjoyed by a person with practically no property of his own (beyond personal belongings like clothing—but even those can be rented)." Friedrich Hayek, *The Constitution of Liberty*, definitive ed. (Chicago: University of Chicago Press, 2011), 208. Hayek ignores the fact that one needs money to rent clothing.

14. See especially *JF*, §§41, 42, and 49.

15. "The second principle applies at the legislative stage and it bears on all kinds of social and economic legislation" (*JF*, 48); see also *TJ*, 145.

16. Carol Rose in discussion at Arizona Law School in 2015 challenged my claim that Rawls's principles of justice apply to private law, including property, saying that she does not see any respect in which it is relevant to the determination of, for example, the law of real property as developed by the common law or subsequently by legislative means. But consider legislative efforts to repeal the common law rule against perpetuities, which itself restricts owners' imposing limits long after their death on the vesting of ownership and control over land and resources (e.g., it prohibits tying up property in trust indefinitely, or for ten generations, before ownership vests in anyone). If the effect of this attempt to control wealth long after one's demise is to limit opportunities and future prospects of the less advantaged members of society, then surely the difference principle would be relevant to deciding the legitimacy of repeals of the rule against perpetuities. Perhaps Rose's point is normative—not that the difference principle cannot be applied to the interpretation or reform of existing property law, but that it is just a bad idea to do so. This is suggested in Rose's "'Enough and as Good' of What?" *Northwestern Law Review* 81, no. 3 (1987): 417–42, where Rose argues that rational utility maximizers behind a veil of ignorance would choose a property system that maximizes wealth and overall utility rather than a property system designed according to the difference principle. This simply questions Rawls's argument for the difference principle. I discuss Rawls's argument and problems with the principle of utility in chapter 4 in connection with property-owning democracy.

17. This is preceded by the claim that "the principles of justice apply to the practice of promising in the same way that they apply to other institutions," and here it is safe to assume that contract and other legal agreements are among the institutions he has in mind, since he refers to the law of contracts immediately thereafter. Later in the same section, Rawls again suggests that the principles of justice apply to contractual agreements when he refers to promises made

"to set up small scale schemes of cooperation and patterns of transaction" (*TJ*, 304) and to "covenants . . . where one party is to perform before the other" (*TJ*, 305).

18. According to the principle of fairness, "A person is under an obligation to do his part as specified by the rules of an institution whenever he has voluntarily accepted the benefits of the scheme or has taken advantage of the opportunities it offers to advance his interests, provided that this institution is just or fair, that is, satisfies the two principles of justice" (*TJ*, §52). Nozick famously denies this principle (with his trivial example of refusing to take a turn playing street music that one daily enjoys) and claims that we have an obligation to do our fair share in a practice we benefit from only if we have voluntarily consented to undertake that obligation. When generalized to social cooperation, Nozick's argument is in effect a rationalization for free-riding, which I believe is integral to an understanding of his (and most other versions of) libertarianism. See chapter 2 herein.

19. Is a non-economic contract among KKK members or other white supremacists not to associate with racial minorities as a condition of membership, with penalties of not just expulsion but also forfeiture of considerable sums of property, void or merely voidable? Some might contend that the forfeiture provision is valid since the association is protected by freedom of association. But unlike exclusion from membership, the financial penalty is not a matter of freedom of association. Why then shouldn't the penalty (if not the entire contract) be held unconscionable, hence void or at least voidable?

20. "We have no notion of a maximum development of these powers." Moreover, "the two moral powers do not exhaust the person, for persons have a determinate conception of the good" (*PL*, 333). See also *PL*, 333–34.

21. For example, the prescribed terms of marriage contracts are designed to cement the union of spouses by publicly defining their relationship as exclusive, as well as accomplish other public (and often non-public) purposes. To enter a marriage, one cannot still be married to another living person, nor can one marry anyone who is a close blood relative or, until recently, a member of the same sex. Marriage contracts cease only upon divorce or death, unless annulled by a court. In previous eras, the husband had a duty to support his wife, and the wife a duty to exhibit obedience toward her husband. There are certain legal requirements regarding the distribution of property that traditionally hold, and still hold unless there is a prenuptial agreement. For example, upon divorce (or death of a spouse), a (surviving) spouse in most states has a right to some proportion of the property (as much as one-half in some states) acquired or earned during the marriage, and sometimes to alimony. Among the mandatory terms of a marriage that cannot be contracted out of are that spouses owe one another fiduciary duties regarding finances and property and have a duty to keep confidential communications private in legal proceedings. It is difficult to see how

any of these constraints and conditions on marital contracts can be regarded as conducive to the maximization of autonomy, moral agency, or the moral powers.

22. Exceptions would be family ties to blood relatives or certain other fiduciary relationships involving legal responsibilities; e.g. parents' duties to support their minor children are not nullified upon divorce or abandonment.

23. See Milton Friedman, *Capitalism and Freedom* (Chicago: University of Chicago Press, 1962), chap. 7, 111–15.

24. In *A Theory of Justice*, he refers to "the important liberty of free choice of occupation" (*TJ*, 241–42) and in *PL* says twice that free choice of occupation is part of the basic liberty of the "independence and security of citizens" (*PL*, 232) or "liberty and integrity of the person" (*PL*, 335). He also affirmed this in conversation with the author. G. A. Cohen questions whether freedom of occupation is a basic liberty for Rawls, in *Rescuing Justice and Equality*, 196–97.

25. *Moose Lodge 107 v. Irvis*, 407 U.S. 163, 179–180 (1972), where the court held (6–3) that a Moose lodge's refusal to serve food to persons on grounds of their race did not violate the equal protection clause since the Moose lodge was a private association and there was no "State Action" merely because the lodge sold alcohol pursuant to a state liquor license. Following the decision, the Pennsylvania Civil Rights Commission successfully sued the Moose lodge, claiming that it violated the state civil rights law; this time the Supreme Court refused to hear the appeal and let the Pennsylvania ruling stand.

26. For a discussion see William G. Buss, "Discrimination by Private Clubs," *Washington University Law Review* 67, no. 3 (1989): 815–53.

27. Nor, he argues, does it protect the fair value of political liberties or fair equality of opportunity.

28. Scheffler, "Distributive Justice," 222.

29. Scheffler, "Distributive Justice," 222.

30. Scheffler, "Distributive Justice," 223.

31. Scheffler, "Distributive Justice," 225. The reason is that the baseline for deciding whether or not the least advantaged are made worse off by a contract rule might arguably be set, not at the current status quo, but at what it would be in a well-ordered society where their position is already improved. One way to address this problem might be to rephrase the weak distributivism clause so that it incorporates a Pareto condition: "Contract law should be designed so as to avoid *worsening the status quo position of the least advantaged members of society given their current position as it exists now under the current law.*"

32. Add to this the fact that (as I've argued in chapters 3 and 4) the difference principle is not the maximizing consequentialist principle it is so often thought to be, but rather a principle of reciprocity that is designed to fairly distribute the social product among those actively engaged in socially productive activity, once prior demands of justice are satisfied (payments for public goods and to future generations, the seriously disabled, etc.).

33. *The Law of Peoples* also incorporates certain non-distributive values, including peace and international cooperation, as well as distributive values, such as the protection of human rights.

34. J. S. Mill, *Utilitarianism*, ed. George Sher (Indianapolis: Hackett, 1979): chap. 5.

35. See Rawls's discussion in *TJ*, §43, of the "exchange branch" of government, which regulates public goods not required by justice (public art museums and the like) according to the principle of efficiency and Wicksell's unanimity criterion rather than the second principle (*TJ*, 249–50).

36. Scheffler, "Distributive Justice," 217–22.

37. Frank I. Michelman, "Property, Utility, and Fairness: Comments on the Ethical Foundations of 'Just Compensation' Law," *Harvard Law Review* 80, no. 6 (1967): 1165–1258; Kronman, "Contract Law and Distributive Justice," ; Gregory Keating, '"The Idea of Fairness in the Law of Enterprise Liability," *Michigan Law Review* 95, no. 5 (1997): 1266–1380; Gregory Keating, "A Social Contract Conception of the Tort Law of Accidents," in *Philosophy and the Law of Torts*, ed. Gerald J. Postema (Cambridge: Cambridge University Press, 2001): 22–71.

38. Ripstein, "The Division of Responsibility," 1822–23.

39. Ripstein, "The Division of Responsibility," 1824.

40. "The ideas of agency and responsibility that animate legal and philosophical thinking about tort are ideas that we must bring to the contract argument, because they rest on considerations that cannot be derived from it" (Ripstein, "The Division of Responsibility," 1829).

41. Ripstein, "The Division of Responsibility," 1821.

42. Ripstein, "The Division of Responsibility," 1842.

43. See the earlier remarks on Rawls's denial that the first principle and the moral powers maximize anything.

44. Stephen Perry contends that Ripstein's own argument for the deontological order of tort law itself involves a consequentialist methodology since in his argument "the choice among different institutional arrangements is simply a choice among different states of affairs." See Stephen Perry, "Ripstein, Rawls, and Responsibility," *Fordham Law Review* 72, no. 5 (2004): 1851.

45. Ripstein, "The Division of Responsibility," 1839.

46. Ripstein, "The Division of Responsibility," 1837n.

47. Kevin A. Kordana and David H. Tabachnick, "On Belling the Cat: Rawls and Tort as Corrective Justice," *Virginia Law Review* 92, no. 7 (2006): 1299. "In our view, the two principles of justice are, in their application, both consequentialist and maximizing" (1280, n. 4). "In embracing distributive principles that are in an important sense maximizing, Rawlsianism has *abandoned* a principled commitment to corrective justice" (1298). See Pogge, "Three Problems with Contractarian-Consequentialist Ways of Assessing Social Institutions," *Social Philosophy and Policy* 12, no. 2 (1995): 258, 263. On my interpretation of Rawls, Pogge's consequentialist interpretation of the difference principle, like his

consequentialist understanding of reasoning in the original position discussed earlier, is mistaken.

48. To this extent, I do not disagree with Kordana and Blankfein-Tabachnick.

49. Thanks to David Blankfein-Tabachnick for this suggestion.

50. *JF*, 48. In *A Theory of Justice* Rawls says, "The second principle comes into play at the stage of the legislature" (*TJ*, 175).

51. Arthur Ripstein, "Private Order and Public Justice: Kant and Rawls," *Virginia Law Review* 92, no. 7 (2006): 1391–1438.

52. See Kronman, "Contract Law and Distributive Justice," and Murphy, "Institutions and the Demands of Justice."

53. An early draft of this chapter was written for a conference on private law at the University of Amsterdam in January 2014. I am grateful to the participants at that conference, particularly Aditi Bagchi, David Blankfein-Tabachnick, Hanoch Dagon, and especially Samuel Scheffler, for their helpful criticisms and advice, as well as to participants in a discussion of this paper at Arizona Law School in February 2015, especially Carol Rose and Thomas Christiano, and once again to Samuel Scheffler and John Oberdiek for advising me on this final version.

PART III

Liberal Institutions and Distributive Justice

6

The Social and Institutional
Bases of Distributive Justice

1. Introduction

This chapter argues that distributive justice is institutionally based. Certain cooperative institutions are basic in that they are necessary for economic production and division of labor, trade and exchange, and distribution and consumption of economic product. These background institutions call for principles of justice to specify their terms and determine the distribution of benefits, responsibilities, and burdens that attend cooperative activity. Primary among these basic institutions are the legal institution of property; laws and conventions enabling sales, exchanges, gifts, bequests, inheritances, and other transfers of goods and services; and the legal system of contract and agreements of all kinds that make transfers possible and productive. Political institutions are necessary to specify, interpret, and enforce the terms of these institutions and render them effective. As such, basic cooperative institutions are primarily social in nature; they are realizable only within the context of social and political cooperation—this is a fixed empirical fact about cooperation among free and equal persons. Given the nature of social cooperation as a kind of reciprocity, distributive justice, I conclude, is primarily a question of social justice too.

The institutional account of distributive justice presupposes that requirements of justice apply to international and global institutions. These requirements include not only procedural and fairness requirements, but also substantive requirements of economic justice. Distributive justice, however, I regard as a distinct form of economic justice.[1] One cannot address the question of whether demands of distributive justice stem from international/global institutions without investigating the particular nature and complexity of these institutions and their role in economic production and commerce. If there are distributive requirements on global economic institutions, they would not replace but would supplement and remain dependent upon the social and institutional bases of distributive justice.

On the institutional account, distributive justice concerns not only the distribution of income and wealth but also the division of economic powers, positions of responsibility, and prerogatives of office (and opportunities to occupy these) among those who take part in and contribute to production and cooperative output. Distributive justice thus includes the appropriate distribution of ownership and control over means of production. Individuals acquire claims to these benefits and responsibilities, I contend, by taking part in and complying with the rules of cooperative institutions and contributing their fair share to economic output. Distributive justice should not then be confused with principles of redress for the alleviation of poverty or principles that remedy people's disabilities and compensate for misfortunes. Distributive justice is not remedial or compensatory justice. Many arguments for global distributive justice are driven by concerns for alleviating desperate poverty and compensating people for misfortunes of birth or accidental circumstance. Poverty and compensation for disabilities and other misfortunes require different principles that apply to the correction of unfavorable conditions and circumstances. Some of these remedial principles may be global in reach. But in an ideal society or world where poverty was eliminated and all disabilities were redressed, there would still be a need for principles of distributive justice to design basic cooperative institutions and determine the fair division of benefits, responsibilities, and burdens among those engaged in productive economic activity.

This understanding of distributive justice differs from others that construe it simply as the allocation of income and wealth independent of its production. I associate distributive justice with a particular problem that gave rise to the term's modern usage. This problem motivated the socialist criticism of capitalism in the nineteenth century. The same problem influenced David Hume's and Adam Smith's political economy and their discussions of justice. The problem has given rise to many precepts of distributive justice, including to each equally or according to contribution, or effort, or "merit," or "the fruits of one's labor." It is the problem of how to fairly organize and distribute economic powers and positions and divide up the resulting joint social product among productive socially cooperative agents. Economic production is a social activity resulting in a cooperative social product. The leading question of distributive justice is, how is the jointly produced social product, and the powers and positions behind it, to be fairly distributed among those who cooperate in productive activity by complying with a society's institutional requirements and making their respective contributions? (Here productive activity should be understood broadly as activity that is socially necessary for economic production across generations and includes childrearing within the family, which is necessary for the reproduction of society.) Whatever we choose to call this problem—whether the problem of "distributive justice" or "the justice of socioeconomic distributions of cooperative social product"—it is distinct from the problems of our duties toward people who are not engaged in socially productive activity, or people with serious disabilities or who are desperately poor, or people who are members of other societies. Since these are different problems, they require their own distinct principles, different from those that should govern the problem of the division of economic powers, positions of responsibility, and the distribution of income and wealth among the members of a society who are actively engaged in productive economic activity. This understanding of the problem of distributive justice informs my argument for its social institutional basis.

2. Alternative Accounts of the Social Bases of Distributive Justice

There have been several recent accounts of the "domestic" or "state" bases—I prefer "social bases"—of distributive justice, each of which, like mine, is influenced by John Rawls. First among these is the coercion view, according to which distributive justice extends its scope only to those who are subject to a state's coercive authority. Second is a political contractualist view, which maintains that citizens' being jointly authors of and subject to a system of laws delimits the scope of arbitrary inequalities and defines the range of distributive justice.[2] Third is a position based in an idea of reciprocity. It says that we owe obligations of egalitarian reciprocity to fellow citizens and residents in the state who provide us with the basic conditions and guarantees necessary to develop and act on a plan of life, but not to non-citizens, who do not.[3] In this section, I briefly discuss these alternatives, in order to provide background for a fourth view, the institutional view.

2.1. The Coercion View

One argument for the domestic bases for distributive justice relies upon the fact of coercion within legal systems. Thomas Nagel and Michael Blake[4] make this argument, and both invoke a contractualist requirement in support of it.[5] Blake contends that coercion is a prima facie violation of individuals' autonomy and must be justifiable to them "through hypothetical consent."[6] Unlike Rawls and Scanlon, Blake sees contractarian justification as relevant *only* within a state, since its role is to justify the use of coercion. As liability to coercion justifies (he contends) equal ability to influence the laws, it also justifies an egalitarian principle of distributive justice among members of the same political society. Since people of one country are not members of or subject to the jurisdiction of coercive laws of another, they have no claim to distributive justice. "Coercion, not cooperation, is the sine qua non of distributive justice."[7]

A guiding thought seemingly behind the coercion argument is that being subject to coercion entitles one to a kind of compensation, including benefits of distributive justice, for restrictions on one's freedom. But if justice requires certain rules of distribution of rights, powers, duties, and so on, why should people have to be subject to the coercive power of the state to be under a duty to comply with these rules and respect others' rights and claims? It is true that coercion is normally needed to enforce and maintain distributive justice. But we can imagine an ideal but still feasible society that is "well ordered" in that its basic institutions satisfy principles of distributive justice that everyone accepts and willingly complies with. In this ideal society, coercive enforcement would not be needed (or at most it would play a minor role). Still, even in the absence of a need for coercive enforcement, the same questions regarding the scope and requirements of distributive justice remain. The presence or absence of coercion is not relevant to deciding these issues in such a society; if not, why should it be relevant in our non-ideal world? The argument from coercion does not seem to provide the right kinds of reasons for the social grounding and domestic scope of distributive justice.

2.2. Nagel's Contractualist View

Though he also appeals to government's coercive authority, it is predominantly the legislative function of political/legal systems that characterizes Nagel's approach to distributive justice. What makes us subject to the law is that we are (ideally or hypothetically) co-authors of the law. One interpretation of the contractualist aspect of Nagel's position is basically Hobbesian.[8] Hobbes maintains that we are all authors of the law in that we *authorize* the "Sovereign" (or the state) to be our sole legal representative, giving it authority to legislate on our behalf. But Hobbesian authorization requires alienation of our original political jurisdiction and even our rights to judge and question the Sovereign's laws and decrees. This is very different from the contractualist co-authorship suggested by Nagel's reference to the general will.[9] If we construe Nagel's political contractualism democratically rather than in Hobbes's way, then the requirement is that laws must be reasonably acceptable to *democratic citizens*, as if they were the product of their (general) will. To meet this, the bases of laws should be justifiable to reasonable and rational persons in terms that they could not reasonably reject in their capacity as free and equal citizens.[10]

Underlying Nagel's political contractualism is the inescapability, or (as he says) "quasi-voluntariness," of laws.[11] By "quasi-voluntariness" Nagel seems to mean that, even if laws were not coercive and we all accepted them, still we must all be socialized and live within a mandatory system of social rules. It is because laws are inescapable in this sense, even if not necessarily coercive, that their bases must be acceptable and justifiable to us.[12] In response to Nagel, Joshua Cohen and Charles Sabel contend that many international economic arrangements are involuntarily imposed upon less advantaged countries on terms that are not acceptable to them. Opting out of these international economic treaties and conventions, such as the World Trade Organization (WTO), the International Monetary Fund (IMF), and the General Agreement on Tariffs and Trade (GATT), and their pervasive influence is not a viable choice for most nations, since they would not be able to engage in trade and export their products if they did so. International or global conformity to these arrangements is nearly as non-voluntary as (national) subjects' conformity to the laws of their land. Hence, they contend, Nagel's appeal to the non-voluntariness of laws is not sufficient to ground distributive justice domestically.[13]

I think Nagel's "quasi-voluntariness" condition is a necessary even if not sufficient condition of social justice; it is a feature of laws and other norms of social justice that they are the kind of (cooperative) rules whose jurisdiction and constant sway are pervasive and inescapable—unlike rules of voluntary associations that one may exit at any time. We cannot voluntarily abandon living in *some* society—there is no state of nature to escape to. But if the jurisdiction of legal and other social rules of justice is inevitable and inescapable—and assuming that direct coercion is not a necessary feature of laws—then we may also have to accept Cohen and Sabel's non-voluntariness argument: global treaties and regulations have a non-voluntary element too that can raise claims of justice, perhaps even distributive justice. But accepting this does not undermine, I believe, the case for the social bases of distributive justice. For that case is largely institutional, based in the non-voluntary nature of certain basic social institutions not existing at the global level, where these social institutions structure, regulate, and suffuse citizens' daily lives (unlike the lives of foreigners) and profoundly affect the kinds of persons they are. It is not simply the non-voluntariness and inescapability of laws and other regulative norms that underlie my claims for the social bases of distributive justice. Rather it is the particular nature of these institutional norms as providing the basis for social and economic cooperation and the pervasive influence they have on our development as free and equal persons and citizens.

2.3. The Reciprocity View

An integral feature of social cooperation for Rawls is reciprocity in the distribution of benefits and burdens that make cooperation possible and productive. Reciprocity is different from mutual advantage, which is explicated entirely in terms of a person's good and what is rational to do. Reciprocity adds a moral component—namely, that cooperative terms are fair, reasonable, and largely acceptable and justifiable to those engaged in cooperation. Andreas Sangiovanni argues for the "state-bases" of distributive justice from an idea of reciprocity. Starting with the luck-egalitarian assumption that justice requires the equal distribution of the consequences of arbitrary natural and social inequalities, he says, "We owe obligations of egalitarian reciprocity to fellow citizens and residents in the state, who provide us with the basic conditions and guarantees necessary to develop and act on a plan of life, but not to noncitizens, who do not."[14]

There are different kinds of cooperation—social, international, global, familial, and cooperation within voluntary associations—and each of these has its own standards of reciprocity in the distribution of benefits and burdens that make cooperation possible and productive. What is peculiar to social cooperation that demands that its own kind of reciprocity be specified in egalitarian terms, while other forms of cooperation—particularly international and global—make no such egalitarian demand? According to Sangiovanni, egalitarianism is grounded in the luck-egalitarian premise that arbitrary and undeserved inequalities in the distribution of resources are to be rectified. He then delimits the scope of the egalitarian requirement by emphasizing the singularity of "reciprocity in the mutual provision of the basic collective goods necessary for acting on a plan of life" that attends membership in the state.[15]

This is a risky strategy since it endorses the very luck-egalitarian premise that global egalitarians rely upon to argue in favor of an egalitarian global distribution principle. Because no one deserves to be born into one country (rich or poor) rather than any other, geographical boundaries are just as arbitrary and irrelevant to distributive justice as are natural and social differences of birth and (mis)fortune. But if *all* undeserved inequalities warrant rectification, why should an appeal to "reciprocity in the mutual provision of the basic collective goods necessary for acting on a plan of life" *totally* overcome this presumption, leaving foreigners with no claim at all? Moreover, cosmopolitan egalitarians will reject the claim that we "do not ultimately rely on [foreigners] for the basic goods necessary to pursue and develop a plan of life"[16] and will insist that reciprocity in this regard is purely a matter of degree. If so, cosmopolitans will argue, Sangiovanni's case for stopping the moral consequences of arbitrary inequalities at the border is jeopardized.

Since it is an essential feature of cooperation, the idea of reciprocity is a significant feature of the institutional approach I advocate. Most institutions are cooperative (prisons in large part are not) and require reciprocity among those who actively participate in them. Sangiovanni's reciprocity view does not strongly support institutional bases for distributive justice. For all that Sangiovanni says, the reciprocity view can be satisfied by a non-institutional allocative principle of justice ("to each equally" or "to each so as to maximize weighted utility, starting with the least advantaged") that makes institutions incidental to distributive justice. An allocative conception may well be a natural consequence of Sangiovanni's luck-egalitarian premise. If it is assumed that justice requires the equal or fair allocation of the consequences of arbitrary inequalities, then it is hard to see why distributive justice should address, in the first instance, the structure and design of basic economic institutions. This approach cedes the playing field to global egalitarianism from the outset by endorsing its luck-egalitarian premise. One is then put in the position of having to find some way to delimit this premise's scope. But the idea of reciprocity in the provision of primary social goods needed to lead a good life does not adequately respond to the cosmopolitan objections that (1) it is insufficient to overcome the presumption of equalizing arbitrary inequalities; and (2) there is sufficient global reciprocity to underwrite the global scope of egalitarian distributive justice.

3. *The Institutional View*

My primary focus is the justice of *cooperative institutions*. By "institutions" I mean (following Rawls) the many social practices of various kinds which are defined and regulated by public systems of rules that specify procedures and rules of conduct, offices, and positions of responsibility and that distribute to participating individuals various rights, liberties, powers, privileges, opportunities, duties, liabilities, and so on.[17]

There are different kinds of cooperative institutions—political, social, legal, religious, international, global, and the like. Most have rule- and decision-making and dispute-resolution procedures, along with sanctions to enforce decisions, and these are all subject to standards of fairness. Also, cooperative institutions engage in the distribution of benefits and burdens of various kinds (rights, powers, duties, liabilities, etc.), and again substantive standards of distribution are relied upon (by participants and observers) to assess the justice of these assignments of institutional benefits and burdens. Standards of fairness and justice differ depending upon the kinds of institution, taking into account their different purposes and roles and the kinds of rights, powers, duties, and so on involved. Thus, we might expect equality of certain rights, powers, and privileges within some institutions, especially political ones, whereas in others, such as armies, churches, families, and educational institutions, equal rights and powers of many kinds may be inappropriate to the institution's purposes and roles.

Hume argued that there are four basic "conventions" that make social and economic cooperation possible and productive.[18] First, rules of property are needed to secure exclusive possession of goods and productive resources, and to specify and assign the incidents of property, including the kinds of rights, powers, duties, and liabilities regarding the permissible uses, control, enjoyment, and disposal of resources and other things. Second, rules of "transfer by consent" make markets, sales and exchange, trade, and the division of labor possible, as well as gifts, bequests, inheritances, and other means of transferring property in possessions. Finally, economic production, trade, and distribution presuppose rules and conventions regulating promising, contracts, and agreements of all kinds. Hume called these three systems of rules the "conventions of justice." Hume also saw government as a fourth convention necessary for social and economic cooperation. Government is needed not simply to enforce the conventions of justice and resolve disputes, but also to legislatively specify and judicially interpret the many procedures and rights, powers, duties, and the like constituting property and other economic institutions.

Hume argued against Locke that none of the conventions of justice (property, markets, and other transfers, agreements of all kinds, and governments) are "natural"; rather they are "artificial"—"artifices" of reason, habit, and imagination. Being conventional, the basic institutions that make social and economic cooperation possible and productive can be specified in different ways. Clearly there are different ways to allocate and define political power, resulting in several forms of government—monarchical, oligarchical, democratic, and mixed constitutions in between. Perhaps not as clearly— because most people take existing property conventions as definitive—the many rules and incidents of property can be specified in multiple ways, so that rights and powers of possession, including "ownership" rights, also are conventionally defined relative to the institutional rules of each society. Since property and the other conventions of justice are not "natural," some general method or principle is needed to specify and assess the rights, powers, and duties that constitute these institutions. According to Hume, the conventions of justice are, or if not should be, designed to achieve "public utility." This explains and justifies, he suggests, such rules as a right of first possession, free exchange of goods and services, the right to possess the fruits of one's efforts and contributions, rights of bequest to one's offspring, and other rules familiar in private property market economies.[19]

The principle of utility is but one way to specify the rules of property, transfer, contract, and other institutions that make economic cooperation possible and productive. Other feasible alternatives include principles of efficiency, libertarian entitlement principles, the difference principle, and so on. The general point is that, even if (as Hayek contends) economic background institutions were to evolve largely unplanned, some standard is at work and is needed to socially specify and critically assess the allocation of economic opportunities, powers, responsibilities, and positions, as well as the distribution of the many rights, liberties, duties, liabilities, and so on that make economic production, exchange, distribution, and consumption possible. The primary question of distributive justice (as I use the term) is, what principles are to be relied upon to decide and assess the manner in which basic social and economic institutions specify the rules and allocate and distribute rights, powers, opportunities, positions of responsibility, duties, liabilities, and so on necessary for productive economic activity?

Now, what role does social cooperation among members of society play in enabling economic cooperation and its necessary background institutions? Economic cooperation is the greater part of social cooperation among the members of a society. Though most people in any society are complete strangers to one another and do not cooperate in other ways, they regularly engage in economic cooperation insofar as they daily enter into productive and commercial transactions, respect and comply with norms of property, markets, contract, and other terms of basic institutions, and form their expectations accordingly. Economic cooperation is fundamentally grounded in and made possible by basic social institutions. Economic agents' transactions, expectations, and daily habits are shaped by the complex system of rules of these background institutions. Margaret Thatcher famously said there is no such thing as "society"; there are only separate individuals. Societies indeed consist of separate individuals, as do churches, governments, families, teams, and other social groups. But what makes separate individuals members of a society, or lesser social group, is that each occupies one or more positions with (specified or implicit) rights, powers, and duties (citizen or subject; manager or laborer; administrator, teacher, or student) and enters into cooperative relationships with others that are defined and regulated according to the rules of the relevant institutions. Primary among the institutions that are distinctive of society and social cooperation are basic social, political, and economic institutions.

Societies are intrinsically political in nature in that they have a political constitution (written or unwritten) and legal institutions enabling society to change existing laws and other social rules and introduce new rules to respond to changing circumstances; judicial procedures for resolving disputes arising under the laws and interpreting their requirements; and executive powers and procedures enabling the administration and (if needed) enforcement of laws, regulations, and decrees. Equally basic to social cooperation are the complex system of rules and institutions that Hume saw as necessary for fruitful economic production, markets, distribution, and consumption among members of society, including the legal institution of property; the system of laws that enable sales, exchanges, bequests, and other transfers of goods and services; the legal system of contract and agreements of all kinds; the myriad laws and conventions defining and enabling corporations, labor unions, legal partnerships, and other joint ventures; and securities laws, negotiable instrument laws, patents, copyrights, and many other institutional mechanisms that make economic cooperation possible. Finally (as Rawls says), the family in some form is also a basic social institution, since it is needed to raise and educate the young, so that society may reproduce itself in perpetuity.

G. A. Cohen contends that Rawls's idea of a basic social institution is ambiguous and that the list of institutions said to be basic seems arbitrarily selective. For example, Rawls says basic institutions have a profound influence on people's lives. But other social institutions also exercise enormous influence over individuals' lives (e.g., religious institutions). Another basis that might be used for distinguishing basic institutions is that they, unlike religious institutions, are legally coercive. But, says Cohen, the family is a basic institution for Rawls and it is non-coercive since familial norms are not enforced by the state but are largely conventional and a matter of free association (among participating adults at least).[20]

Here we have to ignore the fact that all modern governments have bodies of family law that specify and coercively enforce norms of parental control and responsibility to adequately care for children, meet their basic needs, and have them educated. Nonetheless, suppose Cohen's points are conceded. What then is so distinctive about (Rawls's) basic social institutions? The answer is that basic social institutions—like Hume's "conventions of justice"—are those needed to make cooperation among individuals in any society possible and productive. This should be obvious in the case of political and economic institutions. As for the family, even if its internal norms may not be legally specified and coercively enforced to the same degree as the terms of other basic institutions are, still it is a precondition of any ongoing society that it has an institution for nurturing and socializing its young, so that society can reproduce and perpetuate itself over time. Religions, universities, communications, and other (now voluntary) institutions, however necessary they may be for the peaceful and productive cooperation and stability of particular societies, are nonetheless non-basic, since they are not necessary for cooperation among the members of a society in general. Many societies exist and have thrived without these institutions. When necessary for cooperation in a particular society, the function of influential institutions such as religion is often largely "ideological" (to borrow Marx's term)—among other things, they provide the beliefs and motivations members need to comply with the basic terms of cooperation specified by its basic social institutions.

Each society has its own set of basic political and economic background institutions, and these basic institutions (along with cultural traditions) largely distinguish one society from another. Compliance with the rules of these basic institutions, even if generally voluntary, is unavoidable for the members of a society, since these rules are inescapable and structure, regulate, and suffuse their daily lives in innumerable ways—unlike the situation of members of other societies whose lives are structured and regulated by their own system of basic social institutions. Even when emigration is a real option for people (it rarely is), they still must reside within the social framework provided by *some* system of basic social institutions. Conditions resembling a "state of nature," when they exist, result from the breakdown of social and political institutions.

Societies obviously are not separate and self-sufficient—they and many of their members have direct cooperative relationships with other societies and their members, and these can be quite complex. But cooperation among members of different societies presupposes and is dependent upon the basic institutions of their respective societies. What primarily characterizes a society, at least for purposes of justice, is its basic political and economic institutions, and these institutions are independent from those of other societies in that they have different sources of authority and are discrete systems of rules that are legislated, interpreted, applied, and enforced by a society's own political institutions. The rules defining a society's basic institutions largely define the basic terms of social cooperation among members of that society. They specify not just constraints on their conduct, but also the rules and institutions that define legitimate actions and transactions that are a precondition of socially and economically productive activity. These institutions provide the basis for legitimate expectations that political and economic agents form and rely upon in undertaking cooperative activities. Individuals participate in these basic institutions, and a large part of their lives are structured and regulated by them. They form beliefs and expectations based on the institutional rules, and then contribute their labor or possessions and undertake risks in light of these beliefs and expectations.

Any organized group activity involves the creation of benefits, responsibilities, and burdens. What distinguishes cooperation from efficiently coordinated group activity (e.g., prisoners on an assembly line) is that in cooperation each person assumes a share of the burdens of cooperation and is rewarded in turn with a share of the benefits according to some conception of fair terms. Cooperation then normally involves an idea of reciprocity in the distribution of benefits and burdens. Some idea of fair contributions to benefits and fair assumption of burdens conditions any cooperative groups' standards for fair distribution. A fundamental question of justice (if not the fundamental question) is, what are the standards of reciprocity that any society is to use to determine the fair division of benefits and burdens that result from cooperation among members of society with one another? According to the institutional view, distributive justice involves the standards that are to be used to specify, structure, and assess the institutional rules and procedures of the basic institutions that make economic production, trade, and consumption possible among the members of a society. These institutions specify the rules according to which society's members engage in socially productive economic activities and relationships with one another, and form their expectations accordingly regarding their duties and rewards for cooperative compliance. The principles regulating cooperative institutions determine what is generally presumed to be a fair distribution of economic benefits and burdens among society's members who do their part in social cooperation. Whether these distributions are fair is, of course, a substantive question of distributive justice.

4. An Objection and Further Clarification

Now comes the global cosmopolitan who avers that however the terms of basic political and economic institutions regulating society's members' cooperative relationships and expectations are defined, they must distribute a sizable portion of the benefits of a society's cooperative endeavors, if not their burdens, to members of other societies. Global egalitarians contend that the benefits of a society's cooperation are to be equally distributed or at least distributed on equal terms to members of other societies. This is so, even though members of other societies have their own basic institutions defining and regulating their cooperative expectations and socially productive relations, and do not participate directly in any substantial way in the political or economic institutions of other societies.

Why should the basic institutional rules that define the cooperative activities and expectations and socially productive relationships among members of one society extend on equal terms the benefits created by members within that society to members of other societies? Here global egalitarians contend that people are not responsible for the society they are born into; it is a matter of brute luck. Moreover, social cooperation is an ambiguous idea, especially given increasing globalization and the fact that people in one society cooperate—socially, culturally, and economically—nearly as much with people in other societies as among themselves. But the institutional argument for the social bases of distributive justice does not rely simply upon facts of cooperation and reciprocity in general. There are all kinds of reciprocal cooperative relationships among members of the same or different societies—religious, cultural, even economic—that do not give rise to claims of distributive justice. The argument for the social bases of distributive justice rests upon society's members contributing their fair share toward socially productive cooperation according to the rules of the basic social institutions that regulate the political and economic relations of, and claim jurisdiction over and allegiance from, all members of the same society. People living in other societies, no matter the extent of their cooperation with members of one's own society, do not actively participate in the basic institutions of one's own society, nor are they subject to its jurisdiction or responsible for contributing their fair share to social cooperation. Of course, people in different societies engage in economic cooperation across borders, but the institutions that make this possible presuppose and depend upon the basic institutions of social cooperation within each society. Property laws and other basic social institutions within each society provide the grounding and the matter for economic treaties that coordinate and harmonize economic relations among different societies.

Suppose, however, that it be conceded that economic cooperation with members of different societies according to the norms of international or global institutions gives rise to *some* claim of distributive justice, at least with regard to a fair share of income and wealth even if not economic powers, positions, and opportunities. This is not incompatible with the institutional view I advocate. But on the institutional view, it implies at most that distributions extend only to the product of international and global cooperation (mainly the returns on gains of trade) as decided by the specific fair terms of cooperation that specify the common institutions regulative of international or global cooperation. Hence, complex international trade agreements (e.g., within the WTO) can not only be subject to procedural fairness in decision-making and substantive fairness preventing economically powerful societies from taking unfair advantage of less powerful and poorer societies. It may also be that these international or global arrangements give rise to distributive claims on economic product and returns of trade arising out of these economic institutions.[21] But legitimate claims to a fair share of these benefits of international or global economic cooperation do not entail that members of different societies can also lay claim to a distributive share of the benefits (whether income and wealth or opportunities, powers, and positions of office) that is the product of social and economic cooperation among members of a society different from their own.

Here some egalitarian cosmopolitans (e.g., Beitz and Tan)[22] have said that the members of different societies not only cooperate with one another according to the terms of international and global institutions, but also are expected to respect and not interfere with other societies' territory as protected by "international property rights" (Beitz). These demands should be sufficient to entitle other societies and their members to a fair or even egalitarian share of income and wealth resulting from a society's basic social institutions. This allegedly follows from the fact that all are subject to cooperative duties to respect other societies' "right of ownership" (Tan) of their territory and not undermine the integrity of their laws and institutions, submitting to their requirements insofar as they engage in economic and cultural relations with oneself or one's own society.

The general problem with the argument that respect for another society's territory is sufficient grounds for (egalitarian) global distributions is that the argument rests on an extremely diluted, even Hobbesian conception of cooperation, and particularly of economic cooperation. It says, in effect, that societies and their members "cooperate" with each other (socially, economically) so long as they are not in a state of war. But simply because a person (or society) is expected to respect the integrity of another society's territory and socially cooperative relations does not make him or her a participant in others' cooperative endeavors, far less so an equal beneficiary of those rules and subject to their jurisdiction. Simply because I respect the integrity of your home and family does not mean I am a cooperative member of it, nor does it entitle me to benefits your family shares among its members, and neither does it give you any kind of jurisdiction or authority over my day-to-day activities. Even if we accept a diluted conception of cooperation, this entitles parties only to the reciprocal benefits of that particular form of cooperation (namely, respect for one another's territorial boundaries and not undermining one another's laws and institutions). It does not by itself imply a general right to all or even any of the benefits the other party contributes toward and enjoys in his or her cooperative relations with members of his or her own society. The duty to respect another society's territory does not imply a right to a fair or equal share of the benefits created by its members' cooperation according to the terms of their basic social institutions.

Reciprocity is a feature of cooperation of all kinds. It is a truism, but an important one, to say that reciprocity in the distribution of benefits and burdens of cooperation depends upon one's taking part in cooperation itself and complying with the expectations and constraints on conduct which that form of cooperation imposes. Any form of cooperation involves benefits and incentives to engage in mutually beneficial conduct, and at the same time imposes obligations and responsibilities as a condition of conferring these benefits. Reciprocity in the sharing of benefits and burdens is defined by the terms and provisions of cooperation, and these are assessed according to standards of justice appropriate to that form of cooperation. Not all forms of reciprocity are the same, and few of these require egalitarianism in the distribution of benefits. The kind of reciprocity that social cooperation requires is different from the reciprocities of more local institutions, such as families, churches, universities, and professional groups; and all of these differ from the reciprocity required by cooperation among members of different societies and their political institutions. Different kinds of cooperative reciprocity require different regulative principles of justice that provide standards for the legitimate expectations and the distribution of benefits characteristic of a particular form of cooperation. To have a claim upon the institutional benefits of a particular form of cooperation, and to be subject to its particular institutional burdens, requires membership and participation in that particular scheme of cooperation and doing one's fair share in making contributions. Hence, social reciprocity in the distribution of income and wealth, as well as opportunities, powers and privileges of office, and positions of responsibility, requires membership and participation in the political and social institutions that constitute the basic structure of society.

Global egalitarian and other strong cosmopolitanisms deny these claims: participation in and contribution toward sustaining the basic social institutions that make social and economic cooperation among the members of a society possible are not preconditions for having a claim on the benefits of those basic institutions. Reciprocity in social relations is largely if not entirely irrelevant to distributive justice according to global distribution views. It is understandable how classical utilitarians might argue this position, for what matters then is not fairness and reciprocity but maximizing aggregate welfare summed across all individuals in the world. On this view, territorial boundaries and social cooperation, like other distinctions, are ultimately irrelevant to questions of distributive justice, except for their instrumental effect in encouraging greater overall utility. It is also understandable how pure luck-egalitarian conceptions of distributive justice might support such a position; for if membership in one society rather than another is a matter of pure luck, then membership must be morally arbitrary and should be irrelevant to distributive claims. But if the idea of social cooperation—participating in and doing one's fair share to maintain and contribute toward basic social institutions and receiving a fair share of their benefits—is to carry independent weight in matters of distributive justice, then these positions must be mistaken.

It is not part of my argument that the scope of justice, including economic justice, depends upon the presence or need for coercively enforced institutions or relationships. Nor do I contend that the scope of justice, even distributive justice, is limited to members of the same society. Each institution—whether social, global, or local—is subject to procedural and substantive requirements of justice and reciprocity that are distinctive to institutions of that kind. The institutional requirements of justice, including distributive justice, then differ depending upon the kind of cooperation and reciprocity institutions regulate. It is because they are not members of, and do not do their fair share in contributing toward and maintaining the basic institutions of other societies, that members of one society are not entitled to distributive shares of the particular benefits, or are subject to the institutional burdens, of social cooperation created by members of other societies. This does not deny that economic cooperation among members of different societies can raise claims of economic justice, even distributive justice. But these standards of economic justice are different from the standards applying among members of a single society. And even if they do not differ but are the same distributive standards (e.g., egalitarian standards), their reach extends only to the products of economic and cultural cooperation that result from members of different political societies acting according to the rules of international or global institutions; these standards do not entitle foreign persons to the full benefits or burdens that accompany membership and socially productive participation in the basic economic and political institutions of another society.

5. *Economic and Distributive Justice*

To clarify the institutional position, I will elaborate on the distinction between economic and distributive justice. I understand economic justice as a broad range of moral requirements that should structure and regulate cooperative economic relations among persons within society and between societies. Distributive justice is a large part of economic justice, but not the entirety. Distributive justice concerns the principles that should govern the basic institutions that determine (1) the fair distribution of the economic goods, income and wealth, including both consumer goods and the means of production, as well as (2) the fair distribution of powers and prerogatives of offices and positions of responsibility in economic activity, including control over the means of production, and finally (3) the fair distribution of the opportunities to occupy these offices and positions and exercise the powers and prerogatives they involve.

The distribution of economic rights, powers, responsibilities, and opportunities is achieved via certain basic institutions, which might be called "distributive institutions." These have been discussed earlier (property of all kinds, markets and other exchanges and transfers such as bequests and gifts, permissible contracts, negotiable instruments, etc.). Distributive institutions are for the most part legally specified and enforced, but also include other non-legal social conventions.[23] Political institutions are also among key distributive institutions; in addition to their role in legislating, interpreting, and enforcing the rules of the economic institutions just mentioned, they also directly make transfer payments of income and wealth (including wage and other income subsidies and a social minimum) and exercise economic powers of various kinds.

In addition to distributive justice, economic justice involves the standards that should specify and regulate economic activities and institutions that do not directly determine the distribution of income, wealth, and economic powers and positions. For example, monetary policy or laws regulating banking and finance (including capitalization requirements) are governed by standards of economic justice, as are disclosure and other conditions on home mortgages, stock offerings by corporations, and product safety requirements and warranty provisions that cannot be contractually eliminated. Though these laws and regulations have indirect distributive effects, they do not decide how economic opportunities, powers, and positions, and income and wealth are ultimately to be distributed. Terms of trade among different societies also raise questions of economic justice, but not necessarily distributive justice (discussed later).

On the institutional account, a theory of distributive justice is a theory about how to design the basic cooperative institutions that make possible the distribution of income and wealth, economic powers, positions, and opportunities. If these distributive institutions do not exist—and globally they do not—then the subject matter of distributive justice does not exist. There may be a question of justice as to whether these institutions, such as comprehensive global or international property laws, *should* be put into place, but this is not a question of distributive justice. It raises instead the question of whether we are under a positive duty to enter into certain complex kinds of cooperative political and economic relationships with other societies and assume certain duties, in addition to those that are already required by a duty of assistance and other humanitarian requirements of justice (more on this later).

The primary distributive institution is, of course, the complex system of norms of property, for property ultimately determines who has rights, powers, and other claims, as well as duties, liabilities, and the like with respect to income and wealth, including the means of production. The basic institution of property exists in every society and is politically/legally specified, regulated, interpreted, and enforced. There is no legally or politically recognized global or international institution of property to which the terms of principles of justice might apply in order to specify the incidents of property, including rights of use, possession and income, powers of control, duties of conservation, and so on, and to regulate their distribution. There are existing agreements among peoples, under the WTO and other treaties and arrangements, to harmonize certain specific institutions of property, primarily patent law and to a lesser degree copyright. But the harmonization of many separate political societies' own separate property and copyright laws does not constitute a basic global institution of property law with respect to these intangibles—no more than harmonization and cooperation in enforcing extradition laws or narcotics laws constitute a global police force or global legal system with global authority and original jurisdiction. Since there are currently no global or international institutions of property, there is no ground at this time for making claims of global distributive justice on this basis.

What other bases for global distribution requirements might there be? Much has been made of the increasing prevalence of international, transnational, and supranational institutions (WTO, IMF, the World Bank, GATT, the Bank for International Settlements, the Organisation for Economic Co-operation and Development, etc.), and some have argued that these and similar institutions, jointly or severally, provide grounds for claims of global distributive justice. These institutions have an important role with regard to cooperative economic activity among societies and their members, and clearly influence the distribution of income and wealth. They raise many issues of economic justice, regarding fairness of trade relations, reasonableness of conditions for acquiring loans, decent working conditions and workplace safety, the powers and responsibilities of multinational corporations, and the duties of nations that sponsor them to regulate corporations' activities both abroad and at home. Clearly societies and their corporations have a duty of justice not to exploit or take unfair advantage of poorer countries and their resources or workforces, and there are many other duties and requirements of economic justice that apply to trade and trade organizations. But do these international or global trade and other organizations raise concerns of distributive justice of the kind that advocates of global distributive principles contend for, namely, the transfer of income and wealth from wealthier to less advantaged peoples to fit some distributive pattern (often egalitarian)?

I do not believe they do. There is no global parallel to the complex system of basic social institutions in each society that enable the production and distribution of primary social goods that are the object of distributive justice—no global scheme of property, contract, sales, finance, corporation, bankruptcy, and other systems of laws that make up the basic institutions that mainly constitute the basic structure of a society. In the absence of a system of these distributive institutions, there is no basic structure of global economic institutions to which to apply principles of distributive justice. Those international economic institutions that do exist, such as the WTO, do not have original authority or jurisdiction to enact laws; they are secondary institutions in that they originate by treaty or agreement among distinct political societies and presuppose and are dependent upon the basic social and economic institutions of their participating societies. The WTO is a harmonization arrangement that requires participating nations to ensure that their economic policies and laws conform to certain uniform requirements (e.g., eliminating subsidies for industries). There are many different kinds of demands of economic justice that apply to WTO activities. For example, societies that allow corporations chartered under their laws to engage in unfair business practices with less advantaged peoples, or to engage with corrupt governments in practices that exploit a peoples' resources or workforce, are guilty of economic injustice. Societies, jointly and severally, have duties of economic justice to regulate and oversee trade and the business practices of all economic agents working from or within their borders. But the requirements of economic justice that apply to trade and other economic relations differ from requirements that final distributions of income and wealth result in some pattern among participating members or that mandate a global minimum beyond that imposed by humanitarian duties of assistance.

The WTO is not a basic institution of the kind that requires principles of distributive justice to determine the fair distribution of economic powers and product among participating members. Some cosmopolitan egalitarians nonetheless contend that societies have a positive duty to establish a framework of basic institutions that enable poorer societies to engage in economic and other forms of cooperation with other societies. Once these basic cooperative institutions are in place, it is said, duties of distributive justice globally apply.[24]

I agree with the first part of this contention to this extent: Advantaged peoples have a duty to assist what Rawls calls "burdened peoples" with the economic and political development of their society by enabling them to put into place the institutions they need to become economically self-sustaining. The aim of this duty of assistance is to help burdened peoples establish political and economic institutions enabling them to satisfy the basic needs of all their members and become economically independent. But do we have a general duty to engage in economic cooperation, including ongoing trade relations, with other peoples? Assuming a society is economically just in other respects, I do not think it has a duty to engage in cooperative economic relations with every society, especially not economic cooperation of the kind that would require distributive justice. Suppose economic cooperation with a distant society would not be mutually beneficial and would require assuming a net loss for one or more nations. Is there a duty of justice in this case for a society to engage in cooperative activity contrary to the interests of the members of that society, *assuming* that its relationships with other societies are just in other respects? On the assumption that a richer nation has not caused the economic exploitation or isolation of a poorer country, owes it no restitution for past wrongs, and has fulfilled its duty of assistance to that poorer nation, I do not believe the richer nation owes a further duty to engage in economic cooperation with the poorer nation if that requires a net loss. What then of mutually beneficial economic cooperation with poorer societies that nonetheless comes at some cost, insofar as a society could have gained more if it had cooperated with a more efficient but richer supplier? Here I am less sure, but would venture that there is no duty of *justice* to cooperate on these terms (again, assuming the justice of one's own society and its relations with other societies in all other relevant respects).

Perhaps an analogy may prove helpful. In the case of individual relationships, we have duties of civility, respect, and assistance, but we do not have a duty to befriend others or to engage in cooperation of other kinds if it is against our interests. Somewhat analogously, with other peoples, we have duties of civility, mutual respect, and assistance in times of pressing need. Hence, we have substantial duties now to come to the economic assistance of billions of people who subsist on less than a few dollars a day and also to assist their governments in making their society politically independent and economically self-sustaining so that it meets all its members' basic needs. This duty of assistance would involve great costs to ourselves, and perhaps has priority even over increasing the share of income and wealth going to the least advantaged in our own society (assuming they are substantially better off than the least advantaged in burdened societies). But do we as a society also have ongoing duties to engage in economic and other forms of cooperation if it is against our economic and other interests to do so and would come at the expense of our least advantaged (again assuming that our relations with other societies are just in other respects)? Again, I do not think that we do. If I am wrong, and we do have a duty to engage in some forms of economic cooperation with all peoples even if it comes at a cost to ourselves (including our least advantaged), I still do not think that trade and other forms of economic cooperation with all peoples that are morally required are sufficient to give rise to duties of distributive justice. And even if I am wrong about that, and assuming that basic global economic institutions were in place—suppose that various forms of intangible property (patents, copyrights, etc.) were globally applicable and uniformly administered and interpreted—the priority of basic social institutions with regard to claims of distributive justice would remain. Economic justice may well require that the benefits, and the burdens, of this global institutional form of property be fairly distributed among all peoples according to appropriate principles. (Suppose poorer countries were provided with subsidies that came from a tax on patent and copyright profits and/or were granted exemptions that permitted them to produce a restricted amount of patented goods, such as drugs or medical equipment, without having to pay patent fees.) But this requirement of global distributive justice would not extend so far as to nullify or override the social requirements of distributive justice existing among members of other societies. It would not establish a general claim to the social product of other societies of the kind that global egalitarians contend for.

This denies arguments by global egalitarians such as Pogge who contend that any degree of economic cooperation with other societies, no matter how minimal, is sufficient to give rise to full-fledged duties of distributive justice among peoples.[25] Even if the premise were conceded that economic cooperation with other peoples as such gives rise to duties of distributive justice, my contention is that other societies' claims on a share of cooperative product beyond what all have fairly bargained for is limited to a share of the product that stems from the cooperative institution making it possible (gains from trade, etc.). It does not extend to the entire social product of each cooperating people.

Finally, global egalitarians and other advocates of cosmopolitan distributive justice often remark on the pervasive influence and unjust consequences of some international economic agreement or arrangement—such as the WTO under the "Washington consensus"—and then conclude that the injustice of the current arrangement requires principles of distributive justice. I've argued that harmonization of standards under WTO and international regulations of securities, or product safety, or finance, or the law of sales does not by itself give rise to claims of distributive justice. For the basic institutions that are harmonized still have separate sources of political authority, and their jurisdiction ranges still only over members of their respective societies.[26] What is bothersome about current economic arrangements, aside from a history of injustice, is that more powerful nations such as the United States exercise power and threat advantage to inflict standards that unduly benefit themselves and conform to their preferred practices of doing business. But if such standards are fairly enacted according to democratic procedures that do not advantage powerful peoples, then much of the current injustice of international trade relations and other arrangements is potentially minimized. The problem with current WTO and other trade norms and practices is not one of distributive injustice but of economic injustice that gives unfair advantage to richer nations and that allows them to exploit the position of poorer nations and dictate to them economic policies especially beneficial to richer nations.

6. Conclusion

I have argued for the social bases of distributive justice on grounds that distributive justice largely concerns the principles of cooperation needed to design certain basic social institutions that are necessary for any society and that structure and suffuse daily life. I have not discussed Rawls's argument for the priority of the basic structure because of its "profound influence" on individuals' future prospects and the kinds of persons they are and can come to be. Perhaps in the absence of these considerations, the argument from basic social institutions made here is not sufficient to make a convincing case for the social bases of distributive justice. There may be a family of reasons needed to support this conclusion (which is true of other positions as well). I'll conclude with some brief remarks on this further argument.

Cosmopolitan egalitarians contend that appeals to the profound influence of social cooperation are not sufficient to justify the social nature of distributive justice, since global cooperation is increasingly prevalent and influential. I agree that appeals to the profound effects of social cooperation are not sufficient to establish the *exclusive* ground of distributive justice in social cooperation that Nagel and Rawls contend for. International and global cooperation are potential sources of claims of distributive justice too, once a complex web of international or global institutions has developed. But against cosmopolitan egalitarians I contend that the profound effects of social cooperation are sufficient (together with other reasons I've discussed) to justify the social bases of distributive justice with respect to the benefits and burdens that arise from social cooperation according to the terms of basic social institutions. The fact that we, or others, may be profoundly influenced by cultural and even economic exchanges with other peoples does not mitigate the fact that there is something qualitatively different about the effects of membership in a society. Life in the absence of international economic cooperation would be rather austere. In the United States we would have to curtail significantly our profligate use of energy and many raw materials and abandon our enjoyment of many products that we import (approximately 14 percent of the goods and services consumed annually). It would require an extraordinary change in our current living conditions, and for many less advantaged nations its consequences would be even more severe. For this and other reasons, autarky is not a desirable situation for any country.

But the effects of an absence of international cooperation pale when compared with those of an absence of social cooperation. This is not (or not simply) for reasons Hobbes emphasizes. Rather, we are distinctly social beings in that, in the absence of society and social development, we have but inchoate and unrealized capacities, including our capacities for rationality, morality, sociability, even language itself. As Rousseau says, prior to society and socialization, we are but "stupid, limited animals." Without socialization we have only undeveloped and inchoate capacities. Not being members of some society at crucial points in our lives is not then an option for us as civilized beings. It is not simply that social cooperation is inescapable and no longer voluntary for us. Rather, the possibility of voluntary activity itself depends upon our being socialized and educated under the normative influence of society. If our humanity consists in our distinctly human capacities, including our moral and rational capacities of practical reason, then there are profoundly social bases for our humanity. These are strong reasons, together with the institutional reasons here set forth, for affirming the "profoundly social" bases for principles of justice (Rawls). But this argument requires more elaboration than can be provided here.[27]

Notes

1. I understand economic justice as a broad range of moral requirements that should structure and regulate cooperative economic relations among persons and societies. Distributive justice is part of economic justice. This distinction is discussed later.
2. Thomas Nagel, "The Problem of Global Justice," *Philosophy & Public Affairs* 33, no. 2 (2005): 128–29.
3. Andreas Sangiovanni, "Global Justice, Reciprocity, and the State," *Philosophy & Public Affairs* 35, no. 1 (2007): 3–39.
4. Nagel, "The Problem of Global Justice," 113–47; Michael Blake, "Distributive Justice, State Coercion, and Autonomy," *Philosophy & Public Affairs* 30, no. 3 (2001): 257–96.
5. Both Blake and Nagel refer to Rawls's claim that political power is always coercive power. Rawls says this with reference, not to distributive justice, but to the legitimacy of political power (*PL*, 136). Rawls does not argue, as Blake does, that it is government's coercive power that underlies the domestic scope of distributive justice. Instead, I think Rawls's reasons resemble more those discussed in this chapter.
6. Blake, "Distributive Justice, State Coercion, and Autonomy," 284.
7. Blake, "Distributive Justice, State Coercion, and Autonomy," 289.
8. See Sangiovanni, "Global Justice, Reciprocity, and the State," 16.
9. Nagel says that a necessary condition of the "egalitarian requirement" of justice "comes from a special involvement of agency or the will that is inseparable from membership in a political society . . . One might even say that we are all participants in the general will." Nagel, "The Problem of Global Justice," 128–29.
10. This resembles Rawls's principle of political legitimacy (*PL*, 137, 217, 393).
11. Nagel refers to "the ideal of quasi-voluntariness which legitimacy aims at." Thomas Nagel, *Equality and Partiality* (New York: Oxford University Press, 1991), 37.

12. See Nagel, *Equality and Partiality*, 36–37.
13. Joshua Cohen and Charles Sabel, "Extra Rempublicam Nulla Justicia," *Philosophy & Public Affairs* 34, no. 2 (2006), 147–75.
14. Sangiovanni, "Global Justice," 22.
15. Sangiovanni, "Global Justice," 22.
16. Sangiovanni, "Global Justice," 35.
17. See *TJ* orig., 55; *TJ* 47–48.
18. David Hume, *A Treatise on Human Nature*, 2nd ed., ed. L. A. Selby-Bigge and P. H. Nidditch (Oxford: Oxford University Press, 1978), book 3, part 2, chaps. 1–7.
19. Hume, *A Treatise of Human Nature*, 2nd ed., 501–15; David Hume, *An Enquiry Concerning the Principles of Morals* (Indianapolis: Hackett, 1983), sec. 3, "Of Justice," part 2. In the *Enquiry* Hume considers equal division and distribution according to virtue as alternatives to public utility and says they are impractical and exist nowhere for long since they result in general impoverishment.
20. G. A. Cohen, *Rescuing Justice and Equality*, (Cambridge, MA: Harvard University Press, 2008), 133–7.
21. Aaron James, *Fairness in Practice* (New York: Oxford University Press, 2012), argues that more prosperous nations have a duty to share gains of trade with less prosperous nations.
22. Charles Beitz, *Political Theory and International Relations* (Princeton, NJ: Princeton University Press, 1979), 149; Kok-Chor Tan, *Justice, Institutions, and Luck* (Oxford: Oxford University Press, 2012), 154, 158, 163–64.
23. For example, certain market practices or bargaining norms may not be legally specified and are legally permissible; they still are subject to standards of economic and perhaps distributive justice.
24. See Charles Beitz, "Cosmopolitan Ideals and National Sentiments," *Journal of Philosophy* 80, no. 10 (1980): 595ff.; Kok-Chor Tan, *Justice without Borders* (Cambridge: Cambridge University Press, 2004), 59, 169–70.
25. Thomas Pogge, *Realizing Rawls* (Ithaca, NY: Cornell University Press, 1989), 262–63.
26. Here it might be objected that relations between states within a federal union, such as the United States, involve the harmonization of the laws of many semi-sovereign states and that my argument implies that relations of distributive justice should not fully extend across state boundaries in the United States. But the supremacy, commerce, and "full faith and credit" clauses of the US Constitution dictate that the United States is one economic system. The fact that the fifty states all have their own law of sales, contracts, property, etc.—which are all similar if not the same due to common law sources, the Uniform Commercial Code, and other uniform acts—is simply a matter of administrative convenience within the political and economic system of institutions put in place by the Constitution and laws of the United States. Moreover, separate US states do not

have political sovereignty. The Civil War established that there is only one sovereign political authority in the United States. In this respect the United States is different from the European Union, which *is* a union of sovereign states with different cultures and languages. I am grateful to Joshua Cohen and a graduate student in the Stanford Political Theory Workshop in January 2009 for raising this objection, which is also discussed by Richard Miller in his response to this chapter, in "The Cosmopolitan Controversy Needs a Mid-Life Crisis," *Cosmopolitanism vs. Non-Cosmopolitanism*, ed. Gillian Brock (Oxford: Oxford University Press, 2013) 272–93.

27. For further discussion, see chapter 7. For their helpful comments on this chapter, I am grateful to Kok-Chor Tan, Joshua Cohen, Gerald Gaus, Brad McHose, Alistair MacLeod, and audiences at the Stanford Political Theory Workshop and the philosophy departments at the University of Arizona and Queens University.

The Basic Structure of Society
as the Primary Subject of Justice

1. Introduction

Rawls's focus on principles of justice for the basic structure of primary social institutions evolved from his early discussion of practices, social rules, and Humean conventions and his apparent commitment to a version of rule utilitarianism. In his 1955 "Two Concepts of Rules," his stated aim is "to show the importance of the distinction between justifying a practice and justifying a particular action falling under it, and . . . explain the logical basis of this distinction" (*CP*, 20). Though Rawls claims a "logical basis" for the distinction, in later works the parallel distinction between principles for institutions and for individuals, and the primacy assigned to principles of justice for the basic structure, are regarded as moral assumptions required by "the Reasonable" (*CP*, 316–17) that ultimately stem from ideals of persons and society. Rawls's conception of free and equal moral persons, and the social conditions necessary to realize reciprocity and citizens' fundamental interests, are integral to understanding why Rawls assigns primacy to principles of justice for the basic structure of society.

Rawls says that there are two sources for the primacy assigned to the basic structure: the profound effects of basic social institutions on persons and their future prospects and the need to maintain background justice. I discuss the main reasons underlying these considerations for the primacy Rawls assigns to principles of justice for the basic structure. First, it is necessary for the freedom, equality, and independence of moral persons (section 4). Second, Rawls's focus on the basic structure is a condition of economic reciprocity and the just distribution of economic powers, resources, and income and wealth (section 5). Third, the primacy of the basic structure is required by moral pluralism and the plurality of values and by reasonable pluralism, or the plurality of reasonable conceptions of the good among free and equal persons (sections 5 and 6). Before addressing these issues, I discuss the meaning of the primacy of the basic structure (section 2) and the profound influence of the basic structure (section 3).

2. The Primacy of the Basic Structure: What It Means

In the opening pages of *A Theory of Justice*, Rawls declares, "Our topic . . . is social justice. For us the primary subject of justice is the basic structure of society" (*TJ*, 6). The basic structure is "the background social framework within which the activities of associations and individuals take place" (*JF*, 10). More precisely it is

> the way in which the major social institutions fit together into one system, and how they assign fundamental rights and duties and shape the division of advantages that arise through social cooperation. Thus the political constitution, the legally recognized forms of property, and the organization of the economy, and the nature of the family, all belong to the basic structure. (*PL*, 258)

The parties to Rawls's original position choose principles to apply directly to the basic structure of society, to make rules that regulate individuals' and officials' conduct. The first principle of equal basic liberties then applies to the political constitution, to determining and legitimating political procedures for enacting and applying laws and to specifying the constitutional rights of citizens; while the second principle applies to the structuring of social opportunities and the design of the economic system, including ownership and control of the means of production as well as the distribution of income and wealth.

Rawls says the basic structure is the "first subject" (*PL*, 257) and the "primary subject" of principles of *social* justice (*TJ*, 6; *CP*, 156). It is not the only subject of justice, even of social justice. Here Rawls refers to "the need for the division of labor between different kinds of principles" (*PL*, 469). In addition to institutional principles of justice for the basic structure, there are principles of justice for individuals, including the "natural duties" of justice, mutual respect, and mutual aid, and the principle of fairness determining political obligations, duties of fidelity including the keeping of promises and agreements of all kinds, and the like. There are also principles of remedial and compensatory justice (*TJ*, 8), including societal duties to those with severe disabilities (*PL*, 20), which Rawls does not specify. Moreover, "Justice as fairness is a political, not a general conception of justice" (*JF*, 11). The principles of justice do not apply to larger- and smaller-scale institutions and issues or to "lifeboat situations" (*CP*, 156). There are, Rawls argues, different principles of international justice that regulate the relationships between different societies—the law of nations or law of peoples. And there are principles of "local justice" (*JF*, 11) that apply to the structure and regulation of individual relationships and associations within political and global society; these include certain duties and norms of fairness within the family, universities, business firms and labor unions, and other non-public associations.

The primacy of the basic structure also does not mean that social justice is morally more important than these other forms of justice; for example, our duties of social justice do not always outweigh duties and principles of international and local justice. It would be unjust for a government to violate human rights and other requirements of international justice to further justice or prevent injustice within its own society. For example, the difference principle is subject to the duty of assistance owed to burdened societies. A government cannot neglect its duty to contribute its fair share to the alleviation of poverty and economic development of burdened societies in order to pay larger income supplements to the least advantaged members of its own society.[1] Nor can a society violate duties of fairness in trade relations, by taking unfair advantage of vulnerable nations, in order to increase opportunities or income supplements to less advantaged members of its own society.

In saying that the basic structure is the "first subject" of justice, Rawls basically means that the principles of justice for the design and regulation of basic social institutions have to be settled first, before the nature and scope of principles of justice regulating individual conduct, global society, and other private and non-basic public institutions can be fully ascertained. "Justice as fairness starts with domestic justice—the justice of the basic structure. From there it works outward to the law of peoples, and inward to local justice" (*JF*, 11). The primacy of the basic structure means then that principles of justice for the basic structure have a kind of *methodological and regulative primacy* over other principles of justice.[2]

In recognizing a *plurality of principles of justice* that apply to different subjects and institutions, Rawls is not simply saying that different institutions and social arrangements must be regulated by different principles. Almost any moral conception, including utilitarianism, recognizes that the principles and procedures applicable to political constitutions (e.g., one person/one vote and majority rule) would not be appropriate for regulating family life or many other associations. But utilitarianism and other universal moral conceptions see such principles as secondary and as formulated in light of and in order to achieve the aims of a more fundamental or supreme moral principle, such as maximizing aggregate utility. In asserting the primacy of principles for the basic structure, Rawls in effect denies what Liam Murphy has called "monism," the view that there is a single moral principle (or set of principles) that applies at all levels of moral assessment to the justice (or more generally the rightness and wrongness) of all actions, rules, and institutions. In saying there are "different principles for distinct kinds of subjects" (*PL*, 262), Rawls means there are different *first* or *fundamental principles* that apply to and are appropriate for different kinds of social arrangements and institutions. The first principles of social justice are not appropriate for regulating relations among members within families, universities, or global society itself, nor are these principles for associations directly derivable from principles of social justice. Different social arrangements require different principles. What makes these different principles for different institutions "first principles" is that they are not derivative from any principle that is universal in its scope and application.

The primacy of the basic structure presupposes then a kind of *moral pluralism* of first principles of justice, just as it presupposes evaluative pluralism, of values and conceptions of the good. There are different principles for different subjects of justice, and there are different values and moral principles that determine the role of and regulate associations within society. Again, this is a moral assumption Rawls makes, related to "the autonomy of the various elements of society" and ultimately the freedom and equality of moral persons.[3] What prevents this pluralism of first principles from becoming a kind of *intuitionism* that requires balancing first principles of local, social and political, and global justice to determine one's duties "all things considered"? It is the method of determination and justification of these first principles and the *methodological and regulative primacy* Rawls assigns to principles of social justice. The plurality of first principles for multiple subjects of justice are unified by an "appropriate sequence" of determination from the original position (or, in the case of local justice, some other relevant moral point of view), as its conditions of agreement are adjusted to the nature and role of different kinds of social arrangements and institutions. "[T]he parties to a social contract are to proceed through this sequence with the understanding that the principles of each later agreement are to be subordinate to those of all earlier agreements, or else adjusted to them by certain priority rules" (*PL*, 262). The "regulative primacy" of the basic structure means that the principles of justice for the basic structure are to be determined first in this sequence and that, while they do not determine the content of other first principles, they are *regulative* of their scope and content (*PL*, 257–58).[4]

In addition to the plurality of principles for different subjects implicit in the regulative primacy Rawls assigns to the basic structure is a bifurcation between "principles for institutions" of the basic structure and "principles for individuals" that set forth their natural duties, obligations of fairness, and other moral duties (of fidelity, charity, friendship, etc.).[5] Principles of justice for institutions directly apply to and regulate the activities of the basic social institutions and should be used to specify or assess the many legal and other social rules (of property, contract, etc.) that individuals are required to observe pursuant to the natural duty of justice. Principles of justice for institutions do not then apply directly to the regulation of individuals' conduct; rather they apply *indirectly* to individuals via the many institutional "rules for individuals" that they call for. Principles for institutions are used directly to determine and assess the justice of the many laws and conventional norms that constitute the basic institutions of the basic structure. These include provisions of the political constitution, including the specification of political powers, procedures, and a bill of rights; the structure of the economy, including control of means of production and, therewith, laws of property, contract, and other legal measures necessary for economic production, exchange, and consumption; and certain norms that apply to the family regarding the upbringing of children.

Here it is important to emphasize that Rawls's distinction between principles for institutions and individuals does *not* mean that principles of justice do not apply to individuals' conduct. Quite the contrary, they apply *indirectly* to regulations of and restraints on all kinds of individual activity by settling most laws and other social rules of justice that are directly relevant to individuals' day-to-day activities. It is important then not to confuse Rawls's distinction between *principles* for institutions versus *principles* for individuals with his different distinction between *rules* for institutions and *rules* for individuals. These are not parallel distinctions.⁶ The principles of justice for the basic structure are the source of *both* rules for institutions (e.g., constitutional procedures, laws specifying the form of private corporations) and rules for individuals (e.g., laws of property specifying individuals' rights of use, disposal, and income or of permissible and impermissible contracts). Indeed, almost all the rules of justice for individuals are settled by the principles of justice for institutions, and not by the principles of natural duty and fairness for individuals. For example, the complicated rules of property, permissible transfers, and requirements of valid binding contracts that individuals are under a duty to observe are the result of applying the second principle of justice, including the difference principle, to the rules of basic institutions. That we have a moral duty to abide by these institutional rules for individuals follows from the individual duties of justice, mutual respect, and so on, which are principles for individuals; but the rules of property, contract, and so on are themselves the consequence of applying the principles of justice for the basic structure. Principles for institutions are then the source of most rules of justice for both institutions *and* individuals.

This is important because some philosophers have made the mistake of assuming that, since the principles of justice apply directly only to institutions and not to individuals, they do not apply to individuals *at all*—which would mean they do not imply *any* particular rules or duties for individuals. This leads (as we'll see later) to the mistaken argument that the reason Rawls does not apply the difference principle to the regulation of individual conduct is to enable individuals to selfishly pursue their economic and other self-interests without moral constraints. On the contrary, the difference principle applies indirectly to individuals' conduct in all sorts of ways, via the many institutional rules for individuals that it requires.

To sum up, Rawls means at least three things in saying that principles for the basic structure are the first or primary subject of justice. First, there is a *plurality of first principles of justice* that apply to different subjects and institutions, and the principles of justice for basic institutions have "regulative primacy" over these principles. Lesser associations within the basic structure of society have standards of local justice peculiar to their purposes and role, and these are not determined by principles of justice for the basic structure. Nonetheless, these associations must adjust their requirements of local justice to the requirements that the basic structure imposes in order to establish "background justice" in society as a whole (*PL*, 261).[7] Second, within Rawls's contractarian framework, the primacy of the basic structure implies the *methodological priority* of principles of social justice for the law of peoples, principles of local justice, and retributive and compensatory justice. There is an "appropriate sequence" of determination of principles from the point of view of the original position, with the principles of social justice being determined first. Third, the primacy of the basic structure is presupposed by Rawls's distinction between principles for institutions and principles for individuals: principles of justice for basic institutions provide *content* to the institutional rules for individuals that they are under a duty to comply with pursuant to their natural duties of justice and obligations of fairness; moreover, these principles are necessary to maintain *background justice* as individuals freely pursue their aims and associations.

In the following sections I elaborate on these remarks in discussing three kinds of reasons for the primacy of principles for the basic structure. I conclude with a discussion of some frequent objections.

3. The Social Nature of Human Relationships and the Profound Influence of Basic Social Institutions

Rawls discusses two main reasons for focusing on the basic structure of society: the profound influence of basic social institutions on individuals' aims, character, and life prospects; and the importance of maintaining background justice. While the first of these is addressed by considerations relevant to both principles of justice, the second mainly concerns matters of economic justice covered by the second principle.

Before discussing these reasons and related considerations, I should emphasize three points. First, Rawls does not think there is any particular set of considerations providing a decisive argument for making the basic structure the primary subject of justice. "No such decisive arguments are available." As is true of other controversial assumptions he makes, ultimately "everything depends on how the conception of justice hangs together as a whole" in reflective equilibrium (*JF*, 55–56).[8]

Second, like other fundamental ideas he incorporates (free and equal persons, a well-ordered society, reasonableness, reasonable agreement, reciprocity, etc.), the basic structure is not sharply defined from the outset of Rawls's argument, but rather "is initially a rough idea" (*JF*, 12) that is developed in conjunction with other fundamental ideas. "A sharp definition of this structure might have gotten in the way of fitting it into these other ideas" (*JF*, 57). This, too, is related to Rawls's holistic account of justification and reflective equilibrium—of fundamental ideas being provisionally set forth, then elaborated upon and elucidated in a process of discovery and justification of principles of justice, which in turn solidify the meaning of these fundamental ideas. It is only once the principles of justice are set forth and explicated that a clear idea of basic social institutions and the basic structure emerges. This is to say that which institutions are part of the basic structure depends in part upon the *specific content of the principles of justice*, the kinds of requirements they impose upon governments and individuals, and ultimately the ideals of persons and society that these principles realize.

Third, Rawls's focus on the basic structure is integrally tied (in ways to be discussed) to his Kantian form of contractarianism, especially to the ideals of persons and of society that are presupposed by his theory of justice. Rawls says, "Once we think of the parties to a social contract as free and equal (and rational) moral persons, then there are strong reasons for taking the basic structure as the primary subject" (*PL*, 259). In later works Rawls says that the idea of the basic structure is, along with the original position, a "fundamental idea" that is needed to work out the details of the "fundamental intuitive ideas" of society as a fair system of cooperation, free and equal moral persons, and a well-ordered society (*JF*, 10). It is not immediately clear what he means by these remarks. In the following discussion I will try to unravel the various ways in which the freedom and equality of moral persons relate to the primacy given to principles of justice for the basic structure of society.

Now to turn to the first general reason for Rawls's focus on the basic structure: namely, the importance he assigns to "the social nature of human relationships" (*PL*, 278). This is evident in his account of the social contract itself. The primary influence here is Rousseau rather than Locke. There are significant differences in Locke's and Rousseau's natural rights theories of the social contract, which are reflected in subsequent developments of social contract theories. Locke and Lockean views begin with an idea of natural rights and natural property held by fully rational free and independent persons in an apolitical state of nature. Natural individuals are regarded as fully rational, free, independent, and self-sufficient owners who contract to enter political society in order to protect their property in their persons and rightful possessions. The task of Locke's social contract is to work out a morally acceptable solution to the "inconveniences" of a state of nature that is mutually beneficial while preserving individuals' freedom and natural property in themselves as well as their possessions.

Rousseau and his intellectual heirs reject the idea of a state of nature as a baseline for the social contract. Indeed, Rousseau debunks the state of nature as a relevant starting point for assessing the justice of social and political institutions. Natural man, he contends, is not rational or even aware of his natural rights, but is a "stupid limited animal" that acts on instinct from motives of self-love and natural compassion. Natural man's capacities for reasoning and intellect are unrealized in a state of nature, since his needs are few and he has no need to plan for his future. As such, natural man has no need for property or even the ideas of morality and justice. It is only when men enter into society and are able to develop their distinctly human capacities that they require concepts of "mine and thine" and other concepts of justice. Property and economic rights are entirely products of society, responses to the distinct needs and interests of persons living in social contexts. On Rousseau's account of the social contract, the state of nature and natural man's preexisting endowments play little if any role in determining requirements of justice, property, and individuals' entitlements.[9]

Rawls follows Rousseau in holding that the ideas of a state of nature, natural property, and the entitlements man brings to society are simply irrelevant to assessing conceptions of justice. "No sense can be made" of what persons own in a state of nature, or consequently of "that part of an individual's social benefits that exceed what would have been their situation in another society or in a state of nature" (PL, 278). Likewise, since humans are social beings, "[t]here is no question of determining anyone's contribution to society, or how much better off each is than they would have been had they not belonged to it, and then adjusting the social benefits of individuals by reference to these estimates" (PL, 279). In the ultimate dismissal, Rawls says the state of nature is "a historical surd, unknowable, and even if it could be known, of no significance" (JF, 55).[10]

The "social aspect of human relationships" (PL, 278) is the starting point for the primacy Rawls assigns to the basic structure of society. Like Rousseau, Rawls sees our desires and ends, our characters, including our virtues and vices, and many propensities to behavior as products of society. Though we do not begin life as a "blank slate" and clearly have certain natural propensities,[11] our distinctly human capacities (including language, reason, understanding, emotion, imagination) can be developed and realized only in cooperative social interaction. "We cannot view the talents and abilities of individuals as fixed natural gifts" (PL, 269). Though they have a "significant genetic component," they can be developed and realized only under social conditions. Moreover, the particular form of the social conditions under which we live determines not only the direction of their development, but also which talents and natural propensities are realized or left undeveloped.[12] (Michael Jordan's combination of extraordinary abilities to leap and push a large rubber ball into a basket suspended ten feet above the ground would have little use or value in most cultures prior to the middle of the twentieth century.) The same holds true of our desires, interests, ambitions, and final ends. None of these are fixed either. The social conditions under which we develop, including our position relative to others and the means and opportunities available to us, determine the range of options and choices we have in life, and therewith shape our interests and aims, as well as our future prospects.

Rawls regards all this as obvious, and few reasonable and informed persons would deny the effects of society and culture on people's interests and characters. The particular twist that Rawls applies to these plain truths is the fundamental role within society played by the basic social institutions (the constitution of government, property and the economy, and the family). "Everyone recognizes that the *institutional form of society* affects its members and determines in large part the kinds of persons they want to be as well as the kind of persons they are" (*PL*, 269, emphasis added). It is not just "society" and its multifarious influences but the basic social institutions that form the *basic structure* of society that is fundamentally responsible for shaping as well as limiting people's ambitions and hopes, the natural talents they develop and their direction, as well as their future prospects in society.

Obviously, the political constitution and the economic system under which we live have profound effects on our opportunities and future prospects. (Compare people's prospects in Western democracies with those in North Korea.) But here some have claimed that the social institutions Rawls singles out as having such a profound influence on our lives are not limited to those he mentions.[13] For example, the religious institutions prevalent in most societies (in almost all societies until the mid-twentieth century) have an enormous effect on people's interests, aims, and characters. Why isn't the influence of religious institutions, such as the Catholic Church, on the characters of people raised within them equal to or greater than that of the political constitution or economic class they are born into? If the profound influence of basic social institutions is the reason for making the basic structure the first subject of justice and for formulating principles that regulate these institutions, then why shouldn't other equally influential social institutions be incorporated into the basic structure and regulated by principles of social justice as well? The objection is that the class of institutions Rawls includes in the basic structure is unduly restricted and arbitrary.

The answer to this objection is that Rawls's basic social institutions are necessary for cooperation in almost any society, certainly in any complex society under modern conditions. Though religion has and continues to have an enormous influence on many people's lives, it is not in general a precondition of peaceable and productive social cooperation (indeed, it is often the primary source of continual civil strife). Many contemporary societies exist where religion has little or no role in maintaining socially cooperative relations (e.g., Western Europe and Communist China), whereas Rawls's basic social institutions are an integral and essential part of any modern society. Thus, some political framework is needed in any (non-primitive) society for making, revising, applying, and enforcing the social rules that make cooperation possible and for adjudicating disputes arising under them. Otherwise a social group is governed by static customs and is unable to effectively respond to changing circumstances and necessities.[14] (Even prehistorical societies had leaders and procedures for making decisions and resolving disputes.) Further, in order for economic production, trade, distribution, and consumption to be possible, there have to be settled rules of property governing the ownership and control of land, raw materials, and other productive resources, as well as conventions (such as markets and rules of contract and sale) governing the manufacture and transfer of resources and distribution of goods. Finally, any society needs some form of the family to nurture and educate its young and reproduce society across successive generations. No matter how important other social institutions and associations—religious, educational, communications, cultural, athletic, and the like—may be to particular societies, these social institutions and associations are all dependent upon the basic social institutions that specify and secure their property claims and other entitlements, and maintain background conditions for their safe and effective functioning.

Still, the fact that we are social beings, that property is not natural but a social institution, that justice presupposes a web of social relationships, and that basic social institutions exert a profound influence on who we are is arguably not enough to warrant making the basic structure of society the primary subject of principles of justice. Utilitarians also recognize the social nature of humanity, that property is a social convention, and so on; yet this does not prevent them from affirming a first moral principle that applies directly to the justice of individual conduct without the mediation of basic social institutions. An (act) utilitarian might then say: "Of course, the design of basic social institutions is important, but this does not call for unique principles applying only to the basic structure. The principle of utility can just as well determine and regulate the laws and social rules that define basic social institutions as it can the rules of associations and individual conduct, and even specific actions. What's so special about the basic structure, when what ultimately matters is the maximum satisfaction of desires or interests?[15]

Rawls's claims regarding the profound influence of the basic structure cannot be taken in isolation from his other fundamental ideas and moral assumptions. It is the profound influence of basic institutions on persons conceived in a specific way—as free and equal moral persons with fundamental interests in exercising their moral powers—that warrants giving primacy to the basic structure. Here

Rawls's non-consequentialism, his contractarianism, the political values of freedom and equality, and the ideal conceptions of persons and society informing Rawls's constructivism all come into play. If all that mattered, morally, was the maximization of individual utility or some other good state of affairs, then it is understandable why the basic structure of society might be of no special significance. What would then be important is promoting happiness or some other ultimate good, without special regard for society's basic structure. But Rawls rejects the consequentialist position that the fundamental issue in questions of justice is maximizing or otherwise promoting states of affairs. Rawls assumes instead that justice is fundamentally about the nature and moral quality of social relations among persons. The freedom of and equality among persons, and their cooperation on terms of reciprocity and mutual respect, are relations and values of paramount importance. These values provide reasons to focus on the questions of whether and how the basic social institutions governing individuals' social and political relations are to be designed so as to respect individuals as free and equal moral persons. There are indefinitely many forms of society with different basic structures within which people might find their happiness, but it is only in societies where basic institutions take certain definite forms that individuals can live freely and as equals on terms of reciprocity and mutual respect. As opposed to promoting aggregate happiness or some other good state of affairs, it is the moral quality of human relationships and the political/moral values of freedom, equality, reciprocity, and mutual respect that inform the primacy assigned to principles of justice for the basic structure of primary social institutions. These claims are further clarified in the following section.

4. The Basic Structure and the Ideals of Persons and Society

Rawls's constructivism in both its Kantian and its political versions is highly relevant to understanding his focus on the basic structure. Constructivism, as Rawls conceives of it, is a non-consequentialist approach to moral values and ideals. For moral constructivists, morality and justice are fundamentally about relations among persons who interact and cooperate according to rules and institutions that appropriately realize such moral values as human dignity and moral autonomy (Kant); mutual recognition (Scanlon); and respect for others as free and as equal moral persons who cooperate on terms of reciprocity and mutual respect (Rawls). These moral values and ideals are not states of affairs that can be promoted by taking the most effective means to maximize them. Instead they are "principle-dependent" values and ideals to be realized through the interpersonal relations of individuals who interact and cooperate according to principles and rules justifiable by procedures that exemplify these values and ideals. Kant contends that dignity, respect for humanity, and moral autonomy require that we act only on rules that fully rational persons can consent to and will to become universal laws. In Scanlon's contractualism, mutual recognition among persons is realized in interpersonal relations when all persons can justify their conduct to one another by rules that no one could reasonably reject on grounds of objective personal reasons. And in Rawls, the ideal of free and equal moral persons is realized only when society and individuals respect everyone's basic rights and willingly comply with requirements of basic social institutions regulated by principles that would be unanimously agreed to by rational persons in the original position.

Rawls says the original position is a "procedure of construction" that incorporates ideals of persons and society (*PL*, 95). The moral powers, to be reasonable and rational, are "essential interests" of free and equal moral persons (*JF*, 169), but, Rawls says, it makes little sense to maximize the development and exercise of these powers. Instead, these and other values constituting Rawls's complex ideals of persons and society are "modeled in the original position" (*PL*, 48), and then are realized when citizens cooperate according to principles that express these values and are constructed on their basis.

Here is where Rawls's focus on the basic structure becomes relevant. Rawls says the freedom and equality of moral persons "require some public form" and have an "institutional expression" (*PL*, 281). "Once the parties are described in terms that have an institutional expression, then, given the role of the basic structure"—its profound influence on our person and future prospects—"it is no accident that the first principles of justice apply directly to the basic structure."[16] The complex ideal of free and equal moral persons achieves its institutional expression via the equal basic rights and liberties guaranteed by the political constitution, other measures that achieve fair equality of opportunities, and guaranteed economic entitlements satisfying the difference principle. Recall here again the crucial point that the moral conceptions of free and equal persons and a well-ordered society are not states of affairs to be instrumentally promoted or maximized; rather they are ideals to be realized by society's members cooperating according to the rules for institutions and individuals that exemplify the principles of justice constructed from these ideals. Kantian and political constructivism are based in the idea that principles of justice should incorporate the freedom, equality, and moral powers of persons *and that these features of moral persons are to be expressed in basic social institutions themselves* in order to realize this ideal of persons and their social relations.

Accordingly, Rawls says, "Freedom [of moral persons] as applied to social institutions means a certain pattern of rights and liberties; and equal freedom means that certain basic liberties and opportunities are equal and that social and economic inequalities are regulated by principles suitably adjusted to preserve the fair value of these liberties" (*PL*, 280). Rawls elsewhere says that "one main reason" for focusing on the basic structure "is to secure citizens' freedom and independence" (*JF*, 159).[17] One way that moral persons are free is that they have the capacity to be rational: they are capable of forming, revising, and rationally pursuing a rational plan of life and are (held) responsible for their actions and their ends accordingly.[18] The basic liberties are the "institutional expression" of the freedom of moral persons; these liberties are among the institutions necessary to develop and exercise the capacity to be rational and individuals' formation and rational pursuit of their conception of the good. Rawls argues that equal basic liberties of conscience, association, and thought and expression are primary among the institutions that enable individuals to develop and exercise their capacity to be rational, to form and pursue a rational plan of life and take responsibility for their ends and conduct (*PL*, 310–15).

Another main reason for focusing on the basic structure is to guarantee the social and moral equality of persons. "It is only if the basic structure satisfies the requirements of background justice that a society treats its members as equal moral persons" (*CP*, 317). Moral persons are equal in that they all have the moral powers to a requisite minimal degree; the moral powers are then "the basis of equality" (*TJ*, §77). Equality of basic rights and liberties and equality of fair opportunities are the institutional expression of moral persons' equality as persons and as citizens, and the difference principle secures the worth and fair value of the basic liberties for all citizens (*TJ*, 179; *PL*, 280).

Finally, regarding the institutional expression of moral powers of justice, equal political rights of participation and freedom of political thought and expression are institutions necessary for realizing moral capacities for a sense of justice, including our capacities for public reasoning (*PL*, 334–335). Moreover, being publicly recognized as free and equal citizens, as defined by institutional principles incorporating equal basic rights and fair opportunities, is necessary for moral persons' achieving the good of self-respect as equal citizens (318–320).[19]

It is then (Rawls suggests) the ideal of persons and society reflected in the description of the parties and the original position that requires "institutional expression" in the basic structure of society. The central point here seems to be this: it is *only* by acting within a definite institutional framework (of equal basic rights and liberties, fair equal opportunities, etc.), and acting to uphold the justice of these institutions, that we can fully realize and "express our nature as free moral persons" (*TJ*, 501) or (as Rawls puts it in *PL*) realize our political self-conception as free and equal moral persons. We can realize our "nature" (*TJ*) or our "political self-conception" (*PL*) as free and equal moral persons cooperating on terms of reciprocity and mutual respect achieved *only* by affording primacy to principles of justice for the basic structure. And acting upon and for the sake of principles of justice that express our moral and rational nature or political self-conception is the fundamental idea of Rawls's Kantian and political constructivism. This seems to be the general idea behind Rawls's enigmatic claim that a "particular institutional expression" is required by the freedom and equality of moral persons and that "the content of the two principles fulfills this expectation" (*PL*, 281).

Now to complete the comparison with utilitarianism begun earlier: While utilitarianism recognizes the social nature of human relations and the profound effects of basic social institutions, the utilitarian conception of persons does not require any particular institutional expression in the basic structure. Utilitarians take the capacity for pleasure and pain (or the capacity for desire or for happiness more generally) as the fundamental moral fact about individuals; and this capacity can be promoted and satisfied *without any specific institutional framework* and in a large variety of social forms. Rawls's (Kantian and political) ideal of persons and society, by contrast, requires a particular kind of basic structure of society to give this ideal its "institutional expression." It is the profound influence of the basic structure on persons who are conceived in a specific way—as free and equal moral persons with fundamental interests in exercising their moral powers— that ultimately is needed to make sense of Rawls's assumption of the primacy of principles of justice for the basic structure. And once this ideal conception of persons is expressed via institutional principles in the form and content of basic social and political institutions, these principles and the institutional procedures, rights, and duties that result should have regulative primacy over individuals' conduct and pursuits. Otherwise, they cannot realize these ideals or their fundamental interests as free and equal moral persons who cooperate on terms of reciprocity and mutual respect.

Let's assume these considerations support Rawls's claim of the regulative primacy of principles of justice for the basic structure over individuals' conduct within these and other institutions. Some might still insist, in spite of Rawls's constructivism and rejection of consequentialism, that he has yet to establish that his principles of *distributive justice* directly apply *only* to the basic structure and not directly to the governance or assessment of individual conduct. Why should society but not individuals have a moral duty to maximally promote the position of the least advantaged? This brings us to the institutional division of labor and the division of moral labor, two topics discussed in subsequent sections.

5. *Distributive Justice and the Importance of Background Justice*

Rawls says, "The main problem of distributive justice is the choice of a social system" (*TJ*, 242). Here again, as with respecting the freedom and equality of moral persons, a fundamental question of justice, in this case distributive justice, is transformed into a question of the design of basic social institutions. Traditionally distributive justice has been regarded as a problem of "allocative justice," the dividing up of some preexisting bundle of goods or income and wealth (*TJ*, 77). This explains the attraction of such distributive principles as: to each equally; or according to efforts, or contributions, or needs; or to maximize utility. Many classical liberals and libertarians, such as Hayek and Nozick, reject the idea of distributive justice and requirements of "patterned," "end-state," or other allocative distributions. They argue that almost *any* distribution of holdings is just so long as it is the outcome of a historical process of free exchanges and consensual transfers between free, property-owning individuals.

Since Rawls says his position is "egalitarian," it may seem odd that he agrees with the rejection of allocative conceptions and endorses a process-based conception: just distributions are determined, he says, by "pure procedural justice" (*TJ*, §14). This means that distributions are just when they are the outcome of a process where individuals freely engage in economic activity against a background of, and in compliance with, the requirements of fair or just basic economic and legal institutions.

It is because Rawls's view, like those of classical liberals and libertarians, is a process-based conception that relies on markets that many on the left, most notably G. A. Cohen, have argued that Rawls's focus on the basic structure is driven by a concern to justify self-seeking within the capitalist welfare state. Rawls, it is said, agrees with classical liberals in endorsing capitalism; his difference principle is a way to moderate the vast inequalities capitalism inevitably results in, while still allowing economic agents to selfishly pursue their economic interests. A problem with this objection is that Rawls explicitly rejects capitalism, including welfare-state capitalism, since it concentrates economic powers, including ownership and control of productive resources, in the hands of a privileged class. He endorses instead property-owning democracy and liberal socialism, which both guarantee widespread distribution of economic powers and prerogatives as well as income and wealth (*TJ*, xiv–xvi).

The main reason Rawls gives for focusing on the basic structure in matters of distributive justice is that it is necessary to maintain "background justice" via a "social process" that counteracts the tendency of multiple individual transactions to distort the distribution of economic powers, income, and wealth. "Historical process" views such as libertarianism, Rawls says, have "no special role for the basic structure" (*PL*, 262). Libertarians and many classical liberals maintain that, given a historical starting point of just initial acquisitions, almost *any* configuration of holdings that results from a historical process of free exchanges and transfers is also just. Moreover, distributions remain just across generations no matter how unequal the ensuing configuration of assets, so long as the rules of this historical process are uniformly complied with and any deviations are rectified.

The problem Rawls sees in historical process views is that the capitalist "invisible hand" inevitably guides distributions in the wrong direction, not toward but instead away from a fair distribution that exhibits "reciprocity at the deepest level" (JF, 49). A series of historical transactions that are all apparently fair and where all parties comply with their individual duties will tend over time to result in grossly unequal and often distorted outcomes (monopolies, oligopolies, destitution among the poor, etc.). This gives us reason to question the fairness of individuals' bargaining situations and the entire historical process of distribution itself.[20]

Missing from historical process views is a conception of background justice that provides criteria for assessing the fairness of individuals' starting positions, relative bargaining power, and outcomes of economic bargains and of long-term economic trends; the just distribution of economic powers and prerogatives and of income and wealth; and the permissible range of inequalities that may result from transactions among free economic agents. A fundamental role of the economic and legal institutions that constitute the basic structure is to establish and maintain "background procedural justice" (JF, 52, 171) within an "ideal social process" (JF, 57) of economic activity among free and equal moral persons in their capacity as economic agents. *Principles and rules for institutions* specify and regulate basic economic institutions (property, markets, the law of contracts, sales, corporations, finance, etc.) and continually adjust and rectify the inevitable tendencies of markets away from background fairness (via limits on inequalities, income supplements for the less advantaged, and other measures). Individuals freely engage in economic activity according to the *rules for individuals* that regulate uses of property, permissible contracts and other transactions, financial instruments, and so on and prohibit fraud, duress, price fixing, and other violations of justice. Of these rules for individuals Rawls says, "They are framed to leave individuals and associations free to act effectively in pursuit of their ends and without excessive constraints" (PL, 268).

This is the *"institutional division of labor"* (JF, 54, emphasis added) between, on the one hand, the institutional principles and rules of justice that apply to the basic structure and maintain background justice and, on the other hand, the moral principles and institutional rules that apply to the regulation of individual and associational conduct in their particular transactions. Rawls insists on this division of labor between principles and rules for institutions and for individuals in establishing distributive justice for two reasons relating, respectively, to the second and first principles of justice.

First, the institutional division of labor is necessary to maintain "pure background procedural justice" according to the difference principle (JF, 57). Rawls sees a free-market economy as one requirement of economic justice and the difference principle, since markets effectively process limitless information regarding supply and demand and are (normally) more efficient in allocating factors of production, thereby potentially promoting everyone's advantage, including that of the less advantaged. It is significant that the use of markets and the price system to efficiently allocate productive resources does not require, Rawls says, the market distributions of income and wealth defended by classical liberals and libertarians (*TJ*, 239–42). Entitlements to market income depend on rules of property, which specify the extent to which people have rights of income in the resources they own and for sale of their labor. Distributions of income and wealth, along with economic powers and prerogatives, are to be determined by rules of distribution legislated to comply with the difference principle. Accordingly, market distributions of income and wealth, along with the exercise of economic powers, are to be periodically adjusted by taxation and other measures and redistributed as needed to conform to rules of distribution required by background justice (*JF*, 52).[21]

Rawls says the institutional division of labor required by pure procedural justice "allows us to abstract from the enormous complexities of the innumerable transactions of daily life and frees us from having to keep track of the changing relative positions of particular individuals" (*JF*, 54; *TJ*, §14). The problem addressed here is not simply that individual economic agents cannot process limitless information regarding others' economic activities and know whether their economic choices conform to an allocative end-state distribution (such as maximum utility or equality). Because of pure procedural justice, there is no such allocative end-state required; instead, there is a system of background procedural justice, and it is beyond individuals' capacities to achieve and maintain via their individual transactions the system of background justice required by the difference principle.[22] I discuss this further in the following section.

The second reason for the division of labor between principles and rules for institutions, on the one hand, and principles and rules for individuals, on the other, is that this division is necessary for free and equal persons to freely pursue their purposes, commitments, and life plans, "secure in the knowledge that elsewhere in the social system the necessary corrections to preserve background justice are being made" (*PL*, 269). It would be unduly restrictive of individuals' free pursuit of their life plans, as well as their fulfilling special commitments and obligations and other moral duties, to impose an individual duty to promote directly the ends of distributive justice in all that they do—whether this be equality, maximum or maximin utility, or any other allocative distribution. Even if it were not beyond individuals' capacities to know whether their economic choices promote or conflict with allocative patterns, the imposition on individuals of a stringent moral duty to directly promote specific allocative distributions would occupy most, if not all, moral space.

There are two separate considerations at work here. First, there is Rawls's fundamental assumption that there are a plurality of values, moral principles, and reasons for acting in addition to those required by distributive justice. Requirements of distributive justice must accommodate the multiple values, special commitments, and other moral duties and special obligations to particular individuals that we have. Second, given this plurality of values and principles, Rawls contends that essential to individuals' good is that they have the freedom to determine their values and commitments in fashioning their own rational plan of life within the constraints that justice and personal morality impose upon them. The diversity of values and principles has been termed "value pluralism."[23] In *Political Liberalism*, Rawls uses the term "reasonable pluralism" to refer to the diversity of permissible conceptions of the good and comprehensive moral and religious doctrines in a liberal society that respects freedom and equality. The problem is to fashion an account of distributive justice that allows for value and/ or reasonable pluralism—including individuals' free pursuit of a multiplicity of (intrinsically) valuable purposes, activities, and commitments. This is what Samuel Scheffler has aptly called Rawls's "division of moral labor" between the demands of justice and the demands of other values, moral duties, and special obligations and commitments to others.[24]

Here G. A. Cohen and others have replied that the requirement that individuals in their choices and actions promote an allocative distribution such as equality, or the well-being of the least advantaged, or maximum utility, does not coercively restrict individual freedom, for it is not a legal requirement but a moral requirement on individuals' conduct. Individuals can then freely choose to comply with or (selfishly) ignore this moral duty to promote the ends of distributive justice in their choices. Hence there is no undue restriction on individuals' liberty by the imposition of a moral duty to promote a patterned allocation of income and wealth.

Even if Cohen's individual moral duty to promote a specified allocative pattern is not legally enforced, there remains the problem that, in acting according to their freely chosen life plans, special commitments, and other moral obligations, free persons would rarely be in compliance with the strict allocative demands of distributive justice and would be morally adjudged to be guilty of selfishly pursuing their own interests, no matter how beneficent or morally obligatory their actions otherwise might be. In addition to duties of justice, there are a multiplicity of individual moral duties and commitments imposing special obligations on us, and these can be quite demanding in their own right. Moreover, there are many unselfish pursuits and valuable activities that make up individuals' freely adopted conceptions of the good. Rawls is concerned, not simply with the scope of legal liberties and external constraints, but with maintaining the diversity of values and moral principles, as well as the full autonomy of individuals to decide their primary ends and to create and pursue their life plans in compliance with the requirements of justice and other moral duties they have. This is a primary reason for the division of labor between principles and rules that apply to the basic structure to maintain background justice and those principles and rules that regulate individuals' conduct as they freely pursue valuable activities.

This further clarifies the abstract claim addressed in the preceding section, that the ideal of persons as free and equal requires "institutional expression" in the basic structure. Once again, we see that the fundamental justification for the primacy of the basic structure and division of labor between principles for institutions versus individuals is to guarantee both the plurality of values and the possibility of the *full autonomy* of free and equal moral persons—their freedom to create and pursue consistent with justice and personal morality a freely chosen life plan against a background of a plurality of (intrinsic) goods and worthwhile activities. Given Rawls's account of the fundamental interests of free and equal moral persons—to realize their rational and moral capacities— the problem is to find a way to make the moral requirements of (distributive) justice compatible with individuals' being able to live according to their freely chosen rational life plans while conforming to, and even acting for the sake of, justice and other moral duties in their day-to-day activities. The "congruence" of the good and the right, or of rational and moral autonomy, would not be possible were all our actions subject to a moral demand that we maximize social utility, or promote equal (opportunity for) welfare, or promote the well-being or maximum share of primary goods of the least advantaged, or any other stringent allocative principle of justice that is directly applicable to assessments of individual conduct.[25]

6. Clarifications, Objections, and Responses

To clarify Rawls's assumption of the primacy of the basic structure, it may be helpful to briefly summarize and reply to some notable objections.

6.1. Monism versus Dualism

Liam Murphy contends that Rawls's institutional division of labor has no bearing on whether a moral principle applies to either the basic structure or individual actions or to both. As opposed to what he calls Rawls's "dualism," Murphy argues for "monism," the position that fundamental principles of justice should apply directly both to the design of the basic structure and to assessments of individuals' actions. Here his position resembles G. A. Cohen's argument that the difference principle, or some other egalitarian principle of justice, should apply both to basic institutions and to the guidance and assessment of individual conduct. While Cohen's position requires equalizing the consequences of luck and then rewarding people according to effort, Murphy endorses a modified utilitarian "principle of weighted beneficence" to design economic institutions to "maximize aggregate weighted well-being over time; likewise people . . . should act to promote the same thing."[26] Murphy says that, given appropriate institutional liberties that free individuals of the burdens of promoting weighted well-being in their individual activities, individuals are left free and "can for the most part pursue their own interests" without "having to think too much about promoting general well-being."[27] Thus, Murphy, like Cohen, concludes that monism need not unduly constrain individuals' liberty or put unreasonable demands on their conduct.

Murphy's "monism" is a variation on the traditional (act) utilitarian position that the requirement to maximize aggregate utility applies both to individual conduct and to laws and social institutions. Can monism (as Murphy claims) realize the purposes of the institutional division of labor as Rawls conceives of it? This once again is where Rawls's ideal of justice as the regulation of social relations among free and equal moral persons plays a crucial role.

To begin with, if the main purpose of Rawls's distinction between principles for institutions and individuals is to provide for individuals' free determination of their conceptions of the good against a background of a plurality of (intrinsic) values, moral duties, and commitments, then it seems apparent that monism cannot accommodate Rawls's distinction; for monism, as Murphy describes it, is the denial of value and moral pluralism. There is nothing particularly liberal about not legally requiring individuals to maximize weighted well-being (or equality for Cohen) in their day-to-day decisions. Even if we grant that Murphy's (and Cohen's) account has a place for liberal rights, still when individuals act on these liberties and freely pursue their interests, they are not complying with the stringent moral requirements of Murphy's (or Cohen's) principle of distributive justice. They are instead acting in pursuit of the values, commitments, and obligations constituting their conception of the good, which is conduct that rarely would be sanctioned by a monistic principle such as weighted utility that applies to the assessment of all individual actions and institutional measures. Merely having the legal liberty to freely pursue one's own interests instead of conforming to the exacting moral requirements of a stringent, monistic moral principle does not render individuals' free pursuit of their self-determined rational good compatible or congruent (in Rawls's sense) with justice. Personal pursuits, even if excusable on a monist view, nonetheless conflict with the stringent demands of justice on Murphy's account.[28]

The ultimate justification for Rawls's distinction between institutional and individual principles is not simply to leave individuals *legally* free to pursue their own good, including personal commitments, while leaving distributive justice up to background justice. No reasonable conception imposes a legal requirement that individuals must make economic choices that meet requirements of a monistic principle of justice. It is then no surprise that Murphy and Cohen leave individuals legally free to pursue their own interests. The problem is that there is no way to pursue one's individual aims, commitments, and autonomously determined rational life plan and, at the same time, satisfy the stringent requirements of exacting monistic principles. Monistic principles leave no space for the pluralism of intrinsic values and principles, including fundamental moral duties that stem from special relationships and personal commitments, or for the full autonomy of free and equal persons.

6.2. Capitalism, Incentives, and the Institutional Division of Labor

G. A. Cohen and Liam Murphy also argue that Rawls's "dualism" puts no serious demands on people's behavior and leaves people free to pursue their self-interest without requiring them to "promote justice" (conceived as equality on Cohen's account, as weighted beneficence for Murphy, and as maximizing the well-being of the least advantaged on their allocative interpretation of Rawls's difference principle).[29] This criticism ignores the role in regulating individual behavior of the natural duties and other moral duties and obligations people have. On Rawls's account, though individuals have a duty to comply with rules of justice and promote just institutions, they are not under a constant duty always to act to maximize the share of primary goods going to the least advantaged. Why should they be, given the plurality of value and other moral duties and obligations? In addition to duties of justice, individuals are subject to duties of mutual aid and mutual respect; duties of fidelity and obligations of fairness in their dealings with others; special obligations to families, friends, associates, and others; duties of beneficence; and many other moral duties required by Rawls's non-consequentialist, non-monistic position. Nothing about Rawls's position precludes a moral duty not to be selfish or self-aggrandizing or not to take advantage of others; these duties seem part of the natural duties of mutual respect, mutual aid, and beneficence to others. What moral persons are not required to do is maximize weighted beneficence, the position of the least advantaged, or equality, in all their actions and pursuits—for such individual duties would displace other moral duties and obligations we have and would make individual autonomy amid a plurality of intrinsic values, as well as most special relationships and commitments, morally impermissible. We do not live in a monistic moral universe.

Behind Cohen's and Murphy's argument is a serious misinterpretation of the kind of social system that is required by the difference principle. Cohen argues that the purpose of Rawls's institutional division of labor is to free people up to act on their self-interest and engage in "unlimited self-seekingness," while leaving it to principles for the basic structure to redistribute wealth so as to achieve the purposes of distributive justice.[30] The purported purpose of Rawls's "dualism" is to take advantage of capitalist markets' "invisible hand" by providing incentives to people to exercise their undeserved talents in self-interested ways that coincidentally benefit others. The difference principle, regarded purely as an institutional principle, then allegedly serves as Rawls's justification for welfare-state redistributions within a capitalist economy.

Rawls's liberalism requires a market economy, not to accommodate "unlimited self-seekingness," but to guarantee freedom of occupation, association, and fair equality of opportunity and to achieve efficient allocations of productive resources, which are to everyone's benefit. Markets do not, however, provide a substantive criterion for the just distribution of income and wealth for Rawls, unlike libertarianism and classical liberalism. It is the role of the difference principle to adjust and reallocate market distributions so that they meet requirements of background procedural justice. It is a serious misreading then to suppose that the difference principle and the institutional division of labor are intended to accommodate capitalism. Rawls explicitly argues that capitalism, even welfare-state capitalism, is unjust since it concentrates economic powers, including control over productive wealth, in the hands of a capitalist class and denies economic powers and ownership of productive wealth to the majority of citizens (*JF*, 135–40). Instead of capitalism, the difference principle requires either property-owning democracy or "liberal" or "associational socialism" (*CP*, 277). Rawls assumes that, in these economic systems satisfying the principles of justice, neither will there be opportunities for the "unlimited self-seekingness" encouraged by capitalism, nor should individuals be motivated primarily by self-interest and self-aggrandizement. Instead, Rawls argues, citizens' pursuit of their aims and personal commitments will be regulated by their sense of justice, their willingness to comply with justice and other moral duties, and their desire to contribute their fair share to social cooperation. Under social and economic conditions that satisfy Rawls's principles, the institutions of a just society should encourage the development of aspirations that limit individuals' desires for acquisitiveness.[31]

6.3. Rawls's Principles of Justice Are Neither Consequentialist nor Prioritarian

Implicit in Murphy's and Cohen's criticisms of Rawls's institutional division of labor is an assumption that the difference principle is an allocative principle and is either consequentialist and/or prioritarian. They both argue that a fundamental problem with Rawls's institutional division of labor is its implication that the best way to promote the "aim of justice" is *always* to comply with institutional requirements. But, Murphy claims, particularly in non-ideal conditions of a partially just or unjust society, it is often better to bypass institutions and act directly to "promote whatever it is that just institutions are for," whether that be increasing weighted well-being or the position of the least advantaged or some other aim.[32] "Once we accept that the principles that govern the design of ideal institutions *essentially describe means to ends*, the oddness of thinking that justice describes some means to that end but not others becomes rather evident."[33] "It is not credible that what fundamentally matters is that the relevant institutions promote equality or well-being, rather than that equality or well-being be promoted."[34]

Cohen's criticism of Rawls's difference principle is similar: if what is ultimately important is equality, or the well-being of the least advantaged, then it is shortsighted only to apply the difference principle or similar egalitarian principles to institutions but not also to assess and guide the choices and conduct of individuals, requiring that they, too, promote the same ends that the principles of justice are designed to promote.

These arguments misinterpret the nature and role of Rawls's principles of justice, especially the difference principle. To begin with, Rawls's principles of justice for the basic structure are framed as principles for institutions; they are not stated in terms that would apply directly to individual conduct. This is clear in the case of the basic liberties and fair equality of opportunity, which are constitutional requirements. How could I, or any individual, guarantee everyone "a fully adequate scheme of equal basic liberties" or "conditions of fair equality of opportunity"? These demands can be satisfied only institutionally. For example, fair equality of opportunity requires setting up institutions that provide universal educational and healthcare benefits, as well as taxation to limit inequalities of income, wealth, and economic powers. While we surely can respect others' basic liberties and not discriminate unfairly against them in hiring and so on as required by our individual duty of justice, we cannot individually guarantee equal basic liberties and fair equal opportunities for all or take the institutional measures needed to do so. Strictly speaking, it makes no sense to say that these principles of justice should be applied by individuals to their day-to-day activities. Only if it is assumed that these principles for institutions are designed to promote some state of affairs that we are also obligated to promote in our individual conduct does this argument make sense.

Rawls, however, would reject this premise (Murphy's), "that the principles that govern the design of ideal institutions essentially describe means to ends." The first and second principles, including the difference principle, are neither consequentialist nor prioritarian: they are not designed to promote or maximize a state of affairs or "end-state" of equal or maximin distribution of either welfare or primary social goods. Instead the principles of justice are principles of social cooperation that structure social institutions and regulate social relations so that they express and realize an ideal of free and equal moral persons who cooperate on terms of reciprocity and mutual respect that everyone can reasonably accept. If anything is "the end of justice" (Murphy), it is this ideal of persons and of social cooperation. This ideal is not, however, a consequentialist end-state to be maximally promoted, but an ideal that is realized and expressed within social relationships of reciprocity and mutual respect among free and equal persons who act on and from the principles of justice for both institutions and individuals.

Were the difference principle a consequentialist principle,[35] it would imply that the well-being of others is simply a means to maximizing the well-being of the least advantaged (workers). But what reason would an individual or society have to want to maximize *only* the position of least advantaged (*workers*) at the expense of other equally reasonable aims, such as the well-being of the disabled? Rawls implicitly denies the consequentialist reading of the difference principle in saying that the difference principle is a principle of reciprocity that "expresses concern for all members of society," not simply the least advantaged (*JF*, 71).

The difference principle is also not prioritarian in Derek Parfit's sense. Prioritarianism implies that almost any state of affairs in which the least advantaged are better off is preferable to one in which they are less well off. Rawls implicitly denies the prioritarian reading in saying that the difference principle is a principle of "reciprocity at the deepest level." This implies the following: starting with a just status quo, many economic measures leading to states of affairs that make the least advantaged better off are nonetheless unjust since they do not *maximally* or even primarily benefit the least advantaged by making them better off than other alternative measures would.[36] Most economic measures designed to bring about Pareto improvements to a just status quo are in this sense unjust; they unfairly deprive the least advantaged of gains that go to the more advantaged instead.

To connect this discussion with the main point of the preceding section: the difference principle, rather than promoting an end-state of maximal well-being (or maximal primary goods) for the least advantaged, is a principle of democratic reciprocity ("at the deepest level") that fairly structures economic relations (including economic powers and control over productive resources) among socially productive free and equal citizens and then fairly distributes the social product among them. Some principle is needed for this purpose on any account of economic justice. For utilitarians, the principle of utility has traditionally played this role, with the primary focus being on economic efficiency and maximizing total productive output so as to maximize the satisfaction of consumers' desires. Utilitarianism is the traditional justification of laissez-faire capitalism, as well as modern welfare-state capitalism. Murphy's quasi-prioritarian ideal of maximizing "weighted well-being" is simply a variation on the traditional utilitarian argument and justifies a more humane capitalist welfare state. But Rawls is consciously trying to break with this predominant utilitarian/capitalist tradition by imposing, via the difference principle, a requirement of fair democratic reciprocity over efficiency and maximum utility in the economic relations of free and equal citizens and in the distribution of economic powers and resulting income and wealth. This largely accounts for his arguments for property-owning democracy or liberal socialism and his rejection of capitalism of all forms.

This is a complicated subject, better taken up in a discussion of the institutions required by the difference principle itself. But the failure of Cohen and Murphy to focus on Rawls's rejection of capitalism is indicative of their misunderstanding of the role of the institutional division of labor underlying the difference principle.

6.4. Social versus Cosmopolitan Justice

Rawls's principles of justice are intended for the basic structure of *society* and do not apply to global institutions or within lesser domestic institutions. Rawls's account of justice says that, as a matter of reciprocity, a society and its members owe rights of political and distributive justice to members within their own society—to those engaged in social cooperation and subject to the rules of these basic institutions— and not to members of other societies who are subject to different social institutions. Cosmopolitans object to this as an unjustified moral discontinuity. Why should artificial national boundaries make such a difference to the distribution of income and wealth? These are historical contingencies, normally the product of (unjust) wars or ancient marriages; moreover, it is accidental whether a person is born on one side of a boundary or another. Arbitrary contingencies should not matter to justice, since no one is responsible for them.

Some cosmopolitans argue that, since we engage in economic cooperation with much of the world, application of the difference principle should be extended to benefit these other societies. Utilitarians and other monists contend that even this does not resolve the problem of moral discontinuity and arbitrary contingencies; for example, some societies (e.g., Somalia and other burdened societies) have nothing to offer or are incapable of economic cooperation.[37] Institutions, whether social or global, are simply irrelevant to fundamental principles of distributive justice.

The cosmopolitan critique of the social bases of distributive justice is a large topic addressed in chapter 6 of this volume. But insofar as it draws into question the relevance of the basic structure of society to distributive justice, this much should be said: a society has numerous duties of justice to provide benefits to members of other societies, as well as to its own, that are not duties of distributive justice. In *The Law of Peoples*, Rawls addresses the problem of global poverty by imposing on societies a duty of justice (not charity) to assist burdened societies in meeting the basic needs of their members and becoming economically self-sufficient. But for Rawls this is not a question of *distributive justice* as he uses that term. Nor are a society's duties to remedy the disabilities of the mentally and physically impaired, or meet the basic needs of its own poor, or address other arbitrary contingencies (disaster relief, etc.) problems of distributive justice. Rawls's conception of distributive justice is more narrow than other contemporary views; it addresses a specific problem of economic cooperation among members of a society who are subject to its basic institutions. The basic social institutions of any society (including laws of property, contract, sales, corporations, gifts and bequests, etc.) make economic production, trade, distribution, and consumption of product among the members of that society possible. For purposes of distributive justice, Rawls conceives of society's members as normally fully cooperative, which means that they are productive and contribute their fair share to the social product. Given these assumptions, the *fundamental question of distributive justice* for Rawls is this: How is a society to structure the basic social institutions that make economic production possible among socially productive agents, including the division of economic powers and opportunities and control over means of production, and then determine fair shares to the resulting social product of income and wealth that is to go to the economic agents responsible for it?

This is the question that informed the socialist critique of capitalism, with which the idea of distributive justice originates. It is a different question than the question of what a society owes its members to meet their basic needs or to address their natural disabilities and other arbitrary contingencies, or what it owes to members of other societies. These questions raise entirely different issues— of redress, decency, humanitarianism, and the like—and should be addressed by different principles: of remedial or compensatory justice, of assistance or beneficence, and so on. The difference principle is framed to address the specific problem of distributive shares among socially productive economic agents that any conception of justice needs to respond to. The problem with "monism" is that it provides the same answer to all questions of justice and morality, regardless of their differences and regardless of different kinds of relationships (social, productive, associational, familial, cosmopolitan, etc.) among persons.

Once the problem of distributive justice is conceived this way, and the profound influence of basic social institutions on citizens' moral personality and future prospects is taken into account, there seems to be no "moral discontinuity" in distributing the economic powers, opportunities, and income and wealth that result from socially productive activity to the members of society who fully engage in it and do their fair share to maintain basic social institutions. Instead, assuming that a society has satisfied its duties to the disabled and the unemployed, provided educational and healthcare benefits, met the basic needs of its own members, and complied with its duties of assistance to other societies, the "moral discontinuity" would be to apply the difference principle, affording "reciprocity at the deepest level," indiscriminately to the distribution of economic powers, income, and wealth to people who are not "fully cooperative" and engaged in socially productive activity. "Reciprocity at the deepest level" requires not simply membership in society, but also *productive reciprocity*,[38] or doing one's fair share in the assumption of social burdens and creation of social benefits.

Moreover, while there is cooperation among members of different societies and various influential global institutions (the United Nations, World Trade Organization, International Monetary Fund, etc.), there is no global basic structure of basic economic institutions—no global property regime and so on— to which the difference principle might be applied to fashion these institutions; nor is there a global political society or political constitution with the capacity, authority, or legal institutions to globally apply the principles of justice or to create a comprehensive global legal and property system. The global basic structure that exists to regulate trade and other relations among peoples is instead dependent upon the political and economic institutions of different societies and is ideally subject to their joint determination. For these and other reasons, it is for Rawls the basic structure of societies, not of the world generally, that is the source and primary subject of distributive justice.[39]

Notes

1. This assumes that the basic needs of the least advantaged in one's *own* society are met. Rawls says the first principle of justice assumes that citizens' basic needs are met (*JF*, 44 n. 7) and that a social minimum that meets basic needs is a "constitutional essential" (*JF*, 48, 162). The difference principle, he continues, is more demanding and should not be a constitutional essential.

2. Rawls says that "the conception of justice that [applies to the basic structure] has a certain *regulative primacy* with respect to the principles and standards appropriate for other cases" (*PL*, 257–58).

3. "It is the distinct purposes and roles of the parts of the social structure, and how they fit together, that explains there being different principles for distinct kinds of subjects. Indeed, it seems natural to suppose that the distinctive character and *autonomy of the various elements of society* requires that, within some sphere, they act from their own principles designed to their peculiar nature" (*PL*, 262).

4. Again, to say that principles of social justice are regulative of the scope and content of other principles of justice cannot mean that considerations of social justice trump all other moral considerations. Obviously, a society cannot violate the human rights or take unfair advantage of other societies in order to increase benefits to the least advantaged under the difference principle. Moreover, the regulative nature of the principles of justice does not conflict with the requirement that individual shares under the difference principle are subject to a society's first having paid its fair share under the duty of assistance owed to burdened peoples.

5. The principles for individuals Rawls sets forth are the natural duties and the principle of fairness (see *TJ*, §§18–19, 51–52). Natural duties include positive

duties to uphold justice, mutual aid, and mutual respect, as well as negative duties not to be cruel, or injure others, or harm the innocent, or cause unnecessary suffering (*TJ*, 94, 98). The principle of fairness includes obligations of fairness and of fidelity (to keep promises, etc.). Rawls also says we have "a natural duty to bring about a great good . . . if we can do so relatively easily" (*TJ*, 100). Rawls does not intend his lists to be exhaustive (*TJ*, 98). Other negative duties surely would be to not violate others' rights and liberties, including their property; to not steal or commit fraud or engage in other deceptive practices, and other common sense moral prohibitions related to justice.

6. Liam Murphy, I believe, makes the mistake of confusing these two distinctions and assuming that they are parallel. Samuel Scheffler discusses the importance of this distinction in *Equality and Tradition*, chap. 4.

7. For example, while heads of families have the freedom to raise their children according to their own religious beliefs, they do not have the freedom to deny their children the right to an education that teaches them their rights and opportunities as democratic citizens and enables them to develop their capacities so as to become independent and productive members of society. See *PL*, 466–74.

8. Similarly, Rawls says that no specific argument for the principles of justice is conclusive; rather, the argument "depends on judgment—on judging the balance of reasons" (*JF*, 95; see also *JF*, 133, on the "balance of reasons" favoring the difference principle).

9. See in general Rousseau's *Discourse on Inequality*, part 1 on natural man, and his *Social Contract*. See also Rawls's "Lectures on Rousseau" (*LHPP*, 191–248).

10. Rawls is arguing in part against David Gauthier's hybrid Lockean/Hobbesian contract view, which assumes natural property and pre-social endowments and then uses these as a baseline for determining individuals' contributions to society and their entitlements to the "cooperative surplus" due to social cooperation. See *PL*, 278 n. 14.

11. See, e.g., the remarks on evolution and the sense of justice (*TJ*, 440–41) and on the genetic basis for our natural talents (*PL*, 269).

12. "Developed natural capacities are always a selection, a small selection at that, from the possibilities that might have been attained" (*PL*, 270; *JF*, 57).

13. See, e.g., G. A. Cohen, *Rescuing Justice and Equality* (Cambridge MA: Harvard University Press, 2008), chap. 3.

14. On this see H. L. A. Hart, *The Concept of Law*, 2nd ed. (Oxford: Oxford University Press, 1997), chap. 5.

15. See Liam Murphy, "Institutions and the Demands of Justice," *Philosophy & Public Affairs* 27, no. 4 (1999): 251–91.

16. Rawls continues, "The freedom and equality of moral persons require some public form, and the content of the two principles fulfills this expectation" (*PL*, 281).

17. In summarizing the reasons for the primacy of the justice of the basic structure, Rawls says: "This structure comprises social institutions within which human beings may develop their moral powers and become fully cooperating members of a society of free and equal citizens . . . It also answers to the public role of educating citizens to a conception of themselves as free and equal; and when properly regulated encourages in them . . . a sense of being treated fairly in view of the public principles" (*JF*, 57).

18. Because of this capacity to be rational, moral persons have a "higher-order interest" in regulating all their other interests and activities "by reason, that is by reasonable and rational principles that are expressive of their autonomy" (*PL*, 280).

19. All these arguments are in *PL*, lecture 8, "The Basic Liberties and their Priority."

20. "The tendency . . . is for background justice to be eroded even when individuals act fairly: the overall result of separate and independent transactions is away from and not toward background justice" (*PL*, 267).

21. Moreover, for Rawls free markets in allocating labor are a condition of freedom of occupation and choice of careers, freedom of association, and fair equality of opportunity. Markets enable citizens to freely choose their occupations, careers, and where they live and work, and to compete for open positions on fair terms with other similarly talented individuals (*TJ*, 239, 240–41).

22. Cf. Samuel Scheffler, *Equality and Tradition* (New York: Oxford University Press, 2012), 120.

23. Scheffler, *Equality and Tradition*, 116.

24. In two important papers, Samuel Scheffler explains the primacy of the basic structure largely as a reflection of the "division of moral labor" that stems from the "plurality of values and principles" that Rawls's account of justice is designed to accommodate. See Scheffler, *Equality and Tradition*, 116, 125, 134, and chaps. 4 and 5 more generally. Rawls himself refers to "the division of labor between different kinds of principles" (*PL*, 469). See also Kok-Chor Tan, *Justice, Institutions, and Luck* (Oxford: Oxford University Press, 2012), chaps. 1 and 2, on institutions, which is also very helpful. Value pluralism is a thesis about the nature of value and morality, and it is part of a comprehensive philosophical doctrine that is consistent with assumptions made in *TJ*. In *PL* any assumption of value pluralism is replaced by "reasonable pluralism," which is not a philosophical thesis about the nature of value but an empirical assumption that in a liberal society reasonable people will inevitably affirm diverse values, commitments, and religious, moral and philosophical views that impose duties and obligations.

25. From Rawls's Kantian perspective, Cohen's remedy of "personal prerogatives" of unspecified dimensions does not solve this problem (Cohen, *Rescuing Justice and Equality*, 10–11, 61, 71); for in acting on personal prerogatives, though one may be temporarily *excused* from stringent demands of promoting just distributions,

one is not acting on or even in a way that is compatible with the duty to promote justice.

26. Murphy, "Institutions and the Demands of Justice," 263.

27. Murphy, "Institutions and the Demands of Justice," 263.

28. Personal pursuits conflict with justice on Cohen's account as well, though sometimes we are excused from pursuing justice because of "a certain self-regarding prerogative," the scope of which he does not specify. Cohen, *Rescuing Justice and Equality*, 10–11, 61, 71.

29. Murphy, "Institutions and the Demands of Justice," 267.

30. G. A. Cohen, "Where the Action Is: On the Site of Distributive Justice," *Philosophy & Public Affairs* 26, no. 1 (1997): 16.

31. See Joshua Cohen, "Taking People as They Are," *Philosophy & Public Affairs* 30, no. 4 (2001): 363–86.

32. Murphy, "Institutions and the Demands of Justice," 280, 283.

33. Murphy, "Institutions and the Demands of Justice," 282, emphasis added.

34. Murphy, "Institutions and the Demands of Justice," 283.

35. Murphy seems to regard both the difference principle and the individual duty of justice as consequentialist principles. "When pure procedural or 'deontological' theories of distributive justice are incorporated into people's practical lives, they seem to collapse into consequentialist theories." Murphy, "Institutions and the Demands of Justice," 289.

36. For example, start with a just distribution (1) at T_1 that satisfies the difference principle, where the members of the least advantaged group (LAG) have 50 and those of the most advantaged group (MAG) have 250. Two economic regulations are proposed and voted upon by legislators: measure 2 raises the share going to the LAG to 51 with MAG at 350, while measure 3 provides the LAG with 60 and the MAG have 275. It would be an injustice to enact 2 rather than 3 under *both* prioritarianism and the difference principle. But for reasons of reciprocity, it would also be an injustice under the difference principle, but not for prioritarianism, to enact 2 rather than remain with the status quo at 1. (For the difference principle, 3 > 1 > 2, whereas for prioritarianism, 3 > 2 > 1.) According to the difference principle, while society under measure 2 may be richer and more efficient than under 1, and the LAG is better off, still it is unjust, or clearly less just than society at 1.

37. See Murphy, "Institutions and the Demands of Justice," 224.

38. I borrow this term from Stuart White.

39. See Samuel Freeman, *Justice and the Social Contract* (New York: Oxford University Press, 2007), chaps. 8 and 9, discussing the main points in this section. I am grateful to Samuel Scheffler, Chris Melenovsky, Jon Mandle, and David Reidy for helpful discussion and comments.

8

Ideal Theory and the Justice of Institutions

1. Introduction

Amartya Sen's book *The Idea of Justice*[1] orchestrates his many important contributions to political philosophy, social choice theory, the theory of rationality, developmental economics, and other fields, and outlines a relatively new way to reason about issues and disputes of justice. Unlike many predecessors, he doesn't try to provide new universal principles of justice. Instead, Sen describes an impartial method of reasoning that enables us to assess the comparative justice of alternative states of affairs. He relies upon social choice theory together with Adam Smith's idea of the "impartial spectator" and an account of the objectivity of ethical judgments in terms of "their defensibility in an open and free framework of public reasoning."[2]

Sen develops his account by way of extensive comparisons with and criticisms (more than 150 pages) of Rawls's position. His main criticism is that Rawls's theory is "transcendentalist" because it provides universal principles for a "perfectly just" or (as Rawls normally says) "well-ordered society" where everyone accepts and seeks to do what justice requires. Sen is mainly concerned with addressing existing injustices. He considers Rawls's ideal theory irrelevant for this purpose. To address injustices in the real world, it is neither necessary nor sufficient to know what a perfectly just society is. We no more need "transcendental principles" to decide what justice requires than we need the *Mona Lisa* to judge the comparative merits of paintings by Dalí and Picasso.[3] Instead, we should engage in comparative assessment and rank-order realizable alternatives from an impartial point of view. Just as consumers, given their budget constraints, can order their preferences for different bundles of economic goods, we can evaluate and rank alternative states of affairs according to the degree that they embody justice and other social values. We are to set aside our personal interests and biases and occupy the perspective of an "impartial spectator." From this impartial perspective, we are to consider all relevant information and assess the overall advantages and disadvantages in society and their distribution among its members. We then impartially rank realizable social states and choose those judged the best. Sen says that a precondition for the reliability of our choice is that we engage in public discussion with other impartially motivated individuals.

As a practical alternative to guide political deliberation in the United States, Sen's comparative method of evaluating "comprehensive outcomes" seems quite reasonable. Still, the United States is a nation whose revolution and subsequent constitution were deeply influenced by ideal theory, in particular the Lockean doctrine of the social contract. Jefferson's Declaration of Independence is largely drawn from Locke's *Second Treatise*. The Declaration's fundamental ideas and proposals were set forth by Locke and others in the preceding century: all persons are created free and equal; government has its bases and legitimacy in the consent of the people; the people consists of the corporate body of citizens; these citizens have certain inalienable rights, and government forfeits its authority when it violates citizens' inalienable rights; and government's refusal to surrender power signals the people's right of revolution.[4] Sen says that such "transcendental" idealizations are appropriate only for "the grand revolutionary's 'one-shot handbook'" and "would not be much invoked in the actual debates on justice on which we are ever engaged."[5] But it is hard to imagine where liberal and democratic thought, as well as the US Constitution and many subsequent liberal and democratic constitutions patterned after it, would be today without these grand idealizations. The Constitution itself often sounds like ideal theory. "We the People, in Order to form a more perfect Union, establish Justice . . . promote the general Welfare, and secure the Blessings of Liberty."[6] The Preamble's aspiration of a "perfect Union" to "establish Justice" suggests that the Constitution itself envisions (even if it does not incorporate) an ideal of a "perfectly just" society and of political relations. And many social movements and constitutional amendments throughout our history have presupposed an ideal of equality of status and equal rights for all persons that originate in transcendental principles of justice.[7]

In the following discussion, I first address Sen's argument against Rawls's reliance on the ideal theory of "a perfectly just society." I argue that Rawls's theory and principles of justice are not as redundant or irrelevant as Sen contends. In the second part of the essay, I discuss Sen's rejection of Rawls's "institutional approach" in favor of an account of "consequence-sensitive" evaluation of "comprehensive outcomes." I argue that Rawls's institutional approach, without being consequentialist, is also consequence-sensitive in that the principles of justice are designed to realize an ideal of persons and society. I discuss some potential problems with a consequentialist interpretation of Sen's comparative method of evaluating comprehensive outcomes and suggest that a pluralist interpretation of his account (one that combines deontological with consequentialist principles) is not as different from Rawls's approach as Sen intends it to be.

2. *"Perfect Justice" and the Well-Ordered Society*
2.1. The Role of the Idea of a Well-Ordered Society

One of the main themes of Sen's argument against Rawls is the rejection of ideal theory, especially the ideal of a "perfectly just society," which is part of Rawls's and other Kantian and contractarian moral and political conceptions. A distinctive feature of the social contract tradition of Locke, Rousseau, and Kant is an ideal of a "well-ordered society," as Rawls calls it, in which free and equal persons all accept, agree to, and aspire to comply with a liberal and/or democratic political constitution, or more generally with moral principles of justice. Kant and Kantian views also incorporate an ideal of a "realm of ends" in which morally motivated persons all will the same moral rules and successfully realize the achievement of their diverse purposes.[8] Rawls himself uses the terms "perfectly just society" only a few times to refer to a well-ordered society, (*TJ*, 8, 309, 418, 439) but it is important to see what he means by this. Rawls characterizes a well-ordered society as one that is designed to advance the good of its members and is effectively regulated by a public conception of justice. Thus, it is a society in which everyone accepts and knows that others accept the same principles of justice, and the basic social institutions are known to satisfy these principles. Rawls says that "justice as fairness is framed to accord with this idea of society" (*TJ*, 397).

According to this characterization, a well-ordered society is not "perfectly just" in the sense that no one ever disobeys its laws, or even in the sense that it has no unjust laws. Rawls is realistic enough about human propensities to realize that, in any society, no matter how realistically ideal, there will inevitably be some laws that are less than fully just, due to legislators' lack of information, or mistakes in reasoning, or other "burdens of judgment" that affect the application of society's basic principles and its political constitution. What is "perfectly just" about a well-ordered society is (1) that its *basic social institutions* are reasonably just, including the political constitution, laws of property and its transfer, the system of markets and other institutions necessary for economic production, trade, and distribution; and (2) that all society's ("reasonable and rational") members accept the public conception of justice regulating these institution, and all have an effective sense of justice and willingness to comply with its demands, and they normally do so (*TJ*, 397).

The fact that Rawls's parties in the original position are choosing principles for such an ideal well-ordered society has drawn little attention until recently. Most readers have assumed that the parties are choosing principles for our contemporary conditions. Rawls himself was confused about this on occasion.[9] Only in the past several years has commentary and criticism widely taken note of the fact that Rawls's parties choose principles for ideal conditions of a well-ordered society.[10] It is not altogether clear what difference it would make to Rawls's argument for the principles of justice were it assumed that the parties choose principles that apply to our current non-ideal conditions. It is an interesting exercise to conjecture what, if any, difference to Rawls's argument for the principles of justice it would make if the parties chose principles for our own historical conditions now rather than for a well-ordered society. Would it matter to Rawls's argument if we assume that Rawls's parties are located in and are aware that they are choosing principles for our own or some other non-ideal society? Given Rawls's thick veil of ignorance, they still would not know particular facts about their society, their time in history, or their historical circumstances. Why wouldn't they choose the same principles anyway?

With respect to the argument from the maximin rule of choice at least, I do not think the ideal of a well-ordered society plays a significant role. Were the maximin argument the only argument Rawls makes for the principles, as many people assume, then Sen's argument that Rawls's principles are irrelevant to our historical conditions clearly would be wide of its mark. But in spite of all the critical attention devoted to it, the maximin argument is not Rawls's only or even primary argument for the principles of justice from the original position. As Rawls makes clear in his later work, the maximin argument has limited scope.[11] It mainly works against non-liberal conceptions of justice, such as classical utilitarianism and other conceptions (including Nozick's libertarianism) that do not guarantee the basic liberties, equal opportunities, and a social minimum.

But the assumption of a well-ordered society does have important consequences for Rawls's other arguments for his principles, particularly from "the strains of commitment" and from stability (*TJ* orig., 176; *TJ*, 153). Rawls's strains of commitment argument brings out the way in which the argument from the original position depends on the idea of a social contract where everyone binds him- or herself in perpetuity on condition that others do as well. The requirement of choosing principles for a well-ordered society imposes "strains of commitment" on the parties, since it means that whatever principles all choose and agree to in the original position, they must also commit themselves to willingly accept and endorse in society once the veil of ignorance is lifted (*TJ* orig., 176; *TJ*, 153). If the parties to the agreement in the original position were not committed to choosing in good faith and accepting those same principles in society (as the ideal of a well-ordered society stipulates), then some who were dissatisfied with their circumstances might undertake to undermine the application of those same principles once the veil was lifted. This in turn would help defeat Rawls's stability condition (the requirement that principles chosen must be robust enough that disruptions to just conditions do not destabilize society but are met with a tendency to restore justice) (*TJ* orig., 454–58; *TJ*, 398–401). More important, knowing they have this option (of not supporting the principles to which they earlier agreed) might lead the parties to take chances in the original position they otherwise might not take—such as choosing the principle of average utility, in the hope that they fare well in society and, if they do not, then doing whatever they can to undermine those principles. Or they may not accept the same principles of justice and then not agree on any principles in the original position. In this case, the argument from the original position would have no determinate outcome.[12]

Even if Rawls's parties would agree on the principles of justice for non-ideal conditions, the ideal of a well-ordered society still would play a central role in Rawls's theory. For the original position itself is in large part patterned on features of a well-ordered society. This is particularly true of the publicity condition as well as the contract condition (the requirement that the parties unanimously agree and commit themselves to the same principles of justice). As Rawls says, "The reason for invoking the concept of a contract in the original position lies in its correspondence with the features of a well-ordered society . . . Aspects of a well-ordered society are incorporated into the description of the original position by the contract condition" (*CP*, 250).

The idea of a well-ordered society is characteristic of the social contract tradition. It is an ideal of a society in which free and equal persons all publicly recognize and accept the same basic principles of their social and political cooperation. It is in society (not in the original position) where the real social contract is to transpire in Rawls's account. The "artificial agents" in the original position represent real people in a potentially well-ordered society. Their role is to discover the principles that free and equal persons in that ideal society can all publicly accept, agree to, and support. The assumption made by moralized social contract views (Locke, Rousseau, Kant, Rawls, as opposed to Hobbes) is that, since social cooperation is mandatory and political authority is coercive, the members of society (who are regarded as free equals) should be in a position to freely accept the basic principles upon which society is based and which determine the division of social benefits and burdens. If there is no feasible social world in which every reasonable person can accept and endorse the same basic terms of social cooperation, then the ideal of a democratic society of free and equal persons voluntarily cooperating on terms of recognition and mutual respect is seriously compromised.

A second important role of the ideal of a well-ordered society is that it enables Rawls to elucidate the democratic/moral ideal of free and equal rational moral persons. A well-ordered society provides the optimal conditions for such persons' realization of their "social nature" (*TJ*, 95, 403). Rawls seeks to uncover "a conception of justice that is psychologically suited to human inclinations" and also "congruent" with the human good, so that in acting justly we realize "part of our good."

He assumes that we are not purely self-interested egoists, but rather that we have "a social nature," or "moral nature," (*TJ*, 508) which includes a capacity for a sense of justice that enables us to do what justice requires for its own sake. Rawls says (in comparing his project with Chomsky's account of our sense of grammaticalness), "[O]ne may regard a theory of justice as describing our sense of justice" (*TJ*, 41). The role of the ideal of a well-ordered society is that it describes the optimal social conditions for the realization of our sense of justice, which largely constitutes our "social nature" as free and equal moral persons (*TJ*, 95, 458, 500).

Now suppose it is true, as Sen contends (and surely it is to some degree), that we do not need the ideal principles of a well-ordered society to uncover current injustices or to tell us what steps we need to take to improve upon, if not fully rectify, many existing injustices. This still would not bring into question the significance of a philosophical inquiry into the principles of justice that are most suited to our "social nature" and congruent with our good. Moreover, it seems to be an important part of democratic political philosophy to inquire into the principles of justice and social cooperation that would be acceptable to free and equal persons who seek to live together on conditions of reciprocity and mutual respect. Perhaps there are no such principles to fill either of these roles, or perhaps there are several alternatives. This, too, would be good to know. Sen's claim is not, I take it, that these inquiries are idle philosophical speculations of no value simply because they all rely upon an idealization of social and political relationships among people in order to uncover and justify the principles of right and justice. His claim rather is that these inquiries are of no practical significance in determining what justice requires of us here and now. This brings us to Sen's real criticism of Rawls's and similar views.

2.2. Practical Applications

Whatever Rawls's purely philosophical aims might be, does his view have practical implications? And, if so, do they apply to us here and now? Rawls says, in the preface to *A Theory of Justice*, that one of his aims is to ascertain the most reasonable philosophical conception of justice for a democratic society, to supplant what many regard as the governing conception for the past two hundred years, which is utilitarianism (*TJ*, xvii–xviii). Some form of utilitarian reasoning—in the guise of welfare economics, cost-benefit analysis, law and economics, or the like—has long been relied upon by policy analysts, judges, and other government officials. Rawls's aspirations to find an alternative to utilitarianism surely must have gone beyond purely philosophical objectives and included practical applications of his conception of justice as well. Sen, however, argues that Rawls's "transcendental principles" are "redundant" and have no practical application to this world: they are neither necessary nor sufficient to address current injustices in our non-ideal world.[13] This would be a serious charge indeed, if true, since it would consign Rawls's theory of justice to the status of a fascinating philosophical irrelevance (on the order of Plato's model of an ideal society governed by philosopher-kings).

It is questionable whether Sen really sees Rawls's theory as completely redundant or irrelevant. Sen says that he himself accepts the "overriding concern" and "general preeminence"[14] given to liberty by Rawls's first principle of justice, the principle of equal basic liberties. This principle requires "giving personal liberty some kind of real priority" (though not the "extremist lexicographic form chosen by Rawls") over general advantage measured in terms of other social values.[15] Sen also says, "There is no claim here that the capability perspective can take over the work that other parts of Rawlsian theory demand, particularly the special status of liberty and the demands of procedural fairness."[16] These and other passages where Sen affirms in large part Rawls's principle of equal basic liberties suggest that Sen's real dispute with Rawls concerns more the purported irrelevance of the second principle of justice.

But perhaps the "transcendental" feature of Rawls's first principle that Sen rejects is only Rawls's reliance on the ideal of free and equal persons to specify the scope and extent of basic liberties. Rawls employs the ideal of free and equal moral persons in the practical application of the first principle of justice: one role of this ideal of persons is to provide a reference point that enables the further specification and application to particular cases of the first principle of justice.[17] By appealing to the fundamental interests of free and equal moral persons to determine the "significance" of the exercise of the basic liberties in the "two fundamental cases," Rawls provides a method or at least conceptual bases for further specifying the basic liberties and their scope in making constitutional decisions.

Do we really need a "transcendental" ideal of persons and society to justify and apply the abstract basic liberties that Rawls and other liberals generally endorse, including liberty of conscience, freedom of thought and association, liberty and integrity of the person, and equal political liberties? In one sense, of course, we do not, since others—such as Mill and Sen himself—have endorsed a similar liberty principle to Rawls's without resorting to an ideal of persons and society. But the fact that there are others who endorse and have some alternative method for applying a principle protecting basic liberties (by appealing to utility in Mill or impartial evaluation of "comprehensive outcomes" in Sen) does not answer the question of whether an ideal of persons is redundant or irrelevant to the practical application of this principle. This depends upon which theory is closer to being correct or more reasonable, which in turn depends upon whether the application of a principle of basic liberty is better served when it is interpreted by reference to the ideal of free and equal moral persons that Rawls claims is implicit in a democratic society.

Sen, I assume, would deny that Rawls's first principle of justice concerning equal basic liberties is "transcendental," so long as its formulation and justification do not depend upon the contractarian ideals of persons and society but are justifiable and specifiable in some other way. But if Rawls's first principle is not necessarily a transcendental principle in this sense, why can't the same be said of the second principle? Why can't there be some alternative justification of fair equality of opportunity and the difference principle that does not rely upon the ideal of a well-ordered society? Many non-contractarian philosophers endorse the fair equality of opportunity and/or the difference principle without endorsing Rawls's contractarianism. Rawls himself argues in *Political Liberalism* that the principles of justice, including the difference principle, might be endorsed from a variety of perspectives, including Millian utilitarianism and other liberal-democratic consequentialist views.

2.3. Application of the Principles of Justice to Non-Ideal Conditions

Indeed, if we take the principles of justice on their own, ignoring the fact that Rawls appeals to ideals of persons and society to justify and apply them, it is hard to think of reasons why the principles of justice should not apply to non-ideal conditions. There is nothing inherent in any of the three principles that would prevent their being applied to contemporary conditions. This is most obvious in the case of the principle of equal basic liberties. The modern Supreme Court regularly has invalidated majoritarian legislation to enforce similar First Amendment freedoms of conscience, expression, and association and Fourteenth Amendment rights of privacy, freedom of the person, and equal voting rights.[18] So we have direct experience with the protection of many of the basic liberties that are part of Rawls's first principle of justice. And while we have less experience with the achievement of fair equality of opportunity, and only very little experience with anything resembling the difference principle, it is not hard to imagine how they might be applied to current non-ideal conditions. One purpose of fair equality of opportunity is to enable people to cultivate their innate capacities and take advantage of opportunities open to people with similar talents in society. Rawls contends that this principle then requires (among other things) extensive educational opportunities and universal healthcare for all persons in society, so that they can fully develop and adequately exercise their capacities and skills in order to compete for open positions as well as take advantage of benefits of culture and enrich their personal and social lives. While the idea of "fully develop[ing] and adequately exercis[ing]" innate capacities and talents is in need of refinement, this is no impediment to its application to policy and legislative decisions under current non-ideal circumstances. It provides a clear-cut alternative to utilitarian or classical liberal economic reasoning about equality of opportunity that focuses on technocratic values and the pursuit of economic prosperity. Thus, it comes as no surprise that the fair equality of opportunity principle has been relied upon in discussions of just healthcare provision[19] and education policies.

Moreover, fair equality of opportunity puts a limit on the degree of inequality otherwise allowable by the difference principle, or any other principle of distributive justice. Rawls sees it as one of the primary reasons for putting limits on the accumulation of wealth and vast discrepancies in income that are so familiar in US society. It requires, for example, stringent limits on the ability of the wealthy to bequeath or makes gifts of vast sums of wealth to their family members.[20]

As for the difference principle, it is true that its perfect realization would require different economic conditions than those we now have: rather than a capitalist society with vast inequalities that provides a (now shrinking) "safety net," Rawls envisions either a property-owning democracy with widespread ownership of means of production or liberal (market) socialism with social ownership. But the absence of these ideal conditions does not mean the difference principle has no application to our society. In considering alternative tax proposals and in setting the rate of taxation or in deciding whether to enact a substantial negative income tax or guaranteed income supplements, legislators now should take into account the long-term effects of these measures, not just on gross economic output, but especially on the economic well-being of the least and less advantaged. They should choose the alternatives that, in conjunction with existing and foreseeable institutions and policies, better serve the poorer members of society. Applied in this way, Rawls's difference principle supplies a comparative method akin to, but with more substantive content, than Sen's procedural view and can guide legislators in making political decisions and choices among existing alternatives regarding greater comparative justice. These decisions about the rate of taxation and a negative income tax or income supplements may not result in the best measures for achieving a well-ordered society where economic conditions embody the property-owning democracy that Rawls regards as ideal. But such measures are more just than the status quo when tested against that ideal and the principles of justice.

These examples show that Rawls's principles of justice are not irrelevant or redundant in the way that Sen suggests. They have rather straightforward applications to the politics of the present day, which markedly contrast with the current status quo or policies and legislation required by the various versions of utilitarianism often relied upon.

2.4. Transcendental Principles

This raises the question, what makes a principle of justice "transcendental" in Sen's sense? If other conceptions of justice can endorse the same principles of justice without relying upon the ideal of a perfectly just society, and we can envision the application of these principles without appealing to the original position or to that ideal, then the fact that principles of justice are justified within Rawls's or some other social contract view as most appropriate for a well-ordered society cannot render these principles transcendental in the sense of being irrelevant to our current conditions. But this is Sen's primary charge: Rawls's principles of justice are applicable only to the circumstances of the ideal well-ordered society for which they are chosen by the parties in the original position. This seems to be what Sen has in mind in contending that Rawls's principles (or at least the second principle) are "transcendental" and "redundant": they apply only to the circumstances of a perfectly just, or well-ordered, society and are of no relevance to our non-ideal world. As Sen says, "The characterization of spotless justice . . . would not entail any delineation whatever of how diverse departures from spotlessness would be compared and ranked."[21] Likewise, of the absoluteness of the transcendental "right," Sen says that "it does not of course help at all—and that is the central point here—in comparative assessments of justice and therefore in the choice between alternative policies."[22]

Is this an accurate characterization of Rawls's principles of justice? Are they inapplicable to our non-ideal world and of no use in assessing the comparative justice of available alternative laws and policies? As suggested in the preceding section, I do not think so. This is not how Rawls conceived of his principles of justice or the ideal theory of which they are a part, as if they were inapplicable to our non-ideal society. Non-ideal theory in Rawls's sense is not entirely different from ideal theory; rather it is the *application of ideal theory to non-ideal circumstances*.[23] We should appeal to ideal theory, Rawls says, in order to decide what justice requires in non-ideal circumstances (*PL*, 285). It is not as if Rawls imagined that the principles of justice are applicable only to the ideal conditions of a well-ordered society, and some completely different non-ideal theory (such as utilitarianism or some other account of consequentialist or non-consequentialist decision-making) is applicable to the non-ideal world we all live in. Instead, we apply the principles of justice in order to decide which laws and institutions to put into place now, taking into account the degree to which their strict application would be generally acceptable to people and tailoring laws and institutions to realize requirements of the principles of justice to meet our specific social and historical circumstances.[24]

Does this mean that ideal theory is strictly necessary? Surely not to address gross injustices of the kind that Sen is mainly concerned with. We don't need

Rawls's account, or any philosophical account (including Sen's), to identify the measures needed to rectify the gross violations of human rights and many other injustices now existing in the world. But once we take a larger view and think in terms of the social policies and programs that are needed to address many injustices, then ideal theory can play a fundamental, perhaps even necessary role. Ideal theory is, Rawls says, a "necessary complement to non-ideal theory, without which the desire for change lacks an aim" (*PL*, 285). This seems particularly true of the long-term reform of existing social and economic injustices, particularly regarding distributive justice as well as achieving (fair) equality of opportunity in society. And even in the short run, when addressing complicated questions regarding economic policies and regulations, taxation, educational reform, healthcare provision, and so on, and the intersection of some or all of these multiple areas, some guiding objective or principle is needed to unify and coordinate these policies and ensuing legislation. Here the second principle of justice can play a crucial role.

According to Rawls, there are two parts to non-ideal theory: unfavorable conditions and conditions of partial compliance or non-compliance. Unfavorable conditions pose "the problem of how the poorer and less technologically advanced societies of the world can attain historical and social conditions that allow them to establish just and workable institutions" (*CP*, 537). In *A Theory of Justice*, the "general conception of justice"—that all primary social goods are to be distributed equally "unless an unequal distribution . . . is to the advantage of the least favored"—is chosen by the parties in the original position. It applies to unfavorable conditions where civilizations have not advanced sufficiently to sustain the priority of liberty. In discussing the conditions under which the transition to the "special conception of justice" (the two principles with the priority of liberty) applies, there is no suggestion that this cannot take place until the conditions of a well-ordered society exist. Indeed, Rawls suggests that the two principles with the priority of liberty apply to societies once "the basic wants of individuals can be fulfilled" (*TJ* orig., 543).[25]

The second part of non-ideal theory is non-compliance or partial compliance. Rawls says of this part of non-ideal theory (here in connection with the Law of Peoples):

Nonideal theory asks how the ideal conception of a society of well-ordered peoples might be achieved, or at least worked toward, generally in gradual steps. It looks for policies and courses of action likely to be effective and politically possible as well as morally permissible for that purpose. So conceived, nonideal theory presupposes that ideal theory is already on hand, for *until the ideal is identified, at least in outline, nonideal theory lacks an objective* by reference to which its questions can be answered. (*CP*, 555, emphasis added)

Ideal theory "specif[ies] the goals they [well-ordered regimes] should always have in mind and indicate[s] the means they may use or must avoid in pursing that goal" (*TJ*, 556).

There is no suggestion in these passages that the principles of justice are not to apply to the assessment of non-ideal conditions where not everyone accepts the principles of justice. On the contrary, as Rawls says already in *A Theory of Justice*:

> Viewing the theory of justice as a whole, the ideal part presents a conception of a just society that we are to achieve if we can. Existing injustices are to be judged in light of this conception and held to be unjust to the extent that they depart from it without sufficient reason. (*TJ* orig., 246; *TJ*, 216)

Moreover, Rawls is relatively clear that the principles of justice apply directly and in full force to govern the justice of non-ideal conditions, long before the conditions of a well-ordered society are realized (if they ever are) (*TJ* orig., 543; *TJ*, 475). The ideal of a well-ordered society is a theoretical construct that is used to discover what justice requires of us here and now, in this non-ideal world that we live in, and not simply in some future never-to-be-attained ideal world (*TJ* orig., 246; *TJ*, 216). Whether or not we ever achieve that ideal—and most probably we never will—it is still highly relevant to ascertaining the degree of injustice of the status quo, and the knowledge that continuing on the same path without efforts at reform is to be complicit in maintaining injustice. The difficulty and even practical impossibility of attaining an ideal does not imply its irrelevance, and even more so cannot validate the status quo.[26]

But then again, Rawls does not simply think that ideal theory is useful for assessing the nature and degree of existing injustices. At some level, it becomes necessary to redress these injustices if we are to avoid continually enacting stopgap measures that do not really respond to underlying systemic injustice. "In the absence of such an ideal form for background institutions, there is no rational basis for continually adjusting the social process so as to preserve background justice, nor for eliminating existing injustice" (*PL*, 285).

These passages suggest that there are at least two ways in which ideal theory and principles of justice chosen for a well-ordered society can be applied to our own and other non-ideal conditions: first, in order to identify specific injustices and their extent and to critically assess the degree to which a society departs from justice; and second, to provide an objective to work toward that guides the reform of unjust conditions and laws. Except under unfavorable conditions where the general conception applies, there is no suggestion in Rawls's works that principles other than the two principles of justice are to be directly applied to non-ideal conditions in order to fulfill either of these roles. Instead, as he says, "[w]hile the principles of justice belong to the theory of an ideal state of affairs, they are generally relevant" to non-ideal conditions (*TJ* orig., 246; *TJ*, 216). Other than the general conception, the only other principles of justice of non-ideal theory that differ from ideal principles of justice are those that concern retributive justice and punishment, civil disobedience to unjust laws, and other principles that have as their objective eventually establishing conditions of justice defined by the principles of justice.

I conclude that the increasingly common claim, made not just by Sen and others, that Rawls's ideal theory of justice does not apply and is irrelevant to our non-ideal conditions, or that it applies at best indirectly and is an ideal we are to aim for by adopting other more instrumental principles, is mistaken.

2.5. The Claim That Rawls's Principles of Justice Do Not Apply

Perhaps the claim that Rawls's principles of justice do not apply to societies that are not "perfectly just" is meant to suggest the following: in societies where there is not widespread agreement on the principles of justice or on any specific conception of justice, government officials are unable and normally unwilling, because of popular opposition, to *apply* the principles of justice to the process of setting government policies and making and enforcing laws.

In that case, those whose sense of justice is informed by Rawls's principles of justice have to make compromises and think of some strategy in proposing public policies and arguing for legislative and judicial change. These strategies, while they might be designed to promote conditions that bring us marginally closer to the realization of a just and well-ordered society—or, under the current reactionary political conditions, simply to hold the line against creeping injustice—must depart in many ways from the requirements that would be imposed by the principles themselves in a well-ordered society, since those requirements are not generally acceptable or realizable at the moment.[27]

If the widespread non-acceptance of a conception of justice is what is meant in saying that Rawls's ideal theory of "perfect justice" does not or cannot apply to current non-ideal conditions, then this is true of any philosophical conception of justice, Sen's included. Advocates of various versions of utilitarianism, perfectionism, and other consequentialist theories, egalitarianism, libertarianism, socialism, classical liberalism and left liberalism all have to compromise and moderate their aims and demands (if they want to accomplish anything) in making political proposals in the world as it is. They must tailor their proposed policies and laws to what is realistically achievable under the current political environment. But this does not mean that Rawls's theory, or any other, is inapplicable in any significant sense to our current non-ideal circumstances. Rawlsians, like the advocates of all these conceptions, would still insist that their favored conceptions provide the correct criterion for assessing the degree of justice and injustice that exists in current society. Moreover, they would contend that their conceptions should be applied so far as realistically possible to draw up proposed policies and legislative programs.

If this is so, then I cannot discern any significant sense in which Rawls's principles of justice do not apply to us now, in our non-ideal society, for the purpose of (1) determining and critically assessing the justice and injustice of existing laws and institutions, and (2) providing a basis for framing realistically achievable policies and laws to alleviate existing injustices and bring us closer to the ideal of justice implicit in Rawls's view. The same can be said of Sen's conception. Sen, too, conceives of his conception of justice as useful for critically assessing the justice of existing states of affairs and providing a basis for proposing laws that address existing injustices, even though the vast majority of people in US society do not endorse it. That fact of citizens' widespread non-acceptance is also irrelevant to the application of Rawls's theory of justice to current conditions, just as it is irrelevant to the application of Sen's view. If so, then I do not see that there is any significant sense in which Rawls's ideal theory of justice differs from Sen's theory or any other with respect to its applicability to current conditions.

2.6. Is Sen's Criticism of Rawls Inconsistent with His Own Position?

Each moral conception of justice, including Sen's, implies an ideal of what society would be like if its principles and procedures were realized and generally accepted and endorsed by society's members. This thought underlies Rawls's striking claim that "[t]he comparative study of well-ordered societies is, I believe, the central theoretical endeavor of moral theory" (*CP*, 294).

It has been suggested by some that Sen himself, like Rawls, also presupposes an ideal of society and "perfect justice."[28] We've seen that Sen endorses equal basic liberties and normally their priority over other social values. Equality of basic liberties and other rights, it might be said, is surely an ideal principle since it hardly obtains anywhere. The same can be said of equality or even adequacy of crucial capabilities for functioning that Sen advocates.

Sen also relies upon a kind of ideal society—namely, a society of sincere and conscientious deliberators with moral sensibilities, all of whom adopt the point of view of the impartial spectator. They then engage in public reasoning and comprehensive consequential evaluation, which enables them to come to agreement upon, or at least public justifications to one another of, comparative rankings of the justice of alternative states of affairs. Does this suggest that Sen is guilty of inconsistency in his criticisms of Rawls's reliance on "transcendental principles" and an ideal of persons and society? There are indeed substantial idealizations in

Sen's approach. The question of whether he is inconsistent depends on the role of these idealizations in his argument.

The argument that Sen himself presupposes ideal social conditions might focus on the ideal of persons and of public reasoning that Sen's account of impartial consequential evaluation incorporates. Sen explicitly refers to and endorses Rawls's idea of "public reason" and contends that public reasoning and debate among impartial democratic citizens with diverse perspectives is necessary for objectivity and discovering justice's requirements.[29] Public reason is an idea Rawls explicitly draws from Rousseau's social contract doctrine; it resembles Rousseau's idea of citizens' deliberating on justice and the common good and voting the general will (*PL*, 219–20).[30] Public reason presupposes that citizens set aside their own interests and deliberate about justice, common interests, and the public good, and also that they desire do what justice requires. How otherwise can they be motivated to sincerely engage in the impartial public reasoning Sen demands?

Here a critic of Sen's approach might say that Sen condemns Rawls's principles because they are designed for a perfectly just society of citizens who want to do justice. But then Sen implicitly presupposes circumstances at least as idealized as those he condemns in Rawls. How can we expect impartial deliberation on the common good in the current environment? Given the combative state of political discourse, for example the accusations that President Obama was a non-citizen, a Muslim, and a fascist/socialist who advocated "death panels," it is hard to see how Sen's impartial comparative approach is any less transcendental or unrealistic than Rawls's ideal theory.

Is this a fair response to Sen's criticisms of Rawls's "transcendental" theory? It depends upon the role of the idealizations of persons and society that are implicit in Sen's own account. Sen refers at various places to the similarities of his account with Jürgen Habermas's "procedural" account of justice.[31] Habermas's view seems to be that we cannot know what justice is—perhaps even its requirements are indeterminate—until we know the results of (and perhaps even engage in ourselves) an *actual process of ideal democratic deliberation among real people* who are free and equally situated and have (a rather substantial conception of) their basic needs met.[32] On a similar understanding of Sen's account of impartial consequential evaluation, it would indeed be true that his account also supposes an ideal of a society that is inhabited by free and equal persons whose basic needs are met, who are provided adequate (if not complete) relevant information, and who engage in impartial democratic deliberation and public reasoning. If this is Sen's view, in some respects it is even *more* ideal or "transcendental" than Rawls's position. For Rawls nowhere requires that a well-ordered society of morally motivated public discussants must *actually exist* in order for us to discover the principles of justice or what justice requires of us under current conditions. Rather Rawls's account of free and equal moral persons and a well-ordered society are hypothetical ideals, the primary constraint on which is that they be realistically possible given natural human propensities and constraints on social cooperation.

On Rawls's account, we can ascertain what justice requires of us, here and now, by applying the principles that *would be* agreed to among free and equal moral persons who are members of a hypothetical well-ordered society. On the Habermasian idealized procedural view (and Sen's too, to the extent that he endorses a similar procedural view), we cannot ascertain what justice requires of us unless and until we ourselves impartially engage in public reasoning under certain ideal social conditions and accurately assess all relevant information. This may not be a "perfectly just" society in the sense of Rawls's ideal. But in many respects it seems even more idealized and demanding (epistemically if not socially) than the conditions Rawls sets for the discovery of principles of justice. For many, it might seem an exercise in hair-splitting to condemn a position which says that justice requires the application to our society of the principles equal persons would agree to for a well-ordered society, while at the same time endorsing a position which says that justice requires what equally if not even more idealized persons engaged in impartial public reasoning actually do accept for our own society.

But even if we assume that the application of Sen's procedural conception of justice depends on the actual existence of a community of ideal agents engaged in impartial public reasoning, his account still differs from Rawls's position in the following respect: Sen envisions an epistemic ideal of persons who assess the justice of (alternatives in) this non-ideal world, here and now, whereas Rawls envisions an ideal of agents who choose principles, not for this non-ideal world, but for an ideal social world of morally conscientious citizens, the principles of which in turn are to be applied by us now to our non-ideal circumstances. It is that second idealization, the ideal of a "perfectly just society," not the first, the epistemic ideal of impartial and informed choosers, that Sen contests and claims is irrelevant to and redundant for what justice requires in our non-ideal world. He assumes at most what we might call a "perfectly procedurally just society," not, as Rawls does, a "perfectly substantively just society."[33]

So in the end the charge that Sen himself depends upon an ideal of perfect justice is partly true. He does not need an ideal of a perfectly substantively just society, as Rawls does, to *define* what justice requires. At most he relies upon an ideal of impartial and informed deliberators engaged in public reasoning to discover what justice requires of us now. If Sen's situated ideal evaluators had to reason about what the members of an ideal or well-ordered society would accept and agree to in order to decide what justice requires of them in their current circumstances, then the normative content of justice would depend on such an ideal of a perfectly just society. But that is not Sen's position, and that is an important difference with Rawls's position.

Still, my claim has been that none of these idealizations—of principles, persons, their ideal deliberations, or their society and its role in discovering and (in Rawls's case) determining what justice requires of us—makes much difference to either Rawls's or Sen's account of what justice requires of us *here and now*, under current conditions. For Sen, justice requires the realization of states of affairs that are or would be acceptable to ideally defined impartial deliberators engaged in the evaluation of comprehensive outcomes via public reasoning and assessment. For Rawls, too, what justice here and now requires of us is determined by the principles of justice that would be generally acceptable among ideally defined free and equal persons. The fact that Rawls's ideal persons are members of an ideal society and choose transcendental principles for *that society* is irrelevant to the applicability of these reputedly "transcendental principles" to us here and now. There is a difference between Sen's and Rawls's views. But it is not a difference about the scope or applicability to the here and now of principles or evaluations determined by hypothetical persons under ideal conditions of decision.

2.7. Irrelevant Alternatives

A word is in order regarding Sen's analogy of Rawls's "perfectly just" society with the world's most perfect painting. His argument borrows from an axiom of social choice theory, the "independence of irrelevance alternatives": if B is preferred to C, introducing a third alternative, A, that is preferred to both should not affect the preference of B over C. Sen claims that Rawls's description of a perfectly just society is likewise irrelevant to the choice between alternative states of affairs in our world. It is no more relevant than is the *Mona Lisa* to deciding between the relevant merits of a Dalí and a Picasso. Therefore, he concludes, Rawls's principles of justice and the ideal of a perfectly just society, are also irrelevant to our social world.

In *A Theory of Justice* Rawls discusses some of the political and economic institutions that would exist in a well-ordered society (such as property-owning democracy). But for the most part he characterizes a well-ordered society in general terms, simply as a society where everyone accepts the public principles of justice, these principles are realized in society's laws and institutions, and citizens are moved by their sense of justice to comply with these requirements. It is "the principles of justice . . . defining a perfectly just society" (*TJ*, 309), and not a description of this ideal state of affairs itself, that are to be applied to non-ideal circumstances in order to assess injustice and provide objectives to guide the reform of existing laws and institutions. Rawls then does not say that we are to appeal to a description of the conditions and institutions of a well-ordered society itself to assess the justice of current laws and institutions.

In this regard Sen's example of comparing paintings with the ideal best painting is misleading. For Rawls, it is not the ideal state of affairs of a well-ordered society that is to be compared with current states of affairs to see if the latter measures up. Instead it is the principles of justice themselves that are to be applied to and compared with current laws and institutions.[34] The primary role of the ideal of a well-ordered society is to justify the principles of justice; it plays little if any role in the normal application of those principles once justified. Sen's argument should thus be that Rawls's principles of justice (not his ideal of a perfectly just society) are irrelevant to choosing between alternative laws and norms of justice for our own society. But once stated this way, Sen's argument does not appear to be anywhere near as plausible as his claim that we do not need to refer to the *Mona Lisa* to decide between works by Picasso and Dalí; it's simply the wrong analogy. Rawls's principles are highly relevant to decisions on laws and institutions in our own society. And clearly we can apply these principles to assess injustice or our circumstances without comparing the status quo with an ideal state of affairs.

It is not especially difficult to see how the principles of justice are to be applied to existing institutions to assess and reform them and make them more just. In theory, it would be straightforward to apply the principle of equal basic liberties to existing laws and practices, for we already have a model to build upon in the Supreme Court jurisprudence of the past seventy-five years (Rawls appeals to this in his discussion of the application of the equal basic liberties; see *PL*, lecture 8). Furthermore, there is no conceptual difficulty in deciding upon measures that bring us closer to fair equality of opportunity; among those Rawls suggests are universal healthcare, continual educational and retraining opportunities throughout citizens' lifetimes, family allowances, comprehensive childcare and child development programs for the less advantaged, and gradually increasing estate and inheritance taxes to lessen the effects of concentrated wealth. Finally, there are any number of measures compatible with the difference principle that we could institute to reduce the vast inequalities in US society and improve the position of the least advantaged—substantially raising the marginal tax rate on the wealthy, considerably increasing income supplements (such as earned income tax credits and child care allowances), facilitating the organization of labor unions, mandating that workers have co-determination rights on corporate boards, and so on. The reforms that need to be made to institutionalize a property-owning democracy are more difficult, but Rawls envisions the evolution of just economic institutions to be a gradual process, and there is nothing about human nature or "the burdens of judgment" that would prevent the realistic possibility of their achievement.

In all of these cases, there is no need to appeal to a complete description of the institutions of a well-ordered society to do any of this. Sen misconceives the role of Rawls's abstract social ideal to the application of his principles of justice. The ideal of a well-ordered society is crucial to the justification of the principles of justice, but plays at best a subordinate role in their application, and often none at all.

2.8. Conclusion

If the forgoing is correct, and Rawls envisions the principles of justice to apply to our current circumstances for both assessing its degree of injustice and providing objectives to guide legislation and current reforms, then Sen's claim that these principles are neither necessary nor sufficient to determine justice under our circumstances is seriously undermined. I am not sure in what other sense Rawls's principles could be said to be redundant or irrelevant to our circumstances. Of course, there is a trivial sense in which this might be said; namely, Sen has offered us an alternative account of justice that arguably suffices to determine what justice requires of us under current conditions, so we need not appeal to Rawls's principles of justice for this purpose. But it can be said of any conception of justice (including Sen's) that it is not needed because there is an alternative that serves the same role. The relevant question in deciding whether an account of justice is redundant is not whether there is an alternative on offer, but whether that conception of justice is true or most reasonable for assessing justice under our current conditions. Rawls, I have argued, clearly thought justice as fairness meets these conditions. If so, then it seems that his conception would be at least necessary (assuming that it is most reasonable) for assessing how and to what degree our society is unjust and for providing objectives to guide measures that address these injustices. Whether it is sufficient for this purpose depends upon whether it has the internal resources to address current issues. I see no reason to think it does not. I conclude then that Sen's argument regarding the irrelevance and redundancy of Rawls's principles of justice does not succeed.

3. Evaluating Institutions versus Comprehensive Outcomes
3.1. Institutional Realizations and Their Consequences

Rawls says that the first subject of justice is the basic structure of society, which includes the design of such basic social institutions as the political constitution, property, economic markets, and legal and other social conventions that make production, trade, and the distribution of goods and services possible. The role of Rawls's two principles of justice is to specify and assess these basic institutions and their coherence and design in a social system. These "principles for institutions" apply to individuals indirectly by specifying the laws and institutions that citizens have an individual duty of justice to comply with.[35]

Sen rejects Rawls's "transcendental institutionalism." Of institutions he says that "it is hard to think of them as being basically good in themselves, rather than being possibly effective ways of realizing acceptable or excellent social achievements."[36] Instead of an "institutional approach" to justice, he advocates focusing on and evaluating social states of affairs that emerge from institutions and actions. Utilitarianism and social choice theory, he says, take this approach to evaluation and justice. Unlike them, he advocates the evaluation of "comprehensive states of affairs" that focuses not simply on welfare but also on capabilities, liberty, and processes, and even institutions themselves.[37]

Any account of justice must address questions regarding the appropriate rules of institutions that are responsible for the fair distribution of rights and liberties, powers and responsibilities, and other social benefits and burdens. An account that says "promote good consequences" or "realizations" of states of affairs is not an account of justice. As Mill, a consequentialist, says, "Justice implies something which it is not only right to do and wrong not to do, but which some individual person can claim from us as his moral right."[38] Promoting or maximizing good consequences might serve as a criterion for setting up institutions of justice and deciding when there is a just distribution of rights and entitlements; but by itself it is nothing more than the consequentialist moral injunction that collapses justice into larger concerns and lumps its distributional requirements together with considerations of efficiency, welfare, capabilities, and whatever else goes into the good state of affairs to be maximized. Why we should even call a consequentialist theory a "conception of justice" is not clear until we are given an account of the institutions and rules that distribute rights, powers, social positions and opportunities, and income and wealth.[39]

Sen recognizes the importance of rights and institutions to justice. He says, "Any theory of justice has to give an important place to the role of institutions, so that the choice of institutions cannot but be a central element in any plausible account of justice." "However," he adds, "we have to seek institutions that *promote* justice, rather than treating the institutions as themselves *manifestations* of justice, which would reflect a kind of institutionally fundamentalist view."[40]

Rawls's account indeed regards institutions as "manifestations" of the principles of justice, and these principles are not designed to promote or maximize any state of affairs, even just states of affairs. Is Rawls then guilty of "institutional fundamentalism"? Though his principles do not maximally promote states of affairs, Rawls's theory of justice is designed, and his two principles for institutions are "constructed," to realize an ideal of persons as free and equal, reasonable and rational, and of society as socially cooperative relations grounded in reciprocity and mutual respect. Rawls's account is not, as Sen seems to say of "deontological" views in general, impervious to consequences. Sen's distinction between "conse-quence independent deontology and consequence sensitive assessment"[41] should then allow room for Rawls's (and others') consequence-sensitive deontology. Since Rawls's non-consequentialist position is consequence-sensitive—it seeks principles of justice that best realize ideals of persons and of society—it should not be subject the accusation that it is "institutionally fundamentalist."[42]

An example of such a position may be Nozick's libertarianism, which says that no matter how great the inequalities or degree of destitution in a society, absolute property and contract rights always trump the public good and others' basic human needs. Unlike Nozick, Rawls has a conception of individuals' essential good (the exercise of their moral powers and free pursuit of their good), of basic human needs (the primary social goods), and of the common good (justice and social union) built into his account, and he conceives it to be the role of just basic social institutions to achieve these goods for each person (though not to promote them in a consequentialist's sense of taking the most effective means to maximize these goods). Thus, Rawls's account of distributive justice says that economic institutions (property, including control of means of production; contract and commercial practices; markets and other means of transfer; etc.) should be designed and regularly adjusted so as to realize outcomes where the least advantaged class in society is better off than it would be under any other arrangement.

There is no suggestion of inflexible institutional fundamentalism here; instead institutions are subject to periodic and continual adjustment and reform. Similar institutional adjustments apply with the principle of fair equality of opportunity: social entitlements to full educational and job training opportunities and adequate healthcare are to be adjusted to respond to people's circumstances. These are examples of ways in which Rawls's principles of justice are "consequence-sensitive" without being consequentialist, and basic social institutions are flexibly responsive to citizen's social needs without their maximally promoting states of affairs. The charge of "institutional fundamentalism" cannot be made against Rawls, even if it might apply to other non-consequentialist views.

Sen draws a sharp distinction between conceptions like Rawls's that focus on rights and the justice of institutions ("transcendental institutionalism") and conceptions designed to achieve "actual realizations" of beneficial states of affairs (via "realization-focused comparison").[43] Apart from his apparently consequentialist interpretation of "realizations," I do not think the distinction between "institutions" and "realizations" captures a significant difference between Rawls's and Sen's position. Rawls's principles for institutions, while they "manifest" instead of "promote" justice, are nonetheless said by Rawls to "express [persons'] nature as free and equal rational beings"; in acting on and from these principles, Rawls says, we "express our nature as moral persons" and therewith achieve "the realization of our nature as a free and equal rational being" (*TJ* orig., 252, 575; *TJ*, 222, 503). Sen says, "In seeking for perfection, transcendental institutionalism concentrates primarily on getting the institutions right, and is not directly focused on the actual societies that would ultimately emerge."[44] This is not true of Rawls: consequences or outcomes of institutions and the "realizations" of actual societies that would ultimately emerge are highly relevant to Rawls's account of justice. A society that embodies Rawls's principles of justice in its institutions and its political culture realizes reciprocity and mutual respect among equals. By acting on and from these principles, citizens realize an ideal of themselves as free and equal moral persons and citizens. These realizations of ideals of persons and society do not involve maximizing anything or taking the most effective means to promote states of affairs. When government and citizens generally comply with the rules of basic institutions, they are not promoting some state of affairs in a consequentialist fashion, but they nonetheless realize these ideals.

There is then more than one way to attend to consequences and realize outcomes in a conception of justice. Good outcomes are realized by consequentialists by taking the most effective means to maximally promote a state of affairs, one in which the sum total of goods (and perhaps their distribution in distribution-sensitive views)[45] is maximized. For a non-consequentialist such as Rawls, good outcomes are realized when citizens generally abide by the rules of the periodically adjusted institutions specified by principles of justice; then persons realize an ideal of themselves as free and equal moral persons who cooperate on grounds of reciprocity and mutual respect. There is no significant difference between Sen and Rawls regarding concern for consequences or realizations of justice. What might be different is that the means taken to achieve these realizations are differently conceived. Insofar as Sen's position is consequentialist, the means prescribed by his position are instrumental and maximizing; those prescribed by Rawls are not, but are instead (as Sen says of Rawls's principles) "manifestations," which in turn are (as Rawls says) "realizations" of ideals of persons and society. This raises the final issue to be discussed here: To what extent is Sen's own position consequentialist?

3.2. Consequence-Sensitive Evaluation of Comprehensive Outcomes

I conclude with some remarks on Sen's account of "consequence-sensitive" evaluation of "comprehensive outcomes" and its relationship to consequentialism.

Consequentialists traditionally have regarded rights, fairness, justice, and other requirements of the concept of right as instrumental means of promoting (or maximizing) the good, or optimal states of affairs. Moreover, the good itself is conceived (in the modern era) as empirically definable, describable in terms of the natural and social sciences (pleasurable experiences, welfare, exercise of traits of intellect and character, etc.). Sen has long argued for a form of consequentialism that incorporates into the states of affairs to be promoted or maximized complex information regarding not simply well-being, but also capabilities, freedoms, responsibilities, and the fulfillment of individuals' rights, fair procedures, and other deontic requirements. Sen previously called his position "broad consequentialism."[46] He has said, "Consequential evaluation that takes note of freedoms, rights, and obligations—and their violation—would argue that bad things have happened *precisely because* someone's freedom has been breached, and some rights and duties have been violated."[47] "The fulfillment of rights is a good thing to happen—the more the better—as it would be seen in a consequential perspective."[48]

In the *Idea of Justice*, Sen (with one exception) avoids the term "consequentialism" in referring to his account. He says, "The term 'consequentialism' was devised by enemies rather than proponents of consequential evaluation, and it has been invoked mainly to be refuted."[49] He refers to "consequential evaluation" on several occasions in connection with his position, but more commonly he speaks of "consequence-sensitive reasoning" and evaluating "social realizations" and "comprehensive outcomes."[50] He contrasts evaluation of comprehensive outcomes with traditional consequential evaluations of "culmination outcomes" (such as utilitarianism and welfarism more generally), which he rejects; the latter, he says, do not take responsibilities, social processes, and other relevant information into account in assessing and comparing states of affairs.[51]

It is now less clear than previously whether Sen intends to set forth a distinct version of consequentialism or whether he aims for something less ambitious: namely, a method of impartial evaluation for individual agents, policymakers, and public officials that is not tied to any particular moral conception but is compatible with a wide range of such conceptions (including non-consequentialisms that endorse fundamental deontological principles, such as a principle of equal basic liberties, a principle of fair equality of opportunity, or even the difference principle). This modest non-committal approach is suggested when Sen rejects "evaluation of social realizations in strictly impersonal terms"[52] and says that each agent is to take account of his or her own agent-relative as well as agent-independent reasons and concerns in impartial appraisals of what happens in the world.[53]

On the other hand, this *is* a book about justice, and it advocates the assessment of the "comparative justice" of "comprehensive outcomes" and "realizations-based comparisons that focus on the advance or retreat of justice."[54] From the point of view of public officials, citizens, and others expected to make impartial assessments of institutions and their consequences—including appropriate distributions of rights and social responsibilities—their agent-relative reasons and special responsibilities surely must be put aside in their rankings of the comparative justice of laws, institutions, and social states of affairs. This suggests (together with Sen's arguments against Rawls and other deontological positions) that Sen may still endorse a form of consequentialism or at least "consequential evaluation"[55] that includes the fulfillment of rights and responsibilities, as well as institutional arrangements such as fair processes and distributions in the comprehensive outcomes to be realized by society's and individuals' actions.[56] Here I suggest a potential problem in conceiving of "comprehensive outcomes" and the justice of "social realizations" in a consequentialist manner and propose an alternative non-consequentialist way to conceive of Sen's account.

In traditional consequentialism, principles of right and justice are regarded as measures that are instrumental to promoting good consequences (ideally the best); as Rawls says, "[T]he right is defined as that which maximizes the good." In utilitarianism and other standard views, to maximize (or optimize) the good means two things: first, given the good ends to be promoted, we are to take *the most effective means* to achieve them (the simplest, least costly and time-consuming, most probable, etc.); and second, given the means and resources that are available, we are to create as much good as possible (as many good consequences, or the greatest sum total of goodness). The basic idea that we are to *maximize the good* includes both of these conditions.

By contrast with traditional views, the use of the term "maximize" in contemporary economics, decision theory, and social choice theory is, if not ambiguous, at least different from its use in moral philosophy.[57] Arguably the term suggests little more than the consistent ordinal ranking of states of affairs according to people's individual or combined preferences, and individual or social choice of the most preferred ranking. Such rankings by themselves seem to imply little about whether or how people should go about achieving their most preferred situation or maximally ranked state of affairs.[58] The question of whether we are to adopt the most effective means to its realization, or whether there are moral constraints on the measures we can permissibly take to achieve the maximand, is left open by contemporary uses of "maximizing" in economics. If so, then any commitment to consequentialism within modern welfare economics, including social choice theory, cannot be a foregone conclusion. It is perhaps true that most advocates of normative (or welfare) economics are consequentialists (if not utilitarians); but they are not entitled, absent further assumptions and argument, to the consequentialist conclusion that *all* that ultimately matters morally is good consequences and that morality and justice involve taking the most effective means to promote and realize these desirable outcomes.

One objection to a consequentialist interpretation of contemporary welfare economics, including social choice theory, is that the "maximization" (or "optimization") of choice across impersonal states of affairs does not adequately represent or take into account the way we conceive of the normative force of the constraints imposed by individual rights and other requirements of justice and morality.[59] Many consequentialists would dismiss this objection, saying that commonsense intuitions about the normative force of principles of right and justice are mistaken, since rights, fair procedures, and just distributions can be at best instrumental means to achieving good states of affairs. A more sympathetic response to this objection is that information about rights-fulfillments, fair procedures, just distributions, and other deontic moral considerations of justice can be directly incorporated into the states of affairs that are subject to individual and social rankings and action, without misrepresenting the role or importance of these moral requirements in deliberation.

For example, clearly a society where individual rights to freedom of speech, conscience, and association are recognized and respected is morally preferable, other things being equal, to oppressive societies where these and other liberal rights are not recognized; appropriate means ought to be taken to realize these and other liberal rights whenever feasible. The advantage of incorporating in this way (equal) rights, fairness, and other deontic considerations into the outcomes to be realized is that it (seemingly) combines into one account both consequence-sensitive evaluation and recognition of the role and importance of individual rights and requirements of justice in personal and social deliberations and decisions. This problem of addressing the appropriate role and significance of deontic moral norms in deliberation and action seems to have been one motivation underlying Sen's earlier accounts of broad consequentialism and it is carried over into his account of comprehensive outcomes in *The Idea of Justice*.

Still, I believe that the idea of comprehensive outcomes which include the fulfillment of social responsibilities, rights, fair procedures, just distributions, and so on does not by itself address the question of what means are to be taken to achieve "social realizations" of these comprehensive outcomes. Until we are told what role rights, fair procedures, and other deontic constraints and requirements are to have in deliberation and action, incorporating them into the states of affairs that define a social welfare function or comprehensive outcome does not say much of anything about what we are to do or how we are to go about realizing them. Are we to take the most effective means to promote the states of affairs defined by comprehensive outcomes, as is characteristic of traditional consequentialist views, sometimes violating the rights of the few in order to satisfy rights of the greater number?[60] Or do the rights, duties, fair procedures, and other distribution-sensitive deontic requirements that are part of the comprehensive outcomes to be promoted normally put constraints upon the means that may be employed to achieve those same comprehensive outcomes? And if so, how do we determine when such constraints of justice apply to the instrumental promotion of comprehensive outcomes and their relative weight or significance?

These are not questions that Sen directly addresses in his elaboration of consequence-sensitive reasoning about comprehensive outcomes. He is attuned to these issues, since his distinction between culmination and comprehensive outcomes seems in large part designed to address the problem that traditional consequentialism has with affording individual rights and other requirements of justice the appropriate degree of importance that they have in practical deliberation and social decisions. But there remains an ambiguity in his account regarding the role to be assigned to rights and other requirements of justice in practical deliberation and social action. Addressing this ambiguity is important for a number of reasons, not the least of which is that we need to know whether individuals' rights and fair procedures are to be conceived simply as states of affairs to be promoted (by maximizing incidences of rights-satisfactions and compliance with fair procedures) or whether individuals' rights and fair procedures and distributions are to function as genuine constraints upon the means that can be taken to promote these good states of affairs.

May we, for example, restrict the extension of rights to equal opportunities for historically disfavored racial minorities in order to prevent widespread dissatisfaction among white majorities and their ensuing social unrest and subsequent rights-violations of members of the racial minority, as a consequentialist approach suggests? Or can a government violate the rights to freedom of expression of some known individuals who might otherwise express themselves in an incendiary fashion (e.g., by destroying the Koran) in order to prevent or minimize violations of the rights to security of unknown others (e.g., to soldiers in Afghanistan and Iraq)? Or, alternatively, does the fact that individuals have certain basic rights to liberties and equal opportunities normally prevent us from violating or restricting them in order to promote greater rights-satisfactions and other good states of affairs on the whole? These are not easily resolvable issues on anyone's account. Any reasonable non-consequentialist position must admit that violation of the rights of a few may be necessary in supreme emergencies to protect the lives of large numbers of people. But the difference with consequentialist approaches is the recognition that these difficult issues cannot be resolved by employing an algorithm or estimating which alternative involves the greater sum total of rights-satisfactions or other good consequences.

Further clarification of these issues would then greatly add to our understanding of the practical ramifications of Sen's account of justice. The question to be clarified is, once again, whether the states of affairs represented by comprehensive outcomes are themselves to be maximized in the standard consequentialist sense of taking the most effective means to instrumentally realize as much good (including maximizing the incidence of rights-satisfactions and other requirements of justice) as is practicably achievable under the circumstances. Or do the rights and other principles of justice that are part of the comprehensive outcomes to be realized themselves impose independent constraints upon the means that can permissibly be utilized to achieve those same comprehensive outcomes?

If we conceive of Sen's comprehensive outcomes in purely consequentialist terms—as states of affairs that are to be maximized or optimized by taking the most effective means to their realization—then a potential threat of circularity arises from the incorporation of rights and other deontic concepts and principles into the good consequences to be promoted or otherwise realized. Consequentialism is a distinct kind of moral conception, according to which the *sole ultimate principle* of right and justice is to maximize the good. But if so, then it would seem that there is no conceptual space remaining for the claim that there are independent non-consequentialist reasons and principles of right and justice requiring respect for others' rights and fair procedures for their own sake, or that states of affairs where individuals respect one another's rights and fair procedures ought to be promoted for their own sake. For why ought people to conform to these principles of right? Why should respect for just *these* specific rights (of conscience, expression, association, etc.), as opposed to some other list of basic rights, be so important? Why should they be equal? It is not as if individuals should respect one another's rights without reason, independent of other relevant moral considerations. The answer to these questions cannot simply be that individuals' compliance with these principles (respect for basic rights, rules of fairness, just distributions, etc.) promotes good consequences, for then the argument becomes clearly circular. "We should respect others' equal basic rights in order to maximize good consequences, which include respecting others' equal basic rights."[61]

To avoid this circle, the proponent of "comprehensive consequentialism" (as I will call the consequentialist interpretation of Sen's position) would seem to have to concede that respecting these principles of right is intrinsically good and hence the right thing to do for its own sake ("precisely because," as Sen said previously, rights and duties ought to be respected).[62] But in that event, the ultimate good to be promoted itself cannot be described in the absence of an antecedent non-maximizing moral principle of right; deontic principles of right are part of its very definition. But then it no longer seems to be the case that maximizing the good is the *sole* ultimate principle of right, and thus we do not have strictly speaking a consequentialist view. Instead we have a kind of pluralist conception that resembles some form of intuitionism. There are already fundamental non-consequentialist moral principles (requiring respect for rights, fair procedures and distributions, etc.) built into the ultimate good represented by comprehensive outcomes, and these principles must be balanced against other ultimate goods and the measures that instrumentally promote them. What are we to do when required to instrumentally promote fair procedures or respect for rights themselves? What if doing so requires that we violate these same rights and procedures (e.g., violate the rights of a few to protect similar or other rights to freedoms or capabilities enjoyed by the many). Which principle has priority then? To say we should decide this question by maximizing the good provides no answer, for we are trying to decide precisely what that involves. If the moral principles that are part of the maximand are to be given any independent weight at all, then it appears that we have in effect two (or more) separate moral principles at work—a consequentialist principle that tells us to maximize aggregate goodness and a deontological one that tells us to observe fair impartial procedures, respect individual rights, or achieve a just distribution for its own sake. These separate moral principles must be somehow weighed against one another to decide what is right to do. If this is done intuitively and without appeal to some further (non-circular) consequentialist principle, then comprehensive consequentialism is really a non-consequentialist form of moral intuitionism or a pluralist deontological view.

My own view is that in this case we might as well give up any pretense of maximizing the good or promoting the best consequences in the social realization of comprehensive outcomes and face the fact that once principles of right and justice (including just distributions, fair procedures, or equal rights, respect for rights, or fulfillment of duties) are themselves regarded as among the ultimate intrinsic goods to be realized, then we have a full-fledged non-consequentialist pluralist position requiring the intuitive balancing of both teleological and deontological principles. It is only in an attenuated sense that such a comprehensive pluralist position can be said to aim to maximize or promote the best consequences overall. For it can be said of almost any moral conception that it promotes or realizes good consequences in the sense that it requires that people do the best thing overall by conforming to that conception's principles. For example, W. D. Ross's intuitionism might be said to enjoin that we realize the best consequences. Ross requires balancing a prima facie consequentialist principle of benevolence, thus promotion of general welfare, along with prima facie deontological principles of justice, fidelity, gratitude, and so on, to come up with a judgment "all things considered." Understood as a position that assigns intrinsic importance to the fulfillment of rights, duties, and fair procedures apart from their consequences, Sen's position does not seem to differ formally in any significant way from Ross's pluralist intuitionist position; the structure seems to be the same. And Ross's pluralist intuitionism is a standard example of a deontological moral conception.[63]

On the other hand, if Sen really seeks to set forth a consequentialist position in *The Idea of Justice*, as he formerly suggested in his earlier accounts of broad consequentialism, then I believe it is unnecessary and potentially confusing to argue for the inclusion of rights, fairness, and other deontic concepts and principles of justice in the states of affairs to be promoted. For example, suppose one of the goods that are part of the comprehensive consequentialist maximand is said to be equal rights of free expression. Offhand, the value here being promoted would seem to be, not rights-fulfillments per se, but individuals' freedom of expression itself and their having the opportunity to exercise this freedom equally. If so, then it obscures this fact to incorporate a deontological principle of (respect for) *equal rights* to freedom of expression and contend that "we should maximize (respect for) equal rights of free expression." If what Sen really has in mind is maximizing equal opportunities for freedom of expression, or equal or adequate capabilities of certain kinds, then a comprehensive "consequentialism of rights"[64] is really just a roundabout way of arguing for a pluralistic distribution-sensitive position that incorporates equal or proportioned distributions of some goods such as capabilities or important freedoms into the maximand. There is no need to incorporate equal *rights* to capabilities themselves into the maximand to accomplish this equal or proportioned distribution. Instead equal rights (to freedom of conscience and expression or to adequate capabilities) should be brought in as an instrumental principle that promotes the achievement of a state of affairs where individuals enjoy equal (opportunities for) freedom of conscience and expression or to adequate capabilities; but in that case, individual rights and other deontic principles themselves are no longer part of the maximand to be promoted, but are effective instrumental means to its achievement.

Finally, there may be a way to make sense of a comprehensive consequentialism of rights that avoids the circularity problem I mentioned, but I do not think it is a position anyone could sensibly adopt. It is implicit in Nozick's suggestion of a "utilitarianism of rights."[65] Suppose we conceive of rights as detached from persons and then require *maximizing the sum total of rights-satisfying actions*. On this account, the main reason to respect anyone's rights on any occasion is that it results in still greater numbers of rights-respecting actions. This position is suggested (though not intended) when Sen says, "The fulfillment of rights is a good thing to happen—the more the better—as it would be seen in a consequential perspective."[66] The problem with this position is not simply the potential injustice involved (in requiring that the rights of some be violated wholesale to maximize aggregate rights-fulfillments) but also the absurd consequences it entails. For example, in order to maximize the sum total of rights-fulfillments, we should go about manufacturing rights-claims for no other reason than maximizing rights-satisfactions; we should then enter into trivial agreements and make legal commitments to fulfill thousands of promises and contracts we otherwise would not contemplate making, for no purpose other than creating rights in others with corresponding duties that we fulfill. What could be the point of maximizing rights-fulfillments, so regarded?[67] The idea that there is something intrinsically good about the state of affairs of maximum rights-fulfillments without regard to whose rights they are—where rights are regarded as detached from people's projects, relations, and reasons for acting and interacting in particular ways—is peculiar, to say the least. It ignores the fact that rights belong to persons and are special reasons for treating them in certain ways; it also ignores the reasons that people need certain rights, in order to be secure in their persons, to freely pursue and succeed at valuable activities, and to fulfill their purposes. We have even less reason to maximize the sum total of rights-satisfactions than we have reason to maximize the sum total of desire-satisfactions.

For these reasons, I think it is better not to understand Sen's advocacy of consequence-sensitive evaluation of comprehensive outcomes as a consequentialist conception that incorporates rights and other just institutions into the maximand; instead his position is best regarded as a pluralist non-consequentialist conception that requires balancing deontological with consequential principles and reasons to arrive at the best overall outcome, all things considered. But if this is a correct interpretation of Sen's position, then it differs less from Rawls's position than initially seems apparent. The main differences would be Sen's rejection of the priority Rawls assigns to the principle of equal basic liberties over considerations of distributive justice, economic efficiency, and the general welfare; Sen's advocacy of a capabilities approach rather than a primary goods approach to interpersonal comparisons; and Sen's rejection of the difference principle in favor of some other unstated egalitarian principles of distributive justice. But there would be no significant difference in their both endorsing broadly similar fundamental non-consequentialist principles of equal basic rights and liberties, fair procedures, and egalitarian distributive justice.[68]

Notes

1. Amartya Sen, *The Idea of Justice* (Cambridge, MA: Harvard University Press, 2009); hereafter, this work is cited as *IJ*.
2. *IJ*, 196.
3. *IJ*, 16.
4. John Locke, *Second Treatise*, in *Two Treatises of Government*, ed. Peter Laslett (Cambridge: Cambridge University Press, 1997).
5. *IJ*, 100.
6. US Constitution, Preamble.
7. Locke's idealized account of the origin of natural property rights has had an equal influence on US social and political attitudes. See his *Second Treatise on Government*, ed. Peter Laslett (Cambridge: Cambridge University Press, 1988), chap. 5. It provides the basis for many Americans' anti-government attitudes, including their non-social, libertarian understanding of property rights and their full sense of entitlement to whatever they can gain by gift, bequest, and market exchanges. Locke's ideal theory has been put to reactionary as well as revolutionary uses.
8. Immanuel Kant, *Groundwork for the Metaphysics of Morals*, trans. and ed. Mary Gregor (Cambridge: Cambridge University Press, 1998), chap. 2.
9. For example, in the first edition of *A Theory of Justice*, Rawls suggests that once the veil is lifted, "the beneficiaries of unjust institutions . . . may find it hard to

reconcile themselves to the changes that have to be made. But in this case they will know that they could not have maintained their position anyway" (*TJ* orig., 176). Rawls later said, in a 1974 article ("Reply to Alexander and Musgrave"), that this was "incorrect" (*CP*, 252). His reason for conceding error is that this passage "applied to cases of hypothetical transition from unjust societies [which] is irrelevant" (*CP*, 252). Transition cases are irrelevant because the argument from the original position for the principles of justice assumes a well-ordered society where the parties freely accept and endorse the principles of justice, and thus should not have such difficulties reconciling themselves to these principles' demands. Here it should be noted that the fact that Rawls even contemplated the parties choosing the principles for non-ideal conditions suggests my claim that he intended them to apply to non-ideal conditions. His assertion that the passage above is "incorrect" does not alter that fact. The passage, taken from the original edition of *A Theory of Justice*, was deleted in the 1975 German edition, which for the most part comprises the 1999 revised edition of *A Theory of Justice*.

10. See, for example, John Simmons, "Ideal and Nonideal Theory," *Philosophy & Public Affairs* 38, no. 1 (2010): 5–36; and more recently, Gerald Gaus, *The Tyranny of the Ideal*, (Princeton, NJ: Princeton University Press, 2016).

11. "Despite the formal resemblance between the difference principle as a principle of distributive justice and the maximin rule as a rule of thumb for decisions under uncertainty. . . the reasoning for the difference principle does not rely on this rule. The formal resemblance is misleading" (*JF*, 94–95, see also 43n., 96). For "mixed conceptions" of justice (or what Rawls later calls "liberal conceptions") that affirm the first principle, have some conception of equal opportunity and guarantee a social minimum, but have a different conception of distributive justice, the maximin argument does not work.

12. Sen contends without argument that the parties would not agree to the same principles anyway, even assuming they were choosing principles for a well-ordered society, and that the outcome of Rawls's original position is indeterminate (*IJ*, 11–12). My own view is that, correctly understood, Rawls's arguments from the original position are for the most part successful.

13. *IJ*, 15, 100.

14. *IJ*, 63.

15. *IJ*, 299.

16. *IJ*, 299.

17. See *PL*, lecture 8, "The Basic Liberties and Their Priority."

18. See, e.g., *Brandenburg v. Ohio*, 395 U.S. 444 (1969) (on freedom of expression); *Wallace v. Jaffree*, 472 U.S. 38 (1985) (on freedom of conscience); *Griswold v. Connecticut*, 381 U.S. 479 (1965) (on the right of privacy); *Harper v. Virginia State Board of Elections*, 383 U.S. 663 (1966) (on equal protection of voting rights).

19. See, generally, Norman Daniels, *Just Health Care* (Cambridge: Cambridge University Press, 1985), on developing and appealing to the fair equality of opportunity principle to argue for and specify a program of universal healthcare.

20. See *JF*, 51, 53, 161.

21. *IJ*, 99.

22. *IJ*, 100.

23. Rawls says in *A Theory of Justice*: "We must ascertain how the ideal conception of justice applies, if indeed it applies at all, to cases where rather than having to make adjustments to natural limitations, we are confronted with injustice. The discussion of these problems belongs to the partial compliance part of non-ideal theory" (*TJ*, 309). The phrase "if indeed it applies at all" seems at least to leave open the possibility that the ideal conception does not apply to non-ideal circumstances of injustice. But from other things Rawls says about the application of justice as fairness, there is no suggestion that he thinks this is so.

24. My understanding of the direct application of Rawls's two principles of justice to current non-ideal conditions differs also from A. John Simmons's interpretation in "Ideal and Nonideal Theory," *Philosophy & Public Affairs* 38, no. 1 (2010): 5–36. Simmons basically understands the application of the principles of justice to non-ideal conditions in an indirect, almost consequentialist fashion: we are to take the means that are necessary to bring about in the future the conditions of a well-ordered society, even violating basic rights and liberties and fair opportunities of some as defined by the two principles of justice when that is necessary to bring us closer to those conditions ("one step back, two steps forward" as Simmons says). His example is that a non-slave-holding society might institute slavery as the only feasible route to the eventual institutionalization of the principle of equal basic liberties. A crucial element missing from this is that slavery would be permissible only if necessary to make the *slaves themselves* better off. Referring specifically to "transition cases where slavery may be better than current practices," Rawls says in effect that slavery would be permissible only if the alternative was killing the persons who were enslaved. His example is an agreement between ancient city-states to enslave rather than kill their prisoners of war, where servitude is not hereditary and "the slaves are not treated too severely" (*TJ* orig., 248). Simmons's reading also seems to conflict with Rawls's rejection of the utilitarian argument that the gross inequalities and destitution of the working classes created by nineteenth-century capitalism are justified since they markedly improved the position of future generations, including the less advantaged. Rawls says this sort of argument can be justified only if "[u]nder other arrangements the condition of the [nineteenth-century] laboring man would have been even worse" (*TJ*, 264). This passage clearly implies that the difference principle applied to those non-ideal nineteenth-century conditions, as it does to our own non-ideal world.

25. Rawls says in the revised edition, "The equal liberties can be denied only when it is necessary to change the quality of civilization so that in due course everyone can enjoy those freedoms" (*TJ*, 475).

26. This is, I believe, a mistaken inference made by conservative critics of ideal theory. They argue that the enormous difficulties in acquiring the complex knowledge that would inform us of which steps to take to achieve an ideal society shows the irrelevance of those ideas, which in turn should leave us confident of the wisdom of the status quo. See Gaus, *The Tyranny of the Ideal*.

27. For example: Rawls's principle of fair equality of opportunity requires a universal healthcare entitlement that is (assumingly) best realized by a government-administered single-payer plan. But given the current aversion of a majority of US citizens to government-administered programs, the best that can be done to achieve an approximation of universal healthcare is a combination of private insurer, a largely employer-based system subsidized by government, together with the extension of Medicaid for all unemployed. With respect to distributive justice, Rawls's difference principle requires substantial taxation of estates to dilute the effects of economic power and then taxing estates at the receiving end (inheritance taxes) to encourage the breaking-up and wide dispersal of accumulated wealth. But given the animosity toward so-called "death taxes," the best we can do at this point is to hold the line against increasing efforts to repeal the existing system of estate taxes and hope that someday a majority will gradually be convinced of the justice of the wide dispersion of accumulated wealth.

28. See Frances Kamm, "Sen on Justice and Rights," *Philosophy & Public Affairs* 39, no. 1 (2011): 82; "Sen, it might be said, has at least provided a very abstract conception of perfect justice" (95).

29. *IJ*, 122, 196, 392. "Public reasoning and debates are central to the pursuit of justice" (122). "We can take the relevant standard of objectivity of ethical principles to be linked to their defensibility in an open and free framework of public reasoning" (196).

30. Rousseau himself uses the term "public reason"—which he contrasts with individuals' "private" or "own reason"—and says public reason should guide the judgments of lawmakers. See Rousseau's "Discourse on Political Economy," *The Basic Political Writings*, trans. David A. Cress (Indianapolis: Hackett, 1987).

31. See generally Jürgen Habermas, *Between Facts and Norms*, trans. William Rehg (Cambridge, MA: MIT Press, 1996).

32. For example, Habermas says, "Moral justifications are dependent on argumentation actually being carried out, not for pragmatic reasons of an equalization of power, but for internal reasons, namely that real argument makes moral insight possible." Jürgen Habermas, "Discourse Ethics," in *Moral Consciousness and Communicative Action*, trans. Christian Lenhardt (Cambridge, MA: MIT Press, 1990), 57, 68, 147, 151.

33. This distinction is related to Sen's distinction between Habermas's and perhaps his own more "procedural" approach to justice, versus Rawls's more substantive or "normative" approach (*IJ*, 42–44).

34. Gerald Gaus, like Sen, also assumes that applying Rawls's principles involves comparing and ranking social states of affairs according to their approximation to a well ordered society. See Gaus, *The Tyranny of the Ideal*, 246.

35. See *TJ* orig., 115, 334, and *TJ*, 99, 293, on the natural duty of justice "to support and comply with just institutions that exist and apply to us."

36. *IJ*, 83.

37. *IJ*, 86. "Of course the institutions themselves can sensibly count as part of the realizations that come through them, but they can hardly be the entirety of what we need to concentrate on, since people's lives are also involved" (82).

38. J. S. Mill, *Utilitarianism*, ed. George Sher (Indianapolis: Hackett, 1979), chap. 5.

39. An important question here is what kinds of considerations are relevant to deciding fair distributive shares of rights, liberties, powers, opportunities, income and wealth, and other social goods, and to making interpersonal comparisons? Sen famously argues that individual capabilities should be primary among the considerations that are taken into account in deciding distributive shares and making interpersonal comparisons. He contests Rawls's method for deciding distributive shares of primary social goods and making interpersonal comparisons (mainly on grounds that Rawls's institutional account is not sensitive to disabilities, special needs, and variations in people's conversion of primary goods into "functionings") (*IJ*, 260). An interesting question I cannot address here is whether the basic political and economic institutions Rawls focuses on should be attuned to special needs and disabilities at the abstract level that Rawls is concerned with. (Here one relevant question is, why should differences in conversion rates of primary goods matter to the political constitution itself or to structuring basic institutions of property and the economy? These differences matter clearly in deciding how to legislatively address problems of disabilities and basic needs—a problem Rawls speaks to only briefly—but at the level of the constitutional design of basic political and economic institutions, it is less clear what role differences in conversion rates should have.)

40. *IJ*, 82.

41. *IJ*, 210.

42. Sen says at one point that "through defining his principles of justice entirely in institutional terms, Rawls too goes some distance towards a purely institutional view of justice," though not as far as Gauthier and Nozick do (*IJ*, 85). "There is no procedure within the system to check whether the institutions are, in fact, generating the anticipated results" (85n.). This is mistaken; Rawls says that the difference principle achieves "adjusted pure procedural justice," in that economic institutions and their rules are to be regularly adjusted so that shares

going to the least advantaged are maximal. Likewise, the constitutional and legislative institutions and laws needed to realize fair equality of opportunity are subject to continual adjustment to meet changing circumstances.

43. *IJ*, 7–9.

44. *IJ*, 6.

45. For example, William Talbott has suggested a distribution-sensitive form of consequentialism that incorporates "appropriately distributed well-being" into the state of affairs to be maximally promoted. See Talbott, *Human Rights and Human Well-Being* (Oxford: Oxford University Press, 2010).

46. Amartya Sen, "Rights and Agency," *Philosophy & Public Affairs* 11, no. 1 (1982): 3–39.

47. Amartya Sen, "Consequential Evaluation and Practical Reason," *Journal of Philosophy* 97, no. 9 (2000): 494 (emphasis added). This paper develops the position set forth in "Rights and Agency," where Sen also refers to "goal rights systems."

48. Sen, "Consequential Evaluation," 498.

49. *IJ*, 217. Sen notes one exception:

> While I have no great interest in proposing any definition of what consequentialism really is, I should note here that Arjuna's approach [in the *Bhagavad Gita*] is certainly compatible with Philip Pettit's definition of consequentialism . . . "Roughly speaking," Pettit says, "consequentialism is the theory that the way to tell whether a particular choice is the right choice for an agent to have made is to look at the relevant consequences of the decision; to look at the relevant effects of the decision on the world."

> Sen continues, "Since there is no insistence here that the accounting of consequences be confined to culmination outcomes only, ignoring the relevance of agencies, processes or relations, capturable in the picture of a comprehensive outcome, there is no tension in seeing Arjuna as a consequentialist in Pettit's sense" (217–218n.). Sen favorably contrasts the consequence-sensitive reasoning of Arjuna with the purely duty-based reasoning of Krishna.

50. Sen uses the term "consequential evaluation" in referring to his own position at least three times (*IJ*, 213, 216, 217). He also says that "we . . . have to subject democracy to consequential analysis," and we should "look at consequential connections that relate freedoms to obligations" (347, 372). More frequently he refers to the assessment of "social realizations" and the evaluation of "comprehensive outcomes."

51. *IJ*, 22–23, 218, 230.

52. *IJ*, 220.

53. *IJ*, 221.

54. *IJ*, 8.

55. *IJ*, 213, 216–17.

56. *IJ*, 82.

57. Sen discusses the predictive (actual choice) and the normative (rational choice) uses of "maximize" in contemporary economics (*IJ*, 174–78). He also distinguishes between mathematical uses of "maximality (needed for an acceptable choice) and optimality (needed for making a perfect choice)."

58. Thus, in economics, in discussions of consumer choice and ordinal rankings of bundles of goods given their budget constraints, it is not contemplated that economic agents will satisfy their preferences by stealing the goods when they can, rather than paying for them. Instead it is assumed that these presumably rational utility maximizers will respect the constraints imposed by others' legal property rights.

59. Sen's discussion of the role in choice of individuals' commitments to social norms versus their rational pursuit of goals is relevant here (*IJ*, 188–93).

60. The consequentialist response to trolley-like problems is relevant here, since this approach endorses violating the rights to life and security of one person in order to protect the lives and security of two or more persons.

61. Here and in the following discussion I draw on my essay, "Problems with Some Consequentialist Arguments for Basic Rights," in *The Philosophy of Human Rights: Contemporary Controversies*, ed. Gerhard Ernst and Jan-Christoph Heilinger (Berlin: De Gruyter, 2011). My charge of circularity here resembles Sidgwick's response to the claim that virtuous conduct is the ultimate good to be rationally promoted or maximized. Sidgwick says, "If we mean by Virtue conformity to such prescriptions and prohibitions as make up the main part of the morality of Common Sense, [then] to say that 'General Good' consists solely in general Virtue . . . would obviously involve us in a logical circle; since we have seen that the exact determination of these prescriptions and prohibitions must depend on the definition of this General Good." Henry Sidgwick, *Methods of Ethics*, 7th ed. (Indianapolis: Hackett, 1981), 392.

62. See Sen, "Consequential Evaluation," 494.

63. Here it is noteworthy that Sen recognizes that "the substantive gap between some versions of broad deontology and broad consequentialism may not be very great." Sen, "Consequential Evaluation," 479.

64. Sen, "Consequential Evaluation," 499.

65. See *ASU*, 28–29.

66. *IJ*, 498.

67. Minimizing rights-violations would have opposite effects: we minimize prospective violations of rights by failing to exercise or create those rights. The position is also prone to population and other excessive-numbers problems that consequentialists often confront—for example, if the sum of rights-satisfactions ought to be maximized for its own sake, then we would seem to be under a duty to increase population to as many people as needed to maximize the number of rights-satisfying actions. Minimizing rights-violations would require extreme birth control measures.

68. If Sen's position is understood in this non-consequentialist fashion, then it would neutralize some of his criticisms of Rawls's focus on the basic structure and the justice of social institutions. For it would imply that, in the impartial assessment of comprehensive outcomes, distributional principles of justice guaranteeing (equal) basic rights, equal or fair opportunities, and fair distributions and procedures are just as fundamental as are consequentialist principles promoting capabilities, freedoms, welfare, and other relevant goods. While this understanding of Sen seems at odds with his claim that "it is hard to think of [institutions] as basically good in themselves," it nonetheless seems to fit with his claim that "institutions can sensibly count as *part* of the realizations that come through them" (*IJ*, 82–83).

I am grateful to Amartya Sen for his comments on this paper, and to other participants at the Symposium on *The Idea of Justice* at Rutgers Law School in 2011, including David Estlund, Gerald Gaus, Erin Kelly, Rahul Kumar, John Oberdiek, Henry Richardson, and Debra Satz, among others. I am also grateful to John Tasioulas, Jonathan Wolff, Michael Otsuka, and other participants at a colloquium at the University College London Faculty of Laws in 2011, where the third section of this paper was discussed.

9

Constructivism, Facts, and Moral Justification

1. Introduction

In justice as fairness the first principles of justice depend upon those general beliefs about human nature and how society works . . . First principles are not, in a constructivist view, independent of such beliefs, nor . . . true of all possible worlds. In particular, they depend on the rather specific features and limitations of human life that give rise to the circumstances of justice. (CP, 351)

Kant famously advocates an ethics of "pure reason" in which the fundamental principles of moral conduct and their justification are not to contain any empirical concepts. No major twentieth-century moral philosopher was influenced by Kant more than Rawls. Yet Rawls rejects Kant's idea that first moral principles are to be formulated and justified independent of contingent assumptions. Rawls's position might be explained on general philosophical grounds: along with many contemporaries, he rejected the dualisms underlying Kant's and other traditional philosophical positions, including distinctions between analytic and synthetic, pure and empirical reason, necessary and contingent truths, and a priori and a posteriori propositions.[1] But general philosophical reasons of the kind that Quine, Wittgenstein, Dewey, and others relied upon are not the reasons Rawls gives for invoking general facts to justify his principles of justice. His reasons are specific to moral theory, as befits his claim of "the independence of moral theory" from metaphysics and epistemology. And these reasons relate to the one notable exception among Kant's dualisms that Rawls retains: Kant's sharp distinction between the theoretical and the practical uses of reason.

My aim here is to discuss some reasons why general facts should be relevant to a justification of fundamental principles of justice. G. A. Cohen argues the opposing position. He advocates the a priori thesis that, if facts ground principles, then fact-free principles are at the foundation of the structure of the belief of anyone who is clear about what he or she believes and why, just as it is a priori that anyone who is rational maximizes, or satisfices, or whatever.[2]

Cohen's criticism is directed against constructivism in moral philosophy.[3] He says, "Constructivists about justice . . . believe that all sound principles are, as I shall say, fact-sensitive, by which I mean neither more nor less than that *facts form at least part of the grounds for affirming them*." Now strictly speaking, this is not true of Kant's constructivism, for whom the reasons for the "Moral Law" are a priori and based in "pure reason" alone.[4] Nor does Rawls regard "all sound principles" as "fact-sensitive" (e.g., the veil of ignorance and formal constraints of right are not). But Rawls does contend that his "fundamental principles of justice" are based in certain general facts about the human condition. Since Cohen's account of constructivism is closely tied to features of Rawls's constructivism, I will focus on that. I leave aside Rawls's later political constructivism, since it can take no position on the meta-ethical issues Cohen raises. Only justice as fairness regarded as a (partially) comprehensive constructivist position set forth in *A Theory of Justice* and "Kantian Constructivism in Moral Theory" is at issue here.

I discuss three reasons why the first principles of a moral conception of justice should be "fact-sensitive" or presuppose general facts in their justification. First, a conception of justice should be *compatible with our moral and psychological capacities*. It should respond to basic human needs; moreover, given their natural tendencies, conscientious moral agents who affirm the conception should be capable of developing appropriate attitudes enabling them to normally act upon its demands. Second, a conception of justice should provide *principles for practical reasoning* and fulfill a *social role in supplying a public basis for justification* among persons with different conceptions of their good. Third, *a moral conception should not frustrate, but should affirm the pursuit of the human good*. In order to meet each of these reasonable conditions, a conception of justice must take into account facts about human nature and social cooperation in justifying first principles of justice. I argue for this thesis in sections 3–5. Before that, I clarify what Cohen and I mean by "fundamental principles of justice" and what is at stake in this dispute.

2. What Are Fundamental Principles of Justice?

Suppose we were constructed by nature so that we had equal concern for everyone and cared no more for our own well-being than the next person's. We might then, as Hume says, have no need for property and other norms of distributive justice, for then we would be willing to produce and share goods and services without self-concern. Similarly, suppose nature were so bountiful that all our desires could be satisfied without anyone's labor or forbearance—that the objects of our wants would appear "like manna from heaven." Again, we would have no need for property or distributive justice. But circumstances are different. We are characterized by "limited altruism"—we have attachments to particular persons or groups and care more for our own projects and commitments than for others'. Also, there is "moderate scarcity" of goods—enough to meet everyone's needs, but never enough to satisfy all their desires; thus, humans must produce, save, and invest their product to satisfy present aims and future ambitions. These "circumstances of justice" give rise, Hume says, to the "cautious, jealous virtue of justice." Were general facts about humankind entirely different, we might have no need for rules of property and principles of distributive justice that determine who should receive and control income and wealth in exchange for specified contributions.[5] Rawls follows Hume in regarding justice as a particularly human virtue (*TJ*, 109).[6]

It might be replied that none of this shows that the *content* of principles of justice, or what they *require of us*, is either conditioned upon and or justifiable by appeal to facts about human nature. Whether justice requires that we maximize aggregate goodness or distribute goods equally, or according to need, effort, or contribution, or to maximally benefit the least advantaged, or to redress the effects of brute luck, or whatever the criterion—it is *this* question that is not dependent upon facts about human nature but rather upon moral considerations that ultimately are "fact-insensitive." Cohen says, "Ultimate principles cannot be *justified* by facts,"[7] not that they cannot contain any allusions to facts. Yet Rawls explicitly appeals to general facts about human nature (our limited altruism and psychological tendencies of reciprocity) and social phenomena (the chain-connection and close-knitness of economic distributions) to argue that the difference principle is preferable to the principle of utility or a stricter egalitarian principle. As I understand Cohen, this is the problem, namely conditioning the *justification* of principles of justice upon general facts about human propensities, economic tendencies, and social institutions. The problem is that, when facts are invoked to justify principles of justice, these principles then cannot be *fundamental* principles but rather must be the application or extension or "implementation" of fundamental principles to particular factual circumstances. For this reason, Rawls's difference principle cannot be the "fundamental," "ultimate," or "first principle" of distributive justice (all being terms Rawls uses).[8]

In support of Rawls's position, the following four levels of normative principles can be distinguished. They are to be found not only in Rawls, but also in Sidgwick, Mill, Kant, and other major moral philosophers:

(1) *Substantive principles of justice,* which are among the basic principles of conduct (for individuals or institutions); examples include Rawls's two principles of justice, the principle of utility, Kant's Moral Law, W. D. Ross's seven prima facie principles of Right, and Nozick's entitlement principles. I contend that these principles of conduct are fundamental in that they are the ultimate standards that determine if and when actions, laws, and institutions are right or just.

(2) *Principles of justification,* which are among the ultimate reasons and considerations that are used to justify the substantive principles of justice mentioned in (1). These justifying reasons have a different function than providing ultimate standards for right conduct or just distributions; they have primarily an epistemic role. Examples are Rawls's ideals of free and equal moral persons and a well-ordered society, the formal constraints of right (universality, generality, publicity, etc.), and the veil of ignorance, all of which are part of the original position; or Kant's assumption of practical freedom in his "transcendental deduction" of the Moral Law; or Sidgwick's principles of impartial benevolence and of equity (treat similar cases similarly), used to justify the principle of utility; or Harsanyi's impartiality condition and assumptions regarding rational choice and equiprobability of outcomes, used to justify a principle of average utility; and perhaps (as he regards it) Cohen's luck-egalitarian principle. Some account of practical rationality and moral reasoning and justification normally accompanies principles of justification and is utilized in the justification of fundamental principles of conduct for individuals and institutions.

(3) *Principles of application,* which are used to determine what (1) substantive principles of justice require; examples include "equal consideration is to be given to equal interests" in applying the principle of utility; the final three stages of Rawls's "four-stage sequence" for applying the principles of justice; and Kant's categorical imperative procedure for applying the Moral Law.

(4) *Secondary principles and rules of conduct,* which result from the application of first principles of justice in (1); examples are rights of freedom of speech and expression that liberals contend are justifiable by a principle of liberty; the rules of a constitutional, property-owning democracy that Rawls contends are justified by applying the principles of justice; the rules of a capitalist welfare state that welfare economists justify on grounds of the principle of utility; and the duties of fidelity, veracity, and charity justified by many moral conceptions.

Within this four-part schema, epistemic principles of justification (at level 2) do not themselves determine when actions, laws, and institutions are right or just. For example, there is nothing about Rawls's ideal of free and equal moral persons, the five formal constraints of right, the veil of ignorance, and the account of rational plans of life, taken by themselves, that would determine whether one distribution is more just than another or whether socialism, property-owning democracy, welfare-state capitalism, or laissez-faire capitalism is required by justice. Instead, these justificatory principles are among the relevant reasons that must be taken into account in arguing for and justifying substantive principles of distributive justice by way of the original position. It is not the role of these principles of justification to provide the ultimate standard for just distributions. To know what standards to use in deciding which economic institutions or distributions are more or less just, we have to look at the fundamental substantive principles of justice themselves (the difference principle, the principle of utility, libertarian entitlement principles, or some other account of distributive justice).

Cohen holds that so long as a principle has a justification via other "normative principles," it cannot be a fundamental principle.[9] This implies that nothing can be a *fundamental* substantive principle of conduct unless it is itself self-evident or follows from non-factual methodological principles. But the fact that normative justificatory principles (e.g., an impartiality condition implicit in the veil of ignorance) are needed to argue for ultimate substantive principles of justice should not deprive the latter of their status as fundamental moral principles. What *makes* a substantive principle of conduct fundamental is not that it is self-evident or otherwise without normative justification, but that *it is the ultimate standard for determining conduct and there are no more basic principles of which it is an application.* Thus, for Rawls distributions of income, wealth, and powers and positions of office are just when they result from an economy designed to implement fair equality of opportunity and the difference principle. There is no more fundamental principle to which we can appeal to determine just distributions; the second principle is the limit.

Cohen himself distinguishes between "justifying principles" and "regulative principles." He contends that Rawls's principles of justice are regulative principles and that *as such* they are non-fundamental: only justifying principles, like the principles informing Rawls's ideal of free and equal moral persons, can be fundamental principles.[10] But the regulative nature of the principles of justice should not make them any less "fundamental" than the principles used to justify them; for justificatory principles and regulative principles of conduct work at different levels and have different roles. The former are the argumentative ingredients that combine to provide epistemic support for regulative principles. But significantly, they are not adequate by themselves to tell us what we ought to do or how we ought to structure social institutions and relations. Instead, justificatory principles provide fundamental reasons for deciding what are the equally fundamental substantive principles of conduct that regulate what we are to do. This justifying role is taken on in Rawls by the conception of free and equal persons, the veil of ignorance, and other assumptions that go into Rawls's original position; they are among the "restrictions that it seems reasonable to impose on arguments for principles of justice, and therefore on these principles themselves" (*TJ*, 16).[11] Utilitarians such as R. M. Hare and John Harsanyi would argue the same is true of the impartiality assumptions and accounts of rational choice as utility maximization that underlie their impartial choice arguments for a principle of utility. These fact-free principles are fundamental reasons for accepting fundamental substantive principles of conduct. Hence, the fact that substantive principles of justice have a justification should not undermine the claim that substantive principles are the fundamental principles of justice to which we ultimately are to appeal in social and political relations in deciding how to structure institutions and make laws and other rules of conduct. There are no more basic principles, including fundamental principles of justification, which taken by themselves can answer *that* question for us.

But this diverts us from the main issue; which is whether factual considerations can play any role in establishing what I am calling first principles of conduct. Cohen says, "Ultimate principles cannot be justified by facts."[12] Rawls denies this and goes against a long tradition in philosophy of claiming that the justification of fundamental moral principles must depend only on a priori truths. Rawls says, to the contrary, that fundamental principles of justice must invoke and rely upon general facts about human tendencies and social cooperation. His opponents, including Cohen and Habermas,[13] reply that once empirical considerations are invoked to support principles we no longer have a fundamental principle, but rather something less: an "application" (Habermas) or "implementation" (Cohen) of some fact-free fundamental principle(s). In the following three sections I address and take issue with Cohen's and Habermas's claims that only fact-insensitive principles can be fundamental principles of justice.

Why is this issue important? What's the point behind Cohen's "meta-ethical truth" that " [u]ltimate principles cannot be justified by facts"?[14] It might be purely philosophical, akin to Kant's ambition to discover the principles regulative of "pure practical reason" whatever its empirical conditions. Another reason is the fear that appeals to facts make moral principles contingent on circumstances, thereby raising the specter of relativism.[15] But if the facts Rawls appeals to are permanent and apply generally to human beings as such, then there should be no threat of the cultural relativism of moral principles of justice (which is the kind of relativism that matters practically speaking). Finally, a third factor that might be motivating Cohen's critique is that, if his argument regarding facts and principles is true, then it might insulate his luck-egalitarian thesis from recent criticisms. I return to this issue in the concluding section.

3. Justice, Human Needs, and Moral Capacities

The first reason cited earlier for the relevance of facts to first principles of justice is as follows:

(1) A conception of justice (like any moral conception) should be compatible with our moral and psychological capacities. It should be responsive to basic human needs and interests, at least insofar as conscientious moral agents who affirm the conception should be capable of developing appropriate attitudes enabling them to normally and regularly act upon its demands given the constraints of human nature.

A primary example of a fact about human beings that is relevant to fundamental moral principles is the value that we put on self-respect. By "self-respect" I mean a psychological attitude that includes a sense that our individual lives matter and are worth living, that our primary pursuits are also worthwhile, and that we are capable of realizing these pursuits. In traditional societies, a shared religion often provided a principal basis for self-respect, but in a modern democratic society, self-respect generally depends upon others' recognition of a person as an equal citizen. If we were strongly disconnected selves, with little sense of our own good or even of our past or future, we would not be so concerned about either self-respect or others' respect for us as persons; nor would we likely be so concerned about individuals' rights. As Derek Parfit argues, this might strengthen the case for the principle of utility. It is safe to assume that our sense of our personal identity is not based in our having a soul or being an immutable substance. It is a contingent fact whether we are psychologically dissociated, disconnected selves or are "strongly connected" with a sense of ourselves and our good. This suggests that self-respect is a contingent belief and attitude too.

Rawls says that self-respect is perhaps the "most important primary good" (*TJ*, 386).[16] The parties in Rawls's original position consider the effects of principles and institutions on their sense of self-respect in comparing and deciding on principles of justice. Among the bases of self-respect, Rawls contends, are principles and institutions that maintain persons' status as equal citizens, including equal political liberties, equality of fair opportunities, and other equal basic rights and liberties. Why should we be concerned about having *equal* basic liberties and equal fair opportunities rather than *just enough* to do what we need or seek to do?[17] Here the bases of self-respect and our desire to be regarded as equals play a central role in Rawls's argument for egalitarian principles and institutions. Principles of justice are responsive to the "basic needs" of persons who conceive of themselves as free and equal persons. Other primary goods Rawls recognizes (liberties, powers and opportunities, and income and wealth) also have an empirical basis in psychological and social tendencies.

It might be replied that the goodness or desirability of these primary goods is not contingent upon facts. Even if our desire for self-respect depends upon the psychological fact that we conceive of ourselves as strongly individuated selves with a past and a future, still it is good, independent of any such facts about ourselves, that we have such a strong sense of individual self and a concomitant desire for self-respect. Suppose we meet with a tribe whose members have no long-term aims or life plans and little or no sense of individual self, but who live like drones always selflessly serving some dominant communal end (e.g., maximizing the king's pleasures and offspring). We will rightly think this is a bad way for people to live since it results in their exploitation and the violation of their human rights. Even if they do not think of themselves as worthy individuals with their own purposes and separate lives to live, they *should* do so nonetheless, since individual dignity and free self-development and individuality (for example) are fundamental human goods. So, the objection continues, even if Rawls were to rely only upon psychological and social facts to justify the primary goods, they would nonetheless have an independent philosophical grounding in moral values that he does not invoke.

Rawls himself might be interpreted as providing (on the Kantian interpretation; *TJ*, §40) a non-empirical grounding for the primary social goods. The Kantian interpretation suggests that our conception of ourselves as unified selves extending over time with ends and a life plan of our own is not simply a contingent fact, but is rooted in the conditions of rational moral agency, the moral powers, which constitute our "nature as free and equal rational beings." For a person to act and have reasons at all requires having a coherent plan of life and developed moral powers. Otherwise, like a drone, one is a being to whom things just happen and whose behavior is aimless and without reason, or at most a being without self-awareness who does not act but rather engages in activities (like dogs digging bones—there is aim-directed activity but not action).[18] On the Kantian justification of the primary social goods, they are no longer contingent needs of persons who happen to conceive of themselves as we do. They are rather necessary conditions for fully realizing rational and moral agency.

Perhaps then the contingent grounding of primary social goods (and therewith principles of justice) might be replaced in some way by this or some other argument from their necessity. Still, it is not so clear that the relevance of other factual grounds to principles of justice is expendable. Suppose that principles of justice demand more of us than we are humanly capable of doing. It is often argued that the principle of utility makes extraordinary demands on people. A sincere and conscientious utilitarian is a person who should have no special concern for him- or herself and who impartially promotes everyone's interests. But it is beyond our capacities to forgo whatever aims and interests we have and develop a settled disposition *always* to take everyone else's interests *equally* into account and act to maximize overall utility. To contend that we nonetheless *ought* to do so when we by nature *cannot* is to make an unreasonable demand. How can a reasonable morality demand something realistically impossible for people?

One way to mitigate or neutralize the effects of the "ought implies can" requirement is via the indirect application of moral principles. Thus, the principle of utility might avoid the problem of imposing unreasonable demands by "effacing" itself (Parfit) and becoming "esoteric" (Sidgwick). Given the limitations of human nature, perhaps the best way to maximize utility is to inculcate in people a non-utilitarian morality whose rules, when generally observed, in fact create greater utility than any other rules humans are capable of regularly observing. On this indirect and esoteric application of the principle of utility, it can be argued that we indeed are capable of complying with the demands of the principle of utility, by directly observing other moral rules designed to take our limitations into account.

The indirect and "esoteric" application of a moral principle is one way to reconcile "ought implies can" with an overly demanding principle that is beyond human capacities for regular compliance. Sincere conscientious moral agents then are those who are committed to acting on and from the secondary moral rules that best implement the overly demanding principle (e.g., of utility) in light of human nature. This may be one way to defend Cohen's claim that "regulative" principles of justice are not ever fundamental but rather "implement" fundamental principles. Regulative principles might be regarded in the same manner as indirect utilitarians conceive of secondary moral principles; they are applications of more fundamental normative principles that are beyond our capacities to regularly comply with if directly applied. I do not think that Cohen himself would accept the "esoteric" approach to fundamental principles, largely for reasons I discuss momentarily. Next I will discuss features of a contractarian conception of justice that rule out the esoteric approach, and show why facts must be taken into account in the justification of ultimate principles of justice.

4. The Social Role of a Conception of Justice

(2) A conception of justice should provide moral agents with principles for practical reasoning and fulfill a social role in providing a public basis for justification among persons with different conceptions of their good.

To orient the discussion of this second methodological condition, consider Cohen's and Rawls's different conceptions of political philosophy:

(i) "The question for political philosophy is *not what we should do but what we should think*, even when what we should think makes *no practical difference*" (*FP*, 243; emphasis added).

(ii) "A conception of justice is framed to meet the *practical requirements of social life* and to yield a public basis in the light of which citizens can *justify to one another* their common institutions" (*CP*, 347; emphasis added).

These statements reveal a significant difference between Rawls's and Cohen's conceptions of the role of a moral conception of justice. For Cohen, its role is mainly theoretical; in the first instance a moral conception seeks the truth regardless of its practical consequences for social relations and cooperation. Of course, any moral theory seeks truth in the ordinary sense that it is an inquiry into, and justification of, the *correct moral principles*. But if one thinks of moral truth and the role of a moral conception as making potentially "no practical difference,"[19] then it is hard to avoid the idea that principles of justice are prior to and independent of the practical reasoning that we, as moral agents who are situated and engaged in social life, apply to them. Rawls suggests that philosophers who regard moral philosophy as a search to discover the truth of antecedent normative principles are not going to be in a position to see the possibility of constructivism as a distinct method in ethics.[20] For the unmediated quest for true moral principles, pursued as if they are to be discovered by theoretical reason like any other basic theoretical laws or principles, leads to neglect of the arguably equally important conception of the person and its relationship to principles of justice and to neglect therewith of the *social role* of moral principles.

The primary role of a conception of justice for Rawls is a *practical* (as opposed to theoretical) and *social* one. This means: (1) A moral conception is geared to provide, not all possible rational and reasonable beings, but rational and reasonable persons like us, who conceive of ourselves as free and equal moral agents and who are subject to the constraints of human nature, with practical guidance regarding what *we* ought to do. To fulfill this practical role, fundamental moral principles should provide us with principles of practical reasoning that we can reasonably accept and knowingly apply in our capacity as free and equal moral agents. (2) A moral conception has a social role, to provide beings like us with a public basis for justification regarding our moral, social, and political relations. These two conditions on a conception of justice suggest that fundamental moral principles of justice ought to be publicly knowable and generally acceptable to those to whom these principles apply, so that principles can fulfill their practical and social roles as principles of practical reasoning for free and equal moral agents, providing us with practical guidance and a basis for public justification suitable to our status as free and equal persons.

Assigning priority to the practical and social roles of a moral conception rules out formulating a moral conception true of all possible worlds.

Some philosophers have thought that ethical first principles should be independent of all contingent assumptions, that they should take for granted no truths except those of logic and others that follow from these by an analysis of concepts. Moral conceptions should hold for all possible worlds. Now this view makes moral philosophy the study of the ethics of creation: an examination of the reflections an omnipotent deity might entertain in determining which is the best of all possible worlds. Even the general facts of nature are to be chosen. Certainly, we have a natural religious interest in the ethics of creation. But it would appear to outrun human comprehension. (*TJ*, 137–138)

Rawls's point is that there is something misguided in conjecturing a morality for all possible worlds. Moral philosophy should take up the practical perspective of moral agents engaged in deliberation about what they (or groups of which they are members) ought to do. This contrasts with an epistemological point of view of the detached observer who seeks moral truth by inquiring into the way the world (or all possible worlds) really is or ought to be. Constructivism situates the inquiry into moral principles practically by asking not (simply) "What moral principles should I believe correct or true?" but "What principles of justice ought I endorse and act upon in my capacity as a free rational moral agent with human propensities and situated in the social world?"

So conceived, constructivism puts center stage a conception of the person as moral agent and seeks to discover principles of justice that are most appropriate for expressing/realizing this conception. A conception of the person as a free and equal, reasonable and rational moral agent is then interwoven into the content of principles of justice. By contrast, rational intuitionism and related views, due to their direct inquiry into true moral principles unmediated by their social or practical roles, are led to eschew any conception of the person as a central feature of a moral conception. The social role of morality and the related publicity condition on first principles are relevant to this conception of persons. Rawls endorses the following: (A) respect for persons as free and equal moral persons requires that we justify our conduct to them on terms that they can reasonably accept in their capacity as rational moral agents; (B) the freedom and equality of moral persons requires that they be in a position to know and accept the fundamental moral bases of their social relations.[21] I discuss the implications of (A) in this section and of (B) in section 5.

Reasonable acceptability: How do general facts enter into the justification of moral principles, given the contractarian assumption of reasonable acceptability of principles to persons in their capacity as free and equal persons? What does attending to general facts have to do with respect for people as free and equal moral persons? Contractarians influenced by Kant (Rawls and Scanlon are primary examples) contend that to respect persons as rational moral agents requires that the basic moral principles structuring and regulating their relations be justifiable *to* them. Rawls understands this idea (justification to a person) to mean that principles are to be shown to be reasonably acceptable to persons in their capacity as free and equal moral agents with moral and rational capacities and a conception of their good, and in view of general facts about humans and their social relations.[22]

There are a number of ways to work out the contractarian idea of "justification to a person," suggesting potentially several different kinds of contract views. For example, what kinds of knowledge are people presumed to have to whom justifications are made? What are their desires, interests, and moral motivations? Are people presumed to be situated in the status quo, in a state of nature, behind a veil of ignorance, or within an ideal or well-ordered society? I will focus on but one issue, namely: Are we to assume that the hypothetical moral agents to whom contractarian justifications are directed are subject to general facts of human nature and social life and take these facts into account in comparing and deciding on the acceptability of alternative principles? Or are they to leave aside considerations regarding human capacities and social cooperation in deciding whether principles are more or less reasonable? On the one hand, it might be argued that moral persons, who are by definition reasonable and hence morally motivated, should not take into account these facts and instead should agree on principles that apply whatever the facts about their nature and circumstances turn out to be. Then they would be choosing principles true of all (or many) possible worlds. The principles that these hypothetical people could or would agree to would then be designated the most reasonable principles of justice for us. On the other hand, it might be argued that since all moral persons known to us are subject to human tendencies, in justifying principles *to* them we should take into account general facts about human nature such as our tendency to disagreement in philosophical, religious, and moral convictions, our different commitments and conceptions of the good, and the fact that our capacity to act on and from moral principles is constrained by natural psychological tendencies (such as limited altruism). The principles of justice that free and equal moral persons would or could agree to, in light of their distinctly human tendencies and general social conditions, are likely to be quite different than they would be if they did not take into account the human condition at all.

Rawls and Scanlon opt for this second position. Principles of justice are to be justifiable *to* reasonable and rational persons with natural human tendencies and who are subject to normal conditions of social life among beings with different conceptions of their good. It would be unreasonable to impose demands on people that did not take their natural propensities and limitations into account. One consequence of our human nature under free conditions is that we do have different interests and final aims as well as conflicting philosophical, religious, and moral beliefs. For this and other reasons, humans have different conceptions of the good and of what gives their lives meaning. Rawls seeks principles of justice that take these "subjective circumstances of justice" into account and that can gain general acceptance within a feasible social world among reasonable and rational persons constrained by human propensities. The aim is to find the conception of justice that respects us, not simply as reasonable and rational beings, but as distinctly *human* persons who regard themselves as free and equal.

Assume it is a condition of the (philosophical) justification of a moral conception that it be able to fulfill the social role Rawls assigns to it—namely, it should be capable of providing a public basis for justification of social and political relations among persons who are reasonable and rational, who regard themselves as free and equal, and who have different conceptions of the good. To fulfill this role, reasonable people must find a moral conception "reasonably acceptable," meaning (in part) that (1) their human capacities enable them to regularly comply with its demands, and (2) they can accept it for moral reasons and not simply because it is the best compromise they can reach in pursuit of their non-moral interests. A conception of justice must then engage our "moral nature," (*TJ*, 508) including our capacities for a sense of justice. The crucial point here is that, to fulfill a social role of public justification, a moral conception cannot place such great demands upon people's natural capacities or permissible conceptions of their good that it exceeds their capacities for compliance or consistently frustrates their pursuit of their reasonable aims and commitments. Any moral conception that exceeds these factual limitations is unreasonable.

This responds to the problem raised at the end of the preceding section, where I discussed how two-level moral conceptions might satisfy the "ought implies can" requirement by applying fundamental moral principles indirectly to conduct. The problem with this is that, given their social role, moral principles of justice have to serve free and equal persons with a human nature as public principles of practical reasoning that agents themselves can apply as citizens to determine and justify their institutions and actions. It is because of this social role of fundamental principles of justice that the "self-effacing," "esoteric" approach to first principles of justice will not suffice. Sincere, conscientious moral agents have to be capable of understanding, accepting, applying, voluntarily acting upon, and sincerely committing themselves to first moral principles. Their acceptance of and commitment to principles assume that principles are publicly known and fulfill a social role in providing a basis for public justification of laws and basic social institutions. Otherwise principles are unreasonable for free and equal persons; they fail to respect persons as free and equal with the capacities to reason about justice and do what justice requires for its own sake. The idea that basic principles of justice should be publicly knowable and serve a social role by providing a public basis for justification among conscientious moral agents with different conceptions of their good is then implicit in recognition and respect for others as free and equal persons.[23]

To decide on the reasonableness of moral principles means that we need to know a good deal about human psychology, economics, and biology—including the normal stages of development of people's moral sensibilities—in order to determine what people's moral and other capabilities are and the limits of their tolerance of restrictions upon reasonable conceptions of their good. For example, if a moral conception places demands on some people well beyond their capacities for willing compliance (e.g., the least advantaged are denied opportunities and resources necessary to achieving their primary aims in order that those more advantaged may enjoy still greater rewards), then this is a compelling, perhaps sufficient reason for disqualifying that moral conception. (Rawls rejects utilitarianism for this and other reasons.)

5. *Justice and the Human Good*

(3) A moral conception should not frustrate, but should affirm the achievement of essential human goods.

There are different ways to construe this third condition, depending upon how the human good is conceived. I will elaborate on the claim by reference to Rawls's "full theory of the good" in *A Theory of Justice*. Accordingly, (3) becomes the thesis (3'): A conception of justice should enable us to realize (a) the values of community (*TJ*, 456) and (b) our nature as free and equal rational moral beings, making possible the good of individual and moral autonomy. (*TJ*, 452–3, 501) Non-Kantians may find these claims (3' (a) and/or (b)) unacceptable but might still accept the more general claim (3) on grounds of some other conception of the human good.

Rawls's non-consequentialism presupposes that the concepts of "the Right" and "the Good" require different principles. He characterizes the good in terms of rational choice, or according to certain principles of rationality. Generally, a person's good is the rational plan of life that the person would choose under hypothetical conditions of deliberative rationality (with full knowledge of relevant facts, fully understanding the consequences of choice, etc.). Rawls contends that other principles formally characterize morality and the concept of the right. These "reasonable principles" occupy a different position within our practical reasoning than do the "rational principles" providing shape to rational life plans and individuals' good. The role of reasonable principles is to regulate individuals' and groups' pursuit of their rational good and constrain their choice of ends. But if the right regulates and subordinates the good, how can acting right and justly according to reasonable principles be a good or rational activity for a person? The problem of "congruence" of the right and the good is to show that justice and reasonableness can themselves be rational and integral to a person's good (*TJ*, §86). Within Rawls's framework, congruence requires showing that it is rational for each person in a well-ordered society of justice as fairness to cultivate a willingness to do justice *for its own sake*.

A critic might reply that the congruence problem is not essential to deciding the content of first principles of justice,[24] for what justice requires must be independent of the question of whether it is good for us to do what justice requires. Some philosophers have argued that whether or not it is good for any person to do his or her duty is irrelevant to the question of what duty should be.[25] This conception of morality, as detachable from the human good, led Nietzsche to regard "morality" as a calamity for us: being entirely independent of the human good, the constraints morality imposes must stunt the development and exercise of higher human capacities, thus undermining the realization of human flourishing. Why then should we not regard the promptings of our moral sense of justice as neurotic compulsions, resulting from a sense of weakness and inferiority or a fear of authority? The requirement that a conception of justice be "congruent" with the good is responsive to these and similar criticisms. A reasonable constraint on a conception of justice is that its principles and ideals not undermine the human good, but be compatible with, and ideally even affirm, it. If so, then the crucial point for my purposes is that general facts about human nature are integrally related to almost any reasonable conception of the human good. For whether some activity or state of affairs is a good for a person depends upon that person's capacities to engage in or enjoy it.

Now assume that the good for any person consists (at least in part) in that person's exercising and realizing his or her distinctively *human* capacities. This resembles a psychological claim that Rawls calls the "Aristotelian Principle." This "deep psychological fact" (*TJ*, 379) suggests (roughly) that human beings generally enjoy activities that engage the exercise of their realized capacities, and their enjoyment increases the more the capacity is realized and the greater an activity's complexity (*TJ*, 374). (Thus [Rawls's example] assuming a person is equally proficient at chess and checkers, he or she will normally prefer playing chess to playing checkers.) Absent special circumstances, to leave one's mature capacities undeveloped normally results in a life that will be found boring and unsatisfactory. Rawls contends that "accepting the Aristotelian Principle as a natural fact" (*TJ*, 376), it is rational for individuals to realize and train mature capacities and to choose plans of life that in significant measure call upon the exercise and development of their complex human capacities (*TJ*, 376).

Now, relying on the Aristotelian Principle, Rawls appeals to two *intrinsic human goods* in *A Theory of Justice* to confirm and thus justify the principles of justice:

(A) *The Good of Community*: The Aristotelian Principle enables Rawls to argue that the development and exercise of our social capacities for a sense of justice are integral to a person's good, since realizing these capacities enables a person to participate in a social union of social unions.

> It follows from the Aristotelian Principle (and its companion effect) that participating in the life of a well-ordered society is a great good (*TJ* §79) . . . Because such a society is a social union of social unions, it realizes to a preeminent degree the various forms of human activity; and given the social nature of mankind, the *fact* that our potentialities and inclinations far surpass what can be expressed in any one life, we depend upon the cooperative endeavors of others not only for the means of well-being but to bring to fruition our latent powers . . . Yet to share fully in this life we must acknowledge the principles of its regulative conception, and this means that we must affirm our sentiment of justice . . . What binds a society's efforts into one social union is the mutual recognition and acceptance of the principles of justice; it is this general affirmation which extends the ties of identification over the whole community and permits the Aristotelian Principle to have its wider effect. (*TJ*, 500, emphasis added)

The details and soundness of Rawls's argument for the good of a social union of justice are beyond the scope of my discussion. But the general point can be made without the details. Rawls is trying to show how "the values of community" (which would include "solidarity" and "fraternity") are part of the human good. This is a central feature of many moral conceptions of justice, including G. A. Cohen's. Rawls contends that in order to realize the good of community, individuals must act on and from the correct principles of justice. Whether or not one accepts Rawls's justice as fairness, the general point is: assuming that the values of community are partially realized by people *complying with correct principles of justice for their own sake*, then a moral conception that affirms that community is essential to the human good must in turn rely upon general facts about human nature and people's capacities to act on and from the appropriate principles of justice. Thus, when Cohen himself maintains that community, solidarity, and having an "ethos of justice" are human goods (as he suggests elsewhere),[26] then it seems that his principles of distributive justice also must be responsive to human social capacities for justice and for the pursuit and achievement of their good. Otherwise, the purported good of community and the ethos of justice would not be achievable and perhaps would be beyond human reach.

(B) *Moral Personality and Moral Autonomy*: Rawls's second argument for congruence of the right and the good is more controversial, for it stems from Rawls's "Kantian interpretation of justice as fairness" (*TJ*, §40). In general, Rawls's

Kantian interpretation rests upon an account of human agency and practical reasoning: by virtue of the moral powers to be reasonable and rational (our capacities for justice and for a rational conception of the good), we are capable of engaging in practical reason and acting on the reasons that the right (morality) and the good (rationality) provide. These capacities also enable us to form and rationally pursue a conception of our good, and therewith they enable us to unify our lives and provide "unity to the self" (*TJ*, §85). In *A Theory of Justice* Rawls says the moral powers constitute our "nature as free and equal rational beings." The aim of Kantian interpretation and of Kantian constructivism is to depict the principles of justice as derivable from a "procedure of construction" (the original position), which itself "models," "represents," or "expresses" these capacities for moral and rational agency. Kant defines autonomy as acting from principles that reason legislates for itself. One point of Rawls's Kantian constructivism is to provide content to this troublesome idea. Since the principles of justice are "constructed," via the original position, on the basis of the capacities that constitute our "nature as free and equal rational beings," Rawls can say that the principles of justice are among the principles that reason "gives to" or "legislates for itself" out of our nature as free and equal reasonable and rational beings.

The general point for my purposes is that the justification and content of principles of justice are conditioned by the moral powers, these "*natural attributes*" (*TJ*, 444). To be morally autonomous agents who freely design and act upon a conception of the good in compliance with principles that are the product of our moral powers for practical reasoning, we have to take into account the contingencies of human nature and the optimal conditions for the development and exercise of these same capacities. Again, suppose we are empirically constructed so that we do not expect reciprocity from others with whom we cooperate; instead, we have no more concern for our own well-being than that of complete strangers, and our sense of justice is more responsive to (Sidgwick's) principle of impartial benevolence than to Rawls's reciprocity principles. Then it may well be that the principle of utility will be the most suitable principle for the development and exercise of our capacity for a sense of justice, and therewith realizing this essential good. But given human nature, the principle of utility does not express or realize our capacities for justice and the good. It is beyond the capacities of even the most sincere and conscientious utilitarian to regularly act upon the demands of the principle of utility. As Rawls's psychological reciprocity principles state, we tend to form attachments to principles and institutions that do not undermine, but rather support, our pursuit of our good (*TJ*, 415, 433), and normally acquire a sense of justice and willingness to comply with these principles (*TJ*, 429–30). This is good reason for preferring Rawls's principles of justice to the principle of utility, assuming that a conception of justice should be compatible with the human good. And the argument depends upon natural facts about our capacity for a sense of justice, including the fact that it is more likely to be developed and realized by the principles of justice than the principle of utility.

6. Methodological Remarks

Returning now to Cohen, first I will consider very briefly a potential defense of his thesis and then will conclude with some remarks on the practical significance of this issue. Cohen's thesis is that fundamental principles are a priori and "fact-free" and that once facts are stated in support of any principles, they must be secondary principles that are implementations of fact-free fundamental principles. Consider the following defense of Cohen's thesis, suggested by Gideon Rosen.[27] Any allegedly "fundamental" fact-sensitive principle, such as Rawls's difference principle, can be incorporated as the consequent of a complicated conditional statement that has as its antecedent a priori justifying principles (P_n) conjoined with a (conditional) statement of all the facts (F_n) which together justify that fact-sensitive principle (D) (grossly simplifying: $[(P_n \& F_n) \to D]$). This complicated conditional statement does not itself assert the truth of any facts, and thus is itself "fact-free." Now given the added premises F_n stating the facts in the antecedent of this complicated conditional, the fact-sensitive principle D follows (by modus ponens). But if so, then Cohen is correct: any fact-sensitive principle D can be shown to presuppose a fact-free principle in the form of our complicated conditional statement.

I am not sure whether Cohen would accept Rosen's claim as a friendly amendment to his argument. It raises several questions and issues, which I can mention but am not in a position to adequately address here. First, how are we to individuate principles? Is the complicated conditional $[(P_n \& F_n) \to D]$ a principle, or is it a concatenation of numerous fundamental and subordinate moral principles, methodological conditions, conditional facts, and logical connectives and operators? Second, how can this complicated conditional serve as a "fundamental principle" in Cohen's sense? (Could it really be, on anyone's account, self-evident or follow from any reasonable methodological principle, as he requires?) Third, is the complicated conditional capable of serving a public social role as a principle of practical reasoning that individuals and deliberative groups apply (see section 4), or is it simply too long, complicated, and beyond normal comprehension for those purposes? Fourth, does Rosen's claim assume that Rawls's argument for the principles of justice is a deductive argument? If so wouldn't this mischaracterize the nature of the argument from the original position, which surely is not so linear and tightly drawn?[28] Instead, the original position argument comprises a number of distinct reasons and arguments whose conjunction establishes a preponderance of reasons in favor of choosing the principles of justice over all the other alternatives principles considered. Finally, does Rosen's claim presuppose that logical connectives and operators and rules of inference that are part of the complicated fact-free conditional statement are themselves propositional? If so, then this raises the question of whether the logical form of sentences and rules of inference such as modus ponens can serve as premises of arguments or objects of cognition from which we reason. Are they rather not the conditions of judgment and inference that make reasoning possible?[29] Again, one would have to address these and other questions in order to respond adequately to Rosen's claim. It would be interesting to see whether Cohen himself would welcome Rosen's suggestion or regard it as contrary to his purposes.

Finally, what of practical significance is at stake in Cohen's "meta-ethical" argument? Again, Cohen says:

> Certain recent critiques of the "luck egalitarian" view of justice . . . are disfigured by failure to distinguish between rejection of the luck egalitarian view as a proposed principle of regulation and rejection of it at the fact-insensitive fundamental level at which the view is properly pitched . . . [D]ifficulties of implementation, just as such, do not defeat luck egalitarianism as a conception of justice, since it is not a constraint on a sound conception of justice that it should always be sensible to strive to implement it, whatever the factual circumstances may be.[30]

Oddly, this argument parallels Rawls's own remarks regarding luck egalitarianism, or what he calls "the principle of redress"—"to redress the bias of contingencies in the direction of equality" (TJ, 86). Rawls like Cohen says this principle cannot be used by itself to decide distributions, but only in conjunction with other considerations. But rather than contending that the principle of redress is a "fundamental principle" as Cohen does, Rawls says, "It is plausible as most such principles are only as a *prima facie* principle, one that is to be weighed in the balance with others" (TJ, 86). Rawls regards the luck-egalitarian principle as a component of moral intuitionism (in his sense), the view that there are a plurality of prima facie principles to be taken into account and weighed against one another in order to decide what is right or just to do. This seems to be Cohen's contention too; in deciding on the regulative principles of distributive justice for structuring economic institutions and distributing income and wealth, we are to assign appropriate weight to undeserved contingencies, along with other principles, and then redress people's situations as much as circumstances allow. But why call these luck-egalitarian considerations "fundamental principles"? What if the luck-egalitarian intuition is grounded in some more fundamental principle—perhaps, as Rawls conjectures, the difference principle?[31]

Here Sidgwick's account of first ethical principles is relevant. Sidgwick says first principles must be (i) at least as certain as any other moral principles, (ii) of superior validity to other principles, and (iii) really self-evident, deriving their validity, or evidence, from no other principles. This closely resembles Cohen's criteria for fundamental principles. Like Cohen's argument against Rawls, Sidgwick's account of justice is designed to show that none of the principles of justice found in commonsense morality meet his criteria for first principles, and hence must be "middle axioms," or subordinate principles.[32] Suppose Cohen's luck-egalitarian principle, suitably elaborated, meets Sidgwick's conditions. Still, there are further requirements Sidgwick imposes that Cohen's principle cannot meet: (iv) First principles must contain no limitations, or exceptions, or restrictions, unless these are self-imposed, that is, follow from the principle itself and are not simply appended as unexplained provisos. (v) First principles cannot be prima facie principles but must yield judgments of "actual rightness," all things considered. (vi) First principles must *systematize* subordinate principles to organize them into a complete and harmonious scheme. (vii) They must serve for rational agents as an actual guide to practice and cannot be vague, imprecise, or ambiguous. (viii) A first principle must be one that corrects our pre-reflective judgment.[33] Rawls's principles of justice meet these further conditions much better than Cohen's luck-egalitarian principle. (For example, note the parallel between (vii) and the publicity requirement, which requires that first principles serve reasonable and rational agents as principles of practical reason. Sidgwick's requirement in (vii) that first principles be actual guides to practice is one that Cohen's luck-egalitarian principle, regarded as a justificatory principle, cannot meet.) Sidgwick argues, of course, that the principle of utility satisfies all conditions better than any alternative he considers. But Rawls rejects (iii), the requirement of self-evidence, because of his constructivism and reflective equilibrium (and rejects perhaps (i), (ii), and (iv) depending on how they are construed) and argues that the principles of justice are superior to the principle of utility when measured by conditions resembling (v)–(viii), plus other appropriate conditions discussed above.

This is not an argument against Cohen. But it raises the questions (1) what other methodological conditions, in addition to those he mentions, he imposes on a conception of justice; (2) whether, and if so why, he rejects the four further conditions, (v)–(viii), which are accepted by both Rawls and Sidgwick as conditions on first principles; and more generally (3) what conception of practical reasoning underlies Cohen's conception of justice and moral justification.

Finally, Cohen's claim that the luck-egalitarian principle is a fundamental justifying principle leaves open the possibility that Rawls's account of distributive justice may be true when regarded as a principle of regulation in Cohen's sense. This is not far off from Rawls's claim:

> Although the difference principle is not the same as that of redress, it does achieve some of the intent of the latter principle . . . The difference principle

represents, in effect, an agreement to regard the distribution of natural talents as in some respects a common asset and to share in the greater social and economic benefits made possible, by the complementarities of this distribution. Those who have been favored by nature, whoever they are, may gain from their good fortune only on terms that improve the situation of those who have lost out, (*TJ*, 87)

Unlike intuitionists, for whom the luck-egalitarian principle is to be weighed against other relevant principles to decide a just distribution, Rawls regards the principle of redress as a "common sense precept of justice" (*TJ*, §47) that, along with other precepts (to reward people according to their needs, their efforts, and their contributions, among other considerations), is to be accounted for by the difference principle when all relevant considerations are taken into account in reflective equilibrium.

The likelihood that some version of the difference principle is consonant with Cohen's luck-egalitarian principle is also suggested by Rawls's political liberalism.[34] According to it, justice as fairness can be regarded as a "political conception of justice" that fits as a "module" within reasonable comprehensive moral doctrines, which are in an "overlapping consensus" about justice in the ideal conditions of a well-ordered society. So regarded, justice as fairness would be, within these doctrines, clearly derivative and non-fundamental. But political liberalism is not a concession to Cohen's argument. Rather, it avoids such meta-ethical issues and provides another way to regard justice as fairness as the correct conception of justice without disturbing Cohen's anti-constructivist position. I, on the other hand, have tried to make the philosophical case for rejecting Cohen's argument against constructivism, based in an alternative account of moral justification than the one he endorses.[35]

Notes

1. Rawls specifically notes at the beginning of the Dewey Lectures that "[t]here are a number of affinities between justice as fairness and Dewey's moral theory which are explained by the common aim of overcoming the dualisms in Kant's doctrine" (*CP*, 304).
2. G. A. Cohen, "Facts and Principles," *Philosophy & Public Affairs* 31, no. 3 (2003): 233; *FP* in further citations of this work.
3. Cohen restates the argument of "Facts and Principles" in *Rescuing Justice and Equality* (Cambridge, MA: Harvard University Press, 2008). However, all my remarks here are based on "Facts and Principles," since the book had not been published at the time of writing of this chapter. I do not take into account any changes or additions Cohen made in the book.

4. Here I assume the "Moral Law" is Kant's fundamental principle. It's true that the categorical imperative, an instance of the Moral Law, applies to "beings with needs." Similarly, the principle of utility applies to beings like us who are capable of experiencing pleasure and pain. But as I understand Cohen, this factual limitation in the range of application of these principles does not mean that they presuppose empirical facts in their justification. Cohen's position is that *if* there are sensuous beings who have these experiences, their pleasures are to be maximized in the aggregate. This does not require that any such beings actually exist.

5. Hume, An Enquiry Concerning the Principles of Morals, sec. III, pt. I, 20–6.

6. "The circumstances of justice may be described as the normal conditions under which human cooperation is both possible and necessary" (TJ, 109).

7. "Ultimate principles cannot be justified by facts . . . [These] fact-free principles might be self-evidently true, or they might for some other reason require no grounds, or they might need grounds and have grounds of some non-factual sort (they might, for example, be justified by some methodological principle that is not itself a normative principle but a principle that says how to generate normative principles), or they might need grounds but lack them, or . . . they might be judged to be outside the space of grounds" (*FP*, 219).

8. To support his claim that Rawls's principles of justice are not "fundamental principles," Cohen points to the assumption of free and equal persons behind the original position (*FP*, 238) and other fact-free justifying principles implicit in Rawls's argument for the difference principle, such as "one ought not cause too much inequality" (*FP*, 236). This suggests (to Cohen) that Rawls himself relies on more fundamental fact-free principles to justify his principles of justice (that moral persons ought to be treated equally, etc.). Other "fact-free" fundamental justifying principles Rawls invokes that Cohen might have mentioned are the formal requirements of right (including generality, universality, ordering of claims, finality, and publicity), as well as the strong impartiality condition implicit in the veil of ignorance.

9. See *FP*, 219. Cohen says that what makes principles (or reasons) "ultimate" or alternatively "foundational" is that they are at the "summit" in the chain of reasons that justify substantive (or regulative) moral principles. Seemingly for Cohen, only (some) justifying principles can be "ultimate" or "foundational" principles. Also, Cohen says that "constructivists about justice" hold that "*all* sound principles are . . . fact sensitive [and that] facts form at least part of the grounds for affirming them" (*FP*, 213). But in the quote from Rawls that Cohen uses to support this claim, Rawls says, "*Conceptions* of justice must be justified by the conditions of our life as we know it or not at all." Conceptions of justice for Rawls consist of both substantive and justificatory principles regarding morality and practical reason. For Rawls, it is *substantive principles of justice* that must be fact-sensitive, and not all justificatory principles. As Cohen himself notes, many of the assumptions in the original position (the conception of free

and equal moral persons, the veil of ignorance, etc.) are not fact-sensitive in Cohen's sense. On the other hand, *if* Cohen's claim that "[for constructivists] *all* sound principles are . . . fact-sensitive" is meant to be a point about Rawls's *reflective equilibrium*, then it may be true. For Rawls, there are no fact-free foundational principles that are taken as self-evident, necessary, or dogmatically unrevisable whatever new information we might encounter. This is in the nature of establishing a reflective equilibrium of moral principles with considered moral convictions, including fact-sensitive moral convictions, at all levels of generality. Cohen rejects such "holism" but says that "even if true, holism (and quasi-holism) do not threaten my proceedings" (*FP*, 223).

10. Cohen says that his argument "refutes Rawlsian constructivism as a meta-theory of justice" (*FP*, 243). One reason he gives is that Rawls fails to distinguish between "principles of regulation and the principles that justify them" (*FP*, 244). Consequently, "he misidentifies the question 'What is justice?' with the question 'What principles should we adopt to regulate our affairs?'" (*FP*, 244). Rawls's principles of justice cannot be fundamental principles of justice, for these must be principles of justification on Cohen's account.

11. See also *TJ* orig., 18.

12. *FP*, 219.

13. Habermas rejects Rawls's stability argument as part of the justification of the principles of justice, since it appeals to a number of facts about human nature and social cooperation. See Jürgen Habermas, "Reconciliation through the Public Use of Reason," *Journal of Philosophy* 92, no. 3 (1995): 109–31. Rawls replies in *PL*, lecture 9, "Reply to Habermas."

14. *FP*, 219.

15. Thanks to Sebastiano Maffetone for pointing this out.

16. See also *TJ* orig., 440.

17. Harry Frankfurt says of "equality of opportunity, equal respect, equal rights, equal consideration, equal concern, and so on," that "none of these modes of equality is intrinsically valuable" (Frankfurt, *On Inequality* [Princeton, NJ: Princeton University Press, 2015]), 68.

18. David Velleman draws a distinction between action and activity in *The Possibility of Practical Reason* (Oxford: Oxford University Press, 2000), chap. 1, and Christine Korsgaard similarly distinguishes between actions and acts in *Self-Constitution: Agency, Identity, and Integrity* (Oxford: Oxford University Press, 2009) 8–14.

19. *FP*, 243.

20. "A consequence of starting with methods of ethics defined as methods that seek truth is not only that it interprets justification as an epistemological problem, but also that it is likely to restrict attention to the first principles of moral conceptions and how they can be known. First principles are however only one element of a moral conception; of equal importance are its conception of the

person and its view of *the social role of morality*. Until these other elements are clearly recognized, the ingredients of a constructivist doctrine are not at hand" (*CP*, 342).

21. Here freedom is to be taken, among other ways, in the sense of persons' rational autonomy as authors of their rational life plans and their moral autonomy as authors of moral laws. Knowing and accepting moral principles is, of course, a precondition of acting for the sake of moral laws, which is required by moral autonomy.

22. Scanlon has a somewhat different conception of justification to a person, which is tailored to his more general project of providing an account of moral duties we owe to each other. See Scanlon, T. M., *What We Owe to Each Other*, chap. 4–5, (Cambridge, MA: Harvard University Press, 1998).

23. The social role of principles is closely related to T. M. Scanlon's idea that correct moral principles are those that could not be reasonably rejected as a basis for general agreement and justification among people who are conscientious and morally motivated. See Scanlon, *What We Owe to Each Other*, chap. 5. "The contractualist ideal of acting in accord with principles that others (similarly motivated) could not reasonably reject is meant to characterize the relation with others [of mutual recognition] which underlies our reasons to do what morality requires of us" (162).

24. Brian Barry makes this criticism in his review of *PL*, in "John Rawls and the Search for Stability," *Ethics* 105, no. 4 (1995): 874–915.

25. H. A. Prichard, "Does Moral Philosophy Rest on a Mistake?" (1912), in his *Moral Obligation* (Oxford: Clarendon Press, 1949), chap. 1.

26. See G. A. Cohen, *If You're an Egalitarian How Come You're So Rich?* (Cambridge, MA: Harvard University Press, 2000).

27. This reconstructs my understanding of Rosen's argument, which he suggested at the 2006 Philosophy Colloquium at the University of North Carolina. No doubt he could make the argument more persuasively than I do here.

28. I am grateful to Michael Williams for this suggestion. Rawls himself says that, though the argument for the principles of justice aspires to be deductive and incorporate all the necessary premises in the original position, the ideal of rigorous deductive reasoning cannot be attained since in the end "the balance of reasons rests on judgment, though judgment informed and guided by reasoning" (*JF*, 133–134).

29. I am grateful to Jay Wallace and to Mark LeBar for discussion of this point.

30. *FP*, 244.

31. There is nothing on its face that makes the difference principle "fact-sensitive." One might contend that it should be intuitively obvious or "self-evident" that, since the social product is jointly produced and the most advantaged rarely work as hard or experience the gravity of risk that the least advantaged do, fairness requires that the economy be designed to maximize the share going to the least

advantaged over their lifetimes. Regardless of whether this is an appropriate way to interpret the difference principle—as an intuitively obvious fundamental principle (in Cohen's sense) that accounts for our luck-egalitarian intuitions— Cohen's account does not seem to rule it out.

32. Among the subordinate principles Sidgwick discusses are a principle of equal freedom (Henry Sidgwick, *Methods of Ethics*, 7th ed. [Indianapolis: Hackett, 1981], 274ff.) and principles of distribution according to conscientious effort, actual contribution, "fair price," free-market value, etc. (283ff.).

33. For an account of these conditions see *LHPP*, "Lectures on Sidgwick," lecture 1.

34. Cohen has other arguments against the difference principle elsewhere. But his arguments, at least prior to *Rescuing Justice and Equality* (when this paper was written), do not seek to undermine the difference principle itself, only Rawls's interpretation of it as applying directly to the basic structure and only indirectly to individual actions. "Why not apply it directly to both?" (Cohen asks in effect). I address this question in chapter 7.

35. I am grateful to Andrews Reath for his extensive comments and to Tom Hill, Gideon Rosen, Philip Kitcher, and other participants at the 2006 Philosophy Colloquium at the University of North Carolina, Chapel Hill; to Michael Williams, Steven Gross, and other members of the Johns Hopkins Department of Philosophy; to Bruce Brower and others at Tulane University; to Mark LeBar, Alyssa Bernstein, and other members of the Department of Philosophy at Ohio University; to Sebastiano Maffetone and Ingrid Salvatore and others at LUISS in Rome; and to Kok-Chor Tan, Samuel Scheffler, and Jay Wallace, all for their helpful remarks and criticisms.

References

Barry, Brian. *Culture and Equality.* Cambridge, MA: Harvard University Press, 2001.

Barry, Brian. "John Rawls and the Search for Stability." *Ethics* 105, no. 4 (1995): 874–915.

Beitz, Charles. "Cosmopolitan Ideals and National Sentiments." *Journal of Philosophy* 80, no. 10 (1980): 591–610.

Beitz, Charles. *Political Theory and International Relations.* Princeton, NJ: Princeton University Press, 1979.

Blake, Michael. "Distributive Justice, State Coercion, and Autonomy." *Philosophy & Public Affairs* 30, no. 3 (2001): 257–96.

Blinder, Alan. *After the Music Stopped: The Financial Crisis, the Response, and the Work Ahead.* New York: Penguin, 2013.

Bloch, Marc. *Feudal Society.* Chicago: University of Chicago Press, 1964.

Brennan, Jason. *Libertarianism: What Everyone Needs to Know.* Oxford: Oxford University Press, 2012.

Brennan, Jason. "Rawls's Paradox." *Constitutional Political Economy* 18 (2007): 287–99.

Brennan, Jason, Bas van der Vossen, and David Schmidtz, eds., *The Routledge Handbook of Libertarianism.* Routledge, 2017.

Brink, David. *Perfectionism and the Common Good: Themes in the Philosophy of T. H. Green.* Oxford: Oxford University Press, 2003.

Buss, William G. "Discrimination by Private Clubs." *Washington University Law Review* 67, no. 3 (1989): 815–53.

Cassell's New Latin Dictionary. New York: Funk & Wagnalls, 1969.

Cohen, G. A. "Capitalism, Freedom, and the Proletariat." In *Liberty*, edited by David Miller. New York: Oxford University Press, 1991.

Cohen, G. A. "Facts and Principles." *Philosophy & Public Affairs* 31, no. 3 (2003): 211–45.

Cohen, G. A. *History, Labor, and Freedom.* Oxford: Oxford University Press, 1988.

Cohen, G. A. *If You're an Egalitarian How Come You're So Rich?* Cambridge, MA: Harvard University Press, 2000.

Cohen, G. A. *Rescuing Justice and Equality.* Cambridge MA: Harvard University Press, 2008.

Cohen, G. A. *Self-Ownership, Freedom, and Equality.* Cambridge: Cambridge University Press, 1995.

Cohen, G. A. "Self-Ownership, World-Ownership, and Equality." In *Justice and Equality Here and Now,* edited by Frank Lucash. Ithaca, NY: Cornell University Press, 1986.

Cohen, G. A. "Where the Action Is: On the Site of Distributive Justice." *Philosophy & Public Affairs* 26, no. 1 (1997): 3–30.

Cohen, Joshua. "Democratic Equality." *Ethics* 99 (1989): 727–51.

Cohen, Joshua. "Structure, Choice, and Legitimacy: Locke's Theory of the State." *Philosophy & Public Affairs* 15, no. 4. (1986): 301–24.

Cohen, Joshua. "Taking People as They Are." *Philosophy & Public Affairs* 30, no. 4 (2001): 363–86.

Cohen, Joshua, and Charles Sabel. "Extra Rempublicam Nulla Justicia." *Philosophy & Public Affairs,* 34 no. 2 (2006): 147–75.

Coulton, G. G. *Medieval Panorama.* Cambridge: Cambridge University Press, 1955.

Daniels, Norman. *Just Health Care.* Cambridge: Cambridge University Press, 1985.

Dawson, Christopher. *The Making of Europe.* New York: Meridian, 1956.

DelBlanco, Andrew. *College: What It Was, Is, and Should Be.* Princeton, NJ: Princeton University Press, 2012.

Dewey, John. *John Dewey, The Early Works,* vol. 1. Carbondale: Southern Illinois University, 1969.

Duus, Peter. *Feudalism in Japan.* New York: Alfred A. Knopf, 1969.

Dworkin, Ronald. *Is Democracy Possible Here?* Princeton, NJ: Princeton University Press, 2009.

Dworkin, Ronald. *Justice for Hedgehogs.* Cambridge, MA: Harvard University Press, 2011.

Dworkin, Ronald. *Sovereign Virtue.* Cambridge, MA: Harvard University Press, 2002.

Elias, Norbert. *Power and Civility.* Oxford: Basil Blackwell, 1982.

Elster, Jon. "Self-Realization in Work and Politics: The Marxist Conception of the Good Life." In *Alternatives to Capitalism,* edited by Jon Elster and Karl O. Moane. Cambridge: Cambridge University Press, 1989.

Feinberg, Joel. *Harm to Self.* Oxford: Oxford University Press, 1986.

Frankfurt, Harry. *On Inequality.* Princeton: Princeton University Press, 2015.

Freeman, Samuel. "Assessing G. A. Cohen's Critique of the Difference Principle." *Harvard Review of Philosophy* 19 (2013): 23–45.

Freeman, Samuel. "Equality of Resources, Market Luck, and the Justification of Market Distributions." *Boston University Law Review* 90, no. 2 (2010): 921–48.

Freeman, Samuel. *Justice and the Social Contract.* New York: Oxford University Press, 2007.

Freeman, Samuel. "Morals by Appropriation." *Pacific Philosophical Quarterly* 71, no. 4 (1990): 279–309.

Freeman, Samuel. "Problems with Some Consequentialist Arguments for Basic Rights." In *The Philosophy of Human Rights: Contemporary Controversies*, edited by Gerhard Ernst and Jan-Christoph Heilinger. Berlin: De Gruyter, 2011.

Freeman, Samuel. "Property as an Institutional Convention in Hume's Account of Justice." *Archiv für Geschichte der Philosophie* 73, no. 1 (1991): 20–49.

Freeman, Samuel. *Rawls*. London: Routledge, 2008.

Friedman, Milton. *Capitalism and Freedom*. Chicago: University of Chicago Press, 1962.

Friedman, Milton, and Rose Friedman. *Free to Choose*. New York: Harcourt Brace Jovanovich, 1980.

Gaus, Gerald. *The Tyranny of the Ideal*. Princeton: Princeton University Press, 2016.

Gauthier, David. *Morals by Agreement*. Oxford: Oxford University Press, 1986.

Gray, John. *Hayek on Liberty*. Oxford: Basil Blackwell, 1984.

Gray, John. *Liberalism*. Milton Keynes: Open University Press, 1986.

Gray, John. *Two Faces of Liberalism*. New York: New Press, 2000.

Green, T. H. *Lectures on the Principles of Political Obligation*. Cambridge: Cambridge University Press, 1986.

Habermas, Jürgen. *Between Facts and Norms*. Translated by William Rehg. Cambridge, MA: MIT Press, 1996.

Habermas, Jürgen. "Discourse Ethics." *Moral Consciousness and Communicative Action*. Translated by Christian Lenhardt. Cambridge, MA: MIT Press, 1990.

Habermas, Jürgen. "Reconciliation through the Public Use of Reason." *Journal of Philosophy* 92, no. 3 (1995): 109–31.

Hart, H. L. A. *The Concept of Law*, 2nd ed. Oxford: Oxford University Press, 1997. First published 1961 by Oxford University Press.

Hayek, Friedrich. *The Constitution of Liberty*, definitive ed. Chicago: University of Chicago Press, 2011. First published 1960 by University of Chicago Press.

Hayek, Friedrich. *Law, Legislation, and Liberty*. Vol. 2, *The Mirage of Social Justice*. Chicago: University of Chicago Press, 1976.

Hayek, Friedrich. *Law, Legislation, and Liberty*. Vol. 3, *The Political Order of a Free People*. Chicago: University of Chicago Press, 1979.

Holmes, Stephen. *Passions and Constraints*. Chicago: University of Chicago Press, 1995.

Hospers, John. "What Libertarianism Is." In *The Libertarian Alternative*, edited by Tibor Machan. N.p.: Nelson-Hall, 1974.

Hsieh, Nien-hê. "Work, Ownership, and Productive Enfranchisement." In *Property Owning Democracy: Rawls and Beyond*, edited by Martin O'Neill and Thad Williamson. Oxford: Wiley-Blackwell, 2012.

Hume, David. *Enquiries Concerning Human Understanding and Concerning the Principles of Morals*, 3rd ed. Oxford: Oxford University Press, 1975.

Hume, David. *An Enquiry Concerning the Principles of Morals*. Indianapolis: Hackett, 1983.

Hume, David. *An Enquiry Concerning the Principles of Morals*, 2nd ed. Oxford: Clarendon Press, 1970.

Hume, David. *A Treatise of Human Nature*, 2nd ed. Edited by L. A. Selby-Bigge and P. H. Nidditch. Oxford: Oxford University Press, 1978. First published 1960 by Oxford University Press.

Hussain, Waheed. "Nurturing the Sense of Justice: The Rawlsian Argument for Democratic Corporatism." In *Property Owning Democracy: Rawls and Beyond*, edited by Martin O'Neill and Thad Williamson. Oxford: Wiley-Blackwell, 2012.

Jackson, Ben. "Property Owning Democracy: A Short History." In *Property Owning Democracy: Rawls and Beyond*, edited by Martin O'Neill and Thad Williamson. Oxford: Wiley-Blackwell, 2012.

James, Aaron. *Fairness in Practice*. New York: Oxford University Press, 2012.

Kamm, Frances. "Sen on Justice and Rights." *Philosophy and Public Affairs* 39, no. 1 (2011): 82–104.

Kant, Immanuel. *Groundwork for the Metaphysics of Morals*. Translated and edited by Mary Gregor. Cambridge: Cambridge University Press, 1998.

Kant, Immanuel. *The Metaphysical Elements of Justice* Translated by John Ladd. Indianapolis: Bobbs-Merrill, 1965.

Keating, Gregory. "The Idea of Fairness in the Law of Enterprise Liability." *Michigan Law Review* 95, no. 5 (1997): 1266–380.

Keating, Gregory. "A Social Contract Conception of the Tort Law of Accidents." In *Philosophy and the Law of Torts*, edited by Gerald J. Postema. Cambridge: Cambridge University Press, 2001.

Klarman, Michael J. *From Jim Crow to Civil Rights: The Supreme Court and the Struggle for Racial Equality*. Oxford: Oxford University Press, 2004.

Kordana, Kevin A., and David Blankfein-Tabachnick. "Rawls and Contract Law." *George Washington Law Review* 73, no. 3 (2005): 598–632.

Kordana, Kevin A., and David H. Tabachnick. "On Belling the Cat: Rawls and Tort as Corrective Justice." *Virginia Law Review* 92, no. 7 (2006): 1279–1311.

Korsgaard, Christine M. *Self Constitution: Agency, Identity, and Integrity*. Oxford: Oxford University Press, 2009.

Kronman, Anthony. "Contract Law and Distributive Justice." *Yale Law Journal* 89 (1980): 472–511.

Krugman, Paul, and Robin Wells. *Microeconomics*, 2nd ed. New York: Worth, 2009.

Lareau, Annette. *Unequal Childhoods*, rev. ed. Berkeley: University of California Press, 2011.

Locke, John. *Second Treatise on Government*. Edited by Peter Laslett. Cambridge: Cambridge University Press, 1988.

Locke, John. *Two Treatises of Government*. Edited by Peter Laslett. Cambridge: Cambridge University Press, 1997. First published 1960 by Cambridge University Press.

Mankiw, N. Gregory. "Defending the One Percent." *Journal of Economic Perspectives* 27, no. 3 (2013): 21–34.

Marx, Karl. *Karl Marx: Selected Writings*. Edited by David McClellan. Oxford: Oxford University Press, 1977.

Meade, James E. *Efficiency, Equality, and the Ownership of Property*. London: George Allen & Unwin, 1964.

Michelman, Frank I. "Property, Utility, and Fairness: Comments on the Ethical Foundations of 'Just Compensation' Law." *Harvard Law Review* 80, no. 6 (1967): 1165–258.

Mill, John Stuart. *"On Liberty" and Other Essays*. Edited by John Gray. Oxford: Oxford University Press, 1991.

Mill, John Stuart. *Principles of Political Economy*. Indianapolis: Liberty Fund, 2006.

Mill, John Stuart. *Utilitarianism*. Edited by George Sher. Indianapolis: Hackett, 1979.

Miller, Richard. "The Cosmopolitan Controversy Needs a Mid-Life Crisis." In *Cosmopolitanism vs. Non-Cosmopolitanism*, edited by Gillian Brock. Oxford: Oxford University Press, 2013.

Murphy, Liam. "Institutions and the Demands of Justice." *Philosophy & Public Affairs* 27, no. 4 (1999): 251–91.

Nagel, Thomas. *Concealment and Exposure: And Other Essays*. Oxford: Oxford University Press, 2004.

Nagel, Thomas. *Equality and Partiality*. New York: Oxford University Press, 1991.

Nagel, Thomas. "The Problem of Global Justice." *Philosophy & Public Affairs* 33, no. 2 (2005): 113–47.

Narveson, Jan. *The Libertarian Idea*. Philadelphia: Temple University Press, 1987.

Nozick, Robert. *Anarchy, State, and Utopia*. New York: Basic Books, 1974.

O'Neill, Martin. "Free and Fair Markets without Capitalism." In *Property Owning Democracy: Rawls and Beyond*, edited by Martin O'Neill and Thad Williamson. Oxford: Wiley-Blackwell, 2012.

Otsuka, Michael. *Libertarianism without Inequality*. Oxford: Clarendon Press, 2005.

Parfit, Derek. "Equality and Priority." *Ratio* 10, no. 3 (1997): 202–21.

Parfit, Derek. "Equality or Priority? The Lindley Lecture." University of Kansas, 1991.

Paul, Jeffrey. Introduction to *Reading Nozick*, edited by Jeffrey Paul. Totowa, NJ: Rowman & Littlefield, 1981.

Perry, Stephen. "Ripstein, Rawls, and Responsibility." *Fordham Law Review* 72, no. 5 (2004): 1845–55.

Phelps, Edmund. *Rewarding Work*. Cambridge, MA: Harvard University Press, 1997.

Piketty, Thomas. *Capital in the Twenty-First Century*. Cambridge MA: Harvard University Press, 2013.

Pogge, Thomas. *Realizing Rawls*. Ithaca, NY: Cornell University Press, 1989.

Pogge, Thomas. "Three Problems with Contractarian-Consequentialist Ways of Assessing Social Institutions." *Social Philosophy and Policy* 12, no. 2 (1995): 241–66.

Poly, Jean Pierre, and Eric Bournazel. *The Feudal Transformation: 900–1200*. New York: Holmes & Meier, 1991.

Prichard, H. A. *Moral Obligation*. Oxford: Clarendon Press, 1949.

Rawls, John. *Collected Papers*. Edited by Samuel Freeman. Cambridge, MA: Harvard University Press, 1999.

Rawls, John. *Justice as Fairness: A Restatement*. Edited by E. Kelly. Cambridge, MA: Harvard University Press, 2001.

Rawls, John. *The Law of Peoples*. Cambridge, MA: Harvard University Press, 1999.

Rawls, John. *Lectures on the History of Political Philosophy*. Edited by Samuel Freeman. Cambridge, MA: Harvard University Press, 2007.

Rawls, John. *Lectures on the History of Moral Philosophy*. Edited by Barbara Herman. Cambridge, MA: Harvard University Press, 2000.

Rawls, John. *Political Liberalism*, expanded ed. New York: Columbia University Press, 2005. First published 1993 by Columbia University Press.

Rawls, John. *A Theory of Justice*, rev. ed. Cambridge, MA: Harvard University Press, 1999. First published 1971 by Harvard University Press.

Rawls, John. *A Theory of Justice*, original edition, Cambridge, MA: Harvard University Press, 1971.

Ripstein, Arthur. "The Division of Responsibility and the Law of Tort." *Fordham Law Review* 72, no. 5 (2004): 1811–44.

Ripstein, Arthur. "Private Order and Public Justice: Kant and Rawls." *Virginia Law Review* 92, no. 7 (2006): 1391–438.

Ripstein, Arthur. *Private Wrongs*. Cambridge, MA: Harvard University Press, 2016.

Robbins, Lionel. *A History of Economic Thought*. Edited by Stephen Medema and Warren Samuels. Princeton, NJ: Princeton University Press, 1998.

Roemer, John. *A Future for Socialism*. Cambridge MA: Harvard University Press, 1994.

Rothbard, Murray. *Power and Market: Government and the Economy*. Kansas City, MO: Sheed Andrews and McMeel, 1977.

Rothbard, Murray. *Power and Market*. New York: New York University Press, 1981.

Rothbard, Murray. "Society without a State." In *The Libertarian Reader*, edited by Tibor Machan. Totowa, NJ: Rowman & Littlefield, 1982.

Rousseau, Jean-Jacques. *The Basic Political Writings*. Translated by David A. Cress. Indianapolis: Hackett, 1987.

Ryan, Alan. *John Dewey and the High Tide of American Liberalism*. New York: W. W. Norton, 1995.

Sangiovanni, Andreas. "Global Justice, Reciprocity, and the State." *Philosophy & Public Affairs* 35, no. 1 (2007): 3–39.

Scanlon, T. M. "Contractualism and Utilitarianism." In *Utilitarianism and Beyond*, edited by Amartya Sen and Bernard Williams. Cambridge: Cambridge University Press, 1982.

Scanlon, T. M. *Why Does Inequality Matter?* Oxford: Oxford University Press, 2018.

Scanlon, T. M. *What We Owe to Each Other*. Cambridge, MA: Harvard University Press, 1998.

Scheffler, Samuel. "Distributive Justice, the Basic Structure and the Place of Private Law." *Oxford Journal of Legal Studies* 35, no. 2 (2015): 213–35.

Scheffler, Samuel. *Equality and Tradition*. New York: Oxford University Press, 2012.

Schumpeter, Joseph A. *History of Economic Analysis*. Oxford: Oxford University Press, 1954.

Searle, John. *The Construction of Social Reality*. New York: Free Press, 1995.

Sen, Amartya. "Consequential Evaluation and Practical Reason." *Journal of Philosophy* 97, no. 9 (2000): 477–502.

Sen, Amartya. *The Idea of Justice*. Cambridge MA: Harvard University Press, 2009.

Sen, Amartya. "Rights and Agency." *Philosophy & Public Affairs* 11, no. 1 (1982): 3–39.

Sidgwick, Henry. *Methods of Ethics*, 7th ed. Indianapolis: Hackett, 1981.

Simmons, A. John. "Ideal and Nonideal Theory." *Philosophy & Public Affairs* 38, no. 1 (2010): 5–36.

Simmons, A. John. *The Lockean Theory of Rights*. Princeton, NJ: Princeton University Press, 1992.

Smith, Adam. *An Inquiry into the Nature and Causes of the Wealth of Nations*. Indianapolis: Liberty Fund, 1981.

Smith, Adam. *The Wealth of Nations*. New York: Random House Modern Library, 1937.

Steiner, Hillel. *An Essay on Rights*. Oxford: Wiley-Blackwell, 1994.

Talbott, William. *Human Rights and Human Well-Being*. Oxford: Oxford University Press, 2010.

Tan, Kok-Chor. *Justice, Institutions, and Luck*. Oxford: Oxford University Press, 2012.

Tan, Kok-Chor. *Justice without Borders*. Cambridge: Cambridge University Press, 2004.

Tomasi, John. *Free Market Fairness*. Princeton, NJ: Princeton University Press, 2012.

Tully, James. *A Discourse on Property*. Cambridge: Cambridge University Press, 1980.

Vallentyne, Peter, and Hillel Steiner, eds. *Left-Libertarianism and Its Critics*. New York: Palgrave MacMillan, 2000.

Van Parijs, Philippe. "Difference Principles." In *The Cambridge Companion to Rawls*, edited by Samuel Freeman. Cambridge: Cambridge University Press, 2003.

Van Parijs, Phillippe. *Real Freedom for All: What (if Anything) Can Justify Capitalism?* Oxford: Oxford University Press, 1998.

Velleman, David. *The Possibility of Practical Reason*. Oxford: Oxford University Press, 2000.

von Mises, Ludwig. *Liberalism in the Classical Tradition*. Indianapolis: Liberty Fund, 2005.

Waldron, Jeremy. *The Right to Private Property*. Oxford: Oxford University Press, 1988.

Weitzman, Martin. *The Share Economy*. Cambridge, MA: Harvard University Press, 1984.

White, Stuart. "Property-Owning Democracy and Republican Citizenship." In *Property Owning Democracy: Rawls and Beyond*, edited by Martin O'Neill and Thad Williamson. Oxford: Wiley-Blackwell, 2012.

Wolff, Jonathan. *Robert Nozick*. Stanford, CA: Stanford University Press, 1991.

Woodward, C. Vann. *The Strange Career of Jim Crow*. 2d rev. ed., Oxford: Oxford University Press, 1966.

Index